MAVERICK GUIDE TO
OMAN

mav.er.ick (mav'er-ik), *n* 1. an unbranded steer. Hence colloq. 2. a person not labeled as belonging to any one faction, group, etc., who acts independently. 3. one who moves in a different direction than the rest of the herd—often a nonconformist. 4. a person using individual judgment, even when it runs against majority opinion.

The Maverick Guides

The Maverick Guide to Australia

The Maverick Guide to Bali and Java

The Maverick Guide to Barcelona

The Maverick Guide to Berlin

The Maverick Guide to the Great Barrier Reef

The Maverick Guide to Hawaii

The Maverick Guide to Hong Kong, Macau, and South China

The Maverick Guide to Malaysia and Singapore

The Maverick Guide to New Zealand

The Maverick Guide to Prague

The Maverick Guide to Thailand

The Maverick Guide to Vietnam, Laos, and Cambodia

The Maverick Guide to Scotland

MAVERICK GUIDE TO
OMAN

Second Edition

Peter J. Ochs II

PELICAN PUBLISHING COMPANY
Gretna 2000

First edition, January 1998
Second edition, January 2000

ISBN: 1-56554-687-3

In the spirit of
Peachey Taliaferro Carnehan,
Brother to a Prince or fellow to a beggar
if he be found worthy
—Kipling

Information in this guidebook is based on authoritative data available at the time of printing. Prices and hours of operation of businesses listed are subject to change without notice. Readers are asked to take this into account when consulting this guide.

To Evan, Kasthuri, Gwyneth, Kalaivani, and Elspeth, and especially to Letchmi, who is my inspiration and my guide

Maps and illustrations by Peter J. Ochs II

Printed in the United States of America
Published by Pelican Publishing Company, Inc.
1000 Burmaster Street, Gretna, Louisiana 70053

Contents

LIST OF MAPS

LEGEND

≈ Tarmac (asphalt)		▬ Body of water	
～ ～ ～ Graded Track		▪▬▬▪▪ Dry wadi	
•••••• Trail		～～▶ Flowing wadi	
■ Hotel or other building		♂ Mosque	
▲ Restaurant		♁ Church	
○ Village or town		♨ Temple	
▫ Fortress or castle		△ Petrol (Fuel) (remote areas only—maps 20-22)	
* Point of interest		R/A Roundabout	
▨ Mountains		● Shopping center	
⁙ Desert		✪ Capital city	

Preface

It is not worth the while to go round the world to count the cats in Zanzibar. Yet do this even till you can do better, and you may perhaps find some "Symmes' Hole" by which to get at the inside at last. . . . If you would learn to speak all tongues and conform to the customs of all nations, if you would travel farther than all travelers, be naturalized in all climes, and cause the Sphinx to dash her head against a stone, even obey the precept of the old philosopher, and Explore thyself.

—Henry David Thoreau, *Walden*

John Symmes was a retired U.S. Army officer, amateur explorer of the early nineteenth century, and maverick in his own right: he was the chief proponent of a popular theory of the time that the world was not only hollow, but inhabited and accessible by entries somewhere around the poles. Never taken seriously by the scientific community, his ideas were embroidered on by the likes of science-fiction writers Jules Verne and Edgar Rice Burroughs. But getting to the core of an issue to grasp it totally is a reasonable theme, so for now we'll let the metaphor stand.

When the opportunity arose to write a travel guide about Oman (no less, a Maverick Guide), I reflected upon the lives of two men who have served me as mentors and exemplars. I realized in retrospect that these men were mavericks themselves: American transcendentalist Henry David Thoreau and British explorer Sir Richard Francis Burton. Different drummer Thoreau is perhaps the quintessential maverick of American literature while Burton attained his distinction in a lifetime of wanderlust. Although he was knighted late in his life, Burton never rose above the rank of captain, most likely because he raised suspicions among his peers regarding his loyalty every time he immersed himself so completely in a foreign culture.

The popular accolade bestowed on Henry David Thoreau as a world traveler is rather unusual for someone who, except for one trip to Minnesota late in his life, never left his native New England (he was taken by tuberculosis in 1862 at the age of 45). Thoreau's journeys traveled the highways and byways of the mind.

If anybody was a kindred spirit of Thoreau, it would have to be Burton (1821-90). Burton accomplished in his lifetime what it would take dozens of other men to do—he mastered forty languages and dialects; served as intelligence officer for the English army in India; made the holy pilgrimage (Hajj) to Makkah and Medina (as a convert to Islam); entered the equally

9

forbidden city of Harar in East Africa; participated in an expedition to find the source of the Nile River; traveled across the United States and wrote a comprehensive study on the Mormons; served for the British Foreign Office in West Africa gathering enough material on tribal customs for five books; served as consul in Brazil, Damascus, and Trieste; and published extensively with prodigious works of geography and cultural anthropology (43 volumes) as well as over 30 translations of foreign works such as the Kama Sutra and the seventeen-volume *Alf Laylah Wah Laylah,* the 1001 Arabian Nights Entertainments. He was a chameleon, a master of disguise who could pass for a native of any country he entered half an hour after he first arrived. Can there ever be a closer embodiment of Thoreau's vision—master of languages, traveler of all worlds, conformer to all climes—than Burton as his symbiotic alter ego . . . ? It is unlikely that Burton and Thoreau, contemporaries, knew of one another, but if anybody knew the number of cats in Zanzibar, Burton did.

I confess I have not been to Zanzibar, let alone know how many cats are there. But why, of all places, am I rambling on about Zanzibar in the opening to this guidebook about Oman? Fair enough. Read on, traveler. Zanzibar, although today part of the United Republic of Tanzania, was once part of a sizable Omani commercial empire and has played a key role in Oman's past *and* present. Someday I would like to go to Zanzibar and I may very well get there, but if that time is not impending, it's only because I have another task at hand: I have yet to count the Caracal lynx in Oman.

Acknowledgments

I want to thank the people who helped me in this project, especially the following:

Mohammed Noor and the staff at the Department of Tourism of Oman; His Excellency Saif bin Hashil Al Maskary, former Undersecretary for the Department of Tourism (retired); Mr. Salim Al Mahruqi, Information Attaché at the Omani Embassy in Washington; Vijayan Kandeth and all the great folks in the Asha Group; Dr. Milburn Calhoun and Pelican Publishing Company.

I also thank the many friends and colleagues who took interest in my endeavor, gave me wonderful moral support, and contributed whatever knowledge they had about Oman from anecdotal or established sources.

Special thanks goes to His Highness Sayyid Fatik bin Fahar Al Said, who took an interest in my earlier work and whose office was helpful in providing some of the source material for chapter 4.

My most heartfelt thanks goes to the kindly Omani people who have patiently waded through my fumbling Arabic to give me directions to one destination or another and who have graciously given me food and water and a place to pause in my peregrinations, without ever asking anything in return.

Many thanks also to Rob Luscombe, of *Exclusive Adventures into Africa,* who I was fortunate enough to run into at the Asia Travel Market Exhibition in Singapore, for providing the information on Zanzibar.

MAVERICK GUIDE TO
OMAN

The Surrounding Region

1

Why Oman?

> I know one of the Arab lands that is called Oman which is by the sea coast. One
> Haj [pilgrimage to Makkah] from Oman is better than two from other places.
> —The Prophet Muhammed

I first went to the Middle East in 1983 to work for ARAMCO in Saudi Arabia. At the time, I took with me a mental picture of Arabic life that I expected to find, more or less, that was based on notions and hearsay. I had had some previous indirect experience of the Arabic culture from working for companies with Arabic clients in the late seventies and early eighties. The rest of my general knowledge was based on stories that had accumulated since my youth, most notably the legends retold in the 1001 Arabian Nights. These stories had undoubtedly been diluted and perverted by various Hollywood interpretations, and my images were continually counterbalanced by the news of the day regularly emanating from the region. Almost always, the bias was negative. America's perspective was growing more jaded by the minute as we were deluged with stories of loose-cannon despots, political extremists, self-styled religious fanatics, and conniving petroleum lords. All this was, ironically enough, set against a backdrop of rapid cultural change foisted on them by the perpetrators of twentieth-century progress, namely, Western Civilization. One country we *never* heard from was Oman.

The stereotypes that I harbored were bolstered by caveats given to me as I prepared to step into this nether world like a young boy testing the pond surface for skating after the first winter freeze. As my tenure in this foreign clime progressed, I frequently compared notes with fellow "expats" and filed their experiences along with mine for further assessment and reflection. Naturally, we did not look to see whether or not our preconceived notions were true, but only to what degree they were true. We were, after all, living in a foreign culture whose government policy was to minimize cultural contact. We were the outsiders. We were not there to mingle with the local inhabitants; we were just there to perform a certain task and go home. After one year I did just that.

In 1991 the opportunity arose for me to work in Oman. Having chalked up my former experience as a generally positive one (after all I did make it back alive with all parts of me intact), I packed my bags and eight more years of stereotypes and negative news bites. Operation Desert Storm was over. Kuwait had started to recover from the Iraqi occupation. And potentates still rattled their swords. Geographical illiteracy having reached its nadir in this country, one political satirist pronounced, "We live in a country where missiles are built that can find Baghdad on a map while most schoolchildren couldn't." Isolationism appeared to rear its ugly head. Cultural backlash was evident, too: a highly sanitized animated Disney movie loosely based on the Aladdin stories was roundly criticized for accentuating pejorative stereotypes within the setting of the romantic adventure. In all humility, I was ill prepared for what I was about to find. And somewhere in the back of my mind the words of Walt Kelly echoed, "We has met the enemy and it is us."

When I got to Oman, what I discovered in almost no time was more than just a microcosm of the Arab world, but an enchanting, flourishing microcosm of humanity itself. I discovered a country in the midst of a cultural renaissance on the verge of grabbing its singular moment in the sun. I discovered a country with a long and distinguished past that tugs at the roots of our cultural origins. I discovered an ethnic character so unique and diverse that it smashed through every stereotype I have ever known. It gave me pause to think of my own country's multicultural background and how far we have come in the last 200 years.

Everywhere I went in Oman I was met with friendship and hospitality, exuberance and pride, curiosity and zeal. And I discovered many other things:

- A country that, as a political entity, has been around longer than any other nation in the gulf region. Oman is older than the United States (by thirty-three years when the current Al Bu Said dynasty began its course) and extended its arm of friendship a good twenty years before the start of the American Civil War. (For those of you keeping track, the year was 1840, when an Omani vessel first sailed into New York harbor.)

- A country whose underpinnings are, curiously enough, nurtured by democratic principles similar to our own.
- A country that calls upon *all* of its citizens to share the responsibility of carving out its own destiny; where outdated gender biases are put aside in a true spirit of cooperation.
- A country that has celebrated, in its long history, moments of greatness and, in the twentieth century, perhaps has weathered its darkest hour.

When you come to Oman, you will be, as I was, pleasantly surprised at the things you will discover. I will only mention a few because I would hope travelers would like to have the pleasure of discovering a few things on their own. Besides, in all honesty, I haven't found all there is to see yet.

- Historians and archeologists will encounter remnants of civilizations that go back to the beginning of recorded history.
- Photography buffs will find a picture-postcard shot almost everywhere they turn.
- Christians will discover why frankincense was one of the gifts of the Magi and how it came, in all probability, from Oman.
- Theologians will discover a branch of Islam practiced nowhere else in the world, a sect noted for its austerity, sincerity, and tolerance.
- Explorers will discover an ancient boat-building center still surviving and home of the famous Sindbad legends.
- Ethnographers can trace cultural origins of several races to distant parts of the globe and also witness the transition of indigenous nomadic cultures as they enter the mainstream of modern society.
- Geologists can find "textbook quality" examples of rock formations, minerals, and fossils.
- Naturalists will discover a plethora of flora and fauna to observe and study.
- Collectors will be dazzled by contemporary arts and traditional crafts.
- For numismatists and philatelists, a veritable treasure trove awaits.
- Gourmands will never run out of something new to try.
- And a casual traveler can find hospitality at every corner.

There is something for everyone in Oman, from dinosaur bones and butterflies, to simmering sunsets on soft desert sands, to thriving oases and bustling Old World markets. The landscape is sprinkled with over five hundred castles, fortresses, walled cities, and defense towers. There is a deep-seated heritage of the melting-pot variety. Oman is the most heterogeneous of countries on the Arabian peninsula, vibrating with an Arabic undercurrent with African and Asian overtones. Graceful architecture mixes traditional and contemporary styles, breathing a new vitality into the landscape.

The people dress in brightly colored native costumes that exude a refreshing disposition. One traveler in the nineteenth century remarked that the Omanis were certainly the best dressed and most gentlemanly of all the Arabs, something that reflects much more than surface values.

There is something special in the geniality I experience in Oman. I think of the many times I have been invited into the *majlis* (meeting place) of small villages in the interior, whether it was beneath a budding lime tree in a courtyard or inside in a carpeted hall. Our party is cordially offered *khawa* (Omani coffee) and dates, a staple of their agriculture. Language is never an obstacle, even though it may seem a barrier at first. Friendship is the lingua franca here. Old men gesture and raise their cups; genuine smiles belie timeworn faces of privation. Children innocently poke and gambol about. Young ladies who could give Garrison Keillor lessons in shyness sport tentative grins and coyly peek from corners and doorways.

It is an experience I carry with me and cherish very deeply. And I share it because the Omanis would have me share it. That is why I hope you come to Oman—to see an extraordinary country and meet an extraordinary people. And . . . yes, we have met some new friends and they are just like us.

An Old World Rediscovered

"Oh, messenger of Allah, invoke Allah's blessings on the people of Oman." And he replied, "May Allah guide and reward them. . . . May God give them virtue and contentment as well as their daily means . . . expand them for their provisions and increase the bounteousness of their sea . . . inflict not over them an enemy from those not among them."

—A Hadith of Mazin bin Ghadhuba

The Sultanate of Oman is for sure the fastest growing of emerging nations. The fact that in 1970 Oman was such an obscure cultural backwater is enough to send anybody scrambling for his atlas. It is only fair then to introduce the intrepid traveler to Oman by way of a simple geography lesson.

The Sultanate of Oman is a country located in the outermost reaches of the Arabian peninsula. It occupies an area of about 309,500 square kilometers (119,356 square miles), making it roughly the size of the state of New Mexico. The capital city is **Muscat.** (No, the grapes do not come from here! They are French. The name is transliterated from the Arabic *Masqat* and it means "place of anchorage.") The topography is varied, mostly arid desert with rugged mountainous regions in the north and far south separated by the easternmost extension of the ***Rub' Al Khali*** (the Empty Quarter, which takes up most of the lower third of the Arabian peninsula). Barren rock, gravel fields, *sabkha* (salt flats), and rolling sand dunes abound. The largest

section of dunes in Oman being the Wahibah Sands (a stretch of longitudinal dunes 100-200 meters high, 100 kilometers wide, and 200 kilometers
long), they occupy a good portion of **Sharqiyah**, the easternmost province.

The overall climate is extremely arid with the only exception being the
south region of **Dhofar**, which is influenced by the *khareef,* or summer
Indian Ocean monsoon. The eastern seaboard in the north tends to be a bit
more humid than the surrounding mountains as ocean air is trapped along
the coast and prevailing west winds are steered away. Because Oman lies
directly on the Tropic of Cancer, the local weather at times can be some of
the harshest of anywhere on the planet. But during the winter season (or
wet season) temperatures are very pleasant. Sometimes, especially in the
interior at higher elevations, temperatures approach freezing in winter
and places such as **Jebel Shams** can receive a light dusting of snow, but as a
rule, moderate temperature levels prevail. Rainfall is exceedingly light, with
only 100 millimeters (three inches) a year along the coast and 700 millimeters (twenty-one inches) a year in the mountains. Amounts in the south (in
Dhofar) are slightly higher.

The country borders the United Arab Emirates (UAE) to the north, Saudi
Arabia to the west, and Yemen to the southwest. Some of these borders are
hard to reach (except with sophisticated navigational equipment such as
GPS—Geographical Positioning Systems) because they run through particularly desolate regions. However, a permanent border with Yemen was ratified
in 1992 as well as the border with Saudi Arabia in 1991. Oman is bounded by
the Gulf of Oman to the northeast and the Arabian Sea, an arm of the Indian
Ocean, to the southeast. The coastline extends over 1,700 kilometers (1,020
miles). The **Musandam Peninsula,** the northernmost section of Oman, is
separated from the rest of the country by the UAE by a distance of 70 kilometers (40 miles), and midway, within that 70-kilometer span, the town of
Madha declares its allegiance to Oman. There are several small chains of
islands off the northern coast, **Jazir As Suwaidi** and **Jazir Ad Damaniyat;** an
archipelago in the south to the east of Salalah, **Jazir Al Halaaniyat;** and the
island of **Masirah** located due south of the Wahibah Sands.

Oman is divided into several geopolitical regions, which will be used
loosely as a point of departure for this guide. (These areas are further
divided into fifty-nine districts called *wilayats.* Each wilayat is presided over
by a *wali,* or governor.) Here are the major regions, from north to south.

The Musandam Peninsula. This sparsely populated region is a rugged
area of tall cliffs that are likened to the fjords of Norway. Altitudes in this
area rise to about 2,000 meters (6,600 feet). This region serves as the south
edge to the ever vital Strait of Hormuz, the entrance to the Arabian Gulf
(which Westerners call the Persian Gulf), through which one-fifth of the
world's oil supply passes.

The Batinah Coast. This region extends 300 kilometers (180 miles) from Shinas to Seeb and is the country's primary agricultural region. A narrow strip ranging from 8 to 50 kilometers (5 to 30 miles) wide, it derives its limited soil from erosion and deposition of the eastern flanks of the Hajar Mountains. It has been made fertile over the years by reclamation and irrigation. Along with the capital area, this is the densest area of population.

The Hajar Mountains. An extremely rugged chain of *jebels* (*jebel* means "mountain"; *hajar* means "rocky") running from northwest to southeast through the northern third of the country, these predominantly thrust-fault mountains are made up of mostly sedimentary rocks (sandstones and conglomerates, limestones and shales) and ophiolites (oceanic crust and mantle that has been thrust to the surface by tectonic activity). The topography is steep, characteristic of young valley systems, with deep canyons and jagged irregular peaks as well as karst topography (caves and sinkholes). Throughout these mountains are scattered oases surrounding wadi channels (a *wadi* is a riverbed, usually dry but sometimes flowing) with rural populations settled in enclaves within them.

Dhahirah. Beyond the Hajars to the west are the interior foothills and plains abutting the Rub' Al Khali. This sparsely populated region consists of intermittent ridges and salt domes, gravel beds, dangerous *sabkha* (salt flats), and *barchans* (roving sand dunes).

Muscat. The capital region, "the place of anchorage," Muscat is one of the few natural harbors in Oman. Here is the major metropolitan area where one-third of the country's 2,000,000 people reside. Completely surrounded by the forbidding Hajars, Muscat lends a feeling of seclusion.

Sharqiyah. This easternmost end of the Arabian peninsula covers the Eastern Hajars and the Wahibah Sands, a massive area of rolling dunes inhabited by Bedouin tribes. The Hajars run right down to the coast before ending at Sur, affording little room or accessibility all along the coast from Sur to Quriyat. Here the local tribes congregate in coastal communities and concentrate on fishing and farming (if the terrain allows). At Ra's Al Hadd, the easternmost part of the country, the coastline of Sharqiyah turns to the southwest, skirts the southern edge of the Wahibah Sands, and continues on past Masirah Island.

Al Wusta. This central region of Oman is the primary petroleum-bearing region. Coastal settlements are the only signs of life. The interior is increasingly barren as you approach the Rub' Al Khali, and along the northern border are the treacherous salt flats known as the *Umm As Samim* ("mother of poison"). The southern area toward the coast is known as the **Jiddat Al Harasis,** a large expanse of savanna where the Arabian Oryx reclamation project is taking place.

Dhofar and the Nejd. Dhofar is the southern province of Oman. The area's most important city is Salalah, surrounded by a mountain range separating it from the Nejd, a desolate area to the north on the southern fringe of the Empty Quarter. The climate of Dhofar, as mentioned above, is significantly different from the rest of the country.

The overall effect of the landscape—the Empty Quarter and the Hajar Mountains—coupled with the climate is that of insulation. Oman has remained isolated from the rest of the Arabian peninsula for most of recorded history mainly due to these prohibitive atmospheric and geographical conditions. This will be important in a cultural context as well as you will see farther on in this guide.

Oman Tourism in Summary

Scottish merchant Alexander Hamilton wrote in *A New Account of the East-Indies* in 1727, "The Muscati Arabs are remarkable for their humility and urbanity. . . . [One day] I went into the door of a shop to let [the governor] and his guards have the street, which are generally narrow, but he, observing my complexion and garb that I was a stranger, made his guards go on one side and beckoned me to come forward and stood until I passed him."

Oman is a newcomer to international travel and tourism markets. As late as 1986, there was no policy for tourism whatsoever. Throughout the twentieth century Oman was lost to the outside world: political instability, economic despair, and geographical and cultural barriers prevented any kind of contact. Only through the recent developing infrastructure, which caters to many foreign business interests, did a realization come that there was a definite appeal for tourism. However, the government remains cautious. The country has undergone very rapid growth since the 1970s, which is enough to send anyone into future shock. The emphasis has been on preserving Oman's cultural heritage in the wake of this swift expansion. Indeed, there was concern from many quarters that the country's historic identity would be washed away with the onslaught of modernization.

Since the 1980s, the government has been slowly accepting the idea that it can no longer hold on to the cultural purity that isolation affords. Because of Oman's growth and emergence into the modern family of nations and the need to sustain a burgeoning population, priorities have changed. Oman, although it has an economy based on petroleum export, is not oil rich the way Saudi Arabia and the UAE are. The need right now is to diversify the economy away from oil, and one of the best ways it can do that is through tourism. The Omanis realize that their apprehension can be reversed into their biggest asset. Because the country is so culturally rich and national pride is running at an all-time high, the Omanis are now doing what they do best—being themselves in all their cultural brilliance. To be sure, as a nation that has embraced so rapidly the best that twentieth-century technology has to offer, they have also experienced the pitfalls that lack of maturity brings in most developing countries. But the Omanis' strength lies in the depth and breadth of their extraordinary culture. And here is where they excel. The modern world has brought them many things. But for them to keep pace with that modern world and not lose track of who they are in the face of modernization is an extraordinary feat in itself.

This guide will try to acquaint you with what Oman has to offer, insofar as one volume can. I will attempt to give you a comprehensive overview of Oman, of what there is to see and how it came to be, and to impart the information you need to explore this wonderful country. There is also a selected bibliography for more in depth study. In return, I hope that when you come here you will give the Omanis your undivided attention and the same offer of friendship that they will give to you.

- Although Oman is not the first Middle Eastern country to open its doors to tourism, this recent arrival on the international travel scene offers a refreshing perspective of a long-established culture.
- Oman lies at the easternmost extremity of the Arabian peninsula and was a vital link in the old trade routes to the Far East.
- As a nation, Oman is the oldest in the gulf region. The ruling family, the Al Bu Said dynasty, goes back to the 1740s.
- Once a trading empire that extended from Pakistan to Zanzibar, Oman has enjoyed formal relations with the United States since 1840.
- A nation with a history of seafaring, Oman established trade routes with China as early as the eighth century. Its ancient boat-building center of Sur still makes *dhows,* the wooden sailing vessels, by hand and is the home of the famous Sindbad legends.
- Recent archeological diggings aided by a NASA space shuttle and infrared technology have uncovered an ancient trading city buried beneath the desert, once thought to be the lost city of Ubar (T. E. Lawrence called it the "Atlantis of the Sands"). Located near the modern-day village of Shisr, the city was the center for the once-thriving frankincense trade.
- Like America, Oman, more than any other Arab country, has been a melting-pot culture with influences coming from far beyond the Arabian peninsula—from Africa, Asia, and Europe. The culture is therefore rich and colorful.
- Oman is currently undergoing an economic renaissance spearheaded by His Majesty Sultan Qaboos Bin Said. He has turned his country of two million people into a thriving middle-state economy.
- The regional topography displays breathtaking beauty—rugged mountain landscapes (with secluded Shangri-Las) coupled with sweeping

deserts that have played a prominent role in the country's culture and history.
- Oman has over 1,700 kilometers (1,020 miles) of seacoast, sporting a variety of beaches and coves.
- In spite of an arid climate, Oman supports a wide assortment of wildlife.
- The Hajar Mountains, which have effectively isolated Oman from the rest of the Arab world, are home to many local tribes who carve out their rugged existence in this dramatic setting.
- The southern region of Dhofar, in contrast to the north, is lush with vegetation for several months of the year as it is influenced by the summer monsoon coming from the Indian Ocean.
- Although Oman has experienced some of the hottest temperatures on the face of the earth, at least six months of the year the temperatures are agreeable to travelers. The best time to visit Oman is between September and April.
- The tourist can find accommodations ranging from the simplest and most economic to the most luxurious and extravagant.
- The Omanis are a genuine and friendly people who love to talk to visitors. Don't be surprised if you are invited into someone's home for coffee and a chat.

The Confessional

Unlike many other guidebooks, this one contains no advertising, either overt or covert. The opinions expressed—and there are many—are mine. As with other books in the series, no one can use friendship or favors to influence the coverage of personal commercial interests. You may not agree with the opinions expressed, but you will know that it is based on personal experience and is given openly and honestly.

It has not been possible to stay in every hotel that a visitor can use, but the book covers a good range from luxury to basic. Likewise with restaurants and shops—you will end up eating at, or visiting, some places not mentioned in this publication. If they are particularly good, cheap, friendly, or interesting, please let me know about them so that I can visit them before completing the next edition of the guide.

Writing this book has been a terrific adventure for me, no less than my first visit to Oman because every day I find something new to explore. I hope you will come explore this fascinating country. I have tried to make this book a diverse and comprehensive guide. I have not seen it all nor done it all (although I have done most of all there is to do in this book). I hope this serves as a suitable introduction and a worthy supplement to the number of books available in Oman. I welcome comments, suggestions, and criticisms. If you have found a wadi or jebel not mentioned that deserves exploring, tell me about it and we'll see if it can make the second edition. In the meantime, have a safe journey and Happy Traveling.

Getting the Most Out of This Book

This guide is arranged in a pattern similar to that of the other Maverick Guides. It is a tried and tested format that has been used since the 1980s and it enables you to get a good feel for the country and its people while at the same time getting the specifics that are so necessary when you are traveling.

After a chapter on how to reach Oman, how to travel around when you arrive, and how to smooth the basics of government requirements and travel practicalities, there are two chapters on the land and the people, and then specific area chapters. The chapters need not be read in that sequence, of course. However, if you are using the book to plan your trip, I suggest that you read all sections so that you can decide which areas to visit.

Each of the area chapters is divided into eight numbered parts, and after you become familiar with them in one chapter, you will know where to look for these same subjects in each of the other chapters. The categories are as follows:

1. The General Picture	**5. Dining and Restaurants**
2. Getting There	**6. Sightseeing**
3. Local Transportation	**7. Guided Tours**
4. The Hotel Scene	**8. Shopping**

The book has been set up to be used in two ways. First, you should look through it thoroughly before you leave home. Make some plans on the basis of this reading. Decide where you would like to visit and what you would like to do when you are there. Select some hotels, determine if there are some specific restaurants that you will visit, consider which areas have appeal, and make a list of the things you would like to buy while in Oman. Then go and talk to your travel agent. Remember that while travel agents are well qualified to advise on airfares and some package tours, it is unrealistic to expect them to be familiar with details of all destinations around the world. A good agent will appreciate your making informed suggestions and will benefit from the contact names and telephone numbers found inside this guide.

The book is also designed to be used when you are in Oman. The recommendations on sightseeing tours, hotels, restaurants, and shopping will help you in your quest for smooth, fun traveling. The information on sightseeing will help broaden your horizons and encourage you to explore things that most visitors miss. All the sections will help you save time and money as you travel through Oman.

2

Happy Landings

How to Get There

> [My journey to Muscat] started in one of the open-fronted picturesque booths in Dubai's suq where I sat with a small group of people sipping the coffee provided by its hospitable owner. . . . "How do I get to Muscat?" . . . "Go by boom," said one . . . while others audibly took in their breath and uttered evocative phrases to the Almighty as they pondered the question. . . . "I really want to travel overland," I said to my small audience. . . . "Awdh Billahi" (I seek God's protection), an invocation I was later to hear many times. . . . I enquired as to whether I could join a camel party, but all except those carrying rifles, who were presumably of bedu origin, muttered comments and seemed greatly amused.
> —Ronald Codrai, *An Arabian Album:* Travels to Oman, 1948-1955

Given the geographical profile in the previous chapter, it is easy to see that the best way to reach Oman is by air. Road travel to the Sultanate is possible although it is extremely difficult to obtain road passes unless you are already living in the Middle East. There are highway connections with Yemen in the south and the UAE in the north and beyond into Saudi Arabia and other gulf nations, but most casual travelers will find it next to impossible to get past Saudi borders unless they are Muslim and/or participating in the Hajj (pilgrimage). Your best bet is to fly in directly to Muscat, or, if you are traveling from other gulf nations, come down from Dubai or Abu Dhabi via Al Ayn/Buraimi. Remember that you must leave the country the same way you entered.

25

There is a curious setup along the northern border between the Omani city of Buraimi and the UAE city of Al Ayn. While in the UAE, it is possible to move freely between Al Ayn and Buraimi as they are adjacent to each other on the border. Checkpoints in and out of Oman are removed to narrow mountain passes in the Omani interior. Conversely if you are in Oman and want to visit Buraimi, you must obtain the proper road passes from immigration, as well as a visa for the UAE. You can then visit Buraimi and are free to continue on in the Emirates provided that you return to Muscat for your final departure. (You cannot enter Oman by air in Muscat, obtain road passes, drive to Dubai, and leave the Middle East by air from Dubai and vice versa.) Also if you are traveling in Oman by car and you want to visit the Musandam Peninsula, you will have to procure a similar road pass; however, no pass is required if you take a shuttle flight from Muscat to the Musandam.

All of Oman's international traffic is handled by **Seeb International Airport.** Completed in 1973, with substantial upgrades and renovations in 1979, 1986, and 1993 to handle the increasing influx of passengers and cargo, SIA is a completely modern facility with state-of-the-art services. To complement SIA the country now has five additional civil airports located in Salalah, Sur, Masirah Island, and Khasab and Diba in the Musandam. (Prior to 1973, the only airstrip in Oman was a runway between two mountain ridges in what is now downtown Ruwi. Remnants of that strip can still be seen running north-south adjacent to Wadi Kabir.)

Oman is served by an increasing number of airlines with contacts to Europe, the Far East, and North America. The following is a current list of international airlines and their offices in Muscat.

Aer Lingus
OUA Travel Centre
Tel. 708635

Air India
OUA Travel Centre
Tel. 708635

Aeroflot
Bahwan Travel Agencies
Tel. 704455

Air Lanka
Mezoon Travel
Tel. 796680

Air Canada
National Travel & Tourism
Tel. 566046

Air New Zealand
OUA Travel Centre
Tel. 708635

Air France
Bahwan Travel Agencies
Tel. 704838

Air Seychelles
United Travel
Tel. 703303

Air Tanzania
Oman Aviation Services
Tel. 707222

Alyemeda Yemen Airlines
Bahwan Travel Agencies
Tel. 704455

American Airlines
OUA Travel Centre
Tel. 708635

Ansett Australian Airlines
Omani Travel and Tourism Bureau
Tel. 789845

Balkan Bulgarian Airlines
National Travel & Tourism
Tel. 566046

Biman Bangladesh Airline
Oman Travel Bureau
Tel. 701128

British Airways
OUA Travel Centre
Tel. 708635

Cathay Pacific
Omani Travel and Tourism Bureau
Tel. 789818/32/42

China Airlines—Taiwan
Muscat Travel Agency
Tel. 703403

Continental Airlines
Mezoon Travel
Tel. 796680

Cyprus Airways
Blue Falcon Travel & Commercial Co.
Tel. 704440

Damania Airlines—India
Omani Travel and Tourism Bureau
Tel. 789845

Delta Airlines
National Travel & Tourism
Tel. 566046

East West Airlines—India
Oman Tourism & Travel Agency
Tel. 790881

Egypt Air
Mezoon Travel
Tel. 796680

Emirates
Universal Travel & Tourism Agencies
Tel. 786600

Ethiopian Airlines
National Travel & Tourism
Tel. 566046

Flitestar
OUA Travel Centre
Tel. 708635

Gulf Air
P.O. Box 1444, Musandam Bldg.
Ruwi 112
Tel. 707626

Indian Airlines
National Travel & Tourism
Tel. 566046

Iran Airlines
Mezoon Travel
Tel. 796680

Japan Airlines
Bahwan Travel Agencies
Tel. 704455

Jet Airways—India
Mezoon Travel
Tel. 796680

Kenya Airways
National Travel & Tourism
Tel. 566046

KLM Royal Dutch Airlines
OUA Travel Centre
Tel. 708635

Korean Air
Bahwan Travel Agencies
Tel. 704455

Kuwait Airways
Bahwan Travel Agencies
Tel. 704455

LOT Polish Airlines
Eihab Travels
Tel. 796387

Lufthansa
Mezoon Travel
Tel. 796680

Malaysia Airlines
Oman Shipping & Travel Agencies
Tel. 604655

Malev Hungarian Airlines
United Travel
Tel. 703303

Middle East Airlines
Mezoon Travel
Tel. 796680

Northwest Airlines
International Travel Agencies
Tel. 701133

Olympic Airways
Eihab Travels
Tel. 796387

Oman Air
Oman Aviation Services
Tel. 707222

Pakistan International Airlines
Al Darwish Travels
Tel. 792465

Philippine Airlines
Blue Falcon Travel & Commercial Co.
Tel. 704440

Qantas
OUA Travel Centre
Tel. 708635

Royal Air Maroc
Bahwan Travel Agencies
Tel. 704455

Royal Brunei Airlines
OUA Travel Centre
Tel. 708635

Royal Jordanian
Mezoon Travel
Tel. 796680

Sabena Belgian World Airline
Oman Travel Bureau
Tel. 701128

SAS
Mezoon Travel
Tel. 796680

Saudi Arabian Airlines
Omani Travel and Tourism Bureau
Tel. 789845

Singapore Airlines
Mezoon Travel
Tel. 796680

Sudan Airways
Oman Tourism & Travel Agency
Tel. 790881

Swissair
United Travel
Tel. 703303

Syrian Air
Bahwan Travel Agencies
Tel. 704455

Thai Airways
Bahwan Travel Agencies
Tel. 704455

Tunis Air
Blue Falcon Travel & Commercial Co.
Tel. 704440

Turkish Airlines
Azd Travel & Tourism Agencies
Tel. 707303

United Airlines
Omani Travel and Tourism Bureau
Tel. 789850/52

UTA French Airlines
Bahwan Travel Agencies
Tel. 704455

Yemenia
National Travel & Tourism
Tel. 566046

ZAS Airlines of Egypt
Oman Orient for Travel & Tours
Tel. 790400

British Airways, KLM, Air France, and Swissair are the major carriers out of Europe while Gulf Air is now the rising star of international airlines. Oman has a 25 percent share in Gulf Air along with the UAE, Qatar, and Bahrain. Started in 1950 as a taxi service between Manama (Bahrain), Doha (Qatar), Dhahran (Saudi Arabia), and Sharjah (UAE) for the growing petroleum industry, Gulf Air grew into a regular commuter service. They now maintain a fleet of 37 aircraft (including 767s, A320s, and A340s) servicing Europe, Africa, Asia, Australia, and the USA (with scheduled flights to New York and Houston).

Local transportation.

Transportation Within Oman

Domestic Air Travel. The state-owned Oman Air, a fledgling company of Oman Aviation Services, offers internal shuttle flights to the local airports. In addition they now offer extended services to Dubai (UAE), Kuwait, Cairo, Sanaa (Yemen), Karachi (Pakistan), and Trivandrum (southern India).

A Few Driving Tips.

> There are several winds in those seas which are known to sailors to blow in particular directions at certain times. The peculiar knowledge is acquired by theory, practice and long experience. They also have knowledge of certain signs and indications by which they can tell where the wind will be high or not and when a storm can be expected.
>
> —Abul Hassan Ali bin Al Hussayn Al Masudi, tenth century

Many people have heard horror stories of driving experiences in the Middle East. In Saudi Arabia, where every day you take your life into your hands when stepping into an automobile, conditions are probably the worst due to reckless motorists and poor safety enforcement. Driving conditions in Oman are much better. Driving is thankfully on the right and all vehicles are left-side drive, but a few words of advice will be helpful, particularly if you are going to be driving off-road.

First of all, highways and main streets are generally well kept. Road teams can always be seen giving the highways a good cleaning. (Incidentally, you will note the lines of weekend "wadi bashers" extending from the car washes on Friday evening. It is against the law to drive a dirty vehicle and you can be fined.) Speed limits are posted in kilometers per hour and seat-belt use is required.

Drivers in Oman tend to be of two kinds: either extremely cautious (that is, slow) or practicing for the next Daytona 500. There doesn't seem to be any middle ground. Tailgating in the fast lane is common and overtaking becomes a personal challenge. Coupled with this is an unusual amount of pedestrian traffic on the highways. People think nothing of crossing a six-lane divided freeway. So drive defensively. Also be on the lookout for maroon and white candy-striped cars. These are driving instructors and their students and they seem to be at every turn in the road.

Light rain can mingle with oil and lubricants dropped on the road surface, creating slick laminations on tarmac that are as slippery as glare ice. Watch your speed if it starts to shower.

If there is an accident, the law requires that you not move or remove your vehicle from the scene until the Royal Omani Police (ROP) arrive, even if it is stranded across the road and blocking traffic. Accident reports must be filled out; the proper report is necessary for insurance coverage.

Many roads cut across wadi beds. Be aware of this. When it rains, wadis can overflow very quickly. Most wadis will have red and white posts to indicate a wadi course and when it is not safe to drive through. (When you come upon a wadi and the water level has climbed above the white/red demarcation, stop and wait until the water subsides before traveling through.) In severe storms, roads can be washed out. Rain and flash floods can wipe tracks completely away or fill them up with debris. This is not a frequent occurrence on tarmac roads but on tracks and trails its a different story. Sometimes a graded track has to be replowed by teams of bulldozers after a rain before it is passable again.

If you are going to do a bit of off-road driving (wadi bashing) in Oman, it is advisable to travel in groups of at least two vehicles. Off-road conditions vary in this country and are always considered to be in a state of flux. That being said, you will find most off-road tracks in pretty good shape at any given time, with well-traveled, hard-packed gravel. But rain, wind, water, and other natural hazards can change all that very quickly. Sometimes a track degenerates into a boulder field or has been taken over by a watercourse. On steep slopes, use the brake as little as possible and let your gearbox do the work. Well-traveled tracks develop transverse ruts, which give a corduroy effect and a bit of a bumpy ride. Newer tracks tend to be loose under the wheels. Make sure you have good tires and always carry two spares.

Sand driving requires a slightly different approach. Make sure your vehicle is equipped with balloon tires, sand boards, and a shovel. If you don't have balloon tires, you can deflate your tires for about 45 seconds for more traction in the sand. Just remember to refill them at the next petrol pump when you get back on a main road. Some vehicles come equipped with airbags that attach to the exhaust to jack up the rear end if you become stuck. Whatever you do, don't spin your wheels when you get stuck. You will only dig yourself in deeper.

When driving in sand or water, stay in a low gear until you have crossed that section. Trying to change gears while in transit will cause lost momentum and possible stalling. If you do get stuck, start from a higher gear to prevent wheel spinning.

When traversing ridges or sand dunes, cross at right angles to maximize traction. Don't cross over dunes blindly. Take time to inspect the terrain ahead beforehand.

When you drive in Oman, there is always the possibility that you will spot camels on or near the highway. In Salalah you will see them roaming in herds of 100 or more. Their loping gait suggests a lackadaisical attitude and their expression is rather haughty. In all circumstances, if camels are on or near the road, slow down and proceed with caution. Their movements are rather unpredictable. A horn blast could cause them to bolt, although this is unlikely. Just give them plenty of leeway until they decide where they want to go, and wait till they are clear of the road before you pass. An accident with a camel can be serious (for you and the camel!).

If you are not sure of your driving skills but would like to take full advantage of an off-road experience, there is a one-day crash course (sorry) available from the Occupational Training Institute in Qurum. For about $115 (RO 45) they will take you on and off the road and give you all the hands-on tips and guidelines you will need for your venture. Although this course is geared to neophytes, some seasoned vets have also learned a few tips. Contact Tim Mizen or Nick Nielsen at 565380.

Hitchhikers. You will come across them by the roadside frequently. In lieu of projecting their thumbs, however, they stand with their right arms outstretched and wave their right hands from the wrists, palm down. These are invariably good people with no apparent means of transport. Sometimes they are carrying bags. Use your judgment and feel free to help them along their way. A simple "Wayn?" ("Where?") will get you their transit requirements, and they will be most grateful.

Travel Facts and Figures

Weather and Climate.

The heat . . . was so intense that it burned the marrow in the bones, the sword in its scabbard melted into wax and the gems which adorned the handle of the dagger were reduced to coal. In the plains the chase became a matter of perfect ease for the desert was strewn with roasted gazelles. Both the water and the air gave out so burning a heat that fish went away to seek refuge in the fire.

—Abdul Razak, fourteenth century, with hyperbole

As one would expect, the climate in the Middle East can be quite hot. In Oman, some of the highest temperatures on earth have been recorded (over 50 degrees C, 123 degrees F). It is hard to imagine how some of the interior tribes survive in the oppressive heat, but survive they do. Not surprisingly, the Sultan has decreed that all Omanis should wear traditional costumes in public. This has as much to do with pragmatism as it does heritage. The traditional loose-fitting, light-colored garb (for men the single-piece *dish-dasha* with a *kumma* or *massar* headdress—see "Omani Clothing" in chapter 4—and for women a combination of dish-dasha, trousers, and headdresses from head to toe, faces and hands exposed) does much to ventilate the body and protect against heat rashes and sunstroke.

But for six months of the year, the temperatures are downright pleasant. The only distinction is the difference in the humidity between the interior and the coast, the mountains having the much drier air. In the winter months (referred to as the wet season), temperatures in the evening can be cool (7-15 degrees C, 45-60 degrees F); sometimes in the mountains it can dip below freezing and Jebel Shams can receive a light dusting of

Average Maximum Temperature (Coast)

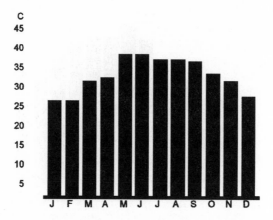

Average Minimum Temperature (Coast)

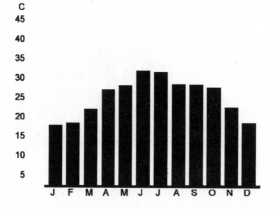

Average Maximum Temperature (Interior)

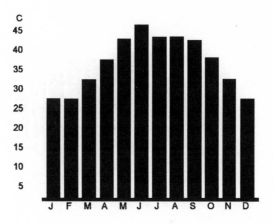

Average Minimum Temperature (Interior)

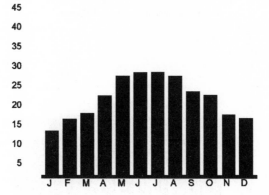

Average Maximum Temperature (Salalah)

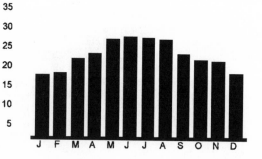

Average Minimum Temperature (Salalah)

snow. And in the summer, while everyone else is sweltering, Jebel Shams, at 10,000 feet, can be a pleasant 25 degrees C.

"After heavy rain, the volume of water flowing through [Wadi Daiqah] must be enormous, and the surging, raging torrent must be a magnificent sight," Col. Samuel Barrett Miles wrote in *Journal of an Excursion in Oman* in 1896. "It not unfrequently happens that travelers and caravans coming from Kuryat [*sic*] are engulfed and overwhelmed by the sudden rise and rush of the stream, as the innumerable tributaries and affluents in a drainage area some 200 square miles, swelling after rain, would concentrate at the gorge with marvelous rapidity and force and form a mighty irresistible wave, destroying everything in its path."

Rain is more prevalent in the mountains than on the coast but it is highly unlikely that you will encounter any precipitation during your relatively short stay. Some places in Oman can go for years without seeing rain. When it does rain, however, watch out! Storms well up and dump buckets of water in a short span of time, usually no more than a half-hour. Cloudbursts are also very localized. In the mountains, it doesn't necessarily have to be inclement overhead. Storms from miles away can send rumbling torrents through ravines and wadis until they reach the sea or disperse into the ground. Roads can be washed out, so it is very important, although this is a rare occurrence, to keep your bearings at all times and know where the high ground is.

In the south, rain and humidity are more common as the summer monsoon washes over the coast from June to October. The days are slightly cooler than in the north but muggy.

Packing and Wearing.

During the day we spent at Muscat . . . nothing could be more delightful. The air was dry, clear and exhilarating. For the previous three or four months the climate had been the same. Muscat has two seasons only—the hot and the cool—each lasting about six months. The hot season is something dreadful; for the black rocks all around give out during the night the heat they store up during the day. The place is a fiery furnace during the whole 24 hours; yet it is not regarded as particularly unhealthy. Possibly the six months of reasonably cool weather, and the complete absence of severe diurnal alterations of heat and cold at any time, keep the public health at par.
—Grattan Geary (editor of the *Times of India*), *Through Asiatic Turkey*, 1878

You will most likely come to Oman during the fall, winter, and early spring months, as the rest of the time is pretty unbearable for most foreigners. Consider packing light, loose-fitting clothing for daytime activity and light sweaters or jackets for the evening. Other clothing will depend on the type of activity you will engage in. Standard sightseeing requires comfortable walking shoes or sandals. Hiking and camping call for a good set of sneakers or hiking shoes. If you are beaching it, tank tops or T-shirts are advisable for men and women along with their standard swimming attire, particularly in public swimming areas. The reason for this is twofold: (1) simple protection from the sun and (2) the Omanis are very modest regarding bathing habits, as you might expect. Skimpy swimming attire is out. The Omanis are very tolerant, but their attitudes toward body exposure conform with the more orthodox views in the Arab world. Swimming attire away from the beach is not appreciated at all.

Men and women should consider modesty in regard to attire. Loose-fitting clothing with minimal exposure is best. Short sleeves are OK, and for women, dresses should fall below the knee. In the evening, sporty, casual wear is sufficient for most venues. Western formal wear (jacket and tie) is usually reserved for business.

Also note that the Omanis are very happy for you to indulge in their culture. They want you to buy Omani clothing and goods to take home and show your friends and family. However, for foreigners to wear Omani clothing in public is considered to be derisive. When you buy that kumma or massar or dish-dasha, don't wear it in public (apart from trying it on for size). An exception to this rule is henna designs for women (see section on clothing). Many foreign women can (and do) try this unique custom. It is not really clothing but decoration. Plus it wears off in a few weeks.

Public Holidays and the Islamic Calendar. Although you can plot your vacation's course quite sufficiently with our Gregorian calendar when coming to Oman, please note that the Islamic calendar is also in effect. The Islamic calendar is a lunar calendar, based on the cycles of the moon. As a result, the Muslim year is 11 days shorter than our solar year and consequently shifts back 11 days every year. It runs in cycles of about 30 years. The Islamic calendar reckons from the year A.D. 622, the year Muhammed fled with his followers to Medina. This year is known as the Hejira, and years that follow it are indicated as A.H. A calendar year consists of 12 months alternating 30 and 29 days, for a total of 354 days. Selected years out of that 30-year cycle are considered leap years, in which 1 day is added to the last month. The following table shows the months of the Islamic calendar and the corresponding dates for the Gregorian calendar for the next 10 years.

The months of the Islamic calendar year are

Muharram (New Year)	Rajab
Safar	Shabân
Rabia I	Ramadân
Rabia II	Shawwâl
Jamada I	Dhû al-Qa'da
Jamada II	Dhû al-Hijjah

AD	1996-97	1997-98	1998-99	1999-2000	2000-01	2001-02	2002-03	2003-04	2004-05	2005
AH	1417	1418	1419	1420	1421	1422	1423	1424	1425	1426
Muharram	May 19, Sun	May 9, Fri	Apr 28, Tue	Apr 17, Sat	Apr 6, Thu	Mar 26, Mon	Mar 15, Fri	Mar 5, Wed	Feb 22, Sun	Feb 10, Thu
Safar	June 18, Tue	June 8, Sun	May 28, Thu	May 17, Mon	May 6, Sat	Apr 25, Wed	Apr 14, Sun	Apr 4, Fri	Mar 23, Tue	Mar 12, Sat
Rabia I	July 17, Wed	July 7, Mon	June 26, Fri	June 15, Tue	June 4, Sun	May 24, Thu	May 13, Mon	May 3, Sat	Apr 21, Wed	Apr 10, Sun
Rabia II	Aug 16, Fri	Aug 6, Wed	July 26, Sun	July 15, Thu	July 4, Tue	June 23, Sat	June 12, Wed	June 2, Mon	May 21, Fri	May 10, Tue
Jamada I	Sept 14, Sat	Sept 4, Thu	Aug 24, Mon	Aug 13, Fri	Aug 2, Wed	July 22, Sun	July 11, Thu	July 1, Tue	June 19, Sat	June 8, Wed
Jamada II	Oct 14, Mon	Oct 4, Sat	Sept 23, Wed	Sept 12, Sun	Sept 1, Fri	Aug 21, Tue	Aug 10, Sat	July 31, Thu	July 19, Mon	July 8, Fri
Rajab	Nov 12, Tue	Nov 2, Sun	Oct 22, Thu	Oct 11, Mon	Sept 30, Sat	Sept 19, Wed	Sept 8, Sun	Aug 29, Fri	Aug 17, Tue	Aug 6, Sat
Shaban	Dec 12, Thu	Dec 2, Tue	Nov 21, Sat	Nov 10, Wed	Oct 30, Mon	Oct 19, Fri	Oct 8, Tue	Sept 28, Sun	Sept 16, Thu	Sept 5, Mon
Ramadan	Jan 10, Fri	Dec 31, Wed	Dec 20, Sun	Dec 9, Thu	Nov 28, Tue	Nov 17, Sat	Nov 6, Wed	Oct 27, Mon	Oct 15, Fri	Oct 4, Tue
Shawwal	Feb 9, Sun	Jan 30, Fri	Jan 19, Tue	Jan 8, Sat	Dec 28, Thu	Dec 17, Mon	Dec 6, Fri	Nov 26, Wed	Nov 14, Sun	Nov 3, Thu
Dhu al-Qada	Mar 10, Mon	Feb 28, Sat	Feb 17, Wed	Feb 6, Sun	Jan 26, Fri	Jan 15, Tue	Jan 4, Sat	Dec 25, Thu	Dec 13, Mon	Dec 2, Fri
Dhu al-Hijjah	Apr 9, Wed	Mar 30, Mon	Mar 19, Fri	Mar 7, Tue	Feb 25, Sun	Feb 14, Thu	Feb 3, Mon	Jan 24, Sat	Jan 12, Wed	Jan 1, Sun
Ordinal number of year in the cycle	7th	8th	9th	10th	11th	12th	13th	14th	15th	16th

Gregorian dates indicate the first day of the Islamic months, e.g. the first day of Ramadan in the year 1424 AH starts on October 27th and the month runs to November 25th 2003 AD.

Shaded areas are leap years.

The most important dates of the Islamic calendar are

Islamic New Year—1st Muharram

The Prophet's Birthday—12th Rabia I

Lailat al-Meiraj—27th Rajab, the night when the Prophet ascended to heaven on a winged mare that bore the face of a beautiful woman with flowing hair

Ramadân—9th month of the Islamic calendar, the month of fasting

Lailat al-Qadr—27th Ramadân, not an official holiday, but a significant day nevertheless, commemorating the night on which Muhammed received revelations that all prayers will be answered

Eid al-Fitr—1st-4th Shawwâl, the breaking of the Ramadân fast

Dhû al-Hijjah—12th month of the Islamic calendar, the month of the Hajj, or pilgrimage to Makkah

Eid al-Adha—9th-14th Dhû al-Hijjah (see below)

In addition to these, Omanis celebrate two holidays on the Gregorian calendar:

July 23—acknowledged as the day Sultan Qaboos came to power in 1970

November 18—National Day (actually Sultan Qaboos's birthday)

Ramadân, the ninth month of the year, is the holy month of fasting. It is a time for introspection and solemn prayer. Every Muslim partakes in a dawn-to-dusk abstention from food and drink. It is not advisable to come to Oman during Ramadân as most services are closed during the day. Government offices run on shortened schedules as well as some businesses. Eateries are closed until sunset. So, before making your travel plans, find out when Ramadân takes place in a given year. (You may refer to the calendar given previously.)

Eid al-Fitr is the holiday directly following Ramadân. It is a very festive and colorful time, as Omanis have broken their fasts to resume their normal life-styles.

Eid al-Adha festivals take place around the middle of the 12th month of the Islamic year, Dhû al-Hijjah, the time of pilgrimage to Makkah. Once again this is a bright and festive time that lasts for several days.

Usually holidays are announced by proclamation shortly before they occur. It is difficult to pinpoint exact dates as many of them pertain to the exact sighting of the new moon. As far as Western dates are concerned, Omanis are very respectful of Western holidays. (I was knocked out by an Omani store that decorated its window with fake snow and Christmas lights before our seasonal holiday.) Business doesn't stop for Western observances. However, expat employees are not cited for absence on major holidays, as employers look the other way.

Mail and Telephone Service. Postal service to and from the Sultanate is fairly efficient, though not the fastest in the world. You can expect incoming letters to Oman to take about two weeks to arrive. (In other words, if you have any urgency, fax if you possibly can or use an international delivery service, which is expensive. There are several international courier services in Muscat, including DHL and Federal Express.) Outgoing mail can take ten days to two weeks to reach the States. If you do mail out, drop your letters at a major post office in Muscat or use the branch office directly opposite the airport (SIA).

In 1994 the Ministry of Posts, Telegraphs and Telephones (PTT) instituted a three-digit ZIP code to facilitate mail delivery. This system has greatly improved the process. But foreigners should note this fact to avoid confusion: There is no local delivery of mail in Oman. Everything is sent to P.O. boxes. Even private residences employ this system. Therefore, a residence in one locale may keep its P.O. box in another.

Postal codes have been allocated by geographical region in the Sultanate while each post office has been allotted a specific code. The first number in the three-digit code represents the region; the following two numbers represent the post office.

GOVERNORATE OF MUSCAT (1—)

Central Post Office (Seeb)	111
Ruwi	112
Muscat	113
Jibroo/Mutrah	114
Madinat Al Sultan Qaboo	115
Mina Al Fahal (PDO)	116

(PDO stands for Petroleum Development of Oman, the national oil company.)

Wadi Kabir	117
Al Harthy Complex	118
Al Amirat	119
Quriyat	120
Seeb	121
Al Maabela	122
Sultan Qaboos University	123
Rusayl	124
Mutrah	125
Oman Commercial Centre	126
Khoula Hospital	127
Seeb International Airport	128
Al Murtafa'a	129

GOVERNORATE OF DHOFAR (2—)

Central Salalah	211
Qairun Hariti	212
Teetam	213
Al Dahareez	214
Al Sa'adah	215
Al Hafa	216
Al Awqadain	217
Taqa	218
Madinat Al Haq	219
Mirbat	220
Tawi Attir	221
Thumrait	222
Sadah	223
Raykhut	224
Dalkout	225
Maqshan	226

AL BATINAH (3—)

Sohar	311
Al Musana'a	312
Widam Al Sahil	313
Al Maida	314
Suwaiq	315
Bidaya	316
Awabi	317
Rustaq	318
Saham	319
Barka	320
Al Tarif	321
Falaj Al Qabail	322

Nakhl	323	Al Akhdar	516
Shinas	324	Al Sinainah	517
Liwa	325	Mahda	518
Al Khaburrah	326		

SHARQIYAH (4—)

THE INTERIOR (6—)

		Nizwa	611
Sur	411	Bahla	612
Al Kamil/Al Wafi	412	Bid Bid	613
Ibra	413	Izki	614
Masirah	414	Lizgh	615
Ja'alan Bani Bu Hassan	415	Birkit Al Mawz	616
Ja'alan Bani Bu Ali	416	Al Hamra	617
Wadi Bani Khalid	417	Adam	618
Sinaw	418	Manah	619
Mudhairib	419	Sumail	620
Mudhaibi	420	Jebel Akhdar	621
Bidiyah	421		
Al Ashkarah	422	**AL WUSTA (7—)**	
Samad Ash Sham	423	Haima	711
Dama Wattaeen	424		

AL DHAHIRAH (5—)

GOVERNORATE OF MUSANDAM (8—)

Ibri	511	Khasab	811
Buraimi	512	Bakha	812
Yanqul	513	Daba	813
Dank	514	Madha	814
Al Araqi	515		

LOCATION OF MAJOR POST OFFICES

Muscat (near the British Bank of the Middle East)—Tel. 738547
Mutrah Business District (next to GTO phone company)—Tel. 708584
Wadi Kabir (Ruwi)—Tel. 786275
Al Harthy Complex (Qurum)—Tel. 563534
Madinat Al Sultan Qaboos (near British Council)—Tel. 697083
Seeb (opposite SIA)—Tel. 510634
Sultan Qaboos University—Tel. 513333
Salalah—Tel. 292933

Incoming packages will be opened and inspected for undesirable materials (contraband, pornography, etc.). Incoming videos are confiscated for screening before they are permitted through (this used to be an involved process that took anywhere from three to six months but now screening is done at the airport and tapes are returned immediately). Note: For Americans it is a good idea not to bother with sending prerecorded videos in or out of the country. VHS recorders and players in Oman use the British system (PAL), which is not compatible with the American standard (NTSC).

Although the best telecommunications are available in Oman, the Western traveler will probably feel that there are still bugs that have to be worked out. Anyone in the entire country is easily reached from abroad by one country code (968) and a six-digit number, but be prepared for occasional delays, crowded lines, and disconnections. Oman is nine hours ahead of New York City, EST, eight hours DST. Public phones are widely available; callers must purchase phone cards, which vary in denomination from one to five riyals. Calls to anywhere in the country are very cheap and foreign calls run at one riyal (U.S.$2.58) a minute depending on the time of day. Discount rates apply late nights and weekends. To place an international call from Oman, dial 00 followed by the country code and the number. (The government allows the monitoring of phone calls without warrant, but it does not abuse this privilege.)

Here are some useful numbers to have handy.

Emergencies: 999
Directory Assistance—Local Information: 198
Directory Assistance—International: 143
International Operator: 195
Time (Arabic/English): 140
Flight Information (arrivals and departures)
Arabic: 1100
English: 1101
Weather
Arabic: 1102
English: 1103
News (including pharmacies on duty)
Arabic: 1104
English: 1105
Foreign Exchange Rates
Arabic: 1107
English: 1106

News Media

Television. The Sultanate operates its own television station with daily programming consisting of news, entertainment (mostly Arabic), children's, and religious programs. Prayers interrupt regularly scheduled programs for brief intervals. There is an English-language newscast at 8:00 every evening.

Most hotels provide satellite services and there is a broad variety of networks to choose from, including CNN, BBC World Service, and Star Network. These networks provide news, sports, and entertainment.

Newspapers and Magazines. There are two dailies published in Oman in English, the *Oman Daily Observer* and the *Times of Oman,* which provide news, commentary, business, and sports. Other papers include the *Gulf News* and *Khaleej Times* (from the UAE) and the *International Herald Tribune.* The following is a list of locally published newspapers and magazines:

NEWSPAPERS (DAILY)

Oman (Arabic)—political
Al Watan (Arabic)—political
Oman Daily Observer—political
Times of Oman—political
Al Shabibah (Arabic)—sports/technical/cultural

MAGAZINES

Weekly

Al Akidah (Arabic)—political
Al Usrah (Arabic)—social
Al Nahdha (Arabic)—political/social
Al Adhwa (Arabic)—political/economic

Fortnightly

Official Gazette (Arabic)—legal

Monthly

Jund Oman (Arabic)—military
Al Omania (Arabic)—social
Al Tejary (Arabic and English)—economic
Al Siraj (Arabic)—cultural

Every Two Months

Al Ghurfa (Arabic and English)—commercial
Al Markazi (Arabic)—economic
Oman Today—tourism

Quarterly

Majalat Al Edari (Arabic)—administrative affairs
Majalat Al Shurtah (Arabic)—police affairs
P.D.O. News (Arabic and English)—petroleum news and features
Rusail (Arabic and English)—industrial
Muscat (Arabic)—municipality working affairs
Regional Municipalities and Environment (Arabic)—environmental affairs

Omani Scouts (Arabic)—scouts and guides activities
Navy Today (Arabic)—military

Half-yearly

Nusoor Oman (Arabic)—military

Annually

A Tribute to Oman—cultural
Pride (Arabic and English)—cultural
Progress—cultural
The Oman Visitor (Arabic and English)—tourism

Occasionally

Resalat Al Masjid (Arabic)—religious

International periodicals include *Time*, *Newsweek*, and *U.S. News & World Report.* Just about any kind of trade magazine can be found in the bookstores and supermarkets if you are looking for reading material. An excellent publication highlighting tourism, related products and services, and scheduled events that comes out every two months is *Oman Today.* On a broader scope there is *What's On*, a tourism monthly published in Dubai.

Metrics and Electrics

The metric system is used throughout Oman, so if you haven't become accustomed to it yet, it's time to brush up.

Temperature. Temperatures are measured in the Celsius scale. For quick conversions see the following chart or use this formula:

$$C = 5/9 \times (F\text{-}32)$$

See also the temperature charts under "Weather and Climate" above for comparison. As a rule, 20-25 degrees C is comfortably warm, 25-35 degrees C is hot, 35-45 degrees is uncomfortably hot, and anything above 45 degrees C can be unbearable. (Temperatures in the desert have been known to rise above 50 degrees C.)

Distance, volumes, weights. It's all metric, so here are

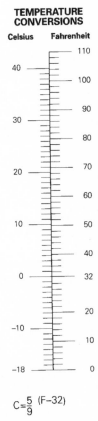

TEMPERATURE CONVERSIONS

$$C = \frac{5}{9}\ (F-32)$$

$$F = \frac{9C}{5} + 32$$

some conversion formulas to impress on your memory. The following should help you make quick mental adjustments.

For distance: 1 kilometer is 0.6 mile (1 mile is 1.67 kilometers). Average speed limits on the highway are about 100 kilometers per hour (60 miles per hour). A meter equals about 39.4 inches. A millimeter equals .03 inches. An inch equals 2.54 centimeters.

For volumes: Liters and quarts are almost the same. A gallon is about four liters and a pint about 500 milliliters.

For weights: 1 kilogram is 2.2 pounds (1 pound is slightly less than half a kilo—0.454 kilograms; a 200-pound man weighs about 91 kilograms).

Electricity. For electricity, Oman uses British standards, which is 220-240 volts at 50 cycles AC, and sockets have been converted to the three-pin flat type. Electricity is abundant along the coast and in major towns in the interior. Only small villages well removed in the interior are without power, but more and more are coming on-line as the Sultanate expands its power grid. The system is efficient and blackouts and brownouts are uncommon, except after heavy rains, when anything is possible. If you bring American appliances to Oman, they must be equipped with power converters and have the proper plugs. If not, most hardware stores can supply the proper plug adapters in Oman.

If you buy an appliance in Oman, it will come without a plug. The plug has to be purchased separately. When buying hi-tech stuff like stereos, make sure they have the proper converters installed (they usually do) so when you take them home you can make the switch from 220 to 110 volts.

Security

> The solicitude evinced for my safety . . . was almost touching, though the descent [into the gorge] could not in fact be called perilous. Indeed, throughout my excursions in Oman, I always had reason to be grateful to the Arabs of my escort, and not unfrequently to the local Arab shaikhs, for their zeal and self-sacrifice on my behalf. They never resented the inconvenience and fatigue I often caused them, but deferred without question to my wishes as to the when and whither; while on any occasion of unusual toil or danger, they seemed to regard my safety and comfort as a main point of consideration.
>
> —Colonel Samuel Barrett Miles; an account of a journey through Wadi Daiqah Gorge in February 1884, from *Journal of an Excursion in Oman,* 1896

The first thing that comes to mind when you think about traveling to the Middle East, as if it is a given, is that there are security risks involved. Is there an element of danger? How safe is it?! When talking about Oman, the only way to answer this question is to confront it head on: *Oman is very safe.* It is one of the safest and most stable countries I have ever visited.

For a very significant reason, Oman has *never* been related to the conflicts and problems that have cropped up elsewhere in the Middle East. (This is explained in detail in the historical overview.) To put it quite succinctly, *Oman is not and never has been a target for terrorist activity, nor is it a breeding ground for extremist politics.* Foreigners need not fear for unwanted reprisals. The people on the whole are quite friendly and there is a substantial security system in place to keep the peace.

To start with, the locals are protected by the **Royal Omani Police (ROP),** a highly skilled police force which is one of the world's most efficient. The ROP is supervised by the Ministry of the Interior and enlists a body of over seven thousand men and women. Along with the standard police force (patrol and detective divisions), the ROP also covers customs, immigration, civil defense, fire fighters, coast guard, prison service, oil security division, and mounted border patrols.

"A man may travel hundreds of miles in this country and never meet with any abusive language and if you happen to be loaded with money in your travels, you need no arms to defend your person, nor any guards to secure your purse," wrote John Jovington in his *Travels* of 1693.

On the local level, crime is very low in Oman because justice is swift. A recent front-page article in one of the Oman dailies gave the Scarlet Letter treatment to the latest batch of convictees by printing their names, stating their crimes, and listing their terms of incarceration. There are few problems with serious crimes such as weapons or narcotics. A word to the wise: don't even think about it.

The Highway Patrol is very efficient. Just ask anyone in Oman who has been caught in a speed trap. These days the ROP defers to high tech in their war against speeding. The old highway stake-outs have been replaced with an automated system that snaps your photo when you whiz by. You subsequently receive a notice in the mail asking you to pay a fine. If you contest it, they will produce the photo and double the fine. (Travelers beware: they can nab you at the airport before you leave.)

"[The Omanis] have a great regard for justice, and an universal toleration for other religions," Capt. Hon. Thomas Keppel testified in his 1825 *A Personal Narrative of a Journey from England to India.*

And the court system is surprisingly fair compared to other Arab countries. I have seen little evidence of favoritism when it comes to dispensing justice. The criminal court system is based on a framework of Islamic judicial practice (*sharia*). Defendants in a case are presumed innocent and cannot be detained unnecessarily. They can be represented by an attorney but there are no public defenders. Trials are non-juried affairs presented before magistrates who decide the issue.

Confinement and punishment in Oman is considered harsh but not abusive or inhumane. Torture, mistreatment, and cruel punishment are not tolerated; incidents are isolated. Executions for capital crimes are rare and subject to ratification by the Sultan. Traditional punishments authorized by Islamic law such as stoning or amputation are *not* imposed. Given the above, it is understandable why a traveler should feel secure in Oman. The crime rate is low and congeniality is high. (I once had a stranger chase me for three blocks to give me a package I left behind.)

On the other side of the coin, safety is as safety does. Don't expect everyone to be a Good Samaritan. Don't leave valuables unattended. Albeit few, there are undesirables lurking in the shadows. Check with your hotel for safekeeping facilities.

On the grand scale, the Sultanate employs an armed force that was established by the Sultan when he came to power in 1970. With the help of foreign military advisors, the Sultan has built up a respectable deterrent force to insure the security of his country. In 1992, there were over forty thousand personnel devoted to the three services, the Royal Army, Navy, and Air Force.

The Royal Army maintains two armored regiments with tank squadrons, reconnaissance and armored car squadrons, eight infantry units, four artillery units, one air defense squadron, one field engineering regiment, and one rifle militia as special security force for the Musandam Peninsula. The army is supplied with American- and British-made armaments.

The Royal Navy fleet consists of province-class missile craft armed with Exocet missiles, Brook-Marine fast attack craft, inshore patrol craft, and amphibious assault craft. The principal naval establishment is the Said bin Sultan naval base at Wudam which contains facilities for training, workshops, repair, and maintenance for the entire navy.

The Royal Oman Air Force maintains a fleet of forty-four combat aircraft of British manufacture. They are assisted by an integrated air control and early warning network. Principal bases are at Thumrait and on Masirah Island, where a training facility is located. Pilots also receive advanced training in Britain.

Oman maintains a collective security with the other gulf nations through its membership in the Arab Gulf Cooperative Council (AGCC, sometimes referred to as the GCC). Along with Bahrain, Kuwait, Qatar, Saudi Arabia, and the United Arab Emirates, Oman has devoted much of its efforts to the improvement of military cooperation and joint participation for the protection of the region. Oman also maintains a "Facilities Access Agreement" with the United States (renewed in 1990). During the Gulf War Oman declared support for the multinational coalition against Iraq. Oman contributed a contingent to Operation Desert Storm and participated in the ground assault on Kuwait. No Omani casualties from combat were reported.

Money and Prices

The monetary unit of the country is the **Omani Riyal** (abbreviated RO). The riyal is divided into 1,000 baizas. Notes are available in denominations of RO 50, 20, 10, 5, and 1, as well as notes for 500, 250, 200, and 100 baizas. Coins appear in 50 and 25 baizas (silver) and 10 and 5 baizas (copper). Note to the incoming traveler: In 1995, the government issued new bills with new designs for *all* denominations (except for the 250 baiza note, which was discontinued). Currently, new bills are in circulation with the old until the old ones are filtered out. When you exchange your money, take some time to examine both old and new bills for their value, which is printed in English and Arabic, as well as markings, to avoid confusion when making subsequent transactions.

One riyal is equal to U.S. $2.58. (Conversely U.S. $1 equals RO 0.387.) The Omani riyal is one of the few currencies in the world that has a greater unit value than the dollar.

The country's monetary system is governed by the **Central Bank of Oman (CBO),** which was established in 1975. At that time the banking laws were formulated to permit and regulate foreign-owned banks in the Sultanate. As of today there are more than twenty commercial banks operating in the Sultanate. Many are listed below.

ANZ Grindlays Bank PLC
Mutrah Business District
Tel.: 703013/704035/705826
Fax: 706911
Telex: 3393 GRNDLY ON

Bank Dhofar Al Omani Al Fransi
Main Office: Mutrah Business
District
Tel.: 790466/67/68
Fax: 797246
Telex: 3900 BDOF ON

Bank Melli Iran
Al Burj Street, Greater Mutrah
Tel.: 710579/708125
Fax: 793017
Telex: 3295 BENKMEL ON

Bank Muscat Al Ahli Al Omani
(SAOG)
Main Office: Mutrah Business
District
Tel.: 703044
Fax: 793536
Telex: 3450 BK AHLAN ON

Bank of Baroda
Mutrah Corniche
Tel.: 714549
Fax: 714560
Telex: 5470 BARODAMT ON

Bank of Oman Bahrain and Kuwait
Main Office: Al Burj Street,
Greater Mutrah
Tel.: 701528/701532
Fax: 705607
Telex: 3920/3674 OBK ON

Bank Saderat Iran
Oman House, Mutrah
Tel.: 793923
Fax: 796748
Telex: 3146 SADERBK ON

Banque Banorabe
Tel.: 703850/704274
Fax: 707782
Telex: 3666 BANO ON

British Bank of the Middle East
Main Office: Mutrah Business
  District
Tel.: 799920
Fax: 704421
Telex: 3110 BBME ON

Citibank N.A.
Mutrah Business District
Tel.: 795705
Fax: 795724
Telex: 3444 CITIBK ON

Commercial Bank of Oman Ltd
  (SAOG)
Main Office: Mutrah Business
  District
Tel.: 793226/27/28
Fax: 793229
Telex: 3275 COMBNKHO ON

Habib Bank A G Zurich
Main Office: Al Tejari Street,
  Mutrah Business District
Tel.: 799876/799865
Fax: 703613
Telex: SWHBIB ON

Habib Bank Limited
Main Office: Mutrah Business
  District
Tel.: 795282/701946/705276
Fax: 795283
Telex: 3283 HABIBBANK ON

Muscat Finance Company Ltd
Main Office: Al Burj St.
  (Rex Road)
Tel.: 799142
Fax: 799141

National Bank of Abu Dhabi
Al Safa House, Mutrah Business
  District
Tel.: 798842
Fax: 794386
Telex: 3740 ALMASRAF ON

National Bank of Oman Ltd
  (SAOG)
Main Office: Mutrah Business
  District
Tel.: 708894
Fax: 707781
Telex: 3281 NBO ON

Oman Arab Bank SAO
Main Office: Mutrah Business
  District
Tel.: 700161/62
Fax: 797736
Telex: 3285 AROMN_BNK ON

Oman International Bank SAOG
Main Office: Al Khuwair
Tel.: 682500
Fax: 682800
Telex: 5406 OMINBNK ON

Standard Chartered Bank
Main Office: Al Jaame Street, Ruwi
Tel.: 703999
Fax: 796864
Telex: 3217 SCBMUS ON

In addition there are three specialized development banks: the Oman Development Bank, the Oman Housing Bank, and the Oman Bank for Agriculture and Fisheries.

All banks offer a broad line of services: checking and savings accounts, currency exchange, travelers' checks, ATMs, etc.

Banking hours leave a bit to be desired: Saturday-Wednesday 8:00 A.M.-12 noon; Thursday 8:00 A.M.-11:30 A.M.; closed Friday. So if you have any banking business to do, get it done as early as possible (before the lines form).

Credit cards such as American Express, Visa, MasterCard, and Diners Club are honored at hotels, restaurants, and shopping areas. Even some of the older *souqs* offer "plastic" services, but if you really want to get into the atmosphere, pay cash after you have haggled for that *khanjar.*

Social Customs and Courtesies

> These Arabians are very courteous in their deportment and extremely civil to all strangers; they offer neither violence nor affront to any; and though they are very tenacious of their own principles and admirers of their own religion, yet they do never impose it upon any.
>
> —John Jovington, *Travels,* 1693

Although the Omanis have been somewhat culturally isolated from the rest of the Middle East you will find a strong undercurrent of Islamic practices with local variations. Omanis enjoy a great deal of personal freedom compared to their neighbors—or their forefathers for that matter. But as a rule of thumb, become familiar with these customs so you will feel as much at home with them as they are with you.

To start with, you have probably heard that everyone in the Middle East is right-handed or trained to be, the left hand being reserved for personal matters and therefore considered "unclean." While this is still true, you will see people in metropolitan areas with latent left-handedness that has been allowed to develop. So if you are left-handed, don't worry. Most Omanis are cognizant of this and receptive. But for formality's sake it is proper and polite to lead with your right hand. When offered food, especially from a communal plate, use your right hand. But left-handers shouldn't have to feel that they automatically have to become right-handed in everything they do.

When shaking hands in the Middle East, do not be put off by the light touch and limp-wristed feel of your acquaintance. This is considered a normal handshake. The hearty, vigorous handshakes that we are accustomed to can be interpreted as signs of hostility and aggression. In Oman, however, you will encounter some people who engage in the Western-style hearty handshake. Sometimes an Omani will accompany his handshake with a hand over his heart to emphasize his sincerity. Also don't be surprised to see men walking hand in hand on the street; it is a common practice and no reflection on their sexual orientation. Kissing between men is also a common greeting, usually consisting of a frontal embrace with a light touch to both cheeks. It is considered a sign of friendship or familial loyalty.

"In Oman . . . the women come freely forward, show themselves and talk like reasonable beings, very different from the silent and muffled status elsewhere. . . . The mutual footing of the sexes is almost European," wrote William Gifford Palgrave in 1868 in his *Narrative of a Year's Journey through Central and Eastern Arabia, 1862-63.*

Omanis are very genial people and welcome conversation. Don't be surprised if they start up a chat with you. Don't feel imposed upon and don't feel intimidated about speaking to men *or* women as long as the conversation stays light, topical, and friendly. Don't talk about subjects such as politics or religion unless they initiate such a discussion, and be careful not to take a contrary position. Be diplomatic if you have to. They do, after all, have their side of the story. They are very fond of their leader, Sultan Qaboos, who has done quite a lot to bring his country into the world community. Omanis are quite proud and happy to be recognized as part of the world family.

In spite of this openness, however, you should be very circumspect when it comes to photography. There are many sights to see and record as part of your permanent memories, and the scenery evokes a picture postcard everywhere you turn. But people, especially in the interior, take a reserved attitude toward photographs. It is not so much superstition as it is modesty and a sense of decorum. For example, it is not considered proper for a woman to allow someone to have in their possession an image of herself, particularly if she is married, as this would upset the limits of propriety and cast aspersions on her. Although you will see publicity photos and the like in brochures and posters, these are typically staged events with people who have granted permission. Do not take photos of people without first requesting *and obtaining* permission. For scenery shots, though, you can snap to your heart's content.

Sometimes people will enjoin you in conversation in solicitation of a handout. Keep in mind that charity plays a more active part of Omani society, as it is the duty of Muslims to be charitable. Use your judgment to assess the situation and act accordingly. You may accept or politely decline as you see fit.

If perchance you are in the interior somewhere and are invited into an Omani home, do not refuse under any circumstances. Even if you happen to be catching a plane soon, don't put yourself in the position of having to refuse an invitation. It is considered very offensive. By the same token, don't hang around waiting for an invite. The Omanis are quite gracious; if the situation arises it will happen quite naturally, which is the best way and most genuine on both sides.

When invited into a home, remove your shoes before stepping into the *majlis* (meeting place). Sometimes the majlis is outside, usually under a tree or shelter of some sort, and delineated by mats. Sit in a manner that does not expose the soles of your feet. To do so is considered rude. In all probability you will be offered *khawa* (Omani coffee), dates, other fruits such as oranges and plantains (a variety of banana), and *halwah,* a delightful confection that is exclusively Omani. (It is quite different from the commercial brands of halva made from crushed sesame in other parts of the Middle East—see the "Omani Food" section in chapter 4.) Once again, do not refuse anything. The portions are small but continual. It is acceptable to refuse any time *after* the first offering. When returning your cup, jiggle it from side to side several times or invert it to indicate you are finished. You may accompany this gesture with a polite nod and your hand placed over your heart.

Most Omanis observe *salah,* prayer, five times a day. In general, men go to the mosque and most women pray at home. (There are segregated prayer rooms at the mosque for men and women.) They are quite gracious when they must interrupt your sojourn to remove themselves to another room and pray. Accept this as part of the routine. They will return shortly to continue your visit as if nothing happened. Visitors are advised that mosques are off-limits to non-Muslims.

In public, Omanis are required to wear their native dress. Loose-flowing garb provides greater ventilation for the body and prevents heat rashes. Visitors are encouraged to buy Omani clothing for souvenirs, but, as mentioned before, apart from fitting, don't wear them in public. Wait until you get home. Also as mentioned before—for practical considerations as well as customary—avoid wearing skimpy or tight-fitting clothes and do not wear bathing attire away from the beach or pool.

If at all possible, do not plan your trip during Ramadân, the Islamic holy month of fasting. Most services are limited, so it is best to avoid traveling to Oman then. Also, Muslims are not allowed to ingest any food or drink during daylight hours. It is considered the utmost offense to eat, drink, or smoke in front of Muslims during this time. Check the Islamic calendar to see when this occurs, as it varies every year.

Another point about the concept of time: Omanis are very forgiving when it comes to punctuality. Although people in the West are tuned in to a fast-paced life-style with demanding schedules, and Oman has adopted that fast-paced style to a certain degree, life there does not go by the clock. Arrangements are *always* kept, but not necessarily when they are scheduled. If there is a delay or postponement, it is assumed there must be a substantial reason, and no further thought is given to the matter. So don't be disappointed or upset if your meeting doesn't go on as scheduled.

Medical Care

Health care and health-care facilities have continually expanded and improved since the inception of His Majesty's economic redevelopment in 1970. Good health was a major priority in the country's redevelopment, and the country has made great strides (see "Sultan Qaboos and the Current Economic Revival" section in chapter 4). The focus has now shifted from treatment to prevention. By 1994 the average life expectancy for Omanis had risen to 68, as infant mortality sank to an estimated 37 deaths per thousand.

The Sultanate employs a full range of medical facilities available to the traveler should the need arise. If you are injured in an automobile accident seriously enough to require treatment, the ROP (police) will see that you are attended to and sent to the proper hospital.

However, if you are taken ill or injured at some time during your trip, you will have to rely on friends, associates, or contacts to get you to a hospital, as there is no emergency ambulance service. Ambulances are only used for transferral between hospitals.

If you have a medical emergency and can get to a telephone, dial 999 (Oman's equivalent to America's 911.) State your name and location and, if possible, the number you are calling from. Explain the nature of your emergency and indicate if police assistance is required. Generally speaking, this is a last resort and unless you are isolated, this action will be preempted by the helpful efforts of just about anybody around you. In an emergency situation, you will be admitted without referral, but you may be transferred to a center that is better equipped to handle your situation. The main hospitals in Oman are:

Royal Hospital
Ghala near the Athaibah roundabout
Tel.: 592888
Specializes in: Blood services
                Geriatrics
                Medical
                       Cardiology

        Endocrinology
        Gastroenterology
        General Medicine
        Nephrology
        Neurology
        Oncology
        Respiratory Disease
        Rheumatology
OB/GYN
        Baby Care Unit
        Maternity
        Ultrasound
        X ray
Outpatient (referrals from other hospitals only)
Pediatrics
Surgery
        Cardio-thoracic
        Cardiovascular
        General
        Orthopedic
        Urology

Al-Khoula Hospital
near Wattayah roundabout, Qurum
Tel.: 560455/Emergency: 563652
Specializes in: Burns
        Neurosurgery
        Orthopedics
        OB/GYN
        Plastics
        Surgery/Trauma

Al-Nahda Hospital
after Wadi Adai roundabout on the Dual Carriageway to Ruwi in Wattayah
Tel.: 701255/Emergency: 707800
Specializes in: Dental
        Dermatology
        Ear, Nose, and Throat
        Opthamology

The **Armed Forces Hospital** (Tel.: 612931) on the Old Nizwa Road is primarily for military personnel and dependents, although the accident and emergency section will provide assistance in extreme emergencies.

The **Sultan Qaboos University Hospital** near Seeb only accepts patients by referral.

In addition to hospitals, there are a number of clinics to provide a wide array of medical services. Hospitals and clinics are identified by a red crescent over the door.

Bausher Clinic
Opposite Royal Hospital, Al Ghubrah
Tel.: 593311
Hours: 7:30 A.M.-2:00 P.M., Sat.-Thurs.
No emergency services available except for pediatrics and OB/GYN

Harub Dental Clinic
Corner of Way 1826 and Way 1805, near Seih Al-Maleh roundabout, Qurum
Tel.: 563217/563814
Hours: 8:30 A.M.-12:30 P.M., 2:30 P.M.-6:00 P.M., Sat.-Wed.
General Dentistry, Oral Surgery

Hatat House Polyclinic
Wadi Adai roundabout, Wattayah
Tel.: 563641
Hours: 8:00 A.M.-12:30 P.M., 3:30-6:00 P.M., Sat.-Wed.; 8:00 A.M.-12:30 P.M., Thurs.
Emergency, Laboratory, Pharmacy

Medident Centre
Madinat al Sultan Qaboos Commercial Centre, Madinat Al Sultan Qaboos
Tel.: Medical-600668, Dental-601668
Hours: 8:00 A.M.-12 Noon, 3:00 P.M.-5:30 P.M., Sat.-Wed.; 8:00 A.M.-12 noon, Thurs.
Emergency on call until 11 P.M., Pharmacy

Qurum Medical and Dental Clinic
Above Salam Stores, Qurum
Tel.: 562198, Pager 910-5907
Hours: 8:00 A.M.-12:30 P.M., 3:30 P.M.-6:00 P.M., Sat.-Wed.; 8:00 A.M.-12 noon, Thurs.
24-hour emergency cover by pager

Beyond that, there are a number of clinics in the interior at strategic locations within the *wilayats* (government districts). If you are traveling on your own and have an emergency, you might take note of local clinics in towns you pass through; if your Arabic is not very strong, they're the government buildings with the red crescent on the signs out in front. If it's beyond regular hours, you might have to raise a fuss to fetch a local doctor.

Muscat area—Muscat Health Centre, Muscat. Tel.: 738563
   Mutrah Health Centre, Mutrah. Tel.: 713539
   Arrahma Hospital, Mutrah. Tel.: 712281
   Ibn Sina Hospital, Wadi Adai. Tel.: 575363
   Quriyat Hospital, Quriyat. Tel.: 645002
   Seeb Health Centre, Seeb. Tel.: 550553
   There are also health centers located in Al Khodh, Dagmar, Hail Al Ghaff, Mazara, Siya, and Yiti.

Batinah Coast—Sohar Hospital, Sohar. Tel.: 840022
   Saham Hospital, Saham. Tel.: 854427
   Wadi Hawasina Hospital. Tel.: 951847
   Shinas Polyclinic, Shinas. Tel.: 847055
   There are also health centers located in Barka, Khabburah, Liwa, Mashaiq, Suwaiq, Wadi Sarami, and Wadi Shafan.

Northern Hajars (facing the Batinah coast)—Rustaq Hospital, Rustaq. Tel.: 875055
   There are also health centers located in Afi, Awabi, Hooen, Nasnah, Nakhl, Wadi Bani Ghaffir, Wadi Bani Kharus, Wadi Hemli, Wadi Mistal, and Wadi Sahtan.

Jebel Akhdar (facing the interior)—Nizwa Hospital, Nizwa. Tel.: 425055
   Sumail Hospital, Sumail. Tel.: 351382
   Bahla Hospital, Bahla. Tel.: 419233
   Adam Hospital, Adam. Tel.: 434033
   Izki Hospital, Izki. Tel.: 340033
   There are also health centers in Al Ghafat, Al Hamra, Al Mamoor, Birkit Al Mawz, Bisiya, and Manah.

Dhahira—Buraimi Hospital, Buraimi. Tel.: 650855
   Ibri Hospital, Ibri. Tel.: 491905
   Yankul Hospital, Yankel. Tel.: 402055
   Wadi Al Jizzi Hospital. Tel.: 668033
   There are also health centers in Al Fayadh, Dank, Hajerrmat, Madha, Mamur, Muqniyat, Sunaina, Ta'nam, and Wadi Fida.

Sharqiya—Sur Hospital, Sur. Tel.: 440244
   Ibra Hospital, Ibra. Tel.: 470022

Bilad Bani Bu Ali Hospital. Tel.: 453011
Wadi Bani Khalid Hospital. Tel.: 485005
There are also health centers in Aiga, Al Aflaj, Al Ayoun, Al Dhahir, Al
Dreez, Al Ghaina, Al Kamil, Al Mudhaibi, Al Ruwais, Al Suwaih, Bidiyah, Bilad
Bani bu Ali, Bilad Bani bu Hassen, Falaj al Mashlikh, Ibra, Qumaila, R'as Al
Hadd, Sinaw, Samad Al Shaan, Tiwi, Wadi Bani Jaber, and Wadi Bani Khalid.

Al Wusta—Al Kahil, Duqm, Haima, Liqbi, Mahoot, Masirah, Soghara

Dhofar—Sultan Qaboos Hospital, Salalah. Tel.: 211555
There are also health centers located in Al Hallaniat, Ashuwaimiyah,
Dhalqut, Ghadow, Hadbin, Hasiq, Haugaf, Jibjat, Khadrar, Madinat Shahan,
Madinat Al Haq, Marsidod, Mirbat, Mudhai, Muqshun, Port Raysut, Qairon
Hairitti, Rakhyut, Rima, Salalah, Shahib Assaib, Sharbithat, Sheleem, Sudh,
Taqa, Tawi Attir, Teytum, Thumrait, and Umbushq.

Musandam—Khasab Hospital, Khasab. Tel.: 660187
There are also health centers located in Bukha, Dibba, Kumzar, Lima,
and Madha.

Pharmacies. There is an extensive network of pharmacies throughout
greater Muscat providing a wide range of medical products—cosmetics, toi-
letries, baby care, health foods, medical and health-related equipment,
health-care and over-the counter products, as well as prescription drugs.
Besides maintaining normal hours, there is a rotation of duty for twenty-four-
hour services. If you have a pharmaceutical emergency, check a local daily
newspaper or the evening news telecast at 8:00 P.M., Oman-TV, for the list of
"on duty" pharmacies for that day. Duty lists are also posted at pharmacies
and clinics, and an "on duty" pharmacy will burn a red light over the door.

Note that many drugs are from Europe and have different names from
their U.S. equivalents. If you bring prescription medications with you, check
with your doctor for generic names to assist the pharmacist in finding the
proper prescription for you.

Pharmacy normal operating hours are 8:00 A.M.-1:00 P.M., 4:00 P.M.-7:00
P.M., Sat.-Thurs.; 4:00 P.M.-7:00 P.M., Fri.

Opticians. There are many licensed opticians providing the latest in opti-
cal products and services for eyeglasses and contact lenses, plus testing,
throughout greater Muscat. There are outlets in all the major shopping
areas operating at regular business hours.

Notes on Health and Safety

The constitution of each one of us had undergone so sad a change. Trouble
and fatigue, sickness and the burning of the fever, went on increasing every day.
This cruel condition was prolonged for the space of four months; our strength

gave way by degrees and the malady increased. . . . I am reduced to such a state
of weakness, O my friend, that the zephyr carries me each instant from one climate to another like the smell of the rose.

—Abdul Razak, fourteenth century

When you come to the Sultanate of Oman, you are most likely entering
the country from a different climate than your own. Because Oman sometimes experiences extreme weather conditions (namely heat) for several
months of the year, it is advisable to come only if you are reasonably fit and
in a good state of health. You are not required to have any special inocula-
tions unless you are coming from a country (or zone) of contagion or poor
health conditions. You should have adequate health insurance to cover
you in the unlikely chance of accident or illness.

If you have pets, it is advisable to leave them cared for at home.

When you come to Oman, you should be aware that it is, apart from
the major urban areas, a rugged wilderness environment, *not* like some
wilderness areas we are accustomed to in the States. For instance, in many
of the canyons and wadis there are no restraining fences or warning signs
to point out a hazardous spot along a trail. (As more tourists come into
the region, the government is taking steps to make the areas more accessible and "tourist-friendly," and local guides are becoming more available.)
Caution and common sense are in effect here, especially if you are a first-
time visitor and traveling on your own. Wadis can be particularly dangerous
if there is any sign of rain, *even if it is not directly overhead.* Flash floods are
responsible for many accidents, and there have been drownings, so it is
imperative to have good bearings and orientation. Know where the high
ground is!

Carry a first aid kit with you to handle small emergencies such as cuts,
bites, burns, or sprains.

If you have never been to an arid region before, don't underestimate
what the heat can do, particularly if you travel here in summer. Bring plenty
of fluids along on your trip, either one of the many brands of local bottled
waters, juices, or electrolyte replacement drinks that are available in many
supermarkets.

Know the difference between *heat exhaustion*—headache, fatigue, mus-
cle cramps—and *heat stroke*—hot, dry skin (no sweating!), which can cause
possible brain damage or death.

Wear appropriate sunblock on your skin and keep exposure of your body
to the sun to a minimum. Wear wide-brimmed hats, sunglasses, and loose-fitting tops and trousers. Good trainers or walking shoes are essential, too.
Rest in the shade whenever you can. If you do get sunburn, a number of topical balms are available.

Malaria is no longer the problem it used to be a short twenty years ago because of the government's program to eradicate the source: the pesky anopheles mosquito. A report in the *Oman Daily Observer* in August of 1996 stated that recorded cases for that year were at about 468, down from about 13,000 cases in 1990. However, malaria has *not* been eliminated. Some areas can be considered high risk, mostly the humid vegetated zones along the coast, or in wadis where the mosquito can breed. Malaria, if gone unchecked, can be fatal. If you have been in one of these areas and begin to run a high fever, seek medical help immediately. Take precautions. Wear long clothes and socks when camping out. Use commercial insect repellents and/or candles and coils. The U.S. Federal Center for Disease Control recommends the use of the prophylaxis mefloquine (the area being choloroquine resistant).

There are a number of creepy-crawly things in the desert that range from just nuisances to serious health threats. The serious ones won't attack unless cornered or provoked and the nuisance ones are just that. The most important dangers are listed below.

Snakes. A wide variety of species live in Oman. Some are venomous, but most are generally more frightened of you than you are of them—they do scurry away on approach and it's OK to observe them at a reasonable distance. It is helpful if you know how to identify snakes, but if you don't, there are books available in Oman on the local reptilian inhabitants. There are several species of water snakes, so before you jump into that fresh pool, toss a stone in to frighten anything away.

Scorpions. Always a crowd-pleaser to the taunters of the squeamish, scorpions can give a very serious sting from the tip of their tail. Although it is very painful, it is rarely fatal except possibly for small children. Scorpions love dozing under rocks, so it is wise to leave rocks and stones undisturbed or, at the very least, inspect them carefully. Painkillers are available at local clinics.

Camel spiders. These are another favorite that sound great in the telling but are rarely encountered. Camel spiders are quite large as spiders go, and they like to attach themselves to a sleeping host (usually camels) and inject a local anesthetic. When the victim wakes, he, she, or it might find a sizable area of flesh missing, ingested by the spider.

Dogs, cats, and other animals. In Oman, dogs and cats do not receive quite the same accord and prestige as they do in the U.S.A. Some local people have them as house pets and employ watchdogs, but there are a number of unkept animals. It is advisable not to approach and pet stray animals. There have only been isolated cases of rabies documented, but since rabies is such a potentially life-threatening disease, it is better to be safe than sorry. The same applies to any feral creature found in the desert, such as foxes. A creature that may appear wounded may actually be sick and infected.

When swimming and diving, be aware that there are a number of undersea nasties that can ruin your day—but don't let awareness spoil your fun.

Jellyfish. In the summer jellyfish proliferate. All varieties are poisonous; they suspend long tentacles beneath them that house nematocysts, which are little triggers that release on touch and inject poison into the victim—intended or not. Even after a storm which roils the waters, tentacles can break off, float around, and sting whatever they come in contact with. Jellyfish washed ashore can still sting even though they're dead. Jellyfish stings can be itchy and painful, but one species found in Omani waters, the box jellyfish, can be fatal. The box jellyfish looks like an inflated bag with four orange spots floating on the surface. Its long stretch of tentacles trailing beneath the surface are deadly. If stung by a box jellyfish, rub the area infected with vinegar or urine (yes, urine!), then rub softly with sand . . . and seek help immediately.

Urchins and corals. Along rocky stretches of coastline, there are urchins, and their stings can be very painful, though not life-threatening. In some areas it is good to wear sneakers while swimming. Corals can also cause problems by giving sharp cuts when stepped on.

Stone Fish and Sea Snakes. These are two very poisonous species, but are not considered threats because they retreat from populated areas and do not attack unless *seriously* challenged. The venom of a sea snake is so potent, one drop can kill ten men. More apt to be encountered by divers than bathers.

Sharks. Now that the bad stuff is out of the way, let's talk about *sharks!* Although there are several varieties of sharks in Omani waters, they invariably stay away from populated areas and shy away from any approach. Divers have noted that the sound emanating from their scuba gear is enough to scare them away. There are no recorded instances of shark attacks in Oman.

Personal Hygiene

All the modern facilities you encounter in the greater Muscat area have Western-style washrooms and toilets. Shower stalls and bathtubs are installed in these as well as the standard Western toilet, paper dispensers, and sometimes a bidet. A plethora of soaps, oils, lathers, and balms are available at all the stores.

In Oman's interior, styles and cleanliness standards vary. Many places have only Asian-style toilets with a pull-chain reservoir overhead, and paper is deferred in favor of a flexible water nozzle or a spigot with a pail and cup. Petrol stations have restrooms which are almost always

Asian-style, sometimes with the plumbing in various stages of disrepair. If you are accustomed to relieving yourself Western style, it would be wise to carry your own roll of paper or tissue, which is easily obtained at local markets.

Government Fiddle-Faddle

Passports and visas.

The Sultan is an Arab of the tribe of the Azd . . . and is called Abu Muhammed ibn Nabhan . . . an appellation given to every sultan . . . no one is hindered from appearing before him, whether stranger or any other. He receives his guests honorably, after the customs of the Arabs, assigns [them] hospitality, and makes gifts according to [their] standing.

—Ibn Battuta, *Travels*

In the past few years, visa requirements have eased in Oman owing to the broadening market for tourism. To enter Oman you must have a valid passport and at least one empty page to stamp your visa. You can apply for a visa through the Omani embassy or consulate of your home country. Express visas are available (24-hour processing time) and are valid for two weeks from date of issue. Business visas take about a week to process and are valid for six months from date of issue and three months from date of entry. Tourist visas can be obtained through travel agencies or your hotel. An application must be filled out (see Sample Application) and submitted in advance of your planned travel. It takes about three to ten days to process the application. You must include at least four passport-sized photos with your application (or a photocopy of your passport with all of the relevant information below). A tourist visa has a validity period of three months with an actual staying period of one month. If you don't receive your visa before you fly, you will obtain a fax copy of it before you leave your country to be presented at the visa booth when you first walk into the terminal. Upon entry to Oman you must stop at this booth to obtain your visa if you don't have the original and proceed to immigration to have your visa stamped.

People with Israeli stamps in their passport or with Israeli passports *are* allowed to enter the country due to the fact that Oman is politically moderate and quite independent. For further explanation, read chapter 4.

Citizens of Arab Gulf countries (GCC nationals) do not need a visa to enter Oman. Non-GCC nationals in the UAE seeking entry via the Oman/UAE border can apply at the Oman Commercial Office in Dubai or the immigration office in Buraimi.

Transit visas, good for twenty-four hours, are available at Seeb International Airport.

Sample Visa Application

Name in Full: _____ Sex: M _____ F _____

Date of Birth: _____ Place and Country of Birth: _____

Occupation/Profession: _____

Nationality/Passport No.: _____

Place and Country of Issue: _____

Date of Issue: _____ Date of Expiration: _____

Permanent Address: _____

_____

_____

If you have visited Oman before, details of last visit:

Visa No.: _____

Date of Issue: _____

Date of Arrival: _____

Date of Departure: _____

Proposed Date of This Visit—From: _____ To: _____

Details of Accompanying Family Members on the Same Passport:

Name: _____ Relationship: _____

Date of Birth: _____ Place and Country of Birth: _____

Name: _____ Relationship: _____

Date of Birth: _____ Place and Country of Birth: _____

Name: _____ Relationship: _____

Date of Birth: _____ Place and Country of Birth: _____

> We . . . walked for six days through an empty plain; on the seventh day we arrived
> in Oman. It is a fertile region with many camels, trees, orchards, enclosures
> planted with palm trees with many fruits of various kinds. We went to the capi-
> tal of that country, the city of Nizwa.
>
> —Ibn Battuta, *Travels*

Once you are in Oman you are free to travel about the country with the following exceptions: If you wish to visit some historical or archeological sites, you might need a permit from the Ministry of Interior or the Ministry of Heritage and Culture to enter. Some sites are undergoing renovations and are for the most part off limits to the general public. Please see this book's "List of Towers and Fortresses" for areas that are currently (as of this book's publication) restricted because of restoration.

The same goes for natural and environmental attractions such as the green turtle nesting areas and the wildlife reserves. Here you will need a permit from the Ministry of Regional Municipalities and Environment to gain access.

Some regions of the country are off limits because they are either government or military installations. For the most part they are well marked and guarded, such as the radar base on Jebel Shams or the military area on the Saiq Plateau (permit required). If you do make a wrong turn down a restricted access road, you will be kindly redirected. (I was once escorted out of a restricted area but not before I was invited to take khawa and dates with the attendant.)

If you wish to visit Buraimi or the Musandam Peninsula by car, you will need to obtain a road pass from immigration and a visa for the UAE. You will then be free to travel on to Dubai or Abu Dhabi in the UAE just as long as you return to Muscat for your final departure.

Non-Muslims should *not* enter mosques or mosque property.

Customs and Duties.

> Most of the Chinese merchant ships take on their cargo at Siraf . . . they then
> sail for Muscat, being the last port of call of Oman . . . In this sea were the moun-
> tains of Oman and the place known as Al-Dardour (whirlpool), a narrow pass
> between two underwater rock formations plied only by smaller ships. The Chi-
> nese do not pass by this place. Here also are the two mountains known as Kaseer
> and Aweer (the Destroyer and the Wrecker). Only a tiny portion of these is visi-
> ble above water. If it passes the mountains safely, the ship will soon arrive at
> Sohar. On the return journey, ships anchor at Muscat to take on sweet water,
> then make sail for India.
>
> —At 'Taji Suleiman, *Silsila Al Tawarikh* (The History Section Annals), 851

Personal items are exempt from duty. Import of arms, narcotics, and pornography is strictly prohibited. Videocassettes and books are subject to scrutiny and can be impounded. As stated before, American videotapes are not worth th bother to bring in or out because of incompatible systems. Visitors are permi ted to carry only one liter of alcohol. Food items may be subject to quarantine

Be sure to save some money for the end of your trip: there is a RO 3 airport tax payable on departure.

Travelers' Guide

Business Hours. Business hours in Oman vary from business to business. The work week is from Saturday to Wednesday, with retail stores open through the weekend.

Government office hours are from 7:30 A.M. to 2:30 P.M., Saturday through Wednesday.

Banks are open from 8:00 A.M. to 12 noon Saturday through Wednesday; from 8:00 A.M. to 11:00 A.M. on Thursday. Banks are closed Friday.

Retail stores open every day between 8:00 and 9:00 A.M. and take an extended lunch break at 1:00 P.M. They reopen at 4:00 P.M. and stay open until 9:00 P.M., keeping their doors open only during the more comfortable hours of the day. On Fridays, retail stores open for the late afternoon-evening session only.

Restaurants stay open till 10:00 or 11:00 P.M., some cafés even later.

Tipping. Most restaurants include a service charge so tipping is not necessary, but feel free to reward your waiter or waitress if you feel that it is warranted. Cabbies are not tipped either although you should establish your fare before you set off. Cabs are unmetered in Oman. A fare of RO 5 between SIA and Muscat is considered reasonable. Short trips, a block or two, are 200 bz.

Getting Around.

> After going up and down a number of narrow streets, or rather lanes, for there is not a genuine street in all Muscat, we entered one differing in nothing from the others . . . [We] stopped at a ponderous gate, close shut and [were told that] this was the entrance to the palace. [Our interpreter] knocked and a little wicket was opened; he spoke a few words and we were invited to enter through a small doorway in the great gate. We found ourselves in a sort of courtyard, around which was built a palace, a very unpretentious, two-story edifice. To our left, close to the gateway, was a good sized room, in which reclined a splendid African lion; the front of the lion's parlour was formed of iron bars similar to those which protect the plate glass of jewelers shops in London . . . Doubtless he is there to strike awe into the souls of people who may seek an interview with the sovereign.
> —Grattan Geary (editor of the *Times of India*), *Through Asiatic Turkey*, 1878

When you are ready to travel throughout the countryside, the best maps available are the ones published by the National Survey Authority (NSA). These maps are available at bookstores and supermarkets in greater Muscat. The Family Bookshops chain is the best. They have outlets in Ruwi, MQ Shopping Center, Muscat Intercontinental Hotel, Qurum (opposite Sabco Center), Rusail, Salalah Holiday Inn, and downtown Salalah on Al Nahdah

Street. There are both English and Arabic versions of the maps. At present there is a map of the Sultanate, 1:300,000 scale; a map of Salalah area, 1:20,000 scale; and a set of four maps for greater Muscat, 1:20,000 scale. These are currently only available in Arabic, but the English versions are being updated and reprinted.

Other country maps by independent publishers are available in the stores.

When asking for directions, be careful. Orientation is not an Omani's strong point. Local maps (the kind on handbills or the backs of brochures advertising various attractions) are usually incomplete, confusing, or contradictory. Spellings are inconsistent. (This is a transliteration problem from Arabic to English more than anything. Many place names have yet to be standardized, although the NSA has tried. "Mutrah" and "Matrah" are the same city, as is "Nizwa" and "Nazwa," "Seeb" and "Sib," "Sohar" and "Suhar," "Azaiba" and "Athaibah." "Ibra" and "Ibri," however, are two different places.)

Signposts with mileages are scattered liberally throughout the country, with more and more appearing every day. But, as mentioned above, spellings and distances are inconsistent. So if a place *sounds* like the one you want to go to, it's probably the right one. Also note that if you are going to the interior, several villages can have the same name. Fortunately, they are usually not in proximity to one another.

In town, common names take precedent over given names. Al Burj Street in Ruwi is called Rex Road because that is where the Rex Cinema once stood. Ruwi Souq Street is also called Ruwi High Street. Al Baladiyah Street is called Honda Road because most auto service centers started there. Honda Road extends all the way through the hardware, plumbing and electrical supply district. The "Dual Carriageway" is actually the Sultan Qaboos Highway running from Muscat to Seeb and up the coast to Sohar. (And I thought all along the Brits were saying "Jewel.") Also, British terminology prevails on the highway—rotaries are "roundabouts," overpasses are "flyovers," and turnoffs or rest stops are "lay-bys."

Also note: Building levels are European style. The first floor is the one *above* the ground floor.

Handicapped Access. Before I left Oman, I had the opportunity to meet an enterprising gentleman, Mr. Mukhtar Al Rawahi, who is the head of the Oman Association for the Disabled. Mr. Rawahi is a paraplegic who led the Omani contingent of disabled athletes to the Para-Olympics in Atlanta for the '96 games. He has been working to make many Omani establishments accessible to the handicapped. While much of Oman may appear daunting to some, there are no limits to where the mind will travel, and where the mind goes, the body can follow. If you need assistance or would like to obtain a list of buildings, hotels, and travel venues that are handicapped-accessible, you can contact:

The Oman Association for the Disabled
P.O. Box 331
Muscat 113
Sultanate of Oman
Tel.: 968-503220   Fax: 968-597657

Embassies and Consulates.

O'Allah, protect for us His Majesty the Sultan,
And the people in our land;
With honour and peace;

May he live longer and supported,
Glorified be his leadership
For him we shall lay down our lives;

O'Oman—since the time of the prophet,
We are a dedicated people amongst the noble Arabs,
Be happy—Qaboos has come,
With blessings of the Heaven;

Cheer up and commend him to the protection of your prayers.
—Oman National Anthem

To start with, before we delve into the list of nations that share formal relations with Oman, it would be worthwhile to describe the symbols that give Oman its national identity. Flags are displayed on all government buildings as well as along motorways and in private homes. The Omanis are very patriotic people and show their pride quite readily.

The national flag of Oman, adopted by Royal Decree on December 17, 1970, is rectangular and consists of three colors—white, red, and green. The first third of the flag extending from the hoist is a vertical red field. The fly consists of three horizontal stripes arranged accordingly: the top two-fifths of the flag is white, the middle fifth is red extending from the vertical red hoist, and the lower two-fifths is green. Emblazoned in silver in the upper left canton is an emblem, a pair of crossed swords with a sheathed Omani dagger known as a *khanjar* superimposed.

The white in the flag symbolizes the dedication of the Omani people to peace and prosperity. The red symbolizes the blood spilled by Omanis protecting their home from foreign invaders (prior to 1970 the flag was all red). The green symbolizes the fertility of the land. The khanjar, traditional weapon of the Omanis, was adopted as an emblem in the eighteenth century.

The following is a list of embassies and consulates as well as other world organizations that maintain offices in the Sultanate.

EMBASSIES

Embassy of the Democratic and
    Popular Republic of Algeria
P.O. Box 216
Madinat Al Sultan Qaboos 115
(Embassy located on Al Inshirah
    Street in Madinat Al Sultan
    Qaboos)
Tel.: 601698
Fax: 694419
Telex: 5054 AMBALG ON

Embassy of the Republic of Austria
P.O. Box 2070
Ruwi 112
(Embassy located in SARCO Show-
    room Building across from Ruwi
    Novotel in Ruwi)
Tel.: 793135/145
Fax: 793669

Embassy of the State of Bahrain
P.O. Box 66
Madinat Al Sultan Qaboos 115
(Embassy located on Way 3017
    near Al Sarooj Petrol Station in
    Shati Al Qurum)
Tel.: 605075
Fax: 605072

Embassy of the People's Republic
    of Bangladesh
P.O. Box 3959
Ruwi 112
(Embassy located on Al Farahidi
    Street in Central Business Dis-
    trict, Ruwi)
Tel.: 708756
Fax: 708495
Telex: 3800 BANGDOOT ON

Embassy of the Sultanate of
    Brunei
P.O. Box 91
Ruwi 112
(Embassy located on Way 3050
    near Al Sarooj Petrol Station in
    Shati Al Qurum)
Tel.: 605075
Fax: 605910

Embassy of the People's Republic
    of China
P.O. Box 315
Ruwi 112
(Embassy located on Way 3051 in
    Shati Al Qurum)
Tel.: 696698/696782
Fax: 602322
Telex: 5114 CHINAEMB ON

Embassy of the Arab Republic of
    Egypt
P.O. Box 2252
Ruwi 112
(Embassy located in Diplomatic
    Area in Al Khuwair)
Tel.: 600411/600982
Fax: 603626
Telex: 2047 ON

Embassy of the Republic of France
P.O. Box 208
Madinat Al Sultan Qaboos 115
(Embassy located in Diplomatic
    Area in Al Khuwair)
Tel.: 604222/266/280
Fax: 604300
Telex: 5163 ON

Embassy of the Federal Republic
of Germany
P.O. Box 128
Ruwi 112
(Embassy located near Al-Nahda
Hospital in Al Hamriya)
Tel.: 702482/702164
Fax: 705690
Telex: 3440 AAMUSCAT ON

Embassy of the Republic of India
P.O. Box 1727
Ruwi 112
(Embassy located in Commercial
Bank Building in Central Busi-
ness District in Ruwi)
Tel.: 702960/957
Fax: 797547
Telex: 3429 INDEMBS ON

Embassy of the Islamic Republic of
Iran
P.O. Box 3155
Al Khuwair 112
(Embassy located in Diplomatic
Area in Al Khuwair)
Tel.: 696944/47
Fax: 696888
Telex: 5066 ON

Embassy of the Republic of Iraq
P.O. Box 262
Madinat Al Sultan Qaboos 115
(Embassy located on Way 1737 in
Madinat Al Sultan Qaboos)
Tel.: 604176/78/79
Fax: 605112
Telex: 5110 IRAQIYAH ON

Embassy of the Republic of Italy
P.O. Box 3727
Qurum 112
(Embassy located on Way 2411 in
Qurum)
Tel.: 564832/560968/564838
Fax: 564846
Telex: 5450 ITALDIRI ON

Embassy of Japan
P.O. Box 3151
Ruwi 112
(Embassy located on Way 2114 in
Madinat Al Sultan Qaboos)
Tel.: 603464/600095
Fax: 698720
Telex: 5087 TAISHI ON

Embassy of the Hashemite King-
dom of Jordan
P.O. Box 2281
Ruwi 112
(Embassy located in Diplomatic
Area in Al Khuwair)
Tel.: 602285
Fax: 601086
Telex: 5518 JORDAN ON

Embassy of the Republic of Korea
P.O. Box 2220
Ruwi 112
(Embassy located near Al Falaj
Hotel in Ruwi)
Tel.: 702322/702458
Fax: 706250
Telex: 3132 GONG KWAN ON

Embassy of the State of Kuwait
P.O. Box 1798
Ruwi 112
(Embassy located in Diplomatic
  Area in Al Khuwair)
Tel.: 699626/27
Fax: 600972
Telex: 5746 KUWAIYIA ON

Embassy of the Republic of
  Lebanon
P.O. Box 67
Shati Al Qurum 118
Way No. 3019, Villa No. 1613
Tel.: 695844/693208
Fax: 695633

Embassy of Malaysia
P.O. Box 3939
Ruwi 112
(Embassy located on Way 1518 in
  Madinat Al Sultan Qaboos)
Tel.: 698643/698329
Fax: 605031
Telex: 5565 MALWKAKIL ON

Embassy of the Kingdom of
  Morocco
P.O. Box 3125
Ruwi 112
(Embassy located on Al Inshirah
  Street in Madinat Al Sultan
  Qaboos)
Tel.: 696152/53
Fax: 601114
Telex: 5560 SIFAMAR ON

Embassy of the Royal Netherlands
P.O. Box 3302
Ruwi 112
(Embassy located in OC Centre
  next to Ruwi Roundabout in
  Ruwi)
Tel.: 705410/420
Fax: 799020
Telex: 3050 NETHEMB ON

Embassy of the Islamic Republic of
  Pakistan
P.O. Box 1302
Al Khuwair 112
(Embassy located behind Al Habib
  Bank in Al Khuwair)
Tel.: 603343/603401/603439
Fax: 697462
Telex: 5451 PAK ON

Embassy of the Republic of the
  Philippines
P.O. Box 420
Madinat Al Sultan Qaboos 115
(Embassy located behind Burger
  King in Al Khuwair)
Tel.: 694857/860/862
Fax: 699718

Embassy of the State of Qatar
P.O. Box 802
Muscat 113
(Embassy located near Al Falaj
  Hotel in Ruwi)
Tel.: 701802/707524
Fax: 794588
Telex: 3460 AL QATARY ON

Embassy of the Federal Republic
of Russia
P.O. Box 80
Ruwi 112
(Embassy located in Shati Al
Qurum)
Tel.: 602893
Fax: 604189
Telex: 5493 ON

Royal Embassy of Saudi Arabia
P.O. Box 1411
Ruwi 112
(Embassy located in Diplomatic
Area in Al Khuwair)
Tel.: 601743/44
Fax: 603540
Telex: 5401 NAJDIA ON

Embassy of the Democratic Social-
ist Republic of Sri Lanka
P.O. Box 95
Madinat Al Sultan Qaboos 115
(Embassy located in Madinat Al
Sultan Qaboos)
Tel.: 697841
Fax: 697336
Telex: 5158 ON

Embassy of the Republic of Sudan
P.O. Box 3971
Ruwi 112
(Embassy located in Diplomatic
Area in Al Khuwair)
Tel.: 697875/699844
Fax: 699065
Telex: 5088 ON

Embassy of the Arab Republic of
Syria
P.O. Box 85
Madinat Al Sultan Qaboos 115
(Embassy located on Al Inshirah
Street in Madinat Al Sultan
Qaboos)
Tel.: 697904
Fax: 603895

Embassy of Thailand
P.O. Box 60
Madinat Al Sultan Qaboos 115
(Embassy located on Road "O" in
Madinat Al Sultan Qaboos)
Tel.: 602684
Fax: 605714
Telex: 5210 THAIEM ON

Embassy of the Republic of Tunisia
P.O. Box 220
Qurum 114
(Embassy located on Al Inshirah
Street in MQ)
Tel.: 603486
Fax: 697778
Telex: 5152 ON

Embassy of the Republic of Turkey
P.O. Box 1511
Qurum 114
(Embassy located on Way 3042 in
Qurum Beach)
Tel.: 697050
Fax: 697053
Telex: 5571 TURCMUSC ON

Embassy of the United Arab
  Emirates
P.O. Box 551
Al Khuwair 111
(Embassy located in Diplomatic
  Area in Al Khuwair)
Tel.: 600302/600988
Fax: 602584
Telex: 5299 EMARAT ON

Embassy of the United Kingdom of
  Great Britain and Northern Ire-
  land
P.O. Box 300
Muscat 113
(Embassy located in Diplomatic
  Area in Al Khuwair)
Tel.: 693077
Fax: 693087
Telex: 5216 PROGROM ON

Embassy of the United States of
  America
P.O. Box 202
Madinat Al Sultan Qaboos 115
(Embassy located in Diplomatic
  Area in Al Khuwair)
Tel.: 698989
Fax: 699778

Embassy of the Arab Republic of
  Yemen
P.O. Box 105
Madinat Al Sultan Qaboos 115
(Embassy located on Way 2840
  behind Intercontinental Hotel
  in Shati Al Qurum)
Tel.: 600815
Fax: 605008
Telex: 5109 ON

CONSULATES

Consulate of Belgium
P.O. Box 808
Muscat 113
(Consulate located near Honda
  Showroom in Wattayah)
Tel.: 563011/562033
Fax: 510079

Consulate of Canada
P.O. Box 1275
Mutrah 114
(Consulate located in SARCO
  Showroom Building across from
  Ruwi Novotel in Ruwi)
Tel.: 791738
Fax: 791740

Consulate of Chile
P.O. Box 415
Muscat 113
Tel.: 561977
Fax: 562469

Consulate of Colombia
P.O. Box 2118
Ruwi 112
(Consulate located on Bait Al Falaj
  Street opposite W.J. Towell in
  Wadi Kabir)
Tel.: 701264
Fax: 797149

Consulate of Cyprus
P.O. Box 603
Muscat 113
(Consulate located in the
  J & B Office Building Near
  Zubair Complex in
  Athaibah)
Tel.: 590200
Fax: 590699

Royal Consulate of Denmark
P.O. Box 1040
Ruwi 112
(Consulate located opposite
  Central Bank of Oman in
  Central Business District in
  Ruwi)
Tel.: 793887
Fax: 707686

Consulate of Finland
P.O. Box 84
Muscat 113
Tel.: 702133
Fax: 703826
Telex: 3278 GETCO ON

Consulate of Mexico
P.O. Box 415
Muscat 113
Tel.: 561977/561417
Fax: 562469
Telex: 5336 MAXOUN ON

Consulate of Mozambique
P.O. Box 783
Muscat 113
Tel.: 594207
Fax: 590542
Telex: 5146 ALAHRAM ON

Consulate of New Zealand
P.O. Box 520
Muscat 113
(Consulate located on Mutrah
  High Street in Greater Mutrah)
Tel.: 795726
Fax: 706443

Royal Consulate of Norway
P.O. Box 89
Ruwi 112
Tel.: 708304
Fax: 793892
Telex: 3214 TOWEL ON

Consulate of Portugal
P.O. Box 1812
Ruwi 112
Tel.: 561400
Fax: 562377
Telex: 5326 ALASFOOR ON

Consulate of Spain
P.O. Box 1990
Ruwi 112
Tel.: 713253/712088
Fax: 711569
Telex: 5235 TALIB ON

Consulate of Sweden
P.O. Box 1
Ruwi 112
Tel.: 708693
Fax: 794283

Consulate of Switzerland
P.O. Box 599
Mutrah 114
(Consulate located opposite Sony
    Showroom in Central Business
    District in Ruwi)
Tel.: 750379
Fax: 799502

WORLD ORGANIZATIONS

Office for World Health
    Organization
P.O. Box 1889
Ruwi 112
(Located in the Ministry of Health
    Building in Al Khuwair)
Tel.: 600989

Office for UNICEF
P.O. Box 3787
Ruwi 112
(Located in the BMW building in
    Al Khuwair)
Tel.: 602624/601398

The following countries have diplomatic ties to Oman but do not have consular offices in the Sultanate.

Albania
Argentina
Australia
Bolivia
Brazil
Bulgaria
Burkina Faso
Burundi
Chad
Comores
Djibouti
Gabon
Gambia
Ghana
Greece
Guinea
Guinea Bissau
Hungary
Indonesia
Ireland
Ivory Coast

Mali
Malta
Mauritania
Mauritius
Mongolia
Nepal
Nicaragua
Niger
Nigeria
Poland
Romania
Rwanda
Senegal
Sierra Leone
Singapore
Tanzania
Uganda
Uruguay
Venezuela
Vietnam

Travel Tips

> Before setting sail, refurbish the Equipment, check stowage of cargo and stores, service the astrolabe and other navigational aids. Consider the voyage as a serious mission, not a pleasure trip.
>
> —Ibn Majid, fifteenth-century Omani navigator

Before you go

- Consider the airline options. Comfort and safety are important. The lowest-priced bargain airfare is not always the cheapest in the long run.

- Stopover options are an important factor in long-haul travel. With the right airfare, you can probably stop at a good destination on the way for little extra cost.

- Travel insurance is a must. It is not advisable to travel to an unknown region without adequate insurance.

- Arrange unlimited medical insurance, including a policy that provides for your evacuation to a Western country in the unlikely event that major medical treatment is required.

- If you are traveling with someone, make sure that both of you are carrying cash ($ U.S.) and some travelers' checks. Dollars will not only get you the best exchange rates, but they are constant.

- Remember this is a tropical climate. Travel light, but be prepared to have some warmer clothes if you are camping out in the interior, especially in winter.

- Get your timing right. A trip in the peak of summer could be abysmal if you are not prepared to deal with the heat, so plan your trip accordingly. Also be aware when Ramadân starts and ends. It is best not to come during that time.

- Don't be late for the airport. Airlines often overbook to compensate for no-shows. If too many people show up, it is often the last arrivals who suffer.

- Watch out for excess baggage. Check with your airline for baggage restrictions because you could be charged a hefty fee if you are over the allowed weight.

While you are away

- Always confirm onward flights as early as possible.

- Understand what your money is worth. Remember that the Omani Riyal has a value over two and a half times the dollar. Remember that in some places you can haggle for a price.

- Report credit card losses promptly. There is a substantial network of banks in Oman, but remember, their hours are limited to morning sessions only.

- Always carry necessary items with you: travel documents, money, medications, etc. in case the airline or hotel or bus misplaces your main luggage.

- Many of the smaller cafés, kiosks, and shwarma stands do not print menus. Ask for what is available or point to a recognizable dish on display. Most vendors will be able to tell you what they cook. It is usually an interesting blend of Omani and Asian-style dishes, almost always spicy, with Sri Lankans taking top prize for spiciest food.

- Always check your valuables with your hotel.

- Tips are only warranted if you feel the service or food was exceptional. Otherwise you don't need to tip, because a service charge is already included in your bill.

- Don't try to break in a new pair of shoes while you are away. Comfort is first priority.

- Since there is a fair amount of oil tanker traffic in the gulf, there is a possibility of spillage of raw crude occasionally washing up on the beaches, in globs that have a tendency to stick to everything they come in contact with. This is not a common occurrence but if you do come across crude on the beach and get some on your clothing or feet, the best solvent/agent for removal is a commercial pesticide called Pif-Paf that is available in all supermarkets and convenience stores. Spray on and wipe off with tissues.

- Be receptive. See and understand how things are done (when waiting in line for bank business, for example). People will explain hierarchies and procedures, and if they sound foreign, just go with the flow. Listen carefully and if you need instructions repeated, ask.

Visit the Region

The main travel corridor to Oman is through the United Arab Emirates, although many flights from Europe, the Far East, and America do fly directly to Muscat. There is talk that the airport in Salalah will become international, thus loosening the bottleneck at Seeb for people leaving the country. Salalah would be able to handle direct flights to the Far East, Africa, and elsewhere in the Middle East. As it is now, they are equipped to handle the biggest of planes and do accept charters from time to time. However, the transition to international is not expected to happen any time soon, as the government needs to shore up the infrastructure.

Gulf Air offers services to just about anywhere in the Middle East, so it is possible to combine trips to, say, Egypt or Turkey, with a sojourn in Oman. In all likelihood, you will probably see Dubai as it is a scheduled stopover on many flights. For those who wish to have a more cosmopolitan experience in the Middle East, Dubai or Abu Dhabi is your stop. Beyond the cities, the UAE does not have the land mass nor the broad natural setting that you find in Oman, although there are books available for the dyed-in-the-wool wadi basher. My feeling is that there is enough to see and do in Oman for any vacation, and the beckoning cities of the UAE do not offer anything that you can't find back home. They are Westernized to the point of lacking any individual identity.

As mentioned before, the only road passages out of Oman are between Oman and the UAE and Yemen. Even so, although there is road service to Yemen, there is no system to accommodate road passage except under certain restricted circumstances (i.e. military). The Omani government is implementing a new 236-kilometer road project that will link Oman and Yemen. Other than that, if you are in Salalah, and you wish to travel to Yemen, you must fly up to Muscat and go to Dubai before flying down to Aden. Road passage is not advisable as the roads deteriorate rapidly after the border and there is little in the way of services for quite a distance. Also, even though the formal relationship with Yemen has normalized, there is not enough contact between the central government and the outlying tribes on the Oman border, who still remain in the aftermath of the 1970s conflagration. Even though the conflict was put to an end in 1975, it is still possible to find armed sentinels and disorganized bands roving the hills along the border. There needs to be a collective effort on the part of both sides to smooth the situation entirely before there can be a free flow of traffic between the two countries.

To travel to the Emirates or Yemen it will be helpful to know the following.

THE UNITED ARAB EMIRATES (UAE)

The UAE is made up of several independent shaykhdoms comprised of the following: Abu Dhabi, Ajman, Dubai, Fujairah, Ra's al Khaimah, Sharjah, and Umm al Qawain. To enter the UAE you must have a valid passport and visa, which can be obtained through your travel agent or the UAE Department of Immigration. Visas are not required for citizens of UAE or nationals of the AGCC. A visa is valid for all shaykhdoms. No vaccinations are required to enter the country. There is no airport tax levied on departure and no import duty. There are standard limits on alcohol, cigarettes, and perfumes imported; restrictions on firearms (proof of permit); and restrictions on fresh food (based on point of origin and possible contagion); but there are no restrictions on foreign currencies. Admission is refused to holders of passports from Iraq, Israel (as well as passports with Israeli visas stamped in them), Mauritania, Sudan, Yemen Republic, and Palestine. Bahraini passports must be endorsed "Citizen of Bahrain" and Kuwaiti passports are denied entry if they have an "article 17, para 2" stamp. Visitors must hold tickets and documents for return/onward destination.

THE YEMEN REPUBLIC

The Yemen Republic (capital: San'a) requires passport and visas for everyone. Holders of Israeli passports are denied as well as passports with Israeli stamps. Visitors must hold tickets and documents for return/onward destination. Vaccination is required against yellow fever and malaria prophylaxis is recommended, but not required. Airport taxes are levied on all foreign nationals (about U.S.$10 for international flights and U.S.$3 for domestic flights). There are limits on alcohol, cigarettes, and perfumes imported. Firearms, illegal drugs, obscene books and magazines, and all products of Israeli origin are prohibited. All currencies are allowed for import.

3

The Land and Life of Oman

Geology

> The effort of nature to provide an outflow for the pent-up waters of the Tyin valley through a mountain range is the most singular specimen of earth sculpture I have seen in Arabia, and consists, in short, of a narrow, winding, vertical-sided gallery or cañon, extending for about six miles . . . excavated through solid limestone rock by the erosive action of water in a period of countless ages. The peculiar character of this chasm, and the grand and picturesque scenery of its surroundings, create an impression on the mind which is not easily effaced. The Arab name for it is the Wadi Thaika, meaning the "Strait or Narrow Torrent."
>
> —Colonel Samuel Barrett Miles, an account of a journey through Wadi Daiqah Gorge in February 1884 from *Journal of an Excursion in Oman,* 1896

Long before the first settlers of lost civilizations came to Oman's shores and began carving their niche in time, before the appearance of man and most other life forms as well, turbulent tides of solid material rose and fell, melted and deformed, submerged, churned, crumbled, and compressed, and rose up again. The resultant *mélange* is the unique display of topographical relief that is Oman's natural history.

To most of us, mountains are symbols of rigidity, fixed, stationary objects, unmoving, unyielding. But to a geologist, whose mind's eye is like a

Oman

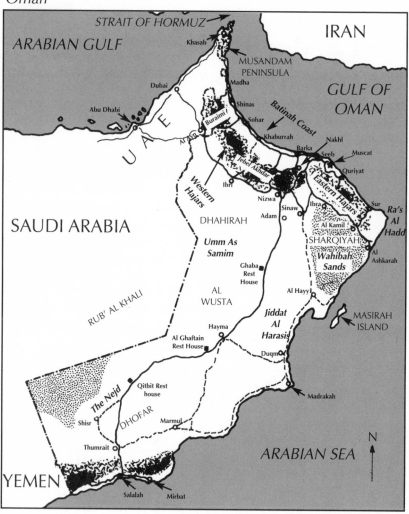

100 km

time-lapse motion-picture camera, mountains are an undulating panorama, a Rubik's Cube of pan-dimensional proportions. We see only one turn or the isolated cataclysmic event—the earthquake, the volcanic eruption—which is nothing more than one scene in the geological play. But the geologist understands just how fluid the land beneath us is.

No doubt the first things you will notice when you come to Oman are the mountains, or in Arabic, *jebels*. The geology of Oman is the singular defining quality of the land, the people, and the culture. Oman is not just a desert, even though the whole of the Arabian peninsula is classified as a desert, and although, acre for acre, there are more tracts of open desert in Oman than anything else. The single most defining quality of the geology of Oman is the jebels.

You can't help feeling intrigued by them. They sequester the country from the rest of the peninsula. They appear to give shelter and protection like the walls of a great fort. They seem barren and unapproachable, but are nevertheless teeming with life. And like most people, you'll probably want to climb them. But before that, a few words are in order about how the jebels of Oman came to be and why they are so important.

The geology of Oman has been relatively unknown for most of recorded history. Few Western travelers have penetrated the jebel flanks in the last couple of centuries, usually only the odd explorer of the Stanley/Livingstone cut of cloth. No one took this part of the world seriously until some sixty years ago when petroleum discovery and exploration dominated the region, starting in Saudi Arabia. Oman was the last country on the peninsula to fall in line. Due to internal problems, exploration did not take place until the 1950s and production didn't start until the late '60s (more in chapter 4). But after the petroleum geologists arrived, word started to spread that there was something special about the geology of Oman.

Today Oman is being revered by amateur and professional geologists alike as a treasure trove of natural history. According to Dr. Samir S. Hanna of Sultan Qaboos University, it would take a lifetime of world travel to observe specimens and features that can be found in Oman: the geology of Oman represents a cross section of almost all the rocks found on our planet.

To start with there are features in the formations that would have to be classified as textbook quality: thrust-fault mountains exposing layer upon layer. Strata formed by the oldest of prehistoric oceans lie here, from deep sea to continental shelf environments. There are formations in Oman that appear in few other places on the planet, such as ophiolites, rocks formed in the lower crust and upper mantle and pushed to the surface. These ophiolites are a source for the minerals olivine, chromite, and serpentine (so called because its smooth texture is like a snakeskin). There is evidence of glacial deposits. There is igneous activity such as basoliths, dikes, and lava flows.

Expansive limestone deposits mean the presence of fossils; dinosaur bones have been unearthed near Sultan Qaboos University, stromatolites (fossilized algae) are found in the Al Wusta, the central region, and petrified wood has been uncovered near Saiwan. Rudists (primitive mollusks) are found in the central desert in heaps. Mollusks, vertebrates, and crustaceans have been found almost everywhere else. Glacial scars over three hundred million years old can be seen in Al Huqf. Karst topography indicates the presence of caves and sinkholes—in the jebels of the Eastern Hajar can be found what has been documented as the world's second largest chamber, Khoshilat Maqandeli (referred to of late as the Majlis Al Jinn cave). There are salt domes in the desert and geodes can be found in the south. Minerals such as copper have been mined since ancient time. Chromite, used in the making of stainless steel, is viable, and tracts of coal in Sharqiyah have been studied for commercial feasibility.

A variety of gems and minerals are also found in Oman, including quartzitic varieties such as rose quartz, crystal, jasper, opal, and cashalong (a rare absorbent stone used to retain high volumes of perfume that disperse over a period of years), and sedimentary specimens such as agate, chalcedony, calcite, chert, flint, limestone, and travertine.

To say that Oman's natural heritage is unique is an understatement. What makes it so special is its accessibility. The first time I ventured to Jebel Shams, the mountain children who ply their family's wares—carpets, yarn and bobbins, sandals, trinkets—ran to us with pockets filled with fossil shells (for a price!). They know what the Westerner likes and they know where to find it. And so it goes that all the trained eye must do when in Oman is to look around and see what there is to see.

This section will give the briefest of overviews of the geology of Oman (more scholarly texts can fill in the gaps much better than I can) and then describe some of the features to be found. In later sections there will be complete descriptions of the regions, broken down into excursions.

Oman is part of the Arabian peninsula, which constitutes a plate: a section of the earth's crust that is loose and shifting. There are many plates covering the earth. Some of these plates are submerged; the ones that are exposed make up the continents. It is believed that long ago in the farthest reaches of geologic time, the continental plates were all together, forming one large continent known as Pangaea. These plates broke up, drifted apart, and randomly came together again, sometimes with dramatic effect. The Indian sub-continent was considered to be a separate plate that crashed into southern Asia, forming the Himalayan mountains.

The Arabian plate met a similar fate, coming to rest (for the time being) at the juncture of Asia and Africa. Further shifting, however, caused the uplift of oceanic strata to the extent of pushing up the underlying material, namely the ophiolites, to the surface, where they remain exposed to this day. Geologically speaking, the mountain ranges in Oman are more closely related to the mountains of Iran than any other part of the Arabian peninsula. They are separated only by the Arabian Gulf, which is viewed by geologists as a recent occurrence in the geological timetable.

The resultant chain of thrust-fault mountains on the eastern side of Oman is no less dramatic than other mountainous regions of the world. Layer upon layer of rock has been exposed, dating back more than a half billion years. And this exposure is continued as the process of erosion—effected by sun, wind, and rain—prevails. A hike into these mountains is a veritable walk through time.

> The ground, of white gypsum powder, was covered with a sand sprinkled crust of salt. . . . I took a few steps forward and [my companion] Staiyun put his hand on my arm saying, 'Don't go any nearer—it is dangerous. . . . Several people, including an Awamir raiding party, had perished in these sands, and he told me once again how he had himself watched a flock of goats disappear beneath the surface.
>
> —Wilfred Thesiger, describing the Umm As Samim, the dangerous sabkha (salt flats) on the western border facing the R'ub Al Khali, *Arabian Sands*, 1956

The other most obvious feature of Oman's environment, synonymously characterized as part and parcel of the Arabic experience, is the desert. Deserts are indirectly influenced by the workings of geologic time insofar as the plates under the desert regions migrated to a particular latitude on the surface. Deserts are the primary result of the climate. A glance at a globe or world map will show you that all of the world's deserts fall at roughly the same latitudes north and south of the equator, namely, the tropics. Prevailing winds and upper atmospheric currents have driven moisture-bearing air masses away from these latitudes. The result is the barren landscapes that are some of the most inhospitable on earth.

Many people's idea of a desert is tinted by the romantic ideal of rolling sand dunes that drift from horizon to horizon à la "Lawrence of Arabia." This is only partially true. The sandy parts actually make up a small fraction of the entire desert. In addition, there are endless rock-strewn boulder fields, parched plateaus, dried ravines and watercourses (called *wadis* in Arabic), and salt flats incapable of sustaining any life whatsoever. Oman has all of these spread throughout the central region of the country. And yes, it has the rolling dunes—the Wahibah Sands—a stretch of longitudinal dunes, 100-200 meters high, that run for 200 kilometers south from the Eastern Hajar to the Arabian Sea.

The northernmost section of Oman is the **Musandam Peninsula.** Jutting out into the Strait of Hormuz, the Musandam is an imposing set of rugged

Aboard a dhow amidst the fjords of the Musandam.

mountains rising 1,500 meters above the water. The peninsula has recently undergone (recent in geologic time, that is) a period of uplift and partial submergence. The rocks are predominantly limestone from the Jurassic Era, cut by deep gorges from the east and west sides that almost separate the tip from the mainland. These valleys once consisted of softer sandstones and shales of the Triassic Era and underlay the Jurassic limestone. Now submerged, they are like fjords and are not seen anywhere else on the Arabian peninsula. One of the fjords, the Khawr Ash Shamm, is over eight miles long. There are few beaches and fewer access roads to the shore from the top. The landscape is extremely rugged although some very plucky natives manage to eke out a life up here. (There is a tourism infrastructure in Musandam, as in most of the country; it will be taken up in a later part of the book.)

South of the Musandam by 100 kilometers or so begin the **Al Hajar Al Gharbi** (the Western Rocky Mountains, or Western Hajars). Running from northwest to southeast paralleling the Batinah coast, the Western Hajars are separated from their eastern counterpart, **Al Hajar Ash Sharqi,** by a natural break known as the Sumail Gap some 80 kilometers west of Muscat. The Eastern Hajars continue running down to and intersecting with the coast at Muscat before continuing on a parallel course to Sur. Before Sur the mountains abruptly halt—the formation ends and does not, as some might suspect, tail off into the ocean. Along this coastal region, in contrast to the Musandam, coastal shelves can be seen indicating some tilting or uplift.

The Hajars are comprised predominantly of limestone which was formed *in situ*, then uplifted, folded, and tilted. Interspersed with these are metamorphic and igneous rocks, including the famous ophiolites. The ophiolites are distinguished by their amorphous shape, lack of stratification, and chocolate-brown color. They can be readily seen surrounding Mutrah, Muscat, and the Al Bustan, as well as in many interior sections.

The main limestone groups (marine carbonates dating to the pre-Permian) form the central scarp of the Hajars, known as **Jebel Akhdar** (Green Mountains). These thrust-fault mountains dip southwest to the interior and are an impressive sight from the coast, as flanks of exposed strata that look impassable rise majestically into the sky (but local villagers know of trails to the summits). The Jebel Akhdar are the highest mountains of Oman, with the mountain popularly known as Jebel Shams rising higher than 10,000 feet. Although the dip to the southwest is gradual, there are many wadi channels that have cut through and eroded the rock. The most impressive of these is **Wadi Nakhr Gorge,** the Grand Canyon of Oman, cutting into the side of Jebel Shams.

Throughout this region are liberally scattered fossils, many exposed by years of erosion (and who knows how many are beneath the surface). Stromatolites are found along the northern side of the jebels, along Wadi Bani Kharus and Wadi Hajir. Mollusks, crustaceans, and crinoids have been found in other basins.

In **Wadi Mistal** (Ghubrah Bowl) beds of glacial till and striated boulders more than six hundred million years old indicate that the Arabian plate once drifted in southern latitudes near the pole.

A series of rocks comprised of limestone and volcanics known as the Exotics makes up a line of ridges along the southwest flank of Jebel Akhdar. **Jebel Misht** and **Jebel Kawr** are the most prominent of these. Their light color makes them stand out from the surrounding ophiolites.

In all cases, the Hajars have been deeply deformed by erosion subsequent to uplift. The tracts of outwash plains to the south are testament to this, as are the hundreds of smaller gorges carved into the rock face, a veritable paradise for geologists and hikers alike.

On top of this, there has been significant karst activity which indicates the presence of caves, sinkholes, and hot springs. In the Western Hajars can be found the **Hoti/Falahi** cave systems near Al Hamra and **Araqi Cave** near Ibri. Further down in the Eastern Hajars is the aforementioned **Khoshilat Maqandeli,** located in a plateau area of Jebel Bani Jabir, and **Muqal Cave,** at the northern end of Wadi Bani Khalid. In Dhofar, the southern region, there is **Tawi Attir,** a massive sinkhole and cave system, as well as caves in Wadi Dirbat.

Hot springs ranging from **Bausher** (outside Muscat) to **Rustaq** have been flowing since ancient times. The area around **Nakhl** is used as a bathing and picnic area and a chemical analysis of the water emerging from the spring has indicated that the water is commercially viable. The spring at Rustaq has been enclosed by a retaining wall and bathing facilities are maintained there. The waters from these springs average about 40 degrees C.

To the south of the Hajars is the broad sweeping plain that is the eastern extremity of the Empty Quarter. This is the largest single land mass in the country. It contains a diverse environment of desert habitats, ranging from sweeping sands to treacherous salt flats to parched gullies strewn with rubble. Towards the coastline the land assumes the shape of a broad lowlying plateau with patches of savanna, the most distinguished region of this being the **Jiddat Al Harasis.**

Further south the land rises gradually to form a broad escarpment over 1800 meters in elevation and barren for the most part until it reaches the extreme southern coast. Here, this scarp breaks off precipitously to the south, forming the narrow shelf on the coastline which is the heart of the southern region of Dhofar. Climatic conditions have transformed this region into the most verdant of the entire country.

Wildlife

FLORA

The residents avoid living in the cities, for the heat in the summer is so great that it would kill them. Hence they go out (to sleep) at their gardens in the country, where there are streams and plenty of water.

—Marco Polo, *Travels*

Despite the inhospitable nature of Oman's arid climate, there is a diversity of plant life that has learned its lessons of survival quite well. Hundreds of species have been cataloged and almost all can be put to good use.

Probably the image most consistent with desert scenery is the palm tree. The date palm is the most common in Oman as it is the chief agricultural crop. There are more than 200 species alone of dates; of these, 20 are commercially viable. Every oasis is a massive cluster of dates. In the Batinah plain and other areas in the north, bananas thrive, and in Salalah coconut palms are cultivated. Wadi Bani Khalid cultivates a variety of red peel banana.

Limes are probably the second largest crop after dates. Interspersed throughout the oases, lime trees provide a distinct break in the pattern of palm fronds. The bright green leaves are radiant and in season they are brightly sprinkled with light green polka dots of the ripening limes. Omani limes are smallish in size—never bigger than a golf ball—and round. The skin is thin but tough and the rich citric taste is enough to compensate for the many seeds that get in the way. Other citrus fruits are grown in Oman, including oranges, grapefruit, and an interesting variety of sweet lemon. Among the vegetation that has been adapted for agricultural use and appears in various settlements in the northern jebels are apples, mangoes, apricots, peaches, pomegranates, almonds, walnuts, garlic, maize, and wild mountain roses, which are cultivated for making rosewater.

> The frankincense and gum-arabic annually exported from Morbat and Dhafar vary from about 3000 to 10,000 maunds (Indian measure) which is nothing to what might be procured, the trees being exceedingly numerous on the mountain declivities and in the valleys inland . . . In this neighborhood is found the aloë tree of Sokotrah, growing out of masses of primitive limestone, apparently without any earth to sustain it.
> —Captain Stansford Bettesworth Haines, *Memoir of the South and East Coasts of Africa*, 1845

Arguably the most famous plant found in Oman—and only in Oman and some regions of East Africa—is the tree that produces a sap used since ancient times as an aromatic and medicinal. The tree is known as the *Boswellia sacra* and the sap it produces is frankincense. Prior to the discovery of oil, frankincense was probably the chief export and economic mainstay of Oman. Over 2000 years ago frankincense was exported at the rate of 3000 tons per year, mostly to Egypt, Greece, Rome, and India. Known to Christians as one of the Gifts of the Magi to the infant Jesus, frankincense in all probability was more valuable than the gold. It undoubtedly came from Oman. Because of its ability to disperse vapors, it was commonly burnt around newborns and infants to ward off disease. In a time of poor sanitary conditions, with no modern medicines to combat infections and bacteria, this was a valuable gift indeed.

Frankincense grows only in the southern region of Dhofar. It is a rather unsightly looking tree, gnarled and windblown, only growing to a height of three to five meters. In the spring, a section of bark is removed to let the sap ooze forth. After a couple of weeks it hardens and is stripped from the tree. It is then sorted by color (bluish-white frankincense is considered the highest quality) and stored before the harvest is sent to market. One tree can yield up to 20 kilograms (about 44 pounds) a season.

In the plains of Oman's interior, acacia trees flourish amidst a variety of grasses, and in the desert, stands of prosopis trees thrive. Called *ghaf* by the local Bedus, there are stretches of single-specie prosopis woodlands running for 140 kilometers in the Wahibah Sands. In some places the canopy is so thick as to provide constant shade. The trees manage to stay green through extensive taproots, which can reach down to 80 meters. They are remarkably resilient to encroaching sand dunes, as what may look like a cluster of trees is actually one tree buried in the sand. Prosopis trees have been estimated to live a thousand years. They are quite versatile: they are used as a fuel source (producing a hot smokeless flame); for fence construction (otherwise they are of poor timber quality); as support for arable soil; and for their products: honey, gum, tannin, and natural medicines.

Other trees lending shade in plains and wadis are the tamarix and zizyphus, or Christ-thorn tree. The desiccated leaves of the Christ-thorn are used in a shampoo, the fruit is edible, and honey is harvested from its small yellow flowers. Flowering trees indigenous to Oman are *cassia fistula,* or golden shower tree and royal poinciana, better known as flame trees. These two flower twice a year (in May and October) with a display equal to any fireworks exhibition.

Surprisingly, there are times when Jebel Akhdar (the Green Mountains) lives up to its name. In the winter and early spring many flowering plants whose seeds have sprouted and taken root show their better side. Varieties of lilies and violets grow along the slopes.

The *qafas* shrub sports a yellow flower that can be seen throughout the spring, while its seeds remain till autumn. They contain a valuable oil; the local people extract it for medicinal purposes. Another flowering tree sought by the locals is the *shu* tree with leafless stems but fragrant pink flowers (attracting many butterflies and bees), which exudes an oil used as an ointment. The *itm* or wild olive can be seen in the higher reaches of Jebel Akhdar. It is noted for its broad gnarled trunks. *But* is a scraggly shrub that produces blue-black berries that natives enjoy eating. They are collected and sold at the Nizwa souq in season. At higher elevations one species of juniper can be found, as well as a bright red bush with yellow flowers, the *berberis.*

Many plants have adapted to desert life in a number of ways. Succulents have a means of retaining every last bit of water they can pull from the ground. One plant, the *boerhavia elegans,* maintains bright red leafless stems which dismember during the hot summer months, leaving only its belowground roots to survive till the following season. Another plant, the Rose of Jericho, cradles its seeds in its dried stems, only releasing them at the touch of the next season's rain. The dried plant resembles a clenched fist and is sometimes called the Hand of Mary. In many cases plants lie dormant for most of the year, waiting for the cooler months to prevail.

Plants related to species found in the Mediterranean and Western Asia apparently arrived with the last Ice Age. These include some wild potatoes and cotton plants. Other plants on the scarp are varieties of bushes, scrub, and smaller trees.

Further south in the jebels of Sharqiyah, a region being considered for a nature reserve, more than 73 samples of previously unknown species of flowering plants and trees have been recently cataloged. But native tribes in these far reaches of the interior have known about them for some time, as they have used by-products of these plants as medicinals, cosmetics, food additives, and other applications over the centuries. The question that has always tantalized botanists—and this is no less true for Oman than any other region—is how many species of plants remain to be discovered.

"Oman is distinguished by its suitability to the many date palms and fruits which grow there, such as banana, pomegranate, lotus fruit and others," recorded Al-Istakhri in *Al-Masalak wah Al-Mamalek* (*The Roads of the Kingdoms*) during the ninth century.

Probably the most diverse area in terms of its flora is a narrow strip of coastline in the southern region of Dhofar. For four months out of the year (June to September) this area is fed moisture from a thick blanket of clouds called the *khareef*, the Indian Ocean monsoon. The clouds overspread an area about 30 kilometers wide and 240 kilometers long before dispersing at the edge of the surrounding scarp. The change in scenery is very dramatic as one enters from the desert in the north along a gradual ascent to the edge of the plateau. The desolate scenery, sometimes referred to as Mountains of the Moon, swiftly changes as you descend 4,000 feet to the coast amidst lush greenery covering the walls of the escarpment, cross a narrow plain of grassland and acacias, and arrive in the urban center of Salalah, where modern agricultural methods have converted the area into a garden city.

It is interesting to note that within this region are pockets of less vegetated areas. These areas came about as a result of deforestation and overgrazing through the years. The moisture-laden clouds of the khareef only drop their loads on wooded areas where a canopy of trees can condense the water and transfer it to the ground, allowing smaller shrubs and flowers to grow. Areas without vegetation, having no gathering ability, do not accumulate moisture.

Nevertheless, the Dhofaris have taken the opportunity to exploit the abundance of vegetation in ways not seen in the north. Besides being able to grow a greater diversity of crops including fodder grasses, plant uses extend to building materials, heat sources, medicines, dyes, cosmetics, tanning agents, fibres, glues, tobaccos, deodorizers, insecticides, and depilatories.

Because diversity is the operative phrase, it is not hard to find species that border on the unusual. One of my favorite haunts is a forest of trees related to the baobabs of Africa, near Wadi Dirbat. In an impressive stand of bulbous trees clinging to the side of the wadi, one tree looks to be 20-30 feet in diameter at the base and is probably over two thousand years old.

Baobab tree in Dhofar.

Beyond that Dhofar offers a plethora of bushes, shrubs, flowering plants, and trees found in the wild including several varieties of orchids, palms and local herbs. Research has discovered that some species indigenous to that area are found nowhere else. One of the most abundant trees, the *Anogeissus dhofarica*, identified in the 1970s, grows only in Dhofar and nowhere else in the world.

FAUNA

Gazelle grazed among the flat topped acacia bushes and once we saw a distant herd of oryx looking very white against the dark gravel of the plain. There were lizards about eighteen inches in length, which scuttled across the ground. They had disc shaped tails, and in consequence the Arabs called them "The Father of the Dollar."

—Wilfred Thesiger, *Arabian Sands*, 1956

In 1972 in the Jiddat Al-Harasis, a plateau region in central Oman west of the Wahibah Sands, the remains of the last Arabian White Oryx (*Oryx leucoryx*) were discovered, bringing to a close their calamitous descent into oblivion at the hands of hunters. With the advent of modern technology on the Arabian peninsula in the early part of the twentieth century, hunting the oryx was no longer a sport—it was a one-way ticket to extinction. The White Oryx, member of the antelope family, was prized for its meat, skin, and horns and in the lawless lands of southern Arabia there would have been no way to save it, were it not for the fact that the Fauna Preservation Society and the World Wildlife Fund had been monitoring the situation for several years. In 1962 a collaboration of scientific teams and local tribes plucked one male and two females from the region near the Oman/Yemen border. They were removed at first to Kenya and then to the Phoenix Zoo in Phoenix, Arizona, where the climate was thought to be best suited for the animal.

These three were joined by donations from the London Zoo, Shaykh Jaber bin Abdulla Al Sabah of Kuwait, and King Saud of Saudi Arabia, bringing the total population in captivity to nine. A captive breeding program was established. Because the group was assembled from a broad genetic base, there was hope that this magnificent creature could be successfully bred in suffucient numbers to be re-established to its native habitat, something that had never before been accomplished.

After hearing of this project, His Majesty Sultan Qaboos pronounced in 1976 that the point of re-introduction should be in the Jiddat Al-Harasis, the spot where the last wild oryx were seen. This news was joyfully received by the Harasis tribes, who wanted to take part in restoring a piece of their natural heritage. By 1980, a group of descendants from the original captive herd had been dispatched to Oman, where they spent several months in an enclosure at Jaaluni in a careful program to acclimatize. In January, 1982, the doors were opened by head ranger Said bin Dooda Al Harsusi, and the Arabian White Oryx was home again in the wild. The Arabian Oryx Sanctuary was established by Royal Decree in 1994, and by 1996 there were approximately 315 oryx roaming the 16,000-square-kilometer reserve. Later that year the World Heritage Committee of UNESCO declared the sanctuary a world natural heritage site.

The White Oryx is a medium-sized antelope with a thick body on spindly legs. It is white except for dark markings on the legs and around the face. The horns are long and slightly arc to almost double the body height. Not sprinters like their swifter relatives, the oryx are more adapted for trekking the long hauls. They move about the desert as they graze, seeking out the areas that provide the best pasture and shade, sometimes feeding at night in summer when temperatures are cooler. Like camels, oryx are known to conserve their water intake. The longest recorded period an oryx has gone between drinks is twenty-two months.

Oryx roam in herds of up to 30 with 1 dominant male, or bull, and a dominant female. Females start calving at about 2 years with a gestation period of about 8.6 months producing 1, and occasionally 2, calves. They may breed twice a year. Calves are weaned at 6 to 10 months and may live up to 19 years.

This is just the first of many success stories that are coming from the Sultanate. The Sultan's record of strong environmental policies for preserving natural heritage go hand in hand with preserving the country's cultural heritage.

> There are plenty of camels, horses, donkeys, mules, oxen and sheep. The country also produces a kind of animal called "flyer across the grass" . . . it is as big as a large cat; over its whole body it has something resembling the stripes of a tortoise shell cat. It has two black ears and its nature is mild, not fierce. If lions, leopards and such wild animals see it, they crouch down on the ground. It is truly king of animals.
>
> —Admiral Zheng He, a eunuch from K'unyang, explorer to the emperor,
> fifteenth century

Mammals. You might think that the camel is the preeminent creature of Oman, and in many ways it still is, but the camel has taken a back seat to technology. Most Bedus drive trucks and four-wheel drives these days, and it's not uncommon to see the camel being given a lift. With their duty as beasts of burden relieved, their chief purposes are relegated to food, milk, and wool sources for the Bedus, racing, and decorating the landscape (for what would a desert be without the camel?).

No less important than the oryx is a species of goat discovered only late last century and found only in Oman, the *Hemitragus jayakari,* or Arabian Tahr. Loosely related to the ibex , the tahr are estimated at around 2,000, making it one of the rarest mammals in the world. Tahr numbers have been decreasing due to hunting and competition with domestic livestock. As a result, a nature reserve has been set aside for protecting the tahr. It is in the rugged jebel region of Wadi Sareen, 45 kilometers southwest of Muscat. The tahr is mostly accustomed to higher elevations, and the steep walls of the jebel provide secluded pockets offering shelter, retreat, and pools of collected rainwater. The tahr, unlike the oryx, needs fresh water on a regular basis to survive.

Tahr are no more than 80 centimeters high with coarse reddish brown hair. The males have dark streaks running along the spine to the tail. The horns are small and curved. Unlike other species of tahr, the Arabian is territorial, with males commanding small herds of females and young. Nesting territories are identified by "scrapes," small patches in the ground dug and cleaned by the male tahrs with their hooves and horns, sometimes 50 centimeters deep.

Government authorities have enjoined locals to serve as rangers of the region to watch and monitor tahr living habits, educate others about conservation and ecology, and bring to justice anyone who kills the tahr or interferes with the tahr habitat. Another area further south in Sharqiyah is also being considered as a nature reserve.

Besides the oryx, the Huqf escarpment in the Arabian Oryx Sanctuary is home to herds of Nubian Ibex, another member of the goat family. The ibex are larger than the tahr and are distinguished by their large, scimitar-shaped horns. The ibex roam the escarpment eating grasses and leaves. A very private animal, the ibex is very shy and difficult to photograph. There are other small populations of ibex in Dhofar Province and on some rocky headlands along the southern coast of Oman.

Other species of mammals that make their home in Oman and are no less welcome are gazelles whose numbers, like the tahr and oryx, were reduced by hunters. These Arabian Gazelles (*Gazella gazella*) enjoy the same protection offered the others. They are more easily seen than ibex and tahr. They can be seen on the plains after rain or in the early morning to eat the dew-soaked grasses. Sand gazelles (*Gazella subguttorosa marica*) are less common. They can be seen, however, in the northern parts of the Arabian Oryx Sanctuary and in the Wahibah Sands.

Rarer still because of their remoteness and timidity are several species of cats: the Arabian leopard, still found in the Dhofar mountains and parts of the Musandam; Gordon's wildcat; and the Caracal lynx, a secretive feline with a sandy brown coat that keeps it well camouflaged in the dry desert surroundings, distinctive black tufts on the ears, and a short tail.

Red foxes are common, as is Ruppell's sand fox. They are species well adapted to desert life. They consume smaller mammals, reptiles, and marine turtle eggs.

Other mammals in the region are desert hares, two species of hedgehogs, several varieties of gerbils, jerboas, mice, and other rodents. Wolves, striped hyenas, and hyrax appear. Fruit bats and the naked-bellied tomb bat are sometimes seen.

Many of the common domestic animals seen elsewhere are in abundance in Oman, including horses, cattle, sheep, goats, donkeys, dogs (the *saluki* is a native breed), and cats. Horses have been traditionally bred, though not in such abundant numbers as in the past. (Apocryphal stories tell of sultans of bygone times with cavalries of 90,000 horses.)

Reptiles and Amphibians. Amphibians of greatest concern are the marine turtles, impressive beasts up to one meter long which circuit the Indian Ocean only to return to the shores of Arabia to lay their eggs on the beaches once a year, before returning to the sea. Females bury massive clutches of over a hundred eggs in the sand, most of which are pilfered by foxes and gulls and, until recently, man. The few who don't make direct contributions to the food chain and are allowed to hatch are subsequently subjects of predation once they reach the open waters. Only a handful of 1,000 eggs ever survive to maturity but those that do are rewarded with a life span of up to 200 years. Mature turtles do not start breeding until after 30 years. Four species of marine turtles use parts of Oman's beaches to lay their eggs; they are the green turtles (*Chelonia mydus*), hawksbill (*Eretmochelys imbricata*), Olive Ridley (*Lepydochelys olivacea*), and the logger-head turtle (*Caretta caretta*). The loggerhead turtle takes Masirah Island as a choice nesting spot. The leatherback turtle can be seen offshore in Oman's waters.

The Ministry of Regional Municipalities and Environment has set in place the infrastructure to protect the nesting beaches of turtles, providing a policy of non-interference but allowing the public to observe the nesting habits with permits for certain restricted beaches. As with the oryx and tahr, local inhabitants have been awarded the task of serving as rangers, monitors, and turtle police.

At this time this is the only formal infrastructure in the Sultanate that allows people to observe a restricted natural environment. The nature pre-serves at Jiddat al-Harasis and Wadi Sarin do not as yet provide public access, though it is hoped in years to come, as species proliferate, there will be mechanisms in place to allow further interfaces between man and nature. Those who wish further information about the nature reserves and natural history of Oman should contact the Ministry of Regional Munici-palities and Environment, Directorate General of Public Awareness and Guidance, P.O. Box 323, Muscat 113, Sultanate of Oman.

Other reptiles in the Sultanate are plentiful. Just ask anyone who has visited Snake Canyon. Snakes appear anywhere in the jebels and wadis. Some are poisonous and some are not. All are generally scared of humans and beat a hasty retreat when alerted, but they will strike out if cornered. The horned viper is poisonous and should be avoided. It has a diamond-shaped head and distinct markings along its body similar to diamond-back rattlesnakes. But although some species are dangerous, they are generally shy and retiring.

Of the many lizards found in Oman the largest and most distinctive is the Monitor Lizard. It usually hunts the smaller lizards and bugs. The spiny tailed lizard is a vegetarian and diurnal. Gekkos can be found on the desert both day and night.

Of the amphibians, newts, salamanders, frogs, and toads can be found skirting wadi banks and hiding under rocks. All are considered harmless and are skittish.

Birds. Oman, quite plainly, is a birders' paradise with over eighty indige-nous species. Regular sightings of transitory birds bring the number of birds seen in Oman to over 435. And the list is growing. The latest, published in 1994 and available from local bookstores and the Natural History Museum, lists all the accepted species and their status.

The Arabian peninsula creates a bridge between Africa and Asia, and its distinctive shape serves as a key landmark for migratory birds, some traveling from as far as the Arctic Circle to roost in southern Africa. Others come from central Asia and the Mediterranean going south, and from Africa going north depending on the season. Some of the attractions to these travelers are the verdant coastlines of Salalah and the Batinah and the small island groups near them, as well as the island of Masirah.

These regions contain *bandars* and *khawrs* (bays and coves) that are teeming with insects, fish, and fruit-bearing plants. Bandar Khayran near Muscat has mangrove-like stands growing in the tidal flats where enclaves of bird species gather. Before dawn they can make a tremendous racket for nearby campers. Khawr Rhori near Salalah is a broad marsh that is a haven for all types of wildlife. The birds think it most appealing as thousands come to feed and move on. There are also nesting areas and shelters in the khawrs, in the wadi channels and jebels, and in the rocky shorelines and islands.

Some regions, such as the Jazir Ad Damaniyat, islands off the Batinah coast, are now being protected by restricted access decrees because of the fragile environment and the damage that can be done by human intervention.

The best times to come to Oman to see the greatest variety of species are in April-May and September-October. Obviously this is when the migratory birds are on the wing. During the summer, the weather is just plain hot as people (and the birds) head for shelter. Winter affords the best time to see the indigenous population.

Varieties of birds include warblers, gulls, terns, doves, crows, bee-eaters, hawks, eagles, vultures, owls, herons, ducks, crakes, kingfishers, parakeets, flamingos, sparrows, weaverbirds, kites, grackles, coots, bush robins, ravens, bulbul, rollers, grosbeaks, kestrels, bittern, shrikes, cuckoos, spoonbills, ibises, plovers, sandpipers, partridge, grouse, and so forth. On a good day, if the timing and location are right, a bird watcher can spot over a hundred species.

Falcons appear in Oman but falconry is not the big sport that it is elsewhere, as in Saudi Arabia. Some tribes in the interior section of Dhahirah raise peregrine and gyre-falcons, but beyond this there is little practice.

Insects. In chapter 2, you can find a list of insects (and arachnids) that you don't want to see in your visit to Oman. This brief section will tell you about the ones you do want to see. Arguably the most beautiful of the phylum Insecta are the butterflies and moths, and Oman, once again, contributes its fair share, much to the lepidopterist's delight. Omani butterflies are either collected or photographed in their habitat in the north and south.

Over eighty species have been classified over the years, almost half of them in the north alone. Butterflies are most plentiful after the rainy season in January and February, but they can be spotted at almost any time except the hottest summer months when only a few species dare to brave the heat. The average lifespan of an Omani butterfly is about three weeks. Varieties include *charaxes, danaidae, nymphalidae, pieridae, lycaenidae,* and *hesperidae,* among others.

Other less interesting insects abound including beetles, centipedes, flies and mosquitoes, ants, and ground-dwelling termites (near Salalah).

> I know of no place equal to Muscat for the abundance and excellence, perhaps too for the variety, of its fish. The water around the ship was continually alive with them . . . thick as gnats in a summer evening.
> —James Fraser, *Travels*, 1821

> Two fin backed whales blow in the harbor: one is named Muscat Tom, visiting the harbor daily for the last 20 years.
> —from the journal of Edmund Roberts, American Special Envoy to Oman,
> 1837

Marine Life. With a coastline that extends for over a thousand miles, it is not surprising that the marine life is abundant, a fact not lost on the locals who have fished these waters for centuries. And with the upsurge of the current economic revolution Omani fisherman are keen to tap this renewable resource.

The long beaches of the Batinah house crustacea and shellfish. Cowries, volutes, cones, and bivalves litter the shoreline as hermit crabs wander from shell to shell seeking a suitable abode. On the coastal shelf in the waters around Muscat, the water is "boiling" with fish. Coral reefs display underwater gardens patronized by colorful showfish. Urchins, slugs, and anemones live along coastal shelves. Eels slither about, including the vicious moray. Deep sea waters produce swordfish, tuna, mackerel, and barracuda, while cetaceans (whales and dolphins) tease the visitors from the land with aerial and aural displays.

During the late summer, the coast is marauded by jellyfish that waft with the tides and put an edge on the delights of frolicking bathers. Crustacea such as prawns, lobsters, and crabs are plentiful and usually wind up on the selling floor in Mutrah's fish souq. Sharks patrol the coast but keep their distance.

To monitor this important aspect of Omani life, the Marine Science and Fisheries Centre was established to help manage fisheries and marine resources. The purpose of this organization is to maximize the efficiency of the industry while keeping close tabs on the environmental aspects of marine life. The center studies abundance, distribution, migration, and qualitative analyses of the catch, mostly commercial varieties of fish. Studies on the impact of algae and plankton are also conducted. Alternative methods for more efficient processing of fish and marine products are also sought.

4

Who Are the Omanis?

Introductory Remarks

> This Sultanate neither belongs to foreigners nor did I get it from their hands. It was left to us by our fathers and grandfathers and I came to it by the will of the people.
>
> —Sayyid Barghash Al-Said, 1871, in a letter to the British Consul at Zanzibar

The development of societies around the region once known as the fertile crescent have influenced the course of subsequent civilizations in many ways. We may not immediately recognize the traces left behind from those years gone by, but with a little investigation and hindsight we can discover them and assemble a model in our mind's eye. The handed-down traditions, preserved in the spirit of the living culture, can be as helpful as relics from ancient times. A tribal dance can yield as much information as a shard of pottery, and a spoken dialect breathes life into a crumbling house of stone.

The "winds of time" is more than just a cliché in the part of the world we call the Middle East. Atmospheric conditions and other natural forces have done much to affect the development of civilizations in ways no one could predict. In retrospect, however, we see the patterns develop. Long before the dawn of civilization, continents creaked and rumbled as they

97

spread across the surface of the earth. Primordial beings gravitated to the areas most habitable and started to learn to control the forces that prevailed over them. The civilizations of the Nile, Tigris/Euphrates, and Indus Valley thrived. But what the winds gave to those civilizations, they also took away. And so societies had to learn to adapt. As the climate in these regions became more and more arid, once prosperous cultures on the fringe of the fertile crescent had to change their priorities. Goods that had been valuable exports were withheld for local consumption while expendable items were sought. Once-common commodities became scarce; inorganic materials, such as copper, marble, and dyes, were the keys to maintaining trade.

The peoples of the Arabian peninsula were the ones that felt the brunt of the climate change first. Their trade with the great empires of the north and east became a lifeline. Because they knew who had what, who needed what, and what they themselves needed, they developed the skills that made them the greatest traders in history. The winds of time and change breathed life into a new culture, one that had shifted its emphasis from goods to services.

Civilizations rose and fell as the peoples of the Arabian peninsula persevered. As the locus of societies expanded, the lifelines from Arabia grew as the hardy traders kept pace. They built stronger boats that could go further and carry more. They learned to plot their course by the stars and devised the mathematics that would be used into the modern day. The unifying link from age to age was the steadfast navigational and trading skills that the outlying civilizations relied upon. It is testament to that fact that the barks and dhows that plied the waters 2,000 years ago, that carried Sindbad to the farthest reaches of the known world and back, are still made by hand today, without drawings or working plans of any kind.

But these ships carried more than cargo. They carried intangibles along with freight: stories. Stories of homelands and stories of strange places. Stories of societies that linked them to other cultures with a bond as strong as any gold coin. Stories that bred traditions and kindled new cultures, assimilated from practices that became ritual. And the winds of time and change that blew then are about to blow again.

Early Civilizations and Pre-Islamic Times

> . . . on the Arabian coast, a type of timber was used in constructing their ships. It is very strong and is not affected if thrown in sea water. Such timber will stay in the water for more than 200 years without being damaged. Out of the water, it deteriorates much faster.
> —Theophrastus, ca. 300 B.C., on the imported Indian teak used in Omani construction

There is no doubt that the Arabian peninsula has enjoyed more verdant times. And there is no doubt that aboriginal societies took advantage of those salad days. It is thought that the name "Oman" derives from the verb meaning to occupy or settle. A man could very easily find a home in Oman. In the pre-dawn of civilization, nomadic tribes settled near flowing wadis and built their homes of stone and branch. The earliest settlements appear to have come from northern Arabia, where tribes of Nazar (Nazarene) were forced to move by extreme drought. They found the wadis of Oman more hospitable. In the surrounding oases they foraged and hunted. There was gazelle and goat to eat, and ostrich for that matter, as bones and shells have indicated. Stone tools such as spearheads, adzes, and knives have been found and dated. Early peoples tamed the goat, the donkey, and the camel. They learned cultivation and developed their crafts, weaving, dying, and pottery. They smelted ore. On the coast they built sailing vessels. They began to trade. Their material wants were satisfied.

The first traces of settlements appear to be in the fourth millennium B.C. Pieces of pottery and funerary jars have been linked to contemporary societies in southern Iran. Elaborate burial mounds have indicated that throughout the eastern Arabian peninsula there was a uniform culture. These beehive tombs, as they are called because of their structural resemblance to a beehive, are found in the area surrounding Ibri. Similar structures are found further south on the Jebel Bani Jabir plateau. The remoteness of the latter suggests the extent to which that society had developed. Beyond that there are not many physical clues of early city life.

Historians have had to go beyond Oman to verify its early existence. Records from Mesopotamia indicate trade with ships from places called Dilmun and Magan in the third millennium. Dilmun, it has been ascertained, was situated on the western shores of the Arabian (which we call Persian) Gulf somewhere between modern-day Bahrain and Kuwait. Magan was located on the outer reaches of the Arabian peninsula, probably near the present-day Omani city of Sohar. It is here that the earliest of copper mines was located; copper as an export commodity exists to this day. The name *magan* in cuneiform texts alludes to shipbuilding ability, as does the Persian *mazoun*. The word *ma-gan* is translated as "ship's skeleton" or "chassis."

Sumerian references to Magan as a seafaring nation touted the worthiness of these early navigators. Accounts from the Indus Valley and the Assyrian Empires, Sumer, and Akkad all attribute the success of their economies to trading with Magan, which provided not only raw materials but also rare woods, spices, and foods brought from the coast of Africa. No less than the cargo they carried, the ships the early Omanis built were commodities themselves, as their reputation as shipbuilders grew. Diorite, a stone known for its hardness and durability, was mined and exported from Oman. Later, the southern cities in Dhofar would add frankincense to their list of valuable exports. The Queen of Sheba, who is mentioned in the Old Testament as presenting gifts of frankincense to Solomon, built her empire on the southern shores of Dhofar. Dhofar is the only spot in the world where the Boswellia tree yields the sap that creates the aromatic. This unique item was in demand from the Nile to across the Mediterranean, to India and beyond, as its value over time was more precious than gold. The great temple of Baal in Babylon alone burned two and a half tons of frankincense a year.

One technical achievement of these early societies was the development of a system to maximize the diminishing water supplies. In the few centuries preceding the Christian era there appeared the irrigation system which is still very much in use today: the *aflaj* (singular, *falaj*). (See Arts and Crafts section later in this chapter.) There are references to the aflaj in the Assyrian Empire during the time of Sargon, and it is known that the design and construction was used widely among early civilizations, from North Africa to as far away as Japan.

The Persians began the first of many occupations of Oman when it was invaded by Cyrus the Great in the fifth century B.C. Omani export was more than just in demand, it was worth controlling. Persian invasion, conquest, occupation, and retreat became the norm over the centuries. Alexander the Great, after hearing of this commercially prosperous region, dispatched expeditionary parties to survey the gulf's nether regions but his early demise curtailed that investigation. As years went on, Oman's reach and reputation grew. Roman historians Pliny and Strabbo refer to a gulf state of "Omana," as does Ptolemy, the Egyptian astronomer and cartographer.

But it was during the second century A.D. that the Persian coastal settlements were displaced by the migrating tribes of central and southern Arabia from the region in Yemen known as Hadramaut. It is believed that this migration was prompted by the collapse of a great dam at Mirab that had been constructed early in the first millennium B.C. These people were known as the Azd, and their leader, who some say was apocryphal, was Malik bin Fahm, a great noble and heroic figure. He is responsible for driving the Persians out of Oman (as far as Sohar) and establishing Qalhat as the first Omani capital. The Persians under Sassinid rule remained in Oman until the dawn of Islam.

Early Golden Ages and the Rise of Islam

By the time of the birth of the Prophet, Muhammed, in 570 A.D., Omani ports continued to prosper. Sohar, Qalhat, Muscat, and Dhofar were frequent ports of call, and further to the north, Julfar, Dibba, and Hormuz flourished. Somewhere in the desert north of Dhofar the overland trading post of Ubar thrived on frankincense, that most valuable of commodities. The Azdi tribes continued to settle in all areas of Oman, and although Arabia was an "economic backwater" by comparative wealth, the people continued to build upon their strength as traders.

In 622 A.D. Muhammed was forced to flee from Makkah with his newfound revelations and a small band of followers, only to return triumphantly several years later. (See Religion section later in this chapter for a more detailed description of the birth of Islam.) With converts answering to Muhammad's call in legion, he began to expand his base and petition the governments of outlying territories.

> I broke the Baajir to pieces when he was a god
> and I rested in the shade
> Al-Hashimi [the Prophet] showed us the falsehood of our ways.
> His religion was not known before.
>
> Traveller, tell Amr and her brothers
> That I, who once claimed Baajir as my god
> Says that the true God has talked.
> —Mazin bin Ghadhuba, in a poem on his conversion to Islam, seventh
> century

The first Omani to convert to Islam was Mazin bin Ghadhuba Al-Tay, who, like many Azdis of the time, practiced a local pagan religion. One day while offering sacrifice to his stone idol, Baajir, he heard a voice telling him that a messenger was about to deliver to him a revelation of the true faith. This also happened on a second occasion, followed by the appearance of a traveler from the Hijaz (western Arabia) who urged him to heed the call of the one true God. Mazin at that time renounced his sins, destroyed the idol, and traveled to Medina where he was converted by the Prophet. In asking for Allah's blessing, he wished that it be bestowed on all the Omani people.

It was then that a merchant from Muhammed's tribe (the Quraish), Amr bin Al-As, traveled to Oman with letters to the joint leaders of Oman at that time—the brothers Abd and Jaifar Al-Julanda—to petition them to join their cause. After convening a council of elders it was decided that the proper course was to embrace Islam. And in a short span of time the Azdi tribes, one by one, fell in line. The only people who did not embrace Islam were the remaining Persian enclaves along the coast. They were subsequently driven out of Oman (but not for the last time). By the time of the Prophet's passing in 632 A.D. (10 A.H.—the Islamic calendar is marked from the start of the *Hejira*, Muhammed's flight from Makkah), Oman and the entire Arabian peninsula had converted to Islam.

Now the Omani navigators had one more intangible export—the word of Allah—to carry to the far corners of the earth. By the seventh century Omani boat builders were producing rugged seagoing vessels capable of long cargo hauls. Sohar was the largest port in Islam and Oman's reach extended as far as Canton, China. Rare goods from the Far East were added to the lists of trade. It is quite possible that the Omanis were responsible for opening the Far East to Islam, as Indonesia and Southeast Asia today have the largest contingent of Muslims in the world.

> Of Oman's relationship with islands of the Far East it was said that on the island of Killeh were wondrous wares: aloes and camphor, sandalwood, ivory, lead, ebony and brazilwood, as well as aromatics of every variety. These goods were transported from this island to Oman, and on the same journey the boats carried Arab goods to India.
> —Abu Zayed Al-Hassan Al Sirafi, *Chronicles of China and India,* eleventh
> century

One Omani navigator of particular note is Sindbad the Sailor, whose embroidered stories have their niche in the fabled *Alf Laylah Wah Laylah,* the 1001 Arabian Nights Entertainments. It is believed that the personage known as Sindbad was born in Sohar, but he may very well be a character compiled from the life and times of many Omani seamen. Nevertheless, embellishments notwithstanding, the exploits of such seamen have to be considered remarkable for that time. (In 1980, British explorer Tim Severin set out to prove that a "Sindbad voyage" from Oman to China was possible using a boat built with only the technology of the time. He constructed the dhow in that fashion, using imported timbers from India and Africa, and the pieces were stitched—not nailed—together with coconut fibre. He then made that voyage of 6,000 miles in seven and a half months. The boat used for that trip, the *Sohar,* now rests at the entrance to the Al Bustan Palace Hotel.)

Closer to home, Omani tribes were spreading out and settling in many regions of the gulf. One spot for an enclave of Azdis was in the Iraqi city of Basra (where the Ibadhi sect was born and eventually spread to Oman—see later section on religion for description of Ibadhism.). The Azdi tribes in Basra were also very influential in spreading Islam to western Asia.

The period after the passing of Muhammed was a critical time for Islam. Divisiveness over conduct and direction spawned civil wars. Factions developed and formed what would become the main schism in Islam. The early days saw many changes in dynastic rule from the Rashidun, or "rightly guided" (title ascribed to the first four caliphs), to the Umayid dynasty to the Abassinids. The location of the seat of Islam shifted from Makkah to Damascus, Syria, to Baghdad, Iraq and back to Makkah. In Oman, one man,

Dhu't Taj Lakit, tried to supplant the ruling Julanda family by apostasy, claiming to be a true prophet. Although he rallied forces and fled to Diba he was eventually defeated, signifying the end of paganism in Oman.

From a social standpoint, local governments developed from tribes or families presided over by a *shaykh,* usually the most affluent member of a family and judged by his peers to be the most capable. The shaykh settled internal affairs, secured peace, and sought means of obtaining prosperity through commercial ventures. The city's income was the shaykh's private purse to use as he saw fit to serve the public interest by creating jobs and activities, placating nomadic rivals, and using his influence to promote unity. Tribes were patrilineal (traced through the male descendent, although there is some indication that some early tribes were matrilineal) and consisted of a nuclear household supported by several lineages. A whole unit combined as a clan. The tribes were the dominant social institutions but since there was no higher bond of organization tying disparate groups together, little is known about ethnographic backgrounds. Sometimes local leaders gave themselves titles such as king or prince without any historical precedent. At times the concept of a unified nation of clans was a far-flung notion at best. (The tribal unit is still the predominant feature of the social landscape today, although it ranges from the nuclear families of the cosmopolitan areas to the isolated clans of the interior descended from aboriginal tribes.)

The only other source of the authority apart from the shaykh came from the *ulema,* or scholars, who elected an *imam,* chosen for his exemplary conduct and strict interpretation of the scriptures, to preside over moral, cultural, and religious matters. He was also called upon to levy taxes and, if necessary, serve as military commander. His power was tied to the tribal structure and in some cases his authority was temporal, but in most areas, especially religious matters, the Imam had final word.

Trade and settlement with the east coast of Africa grew apace. The Omanis were considered the greatest single influence on the African sub-continent. For centuries they traveled to Berbera, Zinj, and as far as Mozambique. Their ports of call included Bandar Moussa, Berbera, Mogadishu, Patta and Lamu, Mombasa, Zanzibar, Qanbaloo, and Kilwa. They traded for gold and iron, aromatics such as ambergris, rare woods such as ebony, teak, and sandalwood, animal skins, and ivory—on which the Omanis had a virtual monopoly when dealing with India and the Far East. Later, slaves abducted from the interior became a valuable trading commodity.

Coastal societies were becoming thalassocracies, i.e., maritime supremacies. They also became more heterogeneous due to a stronger tendency for cultural mixing. The clans of the interior tended to keep to themselves, which created a strange dichotomy that would influence future political developments.

> Kalhat (sic) . . . has a good port, much frequented by merchant ships from India. They find a ready market here for their wares, since it is a centre from which spices and other goods are carried to various inland cities and towns. Many fine war horses are exported from here to India, to the great gain of the merchants.
> —Marco Polo, *Travels*, thirteenth century

The years from the eighth century onward were considered a golden age. Piracy reared its head from time to time, altering the political landscape, but by and large the Omani control of the Indian Ocean corridor was not broken until the sixteenth-century arrival of the Portuguese. Marco Polo made his way across Asia to the Far East in the thirteenth century and Oman did not escape his observation. But even greater than Polo's travels were that of the Tunisian-born Ibn Battuta (1304-1377). From the age of twenty-one, he undertook a lifetime of traveling that took him across most of the Muslim world, to the Far East and back, several times passing through Oman to such far-flung places as China, Sumatra, East Africa and India. Although the later years of his life are obscure, he recorded his travels in the *Rihla,* and they are a stunning record of history, geography, and culture.

European Intervention

> Muscat is a large and populous city. . . . There are orchards, gardens and palm groves with pools for watering them by means of wooden engines. The harbour is small, shaped like a horseshoe and sheltered from every wind. . . . It is a very elegant town with very fine houses and supplied from the interior with much wheat, millet, barley and dates for loading as many vessels as come for them.
> —Alfonso de Albuquerque, *Commentaries,* 1506

The history of gulf societies on the Arabian peninsula has largely consisted of traditional rivalries between merchant classes seeking unification and control, coupled with outside intervention by foreigners. Up until the 1500s, the Persians had posed the most significant threat to Omani security, but a change in the wind was blowing all the way around Africa from the shores of western Europe.

The Portuguese had developed a taste of eastern fineries through their contacts with the Moors. As they became a maritime power, they were determined to beat all comers to finding new trade routes to India. They were also pressed by an inflammatory religious zeal kindled from the days of the Inquisition and their conflicts with the Moors. This explains the atrocities the Portuguese committed upon reaching Omani shores: whole tribes were put to sea in barks covered with pitch and set afire, local leaders had eyes gouged out and noses and ears ripped off, all in a frenzy of crusader mentality.

Ironically it was an Omani mathematician, cartographer, and navigator—Ahmad bin Majid—who was conscripted by the Portuguese to lead Vasco da Gama around Africa to Calicut, India in 1498, thereby unwittingly helping in the downfall of his own people. Da Gama was followed by Alfonso de Albuquerque in 1507, who successfully blockaded the Red Sea and Arabian Gulf as he moved up the coast sacking and burning cities. Qalhat fell when they refused to honor a tax imposed on them. The city never recovered. (The Mosque of Bibi Miriam is the only building left standing today from that great port city.) Likewise with Sur, Quriyat, Muscat, Sohar, and on up the coast to the stronghold at Hormuz: they all fell as the Portuguese worked their way into the gulf, all the way to Bahrain and Kuwait.

Strangely enough, the Portuguese set in motion a pattern that was to be followed by the later "occupations." Even though they had "taken over" a city, they had no intention of colonizing or dominating the area. In fact they disregarded the local population altogether. They simply set up offices in the forts to monitor and control the trade with their newly acquired Far Eastern offices in India. The Omanis, who were left to sort out their own internal squabbles and civil wars, were no match for the Portuguese militarily speaking and were squeezed out from participation. Piracy again flourished for a while (what seemed piracy to the Europeans was "doing anything we can in desperation to maintain sovereignty" to the Omanis). Once the Portuguese had control over the gulf they held it for 150 years. During that time they suffered incursions from Ottoman Turks, who successfully liberated Muscat two times but inexplicably abandoned it. In response, the Portuguese constructed two magnificent fortifications in Muscat over earlier breastworks which overlook the bay: the Jilali and Mirani forts. There they remained, not so much as glancing inland.

By the 1650s, a number of factors—political and economical—made the Portuguese position untenable and they were forced to abandon Muscat, the last of their holdings in Oman. Bahrain, Kuwait, and Hormuz fell as attacks led by Omanis with Persian alliances were more and more successful. The British and Dutch were also in the picture as they vied for naval supremacy and control of the trade. The Dutch established offices on Arabian shores through treaty, not by invasion, and managed to maintain a hold on trade for 133 years after the Portuguese by remaining on friendlier terms with the locals. They made lots of money through their Far East ventures but they pretty much left the Omanis alone. When the winds of fortune changed for them, they too abandoned the gulf.

In 1645 the imam extended an offer to the British East India Company to set up trade facilities at Sohar. The English had been helping the Omanis against their common antagonists, the Portuguese. This began the start of a British monopoly on trade that lasted into the twentieth century. This was also the time of the rise of a very influential family, which was the last great dynasty before the current one: the Al-Ya'ruba.

The Al-Ya'ruba Dynasty

> God has stripped your hearts of mercy and that is your vilest sin . . . who adheres to fundamentals shall not be concerned with side issues. . . . We are the faithful, and shame shall not separate us from you nor admit to us doubt or uncertainty . . . if we live, we live blissfully, and if we die, we die martyrs to our faith.
> —Imam Saif bin Sultan Al-Ya'ruba, in a response to Portuguese threats of reprisals, 1697 (1109 A.H.)

In order to be rid of the Portuguese, the country had to be unified. The man farsighted enough to see this was Imam Nasir bin Murshid Al-Ya'ruba, who was elected to the post in 1624. Through his bitter struggles, he was able to ally the various clans of Oman and maintain supremacy by first reclaiming the coastal regions of Sur and Quriyat. Once he instilled the drive to liberation in his people there was no turning back. Nasir possessed the charisma to keep the people focused on that ideal. Although he never saw his ideal come to fruition—he died in 1649 (1059 A.H.), one year before Muscat fell back to the hands of the Omanis—he is credited with providing the inspiration that restored Oman to a nation state.

The ulema then declared Nasir's cousin, Sultan bin Saif, as imam. He followed through with ousting the Portuguese from Muscat. His relentless attacks on Portuguese vessels in the region over the years insured that they never returned. Sultan also built the great fort at Nizwa and made it his capital. He then built the extended falaj from Izki to Nizwa, the *falaj daris,* the largest single falaj in Oman.

His son and successor Bil'arub built the fort at Jabrin in 1670 (1081 A.H.) and established a college there. But Bil'arub's reign was marred by later quarrels with his brother, Saif bin Sultan. These quarrels distracted Bil'arub from any further efficient leadership. At one point he was forced to flee to the north. Upon returning, he discovered that his brother had acquired a sizable force, enough to take over all the other forts in Oman (except Jabrin). Bil'arub took sanctuary in Jabrin but Saif laid siege, eventually driving his brother to his death in 1693. Bil'arub is buried in Jabrin Fort.

Saif went on to inaugurate a policy of development; his public works restored Oman's previous glory as a mercantile state. With revenues he rebuilt aflaj, planted trees (dates, mangoes, and coconuts), increased crop production of wheat and barley, and introduced honey bees. He rebuilt the Omani fleet and expelled the Portuguese from holdings in East Africa. Upon his death in 1711 (1124 A.H.), he was conferred the title of *Qayd Al-Arth*, "Bond of the Earth."

His son, Sultan bin Saif II, continued his father in good works and in giving fits to Portuguese seamen. Sultan also had a reputation for power, justice, and fair play. It was his habit to wander amongst his people in disguise, usually as a peasant water bearer. When approached once by a stranger demanding water, Sultan asked, "What if I refuse?" The stranger replied, "I would smite thee with my sword were it not for Sultan bin Saif." Sultan was also responsible for extending Omani territory beyond the peninsula to Indian shores and East Africa. When Sultan died in 1718 (1131 A.H.), the period of unity and prosperity that had been created by the Ya'rubas had climaxed. However, the dynasty was to play out a rather protracted and melodramatic denouement that took twenty-six years to unravel.

The problem arose when the ulema came to elect a new imam. Since the Ya'rubas had enjoyed a rather popular and prosperous run, it seemed only logical to nominate the next in line, which was Sultan's son Saif (II). The problem was that Saif was a young boy and not considered old enough to take on the duties and responsibilities of an imam, such as leading the people in prayer. Dissension arose from a distant quarter of the family, who proposed that a more worthy candidate would be Muhanna bin Sultan, who was of age and indeed possessed the right attributes to be imam. He was wise, studious, and careful in thought and execution. But popular sentiment was with Saif, so much so that the ulema feared reprisals if they didn't elect him. What they staged was a conspiracy of sorts by presenting young Saif before the multitude and proclaiming, in Arabic, a phrase that could be taken in two ways. They announced, "Here is young Saif *standing before you!*" (*amamukum*) which sounded like "Here is young Saif, *your new imam*." (*imamukum*). The crowd immediately interpreted the latter and Saif, in their eyes, became imam.

Afterwards, when the tumult had died down, the ulema convened and voted for Muhanna to assume the post. Muhanna ruled very wisely, furthering the prosperity of his predecessors. He abolished customs duties in Muscat and doubled the trade, which led to an economic boom. But public sentiment still ran against him, fomented by Ya'rub bin Bil'arub, son of the late imam. Muhanna's tenure was short-lived. He sought refuge in the fort at Rustaq but was tricked into accepting safe passage out of Oman, whereupon he was abducted, imprisoned, and brutally murdered in 1720 (1133 A.H.).

Ya'rub, in a state of sycophantic contrition, appealed to the ulema to let him be Saif's guardian until he came of age, while he (Ya'rub) was conferred the imamate. But still the people would not have it. Factions broke out along tribal lines, with the Hinawi (Bani Hina) opposed to this latest move. They revolted and overtook Rustaq and the trade routes from the interior to the coast. Ya'rub was compelled to step down and young Saif was named imam again. An uncle of Saif's, Bil'arub bin Nasir, who was responsible for perpetrating the revolt, was appointed his guardian and trustee. But now the Ghafiri tribes (Bani Ghafir) were provoked into opposition. They felt Bil'arub was wielding too much power behind the scenes. Another bitter civil war started and culminated in the deposing of Bil'arub. Bil'arub was replaced by Khalf bin Mubarak of the Hinawis. More importantly, Muhammed bin Nasir, a Ghafiri, was named Saif's guardian.

By now young Saif had reached puberty. The year was 1723 (1136 A.H.). Still not old or mature enough to comprehend all the things that were happening around him, he was content to let Muhammed bin Nasir take the reins. Muhammed forged alliances, built his army, and almost reunited the country, but he tired of his duties (or feigned tiring before the ulema). In response they pronounced him imam, which only prolonged the bloody factionalism. Muhammed bin Nasir and Khalf, his Hinawi rival and counterpart, were subsequently killed in battle.

Finally, in 1728 (1140 A.H.), young Saif was given the imamate for what turned out to be the penultimate time, and it seemed that the country would be united again under the watchful eye of the Ya'ruba dynasty. But the hopes and faith that the people put into young Saif never came to fruition. Saif lacked any real authority and was a miserable statesman. He avoided his duties and thus became a bitter disappointment. The country fractured along the old tribal lines and internecine clashes raged worse than ever. In four short years Saif was cast out of the imamate and replaced by Bil'arub bin Himyar, a distant member of the Ya'rubas. But Saif had not lost face among the Hinawis, who still considered him their leader. Now the country was so divided it would never reclaim the glory of earlier times. The Ya'ruba dynasty was about to come to a close.

Young Saif had to find a way to regain his position as imam. He reckoned that he was not strong enough to do it on his own, so he engaged Baluch mercenaries from Makran (Pakistan) and requested military aid from the shah of Persia. The shah was eager to comply, as he had greater designs on Oman than just mere assistance. With the necessary manpower, young Saif defeated the Ghafiri army led by Imam Bil'arub bin Himyar in 1736 (1148 A.H.). Bil'arub was able to recover and sallied forth against a fresh influx of Persian forces the following year, but with little effect.

Once again, Saif's inexperience led to his downfall. The Persians whom he trusted now began their own occupation, with ideas of complete domination. They imposed their own taxes on the towns they occupied and demanded loyalty to the shah. In desperation Saif appealed to the defeated Bil'arub to reunite with him, restore his seat, and drive out the Persians. With reluctance, Bil'arub agreed. Saif succeeded in reducing the Persian tax but was unable to remove them from Omani soil. The ulema were now completely disenchanted with Saif's fickleness and they removed him from the imamate for the last time (1741/1153 A.H.). He was replaced with Sultan bin Murshid, the last of the Ya'ruba clan. His tenure was also brief and ineffectual. Sultan died two years later fighting the Persians at Sohar.

Saif was now left to reconcile with his own legacy. After he courted the Persians a second time, the Omani people abandoned him completely. Disconsolate and embittered, he retired to the fortress at Al Hazm. Upon hearing of the death of Imam Sultan, he died a broken man. He blamed himself for his mistakes and on his death bed proclaimed, "This is my castle and my grave. I am become an eyesore to everyone, and the quiet of death will be preferable to any happiness which dominion has afforded me." So ended a world with a whimper, but a new world was about to enter . . . with a bang.

The Rise of the Al Bu Saids: "Muscat and Oman"

> One of the Arabs' outstanding traits is their fondness for acts of bravery and the public standing of their heroes. They do not hesitate to rally round their leaders and to confer on them the title of Imam.
> —Rudolf Said-Reute, *The Sultanate of Oman during the Reign of Al-Sayyid Said bin Sultan (1791-1856)*, 1893, about Ahmed bin Said Al-Said

During his second official tenure as imam, young Saif bin Sultan appointed Shaykh Ahmed bin Said Al Bu Said as governor of Sohar. Ahmed bin Said was a vibrant personality, energetic and opportunistic. He was a strong administrator and of good judgment. He kept a high profile with his people and often could be seen distributing sweets to children and the poor. In fact his reputation as a capable leader was so strong that it eclipsed that of his benefactor, Saif. In another one of Saif's about-faces, he tried, unsuccessfully, to have Ahmed assassinated.

Besides his administrative prowess, Ahmed was also a shrewd military tactician. He withstood the Persian onslaught at Sohar for nine months (during which time Imam Sultan died in battle). Taking the situation into account, he accepted a cease fire, which many thought was a surrender. But Ahmed realized this war of attrition was not getting anywhere. His people needed time to recoup their losses and regroup without any further bloodshed. The Persians were suffering from internal strife back home and so a good portion of the army was to be recalled anyway. Ahmed also realized that the ulema needed to fill a vacant seat without the added pressure of warfare.

Seeing that it was time for a change, the ulema pronounced Ahmed as imam. They would be rewarded for their efforts. Ahmed started his rule by removing customs duties, thereby diverting the flow of imported goods away from Persian-held ports, such as Muscat. He captured a Persian-appointed governor to Oman and through a bogus messenger convinced the garrisons in Muscat to relinquish hold of the city. He then planned a huge gathering in Barka to which the Persians were invited. The preparations were so sumptuous that the Omanis complained that they never received such treatment for their own kind. In the middle of a huge banquet on the plain where battalions encamped, Ahmed toasted the Persian military retinue and at the sound of a drum announced, "All those who hold a grudge may take their revenge." In the ensuing massacre, only a handful of Persians survived.

The removal of Persians from Omani land signified the last time that Oman was occupied by foreign parties and the beginning of a new unified state and the start of the dynasty that has lasted to the present day. The year was 1747 (1160 A.H.).

Imam Ahmed, over the course of the next forty years, reunited the country (with the exception of some indignant Ya'rubas who held out at Al Hazm fort and did not relinquish until 1861). He consolidated his power through political alliances and marriages. He rebuilt his army and refortified the garrisons. He restored Oman to maritime supremacy; fleets of cargo vessels enjoyed greater mobility than ever. Ports were secure and ports of call increased. Over half the trade with Africa and the Far East passed through Omani hands. By the time of his death in 1778 (1188 A.H.), Ahmed had restored Oman to the status it had held before the Portuguese intervention.

The ulema replaced Ahmed with his son Said, who was a very religious man but shrank from administrative duties. He was not popular, as early business dealings antagonized the community against him (he had unsuccessfully tried to corner the Omani indigo market in Bahla). Since the tenets of Ibadhism allowed for the division of duties between leaders along religious, administrative, and military lines, he removed himself to Rustaq where he claimed the imamate until his death in 1811 but turned over the hands of government to his son Hamad, who took the title *Sayyid* (a title of respect for a Muslim of noble lineage) and thus became the first sultan in the dynasty. Over the years the country took on a dual nature between the imamate and the sultanate as the country was referred to as "Muscat and Oman," with each faction competing for supremacy and no clear indication for the outside world of who held the upper hand. But Hamad had no such competition from his father. He was a capable leader for eight years but died suddenly in 1792 (1206 A.H.), presumably from smallpox.

> Mascate est une place importante. L'Imam qui y gouverne, et dont la domination s'étend fort avant dans l'intérieur des terres et même sur quelques districts de la côte de Mozambique, est un prince indépendent sous tous rapports. [Muscat is an important city. It is governed by an imam and his control extends to the interior regions as well as colonies along the coast as far as Mozambique, where the prince pledges his allegiance (to Muscat)].
>
> —Talleyrand to Napoleon, 1803

Said then turned the reins over to his brother Sultan and retreated once again out of the public eye. Sultan strengthened the already powerful fleet by adding gunships and sleek cargo vessels. The British and the French took increasing interest in the status of the Omanis and the valuable trade routes. Napoleon Bonaparte looked to expand his dominions but his Egyptian/Syrian campaign was thwarted by the British in 1799. The British now pursued the Omanis for alliance and in 1800 signed a treaty with Sultan giving them broad leverage in the gulf and Indian Ocean. Over the next century that leverage was instrumental in the subsequent exploitation and commercial domination of the Omanis. In East Africa, colonies wanting to divest themselves of suzerainty were now being courted by British merchant vessels.

In any event, Sultan had his hands full trying to cope with other situations. Most of his time was spent in fighting off the Wahhabis, a volatile fundamentalist reform movement that originated in what is now Saudi Arabia and spread through the eastern Arabian peninsula as far as Buraimi, and down the coast in Omani territory as far south as Barka. The Wahhabis were not just the only problem. Qawasimi tribes from the Persian city of Lingeh were also seeking domination of the gulf region, and Sultan had this to deal with as well. Qawasimi marauders had made incursions through the gulf and past the Strait of Hormuz. Omani warships were in constant skirmishes up and down the gulf, which kept Sultan preoccupied. It was in the course of one of his sorties, during an incursion aboard ship in the Arabian Gulf in 1804 (1219 A.H.), that Sultan was shot in the head by a stray bullet. He was buried in Lingeh.

The Reign of Sayyid Said

It was at this time that the Albusaidi dynasty could have taken a turn through a different line of the family (and quite possibly ground to a halt) were it not for the perspicacity and determination of one woman: the Sayyida Moza bint Ahmed Al Bu Said, daughter of the late imam. The country was in a state of shock at the death of Sultan. Being away from the seat of government at the time of his death could have been disastrous—political power throughout the time of the Albusaidis was always a tenuous prospect. Inter-family rivalries, dissident tribes, and outside agitators all conspired to make the role of supreme commander a speculative proposition at best. That Oman was considered an important unified entity at all was based on her commercial prowess more than anything, politics and military might notwithstanding.

At the time of Sultan's death, the question on everybody's lips could very well have been "Who's minding the store?" It was the Sayyida who took control of the affairs of Muscat (the first of many times) and set the country in motion to become the commercial success it was for the next fifty years. Sultan left behind two sons, Salim and Said, half-brothers aged fifteen and thirteen. Although the elder Salim was studious and intelligent, he was retiring, uncharismatic, and rumored to have suffered from seizures. (He later succumbed to paralysis in 1821.) Also, his mother was not Albusaidi. Said's mother was, so Said was considered the higher pedigree. Said was also betrothed to Moza's daughter, making him the favored one. But Said was too young to take the reins of his country, so Sayyida Moza called upon another nephew, Badr bin Saif, to act as regent in the boy's behalf until he came of age. Meanwhile Moza carefully watched the affairs of state (as recounted by her great-niece Emily Said-Reute, née Salma bint Said, in *Memoirs of an Arabian Princess*, 1886):

> . . . she would carry on the government herself until her nephew came of age . . . the ministers had to make their reports to her, and received her instructions and commands every day . . . she closely watched and knew everything . . . and put aside all rules of etiquette; regardless of what people might say she merely wore her [shawl] in the presence of ministers . . . and dressed in men's clothes [on her inspection rounds at night].

Moza's decision to enlist Badr was unfortunately a bad one, as Badr had political aspirations of his own. He had already tried to seize Muscat in 1803, but his attempt was foiled by an astute Banyan (Indian) merchant who reported Badr's clandestine activities to the authorities. Badr was now in self-imposed exile in Qatar. In his retreat he also embraced Wahhabism (whether this was a genuine conversion or a political ploy will never be determined, as other subsequent events prevailed). With Wahhabi aid, Badr was able to hold off any other claimants to the throne. But the proselytizing fervency of his Wahhabi allies went unchecked as preachers roamed the streets of Muscat, terrorizing the tolerant Ibadhi locals (see later Religion section on Ibadhism), threatening them with death if they didn't submit to Wahhabi demands. Finally Badr was commanded by the Wahhabi leader to gather forces and attack the Indian mainland as part of the Wahhabi *jihad.*

Badr was at a loss as to how to react, because he would be making war on Oman's recently formed allies, the British. Once again the Sayyida Moza intervened.

Badr's infidelities had turned the house of Al Bu Said against him. But he would never relinquish his hold of power without a struggle. Moza then conspired with the young Said, now sixteen, to have Badr assassinated. On a pretext to inspect the munitions at Nakhl fort, Badr went to Barka and met Said at Bait al Nu'man castle. There he was promptly killed in strange circumstances by an "unusual discharge of arms." One story has Said and Badr in a dramatic duel to the death with daggers. A wounded Badr escaped but was finished off by Said's horsemen. Said then assumed the government and held it until his death fifty-two years later. He announced to the British that he had assumed power, but the British were slow to respond. They acknowledged his ascendancy a year later when they realized that their fortunes were best served by courting the young monarch.

Sayyida Moza filled in for Said from time to time in his absences from Muscat, showing the acumen that she had displayed in earlier times of crisis. At one instance, through her network of mediators, she quelled a potentially inflammatory disturbance in the interior in 1832. She was a consummate leader, always considered a lady of high esteem.

Said (known as Said the Great in the West, and "The Imam," although he eschewed the latter title) went on to become the longest lived of the sultans of the Al Bu Said dynasty. He was also counted among the best of leaders as his reputation spread to the crown heads of Europe and America. Indeed, few Arab leaders of any time were as well known and respected as Sayyid Said. He provided funds, materials (such as anchors), and services to visiting ships, kept accounts with every passing vessel, and was known to have kept correspondences with American shipmasters who had never traveled to Arabian waters. Rarely has an Arab leader left such a positive impact on a fledgling country half a world away, especially among people who never had the opportunity to know him.

Of Said it was said that he was "a tall and commanding figure, a mild and striking countenance . . . affable and dignified." His biographer wrote:

> Praise be to God through whom Said, the happiest of rulers, attained quiet prosperity and perennial glory, decreeing to him sublime eminence in the sphere of happiness and renown, inasmuch that by the Divine aid vouchsafed to him he subdued the sovereigns of his time, acquired dignity by the battles which he fought with his enemies, conquered with the sword hitherto unknown countries and made a straight road over the dissevered necks of the rebellious.

The traditional outward tolerance of other creeds by Ibadhis was no less marked in Sayyid Said. The Rabbi Jacob Samuel, who traveled to Muscat in

1835 to consecrate the Passover for several Jews, found over 350 Jewish families residing in the Batinah coast. Hindu temples were built to serve the Indian population, and no practice was turned away.

Said was a capable warrior and spent much of his time at sea. Said's private fleet alone consisted of twenty ships. During this time Oman reached its zenith as a commercial maritime power, extending its borders to Pakistan in the north and controlling several ports along the Persian coast and, for a short time, Bahrain. To the south, many cities that had enjoyed earlier Omani colonization fell back in line. Said secured Mombasa from the Mazari. His reach extended all the way to Zanzibar, of which he was particularly fond: he made it his southern capital. (He also had designs on obtaining Madagascar through an arranged marriage with Queen Ranavolana. The queen demurred and instead proffered one of her young daughters. Said courteously backed down.)

Zanzibar was established as an Omani satellite as far back as the eighth century. The Portuguese found large enclaves of Omanis living in Zanzibar when they arrived in the late fifteenth century. Sayyid Said breathed new life into the perennial port. Although he is mistakenly credited with introducing the clove to Zanzibar (it was most assuredly established), it seems there is no doubt that Said made it profitable. He revitalized the rice and sugar cane production and the export of ivory and gum copal. He rebuilt its fortresses and is frequently mentioned by the likes of Burton, Speke, and Livingstone for having contributed so well to their African exploits.

Sayyid Said's influence was also felt by the expanding commerce of the United States, which had been treading Omani waters since the Washington administration. In 1827, American merchant Captain Edmond Roberts, from Portsmouth, New Hampshire, visited Zanzibar after hearing reports of the trade boom in the East African corridor spurred by Omani merchants. He engaged in private talks with Sayyid Said, emphasizing the need for bilateral agreements in trade. The United States and Oman both stood to benefit as the United States, unlike the British and French, had no territorial ambitions abroad and was solely interested in commerce. After concluding talks with the sultan, Roberts returned home with the idea of laying the groundwork for a treaty between the Omanis and the Jackson administration.

This was not the first account of American/Omani contact. In 1790, the Boston brig *Rambler* sailed into Muscat Harbor during the presidency of George Washington. Two years later another Boston-based ship, the *Commerce*, bound for Bombay, shipwrecked on the eastern coast of Oman near Ra's Al Sharbithat, 250 kilometers east of Salalah. The sixteen survivors of the shipwreck then made an overland trek to Muscat, losing half their party in the hazards of the desert. When they arrived in Muscat they were received by Sultan Hamad bin Said, who gave them food and lodging until they recovered from their ordeal and traveled on to Bombay and then home. One member of the crew, Valentine Bagley of Amesbury, Massachusetts, stayed on as a carpenter's mate aboard an Omani vessel before coming home two years later.

After hammering out a draft agreement, Roberts was designated Special Agent and returned, this time to Muscat in 1833, as envoy aboard the *Peacock*. The draft was presented to Said, who accepted it with minor modifications. One of the articles to be amended concerned the treatment of shipwrecked sailors. As a testament to Said's greatness (recalling the 1792 incident), the article was adjusted to read that all costs pertaining to the treatment, recuperation, and repatriation of American seamen, as mandated by Arabic custom and hospitality, was to be borne by the Omani government. The treaty, written in English and Arabic, was signed on October 3, 1833, and ratified by President Jackson in the following year. It was the first trade agreement between Oman and a nation of the Western hemisphere, and it was the second treaty formulated by the U.S. with an Arab state (Morocco being the first in 1820). The agreement gave the Americans broad trading privileges with Oman and its African holdings.

When Roberts was named Diplomatic Agent, he sailed to Muscat again in 1835 with the ratified treaties. Unfortunately his vessel ran aground on some coral reefs near Masirah Island. Roberts dispatched a cutter and seven men to continue on to Muscat. After a harrowing four-day journey, they arrived. Sultan Said immediately dispatched the royal ship *Sultanah* to aid the floundering American vessel. Roberts had managed, by that time, to refloat his ship by jettisoning the heavy guns and was escorted to Muscat by the sultan's ship. In Muscat, ratification ceremonies took place. Before Roberts could sail on to Bombay, the guns he had jettisoned off the coast of Masirah were retrieved by Omani divers and returned to his ship. Sayyid Said's magnanimity was later acknowledged on the floor of Congress and the Americans returned His Majesty's generosity in kind. Richard Palmer Waters of Salem, Massachusetts, was named American consul and dispatched to Muscat.

In 1840, the *Sultanah*, the same ship that came to the aid of Captain Roberts, sailed into New York Harbor laden with cargo along with envoy Haj Ahmed bin Nu'man. (His portrait can be seen hanging in the display of Oman and Zanzibar in the Peabody Museum in Salem, Massachusetts.) The ship's manifest included:

1,000 bags of Omani dates
20 bales of Iranian carpets
100 bags of coffee (mocha)

108 ivory tusks
80 bags of copal (gum resin)
135 bags of cloves
1,000 dried animal skins.

In return, the *Sultanah* brought back china, mirrors and vases, gold thread, muskets and gun powder, and textiles, mostly cotton sheeting. This particular material was very durable and so highly prized in Muscat that it was popularly known as "'Mercani" for its point of origin.

In the meantime, Emissary Nu'man received a "distinction rarely accorded foreign visitors" as he was hosted by the mayor of New York in special celebrations. He was enthusiastically entertained by Americans who were thrilled to see the emissary of such a far-off country. As a special greeting, he was a guest of honor on a train ride from New York City to Hicksville, Long Island.

This was the first of many correspondences with the two countries, which was celebrated 100 years later when Sultan Said bin Taimur was the first sultan to visit the U.S.A. He met with President Franklin D. Roosevelt. The 1833 treaty was updated in 1958 when the United States and Oman signed the new Treaty of Amity, Economic Relations and Consular Rights. The treaty was ratified in 1959 by President Eisenhower and Sultan Said bin Taimur. This was further amended by Sultan Qaboos who, in his accession in 1970, was determined to honor and respect the treaty and long-standing relations between the two nations.

Sayyid Said's reign was long and prosperous. Like no other monarch, he had consolidated and expanded the country's power. He solidified the borders against the Wahhabi invasion. He was the first Omani leader to consider the inhumanity of slavery; he sought alternatives for African slave traders (a difficult prospect to say the least because so many local economies were dependent on the enforced labor). He fathered thirty-six children. One of them, the aforementioned daughter Salma bint Said, married a German nobleman and published a biography of her life and times in Oman, *Memoirs of an Arabian Princess*, under her adopted name of Emily Said-Reute.

Said died in 1856, probably where he enjoyed being most, at sea, en route from Muscat to Zanzibar. On board with him was a son, Barghash, who was then nineteen, and Abdullah bin Salim Al Barwani, a rival Zanzibarian tribal leader and political rabble-rouser whom Said felt obliged to take as a hostage every time he left port. When the ship arrived in Zanzibar, Barghash secretly buried his father in the garden of his southern palace and set in motion plans to usurp the throne. From the time of the Sayyid's death, Oman went into a steep decline and was not to be a major player in world politics until the present day, some 140 years later. The breakup of the Omani empire came about due to a number of factors—one of which was the British, who played no small part.

Division and Downward Spiral

Said's death was not anticipated. He was only sixty-six when he died, and even though he had placed many of his sons in prominent positions, he had not left any clear line of succession. None of his sons had any broad power base with which to run the entire empire effectively. Moreover it is important to note that the Omanis did not in any way consider themselves an empire as much as they were a conglomeration of tribes united by common cause. This is important to consider because of sentiments Said expressed in his letter to the Earl of Aberdeen indicating his wishes for division of power (see below). It was meant to be a delegation of authority within the framework of the state, not the partitioning of an empire, which he did not have the sanction to do.

It is also curious to note that the Ibadhi mechanism of ascendancy by the electoral process (rather than hereditary succession) was ostensibly still in place. It was only rendered inoperative by Said's uncle, the Imam Said, in the 1780s through his abdication of temporal power while retaining religious authority. From Sultan Said's time, it was generally accepted that authority would proceed from the ruling dynasty, even though the electoral principle was quoted by many sides in the succession disputes that followed Said's death. Although the imamate incorporated the electoral process to some degree, it would not be seen again to any great extent until its revival in the current Qaboos administration.

In 1844, twelve years earlier, Said disowned a favorite son, Hilal (because he took to alcohol), and wrote a letter to the Earl of Aberdeen implying that he wanted Hilal to be no part of his future plans. The letter sets forth that one son, Khaled, was to be named *wali* ("governor") of Zanzibar and another, Thuwaini, was to be entrusted with the wilayat of Muscat. By the time of Said's death in 1856, both Hilal and Khaled were dead, the former at sea mustering forces against his father and the latter of pneumonia in Zanzibar in 1854. This left another son, Majid, to orchestrate the affairs of Zanzibar and the African holdings while Thuwaini continued his charge with the office of wali of Muscat. Furthermore, in Said's will there was no mention whatsoever of his wishes for the division of power, only the dispersal of Said's property and personal effects. It was almost inevitable that the country would fracture along geo-political lines.

Barghash, because of his youth and subordination to his brothers, had little or no power base with which to move. Upon Said's death aboard ship, he immediately had a new-found ally: Said's hostage, Abdullah bin Salim Al Barwani. Their cooperation led to a series of intrigues that culminated in Barghash's exile to India. (At one point Barghash was cornered in his estate, where he had stockpiled gunpowder kegs and threatened to blow everybody up if they so much as crossed the threshold. He later escaped the guard by dressing as a woman and—armed to the teeth—posed as a member of the harem. He left in the company of the tallest women—so as not to draw attention to his height—to meet his comrades in arms. After a final battle with combined British and Omani/Zanzibari forces, Barghash was captured.) Abdullah bin Salim, for his perennial exasperations, was cut into little pieces and distributed over the harbor.

At this time the British were very concerned about their commercial ventures. Their chief competitors over the last fifty years had been the French. Now a new player, the United States, had arrived in 1833, and its encroaching commercial ventures were too close for comfort. Like the other commercial empires with footholds in the Middle East, the English, too, wanted a larger piece of the Arabian pie. Seeing that Oman was teetering on the edge of a new period of instability, England, and to some extent France, exploited this new situation to escalate the tension between the brothers Majid and Thuwaini, who were now becoming rivals. Under pretense of acting as mediators, the English and French made secret offers of manpower and armaments, thus fueling arguments and widening the gap between Majid and Thuwaini. Allegations were made that Said had signed documents saying he wanted to split his empire between Muscat and Zanzibar, referring to the long-lapsed Aberdeen letter. Majid and Thuwaini, who were on fairly good terms before the intervention, now were objects of enmity and suspicion in each other's eyes.

They never came to serious blows, as England orchestrated a calculated settlement in 1861 (1278 A.H.) whereupon both brothers agreed to a split, each retaining his respective parcel without fear of reprisals. Known as the Canning Award (after the British administrator in Bombay who formulated it), the imbalance of the respective economies of Zanzibar and Muscat was to be offset by an annual sum of MT$40,000 (Maria Theresa dollars) paid to Muscat as subsidy. Although they were satisfied with this settlement, the animosity between the brothers did not stop. Majid and Thuwaini found ways to alienate each other further through trading blockades and discontinued courtesies.

Muscat was in serious economic decline as the English achieved their goal of "divide and conquer (of sorts)." The city lost most of the Omani fleet which was stationed in Zanzibar at the time of Sayyid Said's death. Following that, many Omani families migrated from Muscat to Zanzibar. In a twenty-year period the population of Muscat dropped from a prosperous 55,000 to 8,000. On top of this, the British, in 1862, had introduced a steamship line that outclassed the Omani vessels and drove them out of competition, leaving the Omanis to resort to slave trade, smuggling, and gun running. Meanwhile the Wahhabis were stirring things up in Buraimi again and Thuwaini's brother Turki rose up against him from Sohar. Unfortunately, Thuwaini did not get along with anybody, including his own family, and in 1866 he was assassinated by his son Salim, who shot his father in his sleep and then assumed control of the country.

Salim's term was very short-lived. He could not win the favor of his people, who could not come to grips with his patricide. This also prompted Zanzibar to discontinue the annual subsidy, which Muscat was using as a remittance to pay the Persians as a rental fee for occupation of Bandar Abbas (in modern-day Iraq). The Persians then revoked their lease and renewed it at twice the rent. Azzan bin Qais Al-Said, a distant relative of the Al-Busaidis, mustered forces against Salim. With no support Salim could not hold center and was forced to flee in 1868 (1285 A.H.). He was later captured and exiled to India, where he died in 1873.

Azzan showed a power and charisma that had not been seen in Muscat in years. Even the British were unsteady about his tenure. They feared he might unite the interior tribes and jeopardize the established order. A self-proclaimed fundamentalist, he expelled the Wahhabis from Buraimi, was proclaimed imam by his own supporters, and set up his own draconian regime. Ironically the imamate he wished to restore was the one renounced by Imam Said in favor of a secular government based on primogeniture and hereditary ascendancy. Nevertheless, Azzan went to extremes. Alcohol and tobacco were outlawed. Mosque attendance was mandatory. Even music of any kind was banned. An attaché in the British consulate was threatened with arrest if he didn't stop playing his concertina. Azzan's severities were not appreciated and he was overthrown by Thuwaini's brother Turki (with the help of British financial and military support) in 1871 (1288 A.H.).

Now that the Sultanate had fallen back into the mainstream of the Al Busaidi family, it appeared that the country would get on the right track. Turki's relationship with his brother Barghash, who had returned from exile in India on good behavior and assumed the leadership of Zanzibar after Majid's passing, was cordial. Britain had agreed to guarantee the annual subsidy. Nevertheless, the early years of Turki's rule were unsettled, mainly because he was in opposition with the remaining of Sultan Said's children. Fortunately for Turki, they were too disunited to do anything about it. Tribal dissents continually surfaced and one unscrupulous advisor made off with a fortune. The treasury was empty and the army restive because their pay was in arrears. Turki was in ill health due to a stroke he suffered in the early 1870s. For a time he retired, appointing his brother Abdul Aziz as regent while he recuperated. But when his health returned Abdul Aziz did not want to relinquish his post and Turki had to take Muscat by force. For a brief period he appeased his opposition with payoffs funded by the British.

Another blow to country was in 1873 when British imperialism took advantage of circumstances to subvert the commercial network by formally abolishing the slave trade. Slavery was always a thorny issue. In the early part of the century when slavery had been banned "to all good Christian nations," Oman became an unexpected beneficiary as increased slavery markets took up the slack and the country's agricultural output increased dramatically. Although the British pursued the anti-slavery issue on humanitarian grounds, it became evident that this was just another manipulative device to break the Omani network of commerce. Later, when Zanzibar became a British Protectorate, the British were faced with economic disaster if they held to their high-minded tenets and looked the other way until slavery was supplanted by modern agricultural methods of the twentieth century.

But it was a sequence of other events that allowed the British to play their trump card. When Sayyid Said moved the capital of his empire from Muscat to Zanzibar in the 1840s, it was recognized that the island was the more productive commercial location. A partition of the Omani state would allow the African side to develop its potential while the British could concentrate their efforts on economic control. First, it was realized that most of the powerful merchant class in Zanzibar was Indian, and since India was already a British protectorate, they could exercise supremacy under the justification that these people were British subjects. Now they made their demand to put an end to slavery. But Barghash was adamant and would not submit to foreign interference. However, outside disturbances and nature intervened.

A war on the African mainland from 1860 to 1865 interrupted the precious ivory trade. Even the American Civil War of the same period caused a precipitous decline in orders from that quarter. A cholera epidemic in 1870 wiped out one third of the population in Zanzibar, where entire slave communities were decimated. And in 1872 a massive freak hurricane rumbled across the island. Over a hundred and fifty Arab and Indian dhows were wrecked in the harbor, many of them laden with cargo. The entire Omani fleet, save one ship which had just sailed out of port, was sunk. Many buildings in the capital were destroyed or damaged. But the devastation to the plantations was worse. In some areas only five to ten percent of the coconut and clove trees survived. New trees would not bear fruit for seven to eight years. The loss of production and revenues was incalculable.

Barghash now had his back to the wall. His fleet was gone. Muscat was too far out of touch and in little position to help anyway. The British threatened a total embargo and Barghash was forced to capitulate. He signed the agreement that abolished the slave trade, closed all the markets, and liberated all existing slaves. Meanwhile, back in Muscat, Turki was obliged to enforce the 1873 treaty although interior farmers were upset at their lower output due to loss of manpower. This caused a further sag in the country's agricultural production, and on top of that, increased animosity between the interior and Muscat.

Turki turned to his brother Barghash in Zanzibar for assistance. Barghash complied, sending his brother many "gifts" of money used to stave off further internal strife. At one point Turki decided to abdicate in favor of Barghash, which would have united the Omani domain once again. Upon hearing this, however, the British talked him out of it.

The last years of Turki's reign were peaceful as he exchanged visits with his brother. Although the nation was staggered by the loss of its commerce to British steamships, the country managed to hang on. Turki, in keeping with his Muslim convictions, managed to distribute two meals a day to the poor. Both Turki and Barghash died in 1888 (1306 A.H.), within months of their final sojourn together, prompting the only peaceful transition of power in the entire century. Although the country was near bankrupt, it managed to remain stable for the time being. The watchful British had squeezed Oman out of the commercial mainstream, as the country was reduced to a subsistence-level economy.

It was about this time during Turki's reign—1879 (1297 A.H.)—that the southern province of Dhofar was annexed to the rest of the country for good, despite an 1895 uprising that was summarily quashed. Dhofar had always been pretty much an autonomous state. Way back in antiquity it had been part of a Yemeni society from the Hadramaut region and was even an enclave for an Ibadhi settlement that had started in Yemen. However, by the thirteenth century, this enclave had disappeared. The ports at Mirbat, Taqah, and Raysut were always prosperous due to the fertile area of the southern plateau and the production of its major commodity, frankincense, which was always in demand. It is not clear how ties were established with Muscat over the ages, but it is very likely that family ties through settlements strengthened an ever increasing bond with Muscat, albeit slowly. There are indications that Dhofar gave allegiance from time to time and may have had some affinity with the Ya'rubas. But for the most part Dhofar continued on its own. It was not until the late nineteenth century that Dhofar fell in with the rest of Oman, and only after a curious set of circumstances that saw it governed briefly by an American.

In the early 1800s, one Muhammed Aqil Ajaibi and his brother Abdu-Rahman were merchants who, with their expanding wealth, controlled the southern coastal waters of Oman. This wealth may have been originally obtained by legitimate means, but later came from piracy and smuggling. Their fleets and revenue increased. Muhammed Aqil had amassed over five hundred slaves from Mozambique for his private army. It was when Muhammed first set eyes on Dhofar that he wanted to settle there, which he later did, recanting his treacheries and abandoning his wayward ways. But in his earlier years his exploits were known and feared up and down the coast. During his days of piracy he had the occasion to capture an American vessel in the Red Sea and take one prisoner as hostage: a ten-year-old American boy. The boy went with Aqil back to Dhofar, where he became a protégé of the pirate and was not only made into one himself but was also converted to Islam, took an Arabic name, and settled along with Aqil in Dhofar. He took a wife, raised a family, and all but forgot how to speak English. He was known as Abdullah Lorleyd.

Aqil had amassed a sizable following and was able to subjugate the local tribes. It was then that he repented his years of plundering and cruelty. He became oddly enlightened and was adored by his subjects as he watched over them lovingly and expanded the wealth of Dhofar. With his new-found altruism he ruled for over twenty years. But he was not to come to a happy end. His early indiscretions had left psychological wounds in his enemies that would not heal, and in the course of time they festered with the thought of revenge. In 1829 Aqil was ambushed and murdered outside of the fort he had built in Mirbat. It was then that his charge, Abdullah Lorleyd, managed to govern for a while, with some success owing to the popularity he had achieved for leading several raids on the tribes in Jebel Qara.

But with the death of Aqil, Muscat took interest, and Sayyid Said dispatched a contingency force to Dhofar. This display was enough for the Dhofaris to capitulate to Muscat authority (in word, at least, if not in deed). Sayyid's ships did not stay long in Dhofar as they were called away to quell disturbances in East Africa. From that point on Dhofar tacitly accepted Muscat sovereignty but still continued to function on its own terms. Nothing is mentioned as to the fate of Lorleyd; he probably faded into obscurity, quite contented with the pastoral life that Dhofar provided. (We do know that he was met by the survey crew of the *Palinarus* and Captain Stafford Bettesworth Haines in 1834 on their excursions along the East African coast.)

For the next fifty years the relationship between Muscat and Dhofar was status quo until an exiled Indian fanatic, the Mopla priest Fadhl bin Alawi, settled in Dhofar and commandeered the settlement into submission. His tenure was brief as Muscat took notice and sent troops in 1879. He was expelled once again and Dhofar formally became part of the country.

Zanzibar, in the meantime, recovered from its recent travesties and continued to prosper—so much so that British attention turned to the island. In 1891 they declared Zanzibar a protectorate. The sultan of Zanzibar was reduced to a mere honorary figure and island jurisdiction was in the hands of the British Consulate. Government policy was dictated through an "old boy" network of hand-picked administrators. It wasn't until 1955 that an Arab Zanzibarian party was able to establish itself and call for general elections. By 1961 they had assumed a majority, prompting a British withdrawal two years later. But seeds of discontent were sown as members of Afro-Sherazi, an ethnic African party allied to the British, rose to power and ousted the Arabs in a bloody massacre in 1964. The Afro-Sherazi went on to declare unity with Tanganyika. The result was the formation of the United Republic of Tanzania with its capital in Dar es Salaam. Leaders from Tanganyika and Zanzibar (the Afro-Sherazi faction) filled in as president and vice president respectively. Thus Arab history in Zanzibar was formally concluded, but many Zanzibarians with Omani roots still thrive there. Many more have returned to Oman with the twentieth-century renaissance.

After Turki's passing in Oman in 1888, his son Faisal became sultan and was immediately put to the task of maintaining the country's tenuous stability. Hinawi/Ghafiri factionalism broke out once again and a rebellion was supported by Hamad bin Thuwaini, the new sultan of Zanzibar at that time. Hamad had lived in Oman for many years, where he gathered a huge following. In 1893 he moved to Zanzibar, prompting a mass exodus from Muscat. In Zanzibar he usurped the throne from Ali bin Said, who had replaced Barghash, and built a very strong power base. In 1895 Hamad turned his sights on Muscat. A successful rebellion was very short-lived as the British came to the aid of the desperate Faisal. In time, Faisal's mistrust of suspected usurpers grew. In later years he kept a caged lion in the courtyard of the palace.

The Twentieth Century: Darkest Hours and Brighter Days

"I have little doubt that the time will come . . . when the Union Jack will be seen flying from the castles of Muscat," wrote Lord Curzon, Viceroy of India, in 1903.

The rest of Faisal's reign was taken up with frequent interior squabbles coupled with the actions of the British and French, who continually vied for Omani allegiance. An outbreak of bubonic plague in 1903 stifled much activity. Shortly after that, the Indian mint, where Oman's currency was manufactured, closed, causing greater economic despair. The interior rallied behind an ex-slave, Sulayamin bin Suwaylim, and the imamate was reconstituted under Salim bin Rashid Al Harthy. Faisal struggled gamely to appease all factions until his death in 1913 (1332 A.H.). It was now the turn for Taimur, Faisal's elder son, to try to reverse the country's fortunes.

The Hinawis and Ghafiris were causing problems again, but this time they were united behind the Imam Salim bin Rashid against Taimur. A rebellion of the interior was eventually defused by an agreement orchestrated by the British and Taimur in 1920. Named "The Treaty of Seeb," it called for the cessation of hostile activity, free movement between the tribes of the coast and interior, an imposition of taxation on goods from the interior not to exceed 5 percent, and a general truce promoting peace and amity. This served the British interest as it ensured political quiescence between Muscat and the interior without the need to dispatch troops. The country's financial woes persisted as Oman remained isolated from the outside world. This was compounded by the strain of the global economic depression of the 1930s: even if they could trade with the outside world, there was little Oman could obtain. Taimur tired of his role and eventually abdicated in favor of his son Said in 1932 (1351 A.H.).

Sultan Said's prime objective was to remove the country's enormous national debt which, to his credit, he was successful in doing. Said's focus, however, left him out of touch with his people. His methods of austerity were by and large too harsh and strangely anachronistic. The years of mistreatment by foreign powers (the Persian occupations, the Portuguese invasion and atrocities, the British meddling) fueled his mistrust of foreigners. He distrusted Western advances in technology as well. Radios, bicycles, and sunglasses (symbols of Western affluence) were banned in Muscat. Electricity was rationed and the gates of Muscat were closed every day at sundown. Even slavery was promoted to stimulate the economy. Communication extended no further than the public notices posted on the bulletin board outside the palace. Fears of reprisals from the interior led him to mistrust his own people. In retribution, education was restricted to a select few. Those who left the country for education outside did so on their own with no hope of returning home. In time his xenophobia drove him to retreat to his southern palace in Salalah.

Said did maintain altruistic intentions, even if he lacked the ability to set them in motion. He realized that one way out of the country's economic dilemma was, like so many other countries in the region, to jump on the petroleum bandwagon. But to allow for exploration teams, he needed the cooperation of the interior, which was not forthcoming. Said sent teams anyway. This provoked the ire of the imam, who felt Said was violating the 1920 accord. A secessionist movement formed in 1954 with support from Saudi Arabian sources but the British intervened on behalf of the beleaguered Sultan and the rebellion was put down. The Treaty of Seeb was abrogated and the imamate was now defunct. Petroleum was discovered in 1964, and in 1967 the first production began. Long-sought revenues began to trickle in. Unfortunately, Said's plans for development were not far reaching enough for him to realize his goal of economic liberation.

Other factors also led to Said's further retreat. In the 1950s and 60s, Marxist separatists in Yemen demanded the overthrow of what they felt was an outdated monarchy. The organization, known as the Popular Front for the Liberation of the Occupied Arabian Gulf (PFLOAG, later renamed the People's Front for the Liberation of Oman), had hoped to put down the monarchy and create a domino effect in the region that would culminate in the establishment of a communist state. Said mistakenly blamed the Dhofaris and subjected them to reprisals for a war that they did not start, compounding their hostility and almost setting in motion the desired outcome of the Marxists. Said was not to see the resolution of this conflict, as other spheres of influence came into play.

Sultan Qaboos Bin Said and the Current Economic Revival

> I promise to you to proceed forthwith in the process of creating a modern government. My first act will be the immediate abolition of all the unnecessary restrictions on your lives and activities. . . . I will proceed as quickly as possible to transform your life into a prosperous and bright future. Every one of you must play his part towards this goal. Our country in the past was famous and strong. . . . Yesterday it was complete darkness and with the help of God, tomorrow will be a new dawn on Muscat, Oman and its people.
>
> —His Majesty Sultan Qaboos, from a speech given to the people on the day of his accession, 23 July, 1970

Said's only issue was a son and two daughters by Dhofari wives. The son, Qaboos Bin Said, was born on November 18, 1940. He spent all his early years in isolation within the royal palace. Wendell Phillips says that his father impressed upon him that he was no different from other Omanis. He was to have no servants; he would have to work or starve. In 1958 at the insistence of the few British advisors Said kept on hand, he reluctantly agreed to send the boy to school in England, first to a private school and then on to Sandhurst, the Royal Military Academy, for his education and grooming. After a tour of duty in Germany the young prince returned to Salalah in 1964, where his newfound worldly views were in conflict with his father's conservative policies. He was requested to again stay within the walls of the southern palace, and he did, for the next six years.

Qaboos spent that time studying the Qur'an and the fundamental teachings of his Ibadhi faith. After taking stock and careful planning, Qaboos was able, with the tacit support of the British, to stage a nonviolent coup d'état in 1970. He asked his father to step down and thereupon took the reigns of the government. Said withdrew to London, where he died two years later. The young sultan now had the gargantuan task of bringing his people back from the depths of despair.

In 1970, Oman was one of the poorest countries in the world, saddled with a barely subsistence-level economy and isolated. Health standards were low and mortality high, education was stultified, and infrastructure, for all intents and purposes, was nonexistent. Qaboos was determined to rebuild his country. This was not going to be a simple task. Oman was not oil-rich like other gulf countries. The oil that had only recently been discovered was slow to come and further investigation was required to find more reserves. But there was enough with which to start building. Qaboos began to put an infrastructure in place. In 1970 there were only 10 kilometers (6 miles) of paved roads in the entire country. Electricity was limited to about 500 customers in Muscat alone. There was one 12-bed hospital run by missionaries, one or two schools, limited telephone service, and mail distribution for the capital area only (anything sent to the interior depended on the goodwill of travelers). It was easier to get to Muscat from Sohar (200 kilometers up the coast) by boat than by land.

Financing the redevelopment was not enough. Qaboos had to enact a stringent economic policy to see that money was spent wisely. And if this were not problem enough, he had to contend with the insurgence of the communist-backed rebels from Yemen without a standing army. (In the preceding lean years, the military had been reduced to a small contingent of palace guards.)

By 1975 the pieces had begun to fall in place. With outside assistance from the Shah of Iran, who dispatched ground forces and air units, the rebels in the south were defeated. Oil production was gradually increasing. The Sultan, on assuming power, had abolished a number of outdated and prohibitive edicts that had been put in place by previous regimes. He began to get a reputation for running a prudent economy as he set his country in motion, pacing it with a series of five-year plans starting in 1976 that carefully plotted the way to recovery. In Mutrah, a suburb of the capitol, the old harbor was dredged and a modern container facility, Mina Qaboos, was put in place to meet the demand for foreign trade. When completed in 1974, it was capable of handling 2 million tons of cargo annually. To promote commercial and industrial development, the Oman Chamber of Commerce and Industry was established in 1973. The chamber serves as a bridge to foreign investors to promote and protect the economic interests of the country.

[The Sultan] wore an elegant brown aba, embroidered with gold thread, and a gold khanjar at his waist. His head bore the multicolored turban that is worn only by the Al Bu Said. "Since 1970 we have come far," the Sultan said as we sipped glasses of the popular iced lime drink called loomey. "A national feeling of working together has developed. This is generating great progress. I am encouraged by the spirit of the returning Omanis. Not only do they bring skills we need, but they make no complaint about the lives they have given up abroad."
—Robert Azzi on Sultan Qaboos in 1972

The country's petroleum reserves grew to over 4.4 billion barrels, modest by many standards, but this was a strong indication that production could last into the next century. Now Qaboos began to concentrate on the most valuable resource of his country: his people. Early projects centered on housing and public services. Electricity and water soon followed as well as a network of hospitals and clinics throughout the country.

In 1970 health care was almost nonexistent. The mortality rate was high and epidemics such as measles and influenza were scourges to entire communities, particularly in the interior. Today there are over fifty hospitals, ninety clinics, and maternity and preventive health care centers and mobile units networking across the Sultanate. The country enjoys a broad-based immunization program; emphasis has shifted from treatment to prevention.

Education was just as important to the young sultan. In the past education had been restricted to a small fraction of hand-picked students (boys only). Prior to Qaboos's accession, Omanis were discouraged from seeking higher education. But this changed in 1970. Education became a paramount issue alongside health care. In the early days the demand was so great that classes were taught in shifts in tents until permanent facilities were established. In an early speech Qaboos pronounced, "[Let] there be education even under the shadow of trees." Teachers were recruited from all over the world. There was a pressing demand for adult education as well.

Women, for the first time in the century, were accorded the privilege of a formal education. Qaboos, recognizing that women are a significant aspect of the labor force and that educated and trained professional women serve as positive role models, was not about to deny one-half of his potential resources. One role model who has made a difference is Ms. Rayya bint Saif Al-Riyami. This spritely senior runs a travel business and a hang-gliding school, is director of Oman's Girl Guides, is a current volunteer in health counseling and family planning (she even holds workshops for men), and in her spare time lends a hand with mothers of handicapped children and recruits volunteers for the association's projects. She has degrees from schools in the U.K. and has been invited by the U.S. embassy to speak to health-care and educational centers in the U.S. She is vivacious, engaging, and one of the most charming persons I have ever met.

Qaboos's most important social objectives in jump-starting the population were to bring peripheral regions of Oman into the mainstream of twentieth-century life. It was also vital to demonstrate that a traditional absolute monarchy need not have the trappings generally associated with it. By the 1990s there were 823 schools for general education in the Sultanate for nearly a half million students, both boys and girls. These consisted of primary schools, prep schools, and secondary schools. Illiteracy was all but eradicated. In addition to general education, there are technical institutes, schools for Islamic study, commercial and industrial schools, an agricultural institute and, in 1986, a university with seven colleges including medical, science, and engineering. Sultan Qaboos University now caters to the needs of more than three thousand students a year.

Beyond petroleum, Oman has other natural resources. Copper has been mined and smelted since ancient times. In recent years significant chromite deposits have been discovered. Chromite is a necessary ingredient in the making of stainless steel. Also, tracts of coal have been discovered in the eastern Hajar Mountains and are being analyzed for viability.

> Of all the gifts which God has blessed us, water is the greatest. It must be cherished and husbanded. Every effort must continue to be made to develop this resource. If extravagance is forbidden by Islam, it is even more applicable to water. Indeed, Islam emphasizes in its teachings that it is our duty to conserve it.
> —His Majesty Sultan Qaboos from the National Day Address, 18 November, 1991

Over the centuries, agriculture and fishing have been a mainstay of the Omani economy. Even now, when 90 percent of the country's exports are based on petroleum, over one-half of the population is engaged in farming or fishing. One of the government's long-term goals is to achieve self-sufficiency in food production. In spite of being an arid climate there is considerable agricultural potential, and modern agricultural methods have increased production of farm produce to meet growing consumption demands. The Hajar Mountains in the north draw larger amounts of precipitation than the neighboring flat regions, and the southern area of Dhofar is affected by regular monsoon rains from the Arabian Sea. Another contributing factor is the use of the aflaj, the network of water channels introduced in ancient times and devised to extract hard-to-reach ground water and distribute it to community farms (see section on the aflaj later in this chapter under "Arts and Crafts").

Dates are Oman's main crop; they are world renowned. In the nineteenth century, date export to the United States alone averaged $110,000/year. Yearly production is up over 150,000 tons. Of more than two hundred varieties of dates grown in Oman, twenty are commercially viable. Limes are also cultivated along with other fruits—mangoes, apricots—and garden vegetables. In the south, bananas, coconuts, and papayas are grown, as well as a number of fodder crops such as sorghum and millet. There is even an interesting variety of sweet lemon.

Livestock makes up another significant source of food. Cattle, sheep, goats, and poultry are raised for meat and dairy products. In Oman today there are over a hundred thousand farms in the country, most of them small family holdings. In 1981 the Public Authority for Marketing Agricultural Produce (PAMAP) was established to promote the internal marketing and

His Majesty Sultan Qaboos Bin Said. (Photo courtesy Ministry of Information)

Bait Al Falaj Fort, site of the Armed Forces Museum. (Photo by Abdullah Al Habsi)

Omani boys dressed up for National Day celebration in Bidiyah. (Photo by Abdullah Al Habsi)

Girl dancers on National Day in Muscat. (Photo by Alan J. Scullard)

A falaj, part of the ancient aflaj network which has provided water to Omanis for more than two thousand years. (Photo by Peter J. Ochs II)

The Muscat InterContinental Hotel. (Photo courtesy of Oman Dept. of Tourism)

The mists of the khareef blow across the hills of Dhofar,
making the landscape lush and green. (Photo by Chris McHugh)

Sparkling pools of Moqal in Wadi Bani Khalid. (Photo by Chris McHugh)

Interior of Al Zulfa Mosque. (Photo by Sulayam Al Abri)

Islamic architecture in one of its finest displays:
Al Zulfa Mosque near Barka. (Photo by Peter J. Ochs II)

Bilad Sayt, a secluded village deep in the reaches of Wadi Bani Awf.
(Photo by Peter J. Ochs II)

Scenic overlook near Fanjah. (Photo by Sulayam Al Abri)

distribution of agricultural products; it has played an ever increasing role in meeting the demand of the country for food. Frankincense also continues to fill a role in the country's agriculture, as it has since ancient times.

It is not hard to see that the people of a country with 1,700 kilometers of coastline would be skilled in the fishing trade. More than 150 species of fish are taken from Oman's waters, from sardines to tuna to shellfish. Smaller varieties are cultivated for use as fertilizer while the larger catches are taken for their food value and by-products. Large-scale fishing ventures have replaced smaller independent fishers and exports are continually on the rise. In 1986 the government set up the Marine Science and Fisheries Centre to study resources and future development as well as provide an academic role in the ecology of the marine environment with emphasis on conservation of ecosystems and endangered species. By 1990 there were over eighteen thousand registered fishermen in the Sultanate.

By the 1990s, Qaboos had accomplished many of his main objectives to establish infrastructure and put his people in touch with a new realm of possibilities. Today there are over 5,355 kilometers of paved roads in the Sultanate and an additional 15,114 kilometers of improved roads reaching out to the most inaccessible villages. There are also links to neighboring Yemen and the United Arab Emirates. There are six airports in the country, with Seeb International Airport servicing the capitol area through more than fifty scheduled flights a week. SIA is implemented with the most advanced radar installations and satellite fiber optics. In addition, Oman has a 25 percent share in Gulf Air which operates between the Middle East and Asia, Africa, Europe, and the United States.

The postal service offers 93 offices and 100 distribution agencies with direct dispatch to 37 countries.

The General Telecommunications Organization (GTO), established by royal decree, maintains 264,716 lines plus nationwide card-phones and a cellular exchange started in 1986. International communications were upgraded in 1986 to standard *A* satellite earth station operating via Intelsat and Arabsat.

Mobile phones were introduced in 1985 and at the end of April 1996 there were 8,352 subscribers with a network capacity of 9,500 lines. In 1997 GTO introduced GSM (Global System for Mobile) phones to the Sultanate. The new system will only cover a limited area in the initial stages and subscribers will continue to use existing systems until coverage is complete.

The government has promoted small-scale manufacture in industrial trades including food and beverage processing, furniture, textiles, paper products, metal products, and electrical goods. The Rusail Industrial Estate was completed in 1985 to accommodate new businesses. Expansion was planned with an additional development in Salalah. Most of the industrial activity is devoted to export. Business policies encourage investors to engage in joint ventures with emphasis on training and job skills for Omanis. Business incentives include guaranteed interest-free loans, customs duty exemption on raw material importation, tariff protection on imports that compete with local products, and a five-year income tax exemption.

Additional industrial estate sites include Sohar in the north, Raysut in the south, and Nizwa, and plans are being laid for others at Sur, Khasab, and al-Buraimi. On the Sohar industrial estate there are currently 12 factories in production and 9 others under construction, while at Raysut there are now 5 factories in production and 13 others are under construction. At Nizwa, Phase I of the infrastructure has been completed.

In business, the Central Bank of Oman controls the country's monetary flow. There are 21commercial banks in Oman (10 local banks and 11 foreign branch offices), three specialty banks for housing and industrial development, and 9 draft and money exchanges. In 1970, Sultan Qaboos established the Omani Riyal as the official currency of the country. Prior to that time the country depended on Indian rupees and Maria Theresa dollars (MT$). Today, the country has assets in excess of one billion riyals (1 RO = $2.58), a net worth of RO 379 million. Working capital stands at about RO 175 million, general reserves at RO 23 million, and other reserves at RO 180 million. The Gross Domestic Product was RO 5,288.2 million by the end of 1995 with an annual growth rate of 3 percent. The budget deficit runs at 10 percent of the GDP with cumulative debts around RO 879 million (1992 figures). The government is financing this debt by drawing on its own contingency funds, doing some commercial borrowing, raising money on international capital markets, and floating government bonds.

By the end of the 1980s Oman had emerged as a middle-income economy after rising from total obscurity and abject poverty. (As a general indicator of growth, the per capita income in 1970 was U.S.$360. In 1980 it rose to $3,100; today, it stands over $7,000.) As a result of this tremendous growth, Sultan Qaboos enjoys an immense popularity with his people. His name is affixed to many public institutions (by acclamation, not by fiat). He enjoys an extremely good rapport with his people and his policy reflects that rapport (see "The Structure of Government" later in this chapter). He maintains a high-profile image by conducting every year a meet-the-people tour. Not the elitist, the Sultan takes the wheel of a Land Rover and, with a train of government ministers at his heels, drives to the interior to discuss problems with regional magistrates. During the National Day festivities which are held each year in mid-November, the Sultan is on hand to usher in a new year of development and prosperity and inspire the people to new and greater accomplishments. They, in turn, come out in droves to extend their gratitude to him.

The Structure of Government

Oman is one of two existing sultanates in the world today (the other being the Sultanate of Brunei). It is noteworthy to describe the political make-up of the country because of Oman's strong and independent character. Surprising as it may seem, Oman is quite different from other Arab regimes. To begin with, Oman is the oldest standing government in the gulf region, as most of the other countries in the region did not coalesce until the twentieth century, around the discovery of petroleum. Oman as a political entity is older than the United States. Oman also has deep-rooted ties with democratic ideals that go back to antiquity—ideals which are not usually associated with developing countries, or with Arab countries for that matter.

The outside world has become all too familiar with the so-called democratic development of some emerging nations. On the road to modernizing and streamlining the power elites, self-governance has been accompanied by instability, uncertainty, and upheaval. To that extent most of these countries have earned the disparaging title of "banana republics." One need not be reminded of the facade of general elections generally used to demonstrate how far a country's political body has supposedly come. Democratic freedom is not "free" in the sense that it automatically falls in the lap of the practitioner. It is a cumulative process that takes time and discipline before it can emerge as a bona fide working system.

The democratizing trends that have emerged on the world scene are usually the result of regional conflicts or grassroots movements brought on by popular dissatisfaction. This is not the case with Oman, although those elements have appeared from time to time. In Oman, mechanisms such as elections and comprehensive legislative authority are viewed as mid- to long-term objectives and so thereby drive the liberalization process.

Oman's political processes have their roots in Islamic traditions. It is those systems that Sultan Qaboos has brought to the fore. It is instructional that the conditions set forth have their underpinnings in the past and are very much a part of the Omani experience, the very meaning of their heritage.

To date, the most outward manifestation of this incremental development is the body known as the Majlis Ash Shura. To understand the workings of the Majlis, it is important to see how the mechanism is derived from the past. Then, in the overall framework of national development as it has been fashioned by Sultan Qaboos, it is possible to see the workings of this unique system. But before the Majlis can be described, it will be helpful to review the structure of the monarchy as it developed over the centuries starting from the source, the foundation upon which all Muslims base their codes: the Holy Qur'an.

The Holy Qur'an is the foundation for conduct for all people, from moral and ethical conduct to civil codes to criminal behavior, and ultimately, the general workings of government. The persons most responsible for disseminating the wisdom of the Qur'an were the religious scholars, the ulema, who set forth a representative as exemplary of this code, the imam ("one who sets an example"). To the Ibadhis, anyone who is devout, just, and competent can fill the role. Their leader must embody these qualities and be an effective administrator as well. If no such candidate was forthcoming, the post could remain vacant until such time as a responsible candidate was found.

The ulema's decision-making process is based on the Qur'anic concept of *shura*, which means "mutual consultation" (a veritable foundation of Western democracy). The shura was a means for dialogue between all levels of society, whether it be between an assembly of scholars or between a leader and his subjects. The Qur'an is not specific as to how the mechanism is implemented; it has left it to the succeeding generations to establish the channels for dialogue. In its more recent manifestations, the concept of shura has been molded into the structure of the government, with innovative twists on the age-old belief. A key point must be made with regards to authority and the concept of shura: Authority is given, not taken. It is vested in one by consensus of all and remains there until those who have vested that power have reason to be disenchanted and see fit to change it.

If the Ibadhi embodiment of Qur'anic precepts of shura are an indication, we can expect to see changes in leadership based on the ability to contribute. The significance of the Omani interpretation, which is the hallmark of their faith, is that their leaders should be recognized on the basis of merit, or not at all. Ironically, the college of the imamate that emphasized the importance of competency over hereditary legitimacy through collective agreement was nullified by outside forces in the 1950s, but the concept of shura has been revived in the workings of Sultan Qaboos, a hereditary monarch who came to power in a *de facto* supplanting of his father and is responsible for changing the face of the Omani government almost singlehandedly.

THE MONARCHY

When Qaboos came to power in 1970, there was a minimal framework to build upon. His father, Said bin Taimur, was a strict autocrat who kept few people within his inner circle, and that included only a handful of British advisors. Qaboos inherited a century-old legacy of stagnation, isolation, illiteracy, and high mortality. There was no standing army (apart from the 400-strong palace guard) and a bitter rebellion fueled by outside agitators in the south. In order to bootstrap his country Qaboos had to create his own infrastructure from scratch. He started by creating a Council of Ministers who would oversee the various internal workings of the government. He then abolished the anachronistic restrictions that had plagued the people and began to develop the country literally from the ground up. In the early days, everything was a priority, but special emphasis was placed on the areas of health, housing, and education. As Sultan Qaboos called to repatriate Omanis who had left the confines of the previous regime for brighter worlds, he began to build his stockpile of experts and specialists whom he could call upon.

As it stands today the government is made up as follows. The Sultan is the head of state and serves as the de facto prime minister. He also is the head of the armed forces, finance, and interior, although he can delegate authority to special representatives. Laws and decrees are issued by the Sultan. Public works are carried out through the system of five-year plans. 1996 saw the inauguration of the country's fifth five-year plan (the first plan began in 1976).

The administrative system beneath the Sultan consists of the Diwan of the Royal Court, the Ministry of the Palace Office Affairs, the Cabinet of Ministers and Secretariat to the Cabinet, Specialized Councils, the Governorate of Muscat, the Municipalities, and the Majlis Ash Shura.

The Diwan of the Royal Court provides for a protocol of internal affairs and advises the Sultan, as well as serving as liaison between the Sultan and the people. The Diwan is the central guiding bureaucracy and also provides a training academy for government officials.

The Cabinet of Ministers is the highest executive authority, deriving its power from the Sultan, to whom it is collectively responsible. The cabinet consists of:

Personal Representative to His Majesty the Sultan

Deputy Prime Min. for Cabinet Affairs

Deputy Prime Min. for Financial Affairs

Min. of National Heritage and Culture

Min. of the Diwan of the Royal Court

Min. of Palace Office Affairs and Head of the Office of the Supreme Commander of the Armed Forces

Min. of Petroleum and Minerals

Min. of Justice, Awqaf and Islamic Affairs

Min. of Higher Education and Vice Chancellor of Sultan Qaboos University

Min. of Interior

Min. of Information

Min. of State and Governor of Muscat

Min. of State for Foreign Affairs

Min. of Communications

Min. of Posts, Telegraphs, and Telephones

Min. of Electricity and Water

Min. of Agriculture and Fisheries

Min. of State and Governor of Dhofar

Min. of Civil Service

Min. of Housing

Min. of Health

Secretary General to the Cabinet
Min. of Regional Municipalities
  and Environment
Min. of Water Resources
Min. of Commerce and Industry

Min. of Social Affairs and Labour
Min. of State for Legal Affairs
Min. of Education
Min. of State for Development
  Affairs

The Secretariat of the Cabinet of Ministers is responsible for the smooth functioning of the government and to see that cabinet decisions are implemented swiftly.

The Specialized Councils consist of:

The Development Council
Financial Affairs
Educational and Vocational Training
Conservation and Pollution Control
Natural Gas

Youth Affairs
Civil Service
Sultan Qaboos University Council
High Committee for Conferences
Tender Board

The Municipalities are the backbone of the country, consisting of fifty-nine regions called *wilayats*. Each wilayat is presided over by a *wali*, or governor. The Ministry of Regional Municipalities and Environment works with the wilayats to improve structures, services, and amenities and to promote public works such as parks, playgrounds, and tree-planting along highways.

The Majlis Ash Shura is an outgrowth of the Consultative Council formulated by His Majesty and is the linchpin of his government reform.

THE MAJLIS ASH SHURA
(MEETING PLACE FOR THE EXCHANGE OF IDEAS)

Foreigners are often misled into thinking that because an Arab country possesses, whether Sultan or Amir, King or President, and it possesses no parliamentary system of democracy, like the House of Commons or the U.S. Senate, then the democratic process cannot exist in Arab countries. This misconception arises from the difficulty faced by non-Arabs when faced with the Arab mind or the Arabic language. In fact, because advisors, tribal leaders, elders, experts, ministers and others are not subject to pressure groups lobbying them in parliament, they often take a much wider view than party politicians whose first objective is to be returned at the next election, sacrificing the long term objective in favor of expediency, and the floating voter.

—Philip Ward, *Travels in Oman*

In the early 1980s, Sultan Qaboos began his policy to "meet the people," which is still in practice, conducted every January. The tours have developed into a national institution as the Sultan leads his entourage of cabinet members to several pre-chosen sites to discuss local politics and problems in a town meeting atmosphere. Although the tours have taken on a symbolic quality and the functional aspects have been supplanted by the more effective and evolved Majlis, the tours are rooted in the tradition of *shura* and serve as a vital link between the Sultan and his constituency.

The Sultan then formulated the State Consultative Council, which was purely an advisory panel made up of members appointed by the Sultan from the government, private sector, and the wilayats. Each appointee was named based on a level of competency. A committee of advisors from the SCC was established to examine the role of consultation between the government and the people, and their report was given to the Sultan. Prompted by global political changes in the late 1980s, the Sultan saw that it was time to take the SCC one step further.

In 1990 the Majlis Ash Shura was created to replace the State Consultative Council. This new body had significant changes over the last. First of all, the new Majlis consisted of representatives from the wilayats only. Membership of the government elite was not allowed, to prevent interference and conflicts of interests. Representatives were to be chosen from the wilayats at large with the selection process directly in the hands of the people. True to Ibadhi tradition, members must show their level of competency or face removal. They are guaranteed free speech except for direct criticism of the Sultan. However, differences of opinions can be aired through ministers or other government representatives. Ethical restraints were put in place to prevent personal exploitation and ensure confidentiality on sensitive issues.

The new Majlis was given broader jurisdiction, including authority over the nation's development policy, social welfare, education, and environmental issues. But it still did not have a legislative mandate. In its inaugural charter the Majlis was charged with "assisting the government in all matters which concern the Omani society and provide all appropriate proposals the Majlis may find necessary to support the society's fundamental values and principles." To this end, the Majlis created five standing committees and keeps the ability to create more as deemed necessary. The committees are:

The Legal Committee
The Economic Committee
The Committee for Health and Social Affairs
The Committee for Education and Culture
The Committee of Services and Development
    of the Local Community

Committees are presided over by an elected chairman and require a two-thirds presence to establish a quorum. Decisions are passed by a simple majority.

Additionally, the Majlis can summon ministers to discuss directly related issues. Ministries must provide all information requested by the Majlis. Questioning and debate with ministers is allowed under certain restrictions, and exchanges are a matter of public domain; i.e., they are televised.

In return, the government is required to present economic and social draft laws to the Majlis for amendment and approval; however, there is no veto power. The Majlis may also initiate its own (non-binding) proposals which, as a matter of course, have been heeded.

In one instance, the body played a major role in establishing a position that has been adopted as national policy regarding the use of television satellite dishes. In Saudi Arabia, for example, satellite dishes are banned outright because of the government's inability to censor programming. The Majlis Ash Shura in Oman was requested by the Sultan to give an advisory opinion. The Majlis, after careful debate, decided that program censorship should be left to individual households and program content should neither be enforced nor prohibited.

In another area the Majlis has been instrumental in developing the legal framework for the resolution of commercial disputes, which was crucial to the country's expansion in international trade and investment. Current legal codes were devised and implemented by the Majlis.

To further fine tune the workings of the Majlis, the Sultan in his 1994 meet-the-people tour solicited recommendations for improving it. On top of that, a 1993 census (the first of its kind) provided an accurate depiction of the country's demographics, which prompted the Sultan to add twenty-one seats to the initial fifty-nine and allocate representatives on a basis of population dispersal. This action redressed the disparity of representation between sparsely populated regions in the interior and the denser coastal regions.

Since the Majlis's inception in 1990, the Sultan has given broad terms for the nomination process at the wilayat level. In 1994 came perhaps the most stunning development (to Western eyes), when the Sultan announced the enfranchisement of women in every aspect of the Majlis's functioning. Women are encouraged to take part in the nomination and the voting process. In the current session there were four nominated women candidates (one led a spirited leaflet campaign in her constituency) and two of them were elected. Given the Sultan's record of encouraging women in all levels of society and the traditional high profile that women in the Sultanate have been accorded, the Omanis were rather nonplussed by Western reactions; they took the development as a matter of course.

Future Prospects

> Oman's heritage has contributed towards the accomplishments of human civilization and has stood on a set of moral facets which provided it with a unique philosophy which has distinguished it with an independent character. Such a philosophy has the inherent strength of depth and wealth that has preserved its essence through the passage of time. Through this philosophy, the Omani heritage has attained a diversity that has bridged the devotion to its roots which the best modernism is a gateway of association between the two. . . . The exposure of our culture to the outside world strengthens its foundation in meeting the changes of the times. Here lies the prime importance of openness to other civilizations. Our association with the rest of the world in this field serves diverse aspects. Such associations have produced a series of exchanges vital to the participating cultures. The resultant studies in historical excavations, exhibitions, cultural weeks, scientific symposia and exchange of expertise are of immense value to the modern generation.
>
> —H. H. Sayyid Faisal bin Ali Al Said, Minister Culture/Life-style on the occasion of the 1994 National Day, the Year of Heritage

The outlook for the government, in spite of recent developments, is not exactly clear. Although the country has achieved spectacular milestones in a short span of time, there are many considerations about the future direction of the Sultanate. In the next twenty years the Sultan will have to take a new tack as the new prosperity creates whole new challenges. Sultan Qaboos has been emphatic that his people are the ones who must control their fate; although his role in bootstrapping the country cannot be denied, he remains self-effacing.

Nevertheless he has forged a national identity that is proud of its cultural heritage and has not fallen into the mainstream of Arabic ideology. As a country justifiably wary of ideological influences, Oman has taken its own path to development and modernization.

The latest step in that progress has now taken place and was announced by Royal decree on November 7, 1996. In this decree, Sultan Qaboos has crystallized the government into a formal system whereby the workings of government are put forth, establishing the system and the framework for the years to come. The framework will essentially retain the monarchy with its mandate to promote the state's policies toward society and the freedoms and responsibilities they entail. In short, the country is now a constitutional monarchy.

Royal Decree No. 101/96 provides for a successor to Sultan Qaboos (a male descendent of Sayyid Turki bin Said bin Sultan, a Muslim, mentally sound and a legitimate son of Omani parents). The decree also upholds the country's integrity and sovereignty by safeguarding its interests and promotes strengthening of ties of friendship with all countries. The country will base its principles on the Islamic code of Sharia and will consolidate and strengthen the principles of Shura (. . . a sound administrative apparatus that will guarantee justice, harmony, and equality for all citizens . . . respect for public order and preserve the best interests of the state.)

The country's economy will be based, as it has in the past, on a free market economy with complete cooperation between the public and private sector. The country will respect freedom of economic activity as long as it serves the public interest and the government will respect private funds and property.

On a social scale the country will promote justice and equality between all citizens, promote the family as the fundamental unit, and provide what it can through education and healthcare to uphold the family, reinforcing strong ties and values and protecting them in time of emergency. People will have the right to practice the work they select and the right to own private property. Freedom of religion (according to established norms), freedom of the press, freedom of speech, and freedom to assemble are also guaranteed. Citizens detained by law will be entitled to legal council and will be presumed innocent until proven guilty of committing crimes. No one will be detained unnecessarily and statements or confessions obtained by duress or coercion will be inadmissible in court. A person will also have the right to redress of grievances.

All foreigners staying in Oman will enjoy protection of their persons and property as long as the society's values and traditions are upheld.

The decree also stipulates the role and duties for the Sultan, his cabinet and ministers, the judiciary branch, and the Majlis Ash Shura, as well as some other general provisions.

The country still has real problems to face. It needs to diversify the economy away from dwindling oil revenues. It faces a massive training and education program, as the latest census revealed that 52 percent of the population is under seventeen, and family planning is now a priority. The climate hampers the further development of agriculture; in fact, over-development in this area has caused problems of its own owing to the scarcity of fresh water.

It will be a challenge for the Omani people to maintain their newfound prosperity. But it is hoped that their answers lie in the values and traditions that once created a great empire. These threads: the egalitarian spirit of shura and emergence of a national identity, the benevolent and paternal role of the Sultan as a unifying force, equal rights for women, the growing participation of the public in government policy, and the respect for family traditions balanced with the need to develop contemporary strategies—are woven into an emerging pattern. As long as the needs of the people are met, the political system expresses the will of the people, and the people respond to the Sultan's call to act responsibly, the prospects for the next twenty-five years may be just as exciting as those of the last.

Religion

Because religion is such a fundamental aspect of the Middle East, it is impossible to enter the region and not be affected by it. You cannot study the region without confronting the religion and the people—head-on. The religion, of course, is Islam, the tenets of which are widely known and greatly misunderstood. With Oman this becomes particularly significant because Omanis practice a form of Islam that does not conform to either of the two main branches that are commonly known (Sunni and Shiite), and hence their outlook differs greatly from that of the mainstream. Omanis are predominantly Ibadhi Muslims, a tiny sect of Islam that is practiced notably in Oman and in a few enclaves in North Africa. It can in fact lay claim to being the oldest of Islamic orthodoxies. To explain how this came about, a brief summary of the origin of Islam will follow.

To begin with, almost everyone knows how Islam started. It was founded by Muhammed bin Abdulla Al Quraish of the Hashimites, a merchant family in the city of Makkah in what is now Saudi Arabia. Muhammed, who was born in 570 A.D., was orphaned at an early age and subsequently raised by first a grandfather and then an uncle who plied the caravan trade. After marrying a wealthy daughter of a local merchant at the age of twenty-five and becoming somewhat handy at the trade himself, he felt compelled to turn his thoughts inward, being materially sufficient and freed from fear of want.

In Makkah during Muhammed's day there was a diversity of religious thought and practice. Christianity and Judaism predominated over a number of polytheistic and pagan cults openly displaying a wide array of rituals. (In Oman there was also this religious diversity. There was even a bishopric in Sohar.) Seeking to escape this ponderous deluge, Muhammed went into solitude where he began to formulate his beliefs into a stream of consciousness that he interpreted as revelations from God delivered to him by the angel Gabriel. This arrangement of thoughts was not a new religion as much as it was a continuation of the Judaic and Christian tradition, now complete and fully evolved into God's revelation to mankind. This assemblage of ideals formed a comprehensive guide to moral, ethical, and spiritual behavior for all humanity. Muhammed called this vision Islam—or submission to the will of God.

The main tenets of Islam are crystallized into the Five Pillars of Wisdom, which set forth a number of acts of proper conduct for every Muslim to demonstrate his or her faith. These acts are:

1) *Shahada*—Pronouncement of faith. "There is no god but God and Muhammed is his prophet."

2) *Salat*—Daily prayer. Every Muslim must perform allegiance to God five times a day—before sunrise, noon, mid-afternoon, sunset, and twilight—with prescribed prostrations accompanying the prayers which the worshiper recites while facing in the direction of Makkah.

3) *Zakat*—Almsgiving. It is the belief that a man is only as rich as his poorest neighbor.

4) *Sawm*—Fasting. During the ninth month of the Islamic (lunar) calendar, Ramadân, Muslims observe a dawn to dusk abstention from food and drink for the entire month. People who are traveling, the weak and sickly, people on medication, pregnant or lactating women, and soldiers on duty are excused as long as they can take up their fast at the earliest convenience. Young children are absolved from participating.

5) *Hajj*—Pilgrimage. At least once in every Muslim's lifetime, he or she is obligated to make a pilgrimage to Makkah at some time during the twelfth month of the calendar year.

In some quarters, a sixth pillar is included, namely *Jihad*, or the struggle to defend the word of God and spread the faith to the world. This is not necessarily by forceful means, but it is usually interpreted as such.

In addition, Muslims are urged to practice virtue of the highest order, refuting pride, calumny, vengefulness, avarice, prodigality, adultery, and the taking of intoxicants, while putting trust in God, to understand his will of patience and modesty, forbearance, sincerity, love of peace, truthfulness, frugality, and benevolence.

During his lifetime Muhammed felt that religion was the focal point of spiritual as well as temporal law. As religion and secular law became fused as one entity, the concept of *sharia*, where all law proceeds from religious law, evolved. This comprehensive structure was the precedent that scholars would rely upon in the years to come as they codified their laws into working systems. This is why the American democratic concept of "separation of church and state" is a concept that is totally foreign to a Muslim. In Islam this does not exist. The church and state are one.

Muhammed gained converts immediately from his family and his nearest associates. Over the years, those closest to him recorded his pronouncements, which make up the main body of Islam's holy book, the Qur'an. Other writings and pronouncements of his followers are contained in the body of works known as the Hadith in which Muhammed discussed with his followers everything from proper conduct to style of writing to correct posture and speech.

But conversion of the pagans and idolaters in Makkah at that time was a different story. Because the economy of Makkah was based in part on a thriving pilgrimage trade, and Muhammed wanted to do away with much of that practice, he drew scorn and persecution from those quarters. In 622 A.D. he was forced to leave Makkah with a handful of followers. He fled north to the city of Yathrib, now known as Medina. It is this year that Muslims proclaim as the start of the Islamic calendar. In Medina, the opportunity arose to settle a long-standing feud between two warring tribes. Here is where Islam first took hold. As Muhammed gained strength through preaching and conversion, he defeated his detractors and eight years later returned to Makkah, triumphant. By the time of his death in 632, Islam had begun to spread throughout the Arabian peninsula in a wave of conversion that is unparalleled in recorded history. Within 100 years of Muhammed's death, Islam was firmly established throughout the Middle East, North Africa, and southern Asia.

Directly following Muhammed's death there was an immediate period of uncertainty as to the direction of this new-found faith. Doctrinal questions of interpretation and line of succession produced factionalism that split Islam into the two major divisions that exist today: the Sunni branch, which is comprised of about 75 percent of all Muslims, and the Shiite branch of about 25 percent. (As previously noted, when talking about Oman, we are dealing predominantly with an altogether different, minor branch of Islam.)

Some people held that the *caliph,* or successor to Muhammed, should proceed in direct lineage from Muhammed's family (this is the Shiite point of view). Others held that any devout and pious Muslim could assume the title (the Sunni perspective). In 654, Ali, Muhammed's cousin and son-in-law, became the fourth caliph. He immediately became embroiled in a bitter civil war with Muawiya, a distant cousin of the third caliph, Uthman. Unable to reach a conclusion in that struggle, Ali decided to take up the offer of arbitration with Muawiya. A small group in Ali's camp thought this was wrong because they believed that Ali's authority proceeded directly from God and that Ali was going against God's will. So incensed were they that they split from Ali's camp and removed themselves to Basra in southern Iraq. They became known as the *Kharajites* (the seceders, the ones who left). The Kharajites emphasized the accountability of the *imam* (another word for caliph) for his actions, which are divinely inspired. Violation of this trust was evidence enough for forfeiture of title. They repudiated Ali because he was in direct contravention of God's orders.

The Kharajites came to be known for their uncompromising stance in doctrinal affairs. Anyone who did not meet their standards was excommunicated, or more often, summarily executed. Naturally, schisms developed within this branch as more moderate Kharajites were themselves denounced as heretics, or worse polytheists, pagans, and infidels. The Kharajites set up their own imamate, rejecting both Sunni and Shiite claims to leadership. Their ruthlessness over the next 100 years only led to their virtual extinction as they became enemies to anyone who did not meet their rigid standards of uncompromising militancy.

Another group that split from Ali's camp at the time of the Kharaji, led by Abdullah bin Ibadh Al-Tamimi, advocated a return to a pure form of Islam, a fundamental belief (without fundamental dogma) that promoted good conduct, strong spiritual values, and, above all, tolerance of all creeds. This became the hallmark of the Ibadhis because they themselves became a persecuted minority (first by the other Kharajites and later by the Sunni and the Wahhabis). At one point Ibadh became the object of bitter enmity by the Kharajites as he disdained their practice entirely. In a letter to their leader he proclaimed that his people were through with the excesses and zealotry, done with exaggerated strictures that treated innocent Muslims as infidels. Abdullah bin Ibadh did not advocate the use of force and discouraged the use of weapons against the authorities. His ideal was to restore the Islamic state to what he felt it had been during the time of the Prophet, which had become corrupted by Uthman and the struggle between Ali and Muawiya.

Abu Sha'atha Jabir bin Zayd, an Omani merchant and colleague of Ibadh, left Oman for Basra, where he adopted the same ideals. He is credited with spreading the influence of Ibadhism throughout Oman. But the crossover did not come easily. Although the Ibadhis practiced tolerance, they, in turn, were not tolerated. The early Ibadhis were persecuted by the Kharajites and no less than the Sunni caliphate itself. Because they would not resort to force they instead assumed the state of *Kitman*, meaning they went underground. All of their activity was circumspect as political circumstances dictated extreme caution. Their meetings were clandestine until they were free of persecution. Attempts to suppress the Ibadhi community in Basra only led to the relocation of the sect. Some settled in Maghreb, which is modern-day North Africa. Others settled in Hadramaut in Yemen, and others still came to Oman. In less than a hundred years the sect had replaced Sunni as the dominant sect in Oman, and Julanda bin Masud became the first Ibadhi imam elected to that post.

The Ibadhi tradition holds that the imam should be elected by a council of scholars (*ulema*). They look to a leader who is exemplary in conduct, demonstrates high moral standards and can defend the community. In sharp contrast to Sunni and Shiite traditions, Ibadhis allow for more than one imam to accommodate different regions. Thus, at one time there were concurrent imams in Oman and North Africa. Also, they reckoned that a permanent visible head was not a necessity when a suitable candidate was not available, or, as in the case of the early days, when they were in the state of Kitman.

Throughout the years, Ibadhism was occasionally suppressed by the Sunni caliphate and the extreme orthodox Wahhabis, but it was never completely wiped out. Ibadhism exists only in Oman (and a few isolated places in North Africa) as Ibadhi enclaves in other regions had disappeared by the twelfth century A.D. The Omanis have developed a strong communal sense which has allowed them to endure. Coupled with the fact that Oman is geographically isolated from the rest of the Arabian peninsula by the Empty Quarter and the Hajar Mountains, the Omanis have led quite an independent existence from the rest of the Muslim world.

Omani Life-style

The society in Oman is still based on strong tribal undercurrents with traditions that extend back to pre-Islamic times. People are largely settled, although there are still nomadic tribes in the interior, notably the Bedouins of the desert and smaller enclaves of mountain people. Changing times in the cosmopolitan areas have had their effect on the tribal system: extended families living together have given way to the nuclear family living apart, but the family bonds are just as strong and enduring.

Family gathering at Nizwa souq.

In the social setting, the family is still the integral unit of society, as reflected by the use of prefixes in names: *Al* meaning "family of," *bin* or *ibn* meaning "son of," *bint* meaning "daughter of," and *bani* meaning "tribe of." Lineage is patrilineal and names can extend several generations in order to clarify the lineage. Thus the Sultan's formal name is Qaboos Bin Said Bin Taimur Bin Faisal Bin Turki Bin Said Bin Sultan Bin Ahmed Al Said.

> As we approached Matrah, we stopped for a fantastic procession. Perched high in a sort of sedan chair, wobbling on top of a camel, sat two young girls, veiled and dressed in orange and gold, and clinging desperately to each other. Around them were women with jewels in their noses and bangles on their arms and ankles, and long pantaloons peeping below gaudy graceful gowns. It was a Baluchi wedding. One of these girls on the camel was the bride; the other was probably a younger sister. The women were friends and relations and they clapped and danced and chattered as they sped her on her way.
> —Barbara Wace, *Geographical Magazine,* 1962

Family ties are the bond that hold communities together. Loyalties are strong and considered sacrosanct. The household is run by the husband/father who has taken a wife to live with him. Although Islam allows a man to take up to four wives, this practice is not usually followed because certain conditions must exist—the first wife must be barren, the husband must be able to provide for and treat all successive wives equally, etc. Most Omanis prefer to remain monogamous.

Marriage in Islam is a civil contract. It is the culmination of events that start with a betrothal arranged by the families. By tradition, a man will marry his first cousin, but nowadays, marriage partners are sought further afield. Even the prospective bride and groom can have input to the betrothal process; there must be mutual consent. A man may propose marriage to a widow or a divorcee on his own. Once the betrothal is established, the groom will offer *mahr*, a gift of money to the family which is to compensate for the loss of their daughter, but is usually spent on items the bride will need in her new home. A portion of that gift is retained in gold for the bride to keep in the unlikely event of a divorce. (Divorce is not very common in Islam; in spite of the widely-held belief that all a man has to do to divorce his wife is to say to her three times, "I divorce you," it's not as easy as that. The sanctions that uphold a divorce are very strict and it is not entered into lightly by any party. Although it may seem easier for the man, a woman can petition a judge for divorce on grounds of non-support, adultery, or impotency.)

A marriage ceremony is performed before a *qadhi*, or judge, who has the participants sign a contract before the members of the families. After the legal ceremony is over, festive gatherings are conducted with separate parties for the men and the women. Everybody attends in their best attire. The women, who dress colorfully anyway (see "Omani Clothing" later in this chapter), are especially resplendent with fine costumes and jewelry as well as henna designs painted on hands and feet. Celebrations can last over a period of several days with different parties and gatherings to celebrate the newlyweds.

This used to be the only way for social mixing in older times, and even then wedding parties were separate affairs for men and women. Nowadays the social structure is changing in cosmopolitan areas, and there are many more occasions than family gatherings for mingling. Sporting functions, parks, and public celebrations, as well as co-education, all provide opportunities for young people to meet. Young women, however, rarely travel unattended, and single dating rarely occurs. Group outings divided along gender lines are the norm and at all times a strict moral code is enforced. Young ladies are expected to be circumspect, modest, decorous, and virtuous above reproach. If this code is broken, the honor of the family is at stake. The slightest implication of impropriety, especially acknowledged publicly, is not just a stain on the woman, but on the whole family's honor. In this regard, the natal family is more important than the married family. An unfaithful wife shames her father and brothers more than her husband. Enforcement of the family honor is paramount.

The age of marriage has risen in recent years. In earlier times betrothals and weddings were made about the time of puberty. But that changed with the installation of the modern state, as many young women would marry in their late teens. Now that age has risen into the twenties as the Sultan has encouraged women to complete their education and participate in the public and private sector as working professionals.

Although gender identities fall into distinct male and female headings, the role of women in Oman is one of much higher profile than in other Arab countries, and much higher than most Westerners imagine. A woman in Oman nowadays receives as much status through her profession as she would through her alliances (family ties). While it is true that a married woman gains status and security once she starts bearing children, especially sons, women gain considerable power through social and professional contacts. They can wield considerable influence on their husband's business decisions and often serve as a guiding force in family matters.

It is important to note that two of Sultan Qaboos's most important social objectives have been to bring peripheral regions of Oman into the mainstream of society and to organize new constituencies, particularly around women and youth. The youth in general are perceived to be the country's most valuable resource, and women are equally important as they constitute half of that potential. Educated, trained, and professional women serve as positive role models not only for their gender but society in general. As previously stated, this is *not* a recent development. Omani women have traditionally enjoyed higher profiles and more active participation in society than in other Arabic cultures.

Birth, as it is with all cultures, is a sacred event. Contrary to popular belief the birth of a female is not looked upon with disdain. This practice probably comes from pre-Islamic times and other countries where female infanticide was practiced. But in Islam, it is a practice that was deeply denounced by the Prophet. A female born into the Omani household is a welcome member indeed.

Death is a solemn occasion. When somebody dies, the body is attended to immediately with washing and anointing of fragrances. It is then wrapped in white muslin and buried on the same day (or within a 24-hour period as the day starts at sunset) during daylight hours. The body is buried in a shallow grave with unmarked stones noting the position of head and feet and is aligned north/south, turned on its side in the direction of Makkah. After a man has died, his widow goes into mourning for a period of four months and ten days, during which time she does not see any male, dresses in old clothes (not necessarily black), and only looks after her own cleanliness, wearing neither makeup or jewelry. Before she returns to normal life she undergoes a ritual bathing before receiving visitors.

> Our achievements this year are brilliant—especially on the football front. To win fourth place in the [under 17 World] championships and for the country to have the best young football player in the world is a major achievement.
> —Ahmed bin Hashal Al Maskery, Secretary General for the Oman Olympic Committee and Director General for GOSCAY (General Organization for Sports and Cultural Activities for Youth)

Anybody who comes to Oman today will find a plethora of sporting activities to do from water sports to running, cricket, volleyball, bowling, equestrian sports, and even ice skating! But the one sport that stands out above all is the national pastime: football (soccer). Everywhere you go you can see leagues in the schools and villages, pick-up games at the beach, or semi-pro and professional games in the stadiums. If you travel to the interior you will find areas almost as sacred as a mosque on a windswept plain or plateau's edge: if it's flat enough, the stones will have been picked up and tossed (or set in lines to demarcate boundaries) with two upright sticks at either end of the rectangular clearing. Here is the pitch, and most likely, boys will be playing on it. Girls will usually watch and not participate in football or other sports. It is not that they are denied, but rather that their modesty and decorum prohibits them.

Omani children are no different from children anywhere in the world, especially when it comes to playing games. They have their own particular variations on some popular pastimes that we enjoyed as youngsters. *Darwaza* is a game similar to our London Bridge Is Falling Down, where players are paired off facing each other with arms extended and raised and lowered to entrap passers-through. The Oman version signifies the opening and closing of the old city gate of Muscat.

Hide and seek games are popular amongst smaller children, especially *Al Khatum,* which involves hidden and found objects. Games of skill similar to Jacks or Pick-up Sticks are played, such as *Talatha-talatha* ("Three-three") or *Khamsa-khamsa* ("Five-five").

Older boys enjoy a game similar to tag called *Al Rhume* in which the one who is "it" is confined to an area circumscribed by a rope held at one end with the other staked into the ground. The other players must retrieve their caps which are left by the stake without getting caught. There is even a game that older boys play called *Solah* which involves hitting an object ball and running to a set point, similar to baseball and cricket.

But what the older boys and men really enjoy is a game of *How-walis.* This is more of a mental exercise that has deep roots in other games of skills and luck such as O-wah-ree and backgammon (which is itself a game of Arabic origin). Small holes in the ground, or cups, have colored stones, beads, or bottlecaps placed into them, two per hole. The players try to maneuver the stones to capture opponents' pieces. Men can be seen playing at the taxi stand on Al Jaame Street in Ruwi; at the beach one can find makeshift gameboards dug into the sand by fishermen.

> Most of them demanded only the bare necessities of life, enough food and drink to keep them alive, clothes to cover their nakedness, some form of shelter from the sun and the wind, weapons, a few pots, rugs, water skins and their saddlery. It was a life that produced much that was noble, nothing that was gracious.
> —Wilfred Thesiger, on the Bedu, *Arabian Sands,* 1956

Perhaps the strongest impression of Middle Eastern culture left on Westerners is that which originates in the Bedouin society. Understandably, many misconceptions about the Bedus arise as their image is distorted in popular movies and fiction. These fiercely independent people have remained nomadic since ancient times; they have roamed the entire width and breadth of the Arabian peninsula. Their habits and customs are firmly ingrained by the harshness of their environment, tempered like a fine steel. They are fervently loyal to one another, remarkably incisive, and as generous a people as you can find. Their moral code is rigid and unassailable but their capacity for compassion is deep. Probably no Westerner has understood the Bedus more completely than explorer Wilfred Thesiger, who

Bedouin woman tending her goats in the souq.

noted once that where he had felt lonely in a teeming London crowd, he never was lonely in the desert in the company of Bedus.

The old world of the Bedouin is not the same as it was twenty or thirty years ago when it was the way it had been for centuries. Although they maintain their independent life-style, the twentieth century has caught up to the Bedouins with a fury. Many old traditions have fallen by the wayside as tribes become more and more absorbed into society, if not willingly, then through the trappings of that modern society. Telephones and pagers have shrunk their world. Camels have been replaced with four-wheel drives. Now they only serve as a source of livestock for milk, meat, and wool or are tendered for racing.

For the hardship and privation the Bedouins (and their mountain counterparts, the Jebalis of Dhofar and the Shawawi of the Hajar) have endured, there is not the slightest trace of embitterment or regret. In spite of all they remain outgoing and generous, knowing that in a land where few things in nature are forgiving, something or someone has to be. If there was an everlasting testament of the Bedouins it would have to be their devotion to life, to their fellow man, and to God.

A List of Notable Omanis

Malik ibn Fahm (leader of Azdi tribes migrating to Oman)
Mazin ibn Ghadubha Al-Tay (first Omani convert to Islam)

Abu Sha'atha Jabir bin Zaid (Omani merchant, first convert to Ibadhism)
Sindbad the Sailor (legendary sea captain)
Ahmad ibn Majid (Omani navigator)
Nasir bin Murshid Al Yaruba (first imam of the Al Yaruba dynasty)

Prominent Imams of the Al Yaruba Dynasty

Sultan bin Saif
Saif bin Sultan
Bilarub bin Sultan
Sultan bin Saif II
Saif bin Sultan II

Shaykh Ahmed bin Said Al Bu Saidi (founder of the Al Bu Said dynasty)

Early Albusaidi Sultans

Hamad bin Said
Said bin Sultan (Said the Great)

Sayyida Moza bint Ahmed Al Bu Said (daughter of Ahmed and distinguished lady of the court)

Later Albusaidi Sultans

Thuwaini bin Said
Turki bin Said
Faisal bin Turki
Taimur bin Faisal
Said bin Taimur
Sultan Qaboos Bin Said

Sultans of Zanzibar

Majid bin Said
Barghash bin Said

Omani Clothing

"[The Omanis are] the cleanest, neatest, best dressed and most gentlemanly of all the Arabs," wrote James Buckingham in *Travels in Assyria, Media and Persia,* 1829.

Omani dress is a distinctive outgrowth of the traditional Arabic costume that is familiar to Western eyes. In fact, the Omani national dress is so ethnically diverse, it is unique in Arabic culture. Styles and habits are surprisingly different, particularly in women's clothing, which is so colorful that it can only be described as a flower show run amok.

To start with, the men wear white or off-white attire known as a *dish-dasha,* an ankle-length gown with long sleeves and no collar (which differs from other Arab states). A tassel several inches long, called a *kashkusha* or *frakha,* descends from the right side of the neckline and is usually saturated with perfume or incense. In earlier days the dish-dasha had a breast pocket on the left, but nowadays that has been replaced in favor of side pockets waist-high in the seam. The dish-dasha is fastened by several buttons or studs ascending to the neck in the front. Beneath the dish-dasha is a wrap called a *wizar* or *lunghi,* similar to the Far Eastern sarong, which is wrapped around the body from the waist. The wizar can be plain or printed cloth, or a plaid weave. There are some regional variances to the dish-dasha, such as the ones from Sur which are gathered into pleats in the front toward the neckline, and in Dhofar where the dress takes on an African quality.

On formal occasions the man will wear the traditional *khanjar,* a dagger attached to a belt. The sheath to the khanjar is decorated with ornate silver thread, while the hilt is made from wood, metal, or bone depending on the region or tribe. Next to the khanjar there may be a small silver container containing *kohl,* an eye shadow used by desert travelers to reduce glare, and a pair of tweezers for extracting thorns and slivers.

The headdress of the men is particularly distinct. It comes in two forms, the *kumma* and the *massar.* The kumma is an embroidered flat-topped brimless cap that is almost cylindrical in shape. It is almost always ornate with bright floral and geometric stitched patterns. In fact, no two kummas look alike. Handmade kummas can take up to a month to stitch. The best ones can cost as much as RO 80 (U.S. $206), but there are also cheaper machine-made varieties.

The other, more formal headdress is the *massar,* a square cloth usually made of cotton or wool with ornate elegant patterns woven into the material. To be worn properly, the massar is folded into a triangle and placed over the head towards the center of the hypotenuse with the ends trailing down each side. Then, each end is wrapped around the head and tucked so the final appearance is like a turban. Various ways of wrapping, tucking, and tilting the massar identify the region the wearer hails from. In Muscat, for example, the massar is tightly wrapped with no loose ends and squarely placed with a distinct banding of the patterned material. Bedouins prefer a looser wrap sometimes fastened with a rope made of goat hair. Other areas show a stylishly positioned knot or dangling loose ends to the left or right. Sometimes a man will wrap a massar around his kumma, thus making it form-fitted and easier to take off and on as the massar retains its shape.

Finally, for strictly formal occasions, the men will wear an outer cloak called a *bisht*. It is usually black or some dark color and is embroidered with gold thread along the edges. It is worn across the shoulders and fastened at the neck.

Women's clothing is far more fascinating and is easily the most distinctive and attractive anywhere on the Arabian peninsula. Omani women have traditionally worn colorful, attractive clothing; it is believed that the policy for women to wear black in public is an imported tradition from other regions. In Oman, women dress modestly, in keeping with their Ibadhi beliefs, but they are nevertheless alluring. Contrary to other Arabic countries, Omani women are seldom veiled, as tradition holds for face and hands to be exposed. Only in the more orthodox region of Dhofar and among the Bedu tribes will there be a higher percentage of covered faces. The Bedu women of the Wahibah Sands, in lieu of a veil, wear a *birqa*, or mask, which is usually black but sometimes metallic blue or gold and covers most of the face except for large eye holes exposing cheeks and forehead. Sometimes the chin remains exposed and the face is decorated with saffron and other dyes.

A word or two on the birqa: it is not a sign of repression. Among the Bedu, it is not an instrument of domination by males to keep the women "in their place" nor is it required by the men to be worn. The women dress modestly out of habit and adherence to *their* sense of morality. They consider the mask to be alluring and seductive; it is part of the ensemble. Young girls look forward to wearing the mask when they reach puberty. Asking a Bedu woman why she wears a mask is like asking a Western woman why she wears a blouse.

Female dress is varied, according to region, around a basic ensemble. This ensemble consists of three pieces: a loosely fitted dish-dasha that falls just below the knees; *surwal,* which are baggy trousers gathered at the ankle; and a headdress or combination of headdresses in a variety of styles: the *lihaff,* a piece with simple embroidery that is attached at the top of the head and extends to the back, the *wiqaiah,* a larger piece, more colorful and richly embroidered, usually reserved for special occasions, and the traditional shawl which is sweeping, colorful, and worn over the other pieces, sometimes from the head and sometimes from the shoulders. In some areas the headdress is fastened to expose only the face, in others the neck is exposed. Occasionally the women will wear a sheer version of the Saudi Arabian *abaya* as an outer garment in public, but this is generally worn from the shoulders.

The fabric of this clothing is always very bright and colorful, utilizing exotic prints or ornate hand-stitching in gold and silver threads. The trousers are richly embroidered at the ankle in floral and geometric patterns that extend up and open at the knee. Embellishment on the dish-dasha starts from rectangular panels around the bodice and extends along all the borders. Color combinations are wildly innovative as the women seem to make anything work to their advantage. The final ensemble is adorned with a patterned shawl or wiqaiah, or both, held in place by concealed pins, or in the case of formal occasions, elaborate gold tiaras. The women further complement their outfits with rings, necklaces, anklets, bangles, and, in some regions, the *Al Murriyah*, a long necklace to which is attached a small box containing inscriptions from the Qur'an.

As a final piece of decoration, Omani women engage in an age-old tradition of staining their hands and feet with henna, a dye extracted from a local shrub (*Lawsonia inermis*). This is usually done by a beautician with an artistic flair. A solution of henna dye and lemon juice is applied to the hands and feet, painted in very elegant floral designs. When the henna dries and is rubbed off, a deep reddish brown stain remains, looking like a monochrome tattoo but lasting only a few weeks as continued washing wears the stain away. Sometimes men in the interior will have their fingertips, hands, or feet stained in a uniform manner with no decoration. This practice is also reserved for special occasions and festivals.

It is unfortunate that in the downplaying of cultural stereotypes, instances of creative expression are overlooked. As we have seen, the overall picture of Omani identity and heritage has been mistakenly merged with other inaccurate impressions of the Middle East. No wonder it is easy to miss out on these beautiful and expressive traditions. The encouragement and preservation of these life-styles can only stimulate the observer, inspire the creator, and dispel misleading stereotypes.

Omani Food

> Batinah limes headed the list [of supplies] which did not surprise me as I had already many times enjoyed them myself squeezed over cooked fish. . . . Then there was charcoal from the interior of Oman, fresh fruit and vegetables according to season and the arrival of the caravans carrying the produce and, if they could be afforded, some eggs, a few chickens and the odd goat or two. If a nakhuda [captain of the vessel] was feeling particularly benevolent, honey and halwa and even nuts were available. Honey and sugar spread over a dish as vermicelli—delicious!
>
> —Ronald Codrai, *An Arabian Album: Travels to Oman, 1948-1955*

To see the diversity of food in Oman today, from elegant international cuisine to American fast food, it is not hard to understand that Oman was a hub for the food trade. And from there it is not hard to assume that they would develop an intriguing cuisine of their own based upon all the foreign goods and spices they traded for, as well as their own contributions to the country's larder.

Carrying provisions in a rural village.

Omani food has a delicacy all its own that is very earthy and satisfying. Staples consist of rice, meat, bread, fish, fresh fruit (especially dates), and Oman's own particular brand of coffee. Omani meals are served with a great deal of tradition and care. It is best that the first-time traveler to an Omani repast be careful and pay attention!

The first thing you will undoubtedly sample in an Omani home is the coffee, which is called *khawa*. Khawa is unlike Western coffee in that it is a mixture of ground coffee beans and cardamom. In the desert, khawa is brewed on an open fire or brazier and seasoned with a few drops of rosewater and a pinch of saffron. It is served from a pot with a long curved spout and poured into small cups without handles. The cups hold no more than an ounce or two and the server will continually refill your cup until you shake it from side to side or invert it, indicating that you want no more. Khawa is not taken with cream or sugar. It is very aromatic and has a bitter taste. (In restaurants you can sample khawa with a bit of sugar to gradually acquire a taste for it.) As mentioned in the section on customs, you may refuse after your first serving.

The next food that you will be obliged to sample are Omani dates. Dates are cultivated throughout Oman (up to twenty varieties) and although you may at first have them fresh, Omani dates are used in a number of ways. Date honey is a syrup that can be used in cooking or on desserts. Dates are used in salads, with meats and fish, cooked or uncooked. You might have fresh dates sprinkled with cumin or as a stuffing for a vegetable dish. Ripened dates are very sweet with a mealy texture. The riper the date, the sweeter. Dates are dried and stored as they retain their food value over a period of time.

As a food, dates have been harvested since the earliest of times. They are a nutritional staple for people in the Arab world. In times of drought, dates are a prime source of energy. Technically called a drupe, the date grows on a palm tree known as the *Phoenix dactylifera* and is found in most tropical regions of the world. Dates were introduced to China in 300 A.D. by the Iranians and appeared on western American shores in the 1700s, compliments of the Spanish.

The date palm is a bisexual plant, so the female has to be fertilized with the pollen of the male, which can be very tedious for the date farmer. There are two seasons a year for harvesting dates in Oman.

Next to dates, limes are the second most important crop. Limes are used as a food additive or served as a juice mixed with water or club soda. You can add sugar or salt to taste. At almost every meal in most restaurants, fresh lime slices are added to squeeze over your entree or salad to bring a delightful taste to the food. (Most of us back home are accustomed to fancy salad dressings to accompany our fresh greens—a trip to any salad bar will tell you that. In Oman a salad is very simple: a few sliced greens, usually lettuce, cabbage, cucumber, onion, and sometimes tomato with a slice of lime on the side. This may sound a bit pedestrian, but once that lime is squeezed over the greenery, you need do nothing more except eat. The lime is enough to make the salad incredibly tasty.)

Other fruits such as oranges, mangoes, papaya, bananas, and coconuts are served at Omani tables.

Because Oman was and is at the center of the spice trades, spices are an integral part of Omani food. However, the food does not take on the "spicy-hot" taste that is experienced in countries further east. Omani spices used in cooking usually center on cumin, black pepper, cloves, cardamom, and cinnamon. They are ground and added to meats and poultry in a variety of ways. A mixture of these spices is called *bizaar*.

Meats are a common part of the Omani diet, mostly beef, mutton, goat, poultry (chicken), camel (amongst the Bedu), and fish (but obviously no pork products). The most popular form of meat that is usually reserved for festivals, notably Eid al Fitr and Eid al Adha, is a dish called Shuwa, the preparation of which is a most elaborate process and is described in *A Taste of Oman—Traditional Omani Food* by Marcia Stagath Dorr:

> A large fire pit must be dug in the usually very hard and stony earth. Additional stones are used to line the pit, and a lid is fashioned out of wood or metal. A very hot fire is then built using the largest pieces of wood available. Meanwhile the meat is prepared according to individual interpretations of the following traditional Omani recipe:
>
> The [beef or goat or mutton] may be cut into pieces but is usually left as a whole roast. It is then basted with [date honey] and/or sprinkled with the juice of fragrant Omani lemons, salted according to taste and seasoned generously with bizaar. Less traditional ingredients such as garlic, ginger, and chilis may be added.
>
> After the preparation, the meat is wrapped in banana leaves, if available, and securely sewn into sturdy sacks made of natural fiber. Sacks woven from palm leaves especially for this purpose can be found in many souqs, although empty rice sacks and other substitutes are just as frequently used.
>
> When the fire is glowing red-hot, the sacks of meat are dropped into the fire pit which is immediately covered with the lid or large stones and finally insulated with a thick layer of earth and gravel. This extinguishes the fire while retaining the heat. The meat is then left in the pit to cook very slowly up to two days. The result is a deliciously spicy, succulent roast which is served hot on a very large communal platter. Shuwa is usually eaten on the second or third day of Eid.

Another meat dish served on the holidays is *Mishkak*, which is similar to Shuwa, but consists of small bits of meat skewered on kabobs of date palm fronds and cooked over a hot fire.

Because the waters of Oman are filled with such a variety of fish, Omanis have learned to prepare a number of them for their diet: grouper, shark, tuna, sardines, cuttlefish, and shellfish. Fish is prepared in much the same way as smaller cuts of meat or chicken. Smaller fish are used as additives and flavorings for other dishes.

Rice, potatoes, or bread will almost always accompany the main meal, which is taken early in the afternoon. *Harees* is a boiled wheat flavored with chicken and tomato, seasoned with lime, cumin, and pepper, served with ghee (clarified butter), and garnished with fried onion slices. *Kabuli* is a hearty combination of meat, potatoes, and rice (or sometimes lentils and chickpeas) flavored with *bizaar,* garlic, onions, and raisins (chopped dates and nuts are another variant). Harees and kabuli are always a part of the day's main meal. Breakfasts consist of light snacks of porridge made from grains. In the desert, this would be accompanied by goat's milk. Cosmopolitan Omanis, however, rely on the plethora of processed and fresh foods made available in modern markets.

The most distinctive of desserts is a sweet that is truly Omani in every way. It is called *halwah* and should not be confused with the Lebanese confection, halvah, made from ground sesame with added flavors. The preparation of halwah is long and tedious, as it is usually made in large quantities, stirred in large vats before being poured into individual containers. The main ingredients to halwah are light and dark sugars, water, starch, ghee, rosewater, cardamom, nutmeg, and almonds. The mixture of these items is cooked, strained, and blended in repeated steps until the halwah is a thick gelatinous consistency. The result is a unique taste that you can't quite put your finger on but is very intriguing.

At the end of any formal gathering with much food and drink, the host will pass around a small brazier of burning coals on which frankincense, but sometimes other mixtures of aromatics called *bokhur*—sandalwood, myrrh, jawi (an aromatic resin), and dhufran (the powdered opercula from certain species of snail)—are placed. As it passes by, the visitors allow the smoke to waft into their clothing and hair. This is also the signal that the evening's festivities have come to an end and it is time for the guests to thank the host and depart in a breeze of olfactory delight.

Arts and Crafts

The skills demonstrated by Omani people are deeply tied to their struggle for survival in a turbulent land. They have had at their disposal limited amounts of raw material to build, shape, and weave their material industry. They simply made do with the best of what they had. Once they established their reputation as traders, if they didn't have the raw material, they could most likely procure it. All the traditional crafts have evolved directly from their utilitarian function and are still carried on today, albeit in a dramatically changing setting where technology is rapidly obscuring the links to the past. Realizing this, the Omanis are doing everything possible to preserve their valuable cultural heritage. The government has established training centers to keep the old traditions alive. In doing so they create new markets in which to sell local goods. Tourism will be helpful in this area.

The two most prominent Omani traditions are artisan class skills, shipbuilding and aflaj construction. While these are technological advances from a bygone time, one still plays an important functional role today: the aflaj. Shipbuilding in the traditional fashion has been relegated to the past, since Omani vessels were outclassed by British steamships in the 1800s. But the aflaj system is still one of the most efficient systems for distributing water through the rugged parched terrain. It has to be efficient. It's been used for over 2,500 years.

AFLAJ

And unto Eber were born two sons; the name of one was Peleg, for in his day was the earth divided.
—Genesis 10:25, biblical reference to the division of property upon which the aflaj system is based

The story goes that the Prophet Da'ud (David), father of Suleiman (Solomon), flew on a magic carpet over Oman and commanded an army of Jinn (genies) to construct the intricate network of channels that course above and below ground and provide Oman with its life source. (In some areas the aflaj are even referred to as *da'udis*.) Other historians have a not quite so lofty approach. While the exact point of origin cannot be traced, they know that aflaj and their derivatives have been used in societies since ancient times with the earliest records coming from the Assyrian Empire and the court of Sargon II (700 B.C.). Similar structures have appeared from China to Africa and throughout Persian and Arabian lands. Whether it was an imported or native idea in Oman is not exactly clear. But by the early years of Christianity, Persian societies transplanted to Oman were employing the aflaj.

By Islamic times the aflaj were well established, as were the stories. It is believed that the aflaj were so big that the caliph in Baghdad threw his cane into the Euphrates River . . . and it turned up in a cistern in Oman. Another story holds that an intermittent falaj became that way because the leader of the Jinn was overtaken by the beauty of a daughter of a wealthy landowner and proceeded to kidnap her and take her to his ethereal plane. To compensate for his crime he let the spring flow whenever the men of the village walked down to the aflaj to collect water. Today, some water diviners call upon the spirits of Suleiman and Da'ud to bless them with an abundant supply of never-ending springs. (Aflaj is the plural form; falaj is the singular form and thus means one channel or subset of channels. The word *falaj* derives from a Semitic root, *plg,* that denotes division. The Arabic word signifies the division of property, which suggests a means for distributing water.)

As marvelous as these stories may be, they don't match the physical marvel that constitutes the construction of the aflaj. The aflaj of Oman are networks made up of thousands of kilometers delivering 900,000,000 cubic meters of water per year (238 billion U.S. gallons)—70 percent of the country's total water consumption. Fifty-five percent of all Omani farms are irrigated by aflaj. (This relatively low number represents the effects of technological change in recent years, as many more farms in the Batinah region and Dhofar rely on modern irrigation methods.)

At the heart of this seemingly complex structure is a simple and elegant principle: gravity. The hydraulics of this system are based on the simple flow of water from high places to low—and all of the principles used in the aflaj had been established by 1,000 B.C. The aflaj tap the water supply deep in the aquifers of the jebels and transfer it to the outlying farms. Even in periods of extreme drought, the aflaj never run dry. Still, to construct a falaj is a major accomplishment in itself: a good portion of the aflaj network is *underground.* One of these is a *qanat* falaj. A falaj constructed alongside of and tapping into wadi beds is called a *ghayl* falaj.

The artisans who construct aflaj are known as *awamir* and hail from a tribe located near Izki. The exclusivity of their class owes to the extreme level of danger attached to aflaj construction: To begin with, the awamir has to dig a well, the first of a series of wells called the *Umm al Falaj* ("mother well"), which can be up to 60 meters deep. Then a downsloping chamber, or gallery, is carved out of the bedrock to collect water. After that a series of vertical shafts are dug downstream in the direction of the flow to extend the tunnel until it reaches a point where it can flow on the surface. These shafts are useful later on for aflaj inspection and maintenance. Herein lie the dangers. The chances of cave-ins and rock slides are high. Poor ventilation and stifling heat impede construction and the chance of flooding when chambers are connected is great. In Persia, the aflaj were simply known as "the murderer."

The output from this exhausting work is no less daunting. One kilometer of tunnel a half-meter wide means the removal of 3,000 to 4,000 tons of material. Above ground, the series of vertical shafts pointing to the source looks like a string of bomb craters.

But on the other end the work takes on a refined quality as the surface channels, formerly of mud and brick but nowadays reinforced with concrete, snake through the farmland in an intricate network of conduits, reservoirs, and cisterns. The awamir even employ inverted siphons to traverse wadi beds. The hierarchical flow suggests that the first point of emergence of the falaj is the point where water is drawn for drinking and cooking. The access to this section of falaj is unrestricted. Next come segregated bathing areas for men and women with enclosed bath houses. Further on is reserved for cleansing the dead before burial, as well as sites for washing clothes and utensils, before reaching the farm plots. At the point of dispersal, the individual plots are rationed water, each plot being allotted a number of *athar* ("shares"), using an old system of accounting based on the size of a given plot and the influence of the owner. Water is apportioned using "falaj clocks," sundials with gradations on them to determine how long a plot receives its share. Stones wrapped in cloth and mud are used to block channels and divert flow. All the water is fairly distributed. Shares of water may be bought and sold at auction. And as may be assumed, the water accountant (*bidar*) plays a very important role in the village.

Aflaj have been constructed through and under towns, and under forts and mosques, although distribution to individual homes is rare. The shaykh is likely to live in a house situated near the source of the aflaj to indicate his prominence and ability to settle disputes over water rationing. The Falaj al Kamil near Rustaq is a fascinating underground maze of dimly lit corridors once thought to extend 32 kilometers (19 miles). At the Al Hazm fort near Rustaq there is even a network of dummy channels to confound enemies when the occupants were holed up inside and needed a constant supply of water.

SHIPBUILDING

> The type of boats built here is made from coconut wood and the leaves of the date palm. After the wooden planks have been sawn they are stitched together using rope made from coconut fibre in the manner in which ropes are woven from palm fronds. Oman is famed for a type of grease used for sealing the breaches in the boats. There are also larger boats which they build from local or imported woods. Omani sailors travel the Indian Ocean and the Arabian Sea in these boats, carrying goods and precious wares as far as the coasts of Africa, India and China. And they bring back with them the merchandise of these countries.
>
> —Al-Idrisi, *Wasa Al-Hind,* twelfth century

The legacy of shipbuilding and navigation left to Western civilization by Arab peoples is tremendous. Their contribution to the craft is underscored by the fact that much of their terminology and technology, in some form or other, is still used today (Al-gebra, the mathematical study of indeterminate values as applied to the geometry of distances; Al-deberan and Deneb, names of prominent stars in the sky used for navigation; the use of lateen (triangular) sails to tack against the wind, to name a few).

By the dawn of Islam, Omani seamen had mastered the seas with their wondrous sailing vessels. They assembled their boats from fine materials imported from India and Africa. Shipbuilding centers in Sohar, Sur, and Dhofar were thriving. Stories of fantastic voyages (that were fantastic in their own right with no embellishment) filled books and carried on by word of mouth over the centuries. The skills of Omani shipwrights were unrivaled. They assembled boats over 120 feet long that weighed 500 tons. They never worked from plans, just by eye and memory. Their ships were made of imported teak woods for the hull and palm trees for the mast. They were stitched (not nailed) together with coconut fiber and caulked with natural oils and animal fat.

Even when iron nails were introduced into shipbuilding, they were resisted by the superstitious Arab shipwrights. One of the legends from the Arabian Nights tells of a new-styled boat fastened with iron nails. It was reduced to flotsam when it passed over a huge undersea "magnetic mountain" which pulled the nails out of the boat and left it to fall to pieces.

There was also the belief that if a barren woman could leap across a newly laid keel she could then conceive. But in order to appease the spirits of the waters (*efreeti*), a life had to be taken in return, presumably one of the ship's carpenters, or worse, the future captain. When a keel was laid there was a mad scramble to assemble the boat around it in case a childless woman happened to be in the vicinity.

Today shipbuilding in Oman is but a dim shadow of its former prominent self. The great Omani sailing vessels were outstripped by steamships in the nineteenth century and by lightweight, high-powered synthetic boats in the twentieth century. Now only a handful of the great craftsmen remain in Sur, maintaining a trade that has become obsolete. But they still build a few smaller vessels used by local fishermen.

Collectively called dhows, which is a Western term adapted by the Arabs, these boats displayed a diversity of styles and uses, but only a few are built today. Some of these are:

Baglah—One of the largest ocean-going vessels, it was a primarily a cargo vessel with a payload of up to 400 tons. The larger versions had copper-plated hulls, up to three masts, and a square stern with a high poop deck (giving it a resemblance to a Spanish galleon). The last Baglah was made in Sur was in 1952.

Sambuq—One of the oldest and most prestigious ships in Oman, the Sambuq was used as a fishing vessel. It had a low sleek bow with a high flat stern, 80 feet long, and could carry 150 tons. Sambuqs were still made the old-fashioned way, stitched, not nailed, up until the 1960s.

Ghanjah—Similar to the Baglah but more Indian in design with its distinguishing feature being the ornamentation. There are two Ghanjahs remaining in Oman today.

Shu'i—Smaller than the Sambuq (30 feet), the Shu'i is still used today as a fishing vessel, known for its light weight and maneuverability. Most Shu'is made today are fitted with engines.

Boom—Largest of boats before the European invasion, the Boom was 120 feet long, 30 feet wide, and carried cargo all the way to China. With a high prow and pointed stern, the boom could carry 400 tons of cargo. It could be fitted with up to three masts and was a veritable workhorse. The last Booms were built in the 1970s.

Badan—A versatile light craft, double-ended like the Boom, with no deck, the Badan was a popular fishing and passenger boat. Because of its flat bottom and shallow draft, it could maneuver through shallow coastal waters and could be easily managed by a crew of seven.

Jalibut—Derived from the British "Jolly boat," European in style, it was used for fishing, cargo and pearl diving. Fifty feet long with a single mast, it could carry up to 75 tons.

Bateel—A distinctive boat with a high stern and over 70 feet long, the speed and maneuverability of the Bateel made it useful as a warship as well as a cargo vessel. The Bateel can be seen today, used as a fishing vessel in the Musandam.

WEAVING AND DYING

In the interior sections of Oman, villagers and nomads continue their age old practice of weaving, but as with other crafts, these have been deeply affected by changing technology. There are still a few traditional weavers left; they have gained new markets in the expanding tourism trade.

In earlier days cloth was made from a number of fibers, mostly hair, wool, and cotton. Hair fibers were gathered from long-haired goats and camels, while wool was gathered from sheep. The goat hair comes in a selection of colors, notably black, browns, and greys. It produces a rough prickly yarn that is difficult to spin but very durable. Camels are the one-humped or dromedary variety and have typically short hair. However, longer strands can be gathered from the shoulders and hump. Most are beige in color, but a few from the south are black. Sheep's wool is strictly secondary as a hair fiber. Sheep are not bred in Oman for their quality of wool; whatever wool is used is sometimes imported.

Much is the same for cotton. Omanis used to cultivate and spin their own cotton but now that practice has virtually disappeared. Cotton fabrics are imported, as well as ready-made clothing from India and the Far East.

Other plant fibers that are still extensively used are reeds and palm fronds. These are braided and stitched to make mats, baskets, pouches, fans, furnishings, and other household articles. Spinning of fibers is mostly done by hand on small spindles. Spinning wheels never caught on in Oman because the spinners were usually nomadic.

Once the yarn was spun it was ready for dying. Camel and goat hairs remained undyed, but wool yarn was dyed using a combination of natural and synthetic agents. When the yarn was skeined it was mixed with alum which served as a fixative. Colors were made from pigments from local vegetation. Red dye was produced from the roots of madder which were crushed into a powder and added to a mixture of boiling water and lime juice. Color gradations could be produced by successive dipping into the dye.

Purple colors could be obtained from the shells of murex, a whelk found off the coast of Masirah. The dye was extracted from the mucous gland and produced several shades of color ranging from maroon to purple and blue-violet. Yellow was obtained from a complex mixture of local plants. Indigo dye has been manufactured for many generations and is still made today, although there are only two or three dyers left in Oman. The neel plant which grows around Nizwa provides the principal agent in the making of the dye today. (In the early days of Albusaidi rule, the Imam Said bin Ahmed tried to corner the indigo market and create a monopoly, which led him to fall into disfavor with his people.) Many of these colors have been replaced by synthetic imports.

POTTERY

The earliest pots from Oman date back to the third millennium B.C. Pottery is still a mainstay for the people in Bahla and, to a lesser degree, Salalah, where the quality of the clay is not quite as good, but the craft is well established and techniques are sophisticated. Pots are still thrown on a foot-driven wheel and baked in large mud-brick kilns. The potters create a variety of earthenware for decorative or practical purposes, from huge jugs for storing dates to incense burners, water jars, bowls, coffee pots, and even roof tiles and gutters.

JEWELRY

Jewelry is an essential part of the Omani costume. The artisan craft has its roots in antiquity. Omani gold and silversmiths are quite innovative when it comes to fashioning jewelry, particularly the Bedu craftsmen who fashioned baubles and bangles from whatever materials they could get their hands on: coins, bells, chains, etc. Gold and silver do appear in small quantities in Oman, unlike copper which is plentiful, and so most of the gold and silver used is imported.

The outcome of the smithy's efforts is intricate and ornate work in a wide array of designs. From head to toe there seems to be no end to the ways a lady can show off her finery: headpieces, earrings and nose rings, necklaces and pendants, rings for every finger and thumb, armlets, bracelets, anklets, amulets. It is no wonder that the adornment leaves the wearer weighted down.

For the men, the silver filigree on the hilts and sheaths of their khanjars (daggers) and swords is no less inspiring. Intricate geometric patterns dazzle the eye. Tribes are identified by signature patterns. Even simple utilitarian items receive special treatment. Silver toothpicks, tweezers, and earspoons do not escape the creative eye of the craftsman.

UTENSILS

Just as ornate as the jewelry are the many household items smelted and forged from local metals of copper, tin, and brass. The most distinctive and prolific is probably the coffee pot. The traditional Arabic pot is reproduced in Oman with its trademark hourglass shape, high domed rim, and long curving spout. Pots from older days were fitted with dangling ornaments and hollow lids to place pebbles inside: raucous alarms that might indicate someone sinister was trying to slip a Mickey Finn into the drink. Other household items such as bowls and trays, incense burners, rose-water sprinklers and pots are made.

Nowadays the families use plain aluminum kitchen utensils for their cooking, but the ornamental variety are still made for decoration. Every Omani household has a treasure or two proudly on display on a shelf or table or chest. There is also a thriving market for these items; they can be found in many souqs.

ARCHITECTURE

Arabic architecture is renowned for splendid symmetry, design, and detail. And it is no less prominent in Omani building than in other Arabic countries. Their buildings are solid edifices of whitewashed mortar and stone, highlighted with soft curving arches and decorated with eye-catching patterns in window screens and doorways. Eaves and porticos display traditional Arabic geometries. On many buildings, particularly the doors and windows, highlights of bright colors appear. Interiors are vast open rooms that give the look and feel that the building is bigger from the inside than from without. The architecture is influenced by Portuguese styles as well as Indian. Trade brought fineries and styles from far flung corners of the world.

In the interior and other coastal cities, bare simplistic styles are the rule, but buildings are no less rugged. Mud brick reinforced with thatched palm and stone cottages grab onto hillsides, in wadi clefts and perched on shorelines. The basic pattern of a home is a central courtyard surrounded by the various rooms, the majlis, the harem, kitchen, and sitting rooms. In cliffside villages space is at a premium, so the houses take on a cozy feeling. Building appears to be haphazard as villages grow and paths intersect and weave around new structures. A village may decline with the rate of its local productivity. Lean years lead to abandonment of sections or entire towns while prosperous years bring a rash of development in any direction that accommodates it.

One village of note that is attracting the attention of the cultural renovation committees is a particularly elaborate but abandoned village near Ibra. Not quite as run down as most, with elaborate structures, doors, and windows and a round tower with square rooms inside, Al Mansfah represents a vital link with Oman's cultural past. With renovations due to start, Al Mansfah will be off limits until reconstruction is complete.

WOODEN CRAFTS

Besides shipbuilding, wood carvers lend their craft to other forms of display. Probably the most prolific of these are the fantastic wooden doors that can be seen in every village and town. The woodcarvers who spent so much time carving elaborate designs on the poop decks and sterns of Omani boats turned their hammers and chisels on the universal symbol for "home." Even the simplest of structures will have an ornate wooden door as a sign of the geniality of the owner inside. The wood is usually imported from India or Africa and is a very durable hardwood such as teak. Most wood carvings are geometric designs, sometimes interspersed with quotations from the Qu'ran and perhaps the owner's name over the frame.

One of the most important items in the home, since there were few furnishings altogether, was the chest. It is usually made of wood, ornately studded and inlaid with brass. The chest, curiously enough, is not wholly Omani, but evolved from the many kinds of chests used as transport containers from the various ports that served Muscat, Sohar, and other coastal cities. Although Omanis designed and built chests of their own, collecting chests from far off ports became a bit of a hobby. Herein lies the variety in style and ornamentation that was imitated. Many kinds of chests, both local and foreign, can be found lurking in antique dealer's shops.

Early chests left behind by the Portuguese, who used them to carry ammunition, were thick and heavy, made from Brazilian mahogany with crude iron fixtures. Shirazi chests from Iran were in such demand by wealthy traders that they are hard to find in Oman today, but they are identified by their ornate floral engravings and brass escutcheons. They were used to transport carpets in their heyday. Surat-style chests from India mimicked the Shirazi style but were less ornate. Malabar chests from India were decorated with a combination of floral and geometric designs; although they were inlaid with brass they were not studded.

The Omanis used chests for a number of practical purposes, mostly for storage of valuables, but the most common was the bridal chest that developed around the eighteenth century. Chests were often passed down through the families, usually from mother-in-law to daughter-in-law, filled with precious items—money, silks, jewelry—and were part of a trousseau for the bride. Many of these chests came from the port cities where local wood carvers would redesign discarded transport containers to suit the needs of a specific customer. Some chests have added ornamentation, compartments, and a secret drawer or two.

MUSIC

Drums were beating, and the crowd swayed left and right to their rhythms; quivering sword blades flashed in the sun as sword dancers leapt hither and thither, and low chanting grew loud as we approached. Swinging round to form a corridor for us, the tribesmen, holding their rifle butts to their hips for the *feux de joie* sent a hail of friendly bullets pinging over our heads. We went on to where the Amir stood, before the fort, on a carpet placed in the large open square, a favourite position for witnessing the horsemanship and camel-racing that now took place. . . . A dozen horsemen galloped past, now in this formation, now in that, curvetting and firing their rifles at the same time, or racing in pairs down the straight . . . chanting heroic verse, an ancient Badawin custom deriving from the mighty Antar of antiquity: "We have filled every quarter with fear till mankind grovels before us." (Chorus) "God is Great." "We have excelled the Pleiades (Thuraiyya) in its zenith." "God is Great." "And whosoever approacheth us seeking trouble shall find us brave as lions." "God is great."
—Bertram Thomas, *Alarms and Excursions in Arabia*, 1931

Omani music does not have a strong identity of its own. Ibadhism in the past did not encourage singing and dancing, although it existed in primitive forms. What musical character exists in Oman today comes from outside sources, notably the Zanzibarian connection. A lot of the ethnic music heard today is of rhythmic African quality with a lot of percussive instruments. Horns and pipes resemble instruments heard from points to the south and west along the African coastline.

Some coastal towns—notably Sur, through its connection with foreign trade—have adapted as their own the use of an instrument that is associated with an altogether different cultural heritage: the Scottish bagpipe. It seems that the bagpipe arrived about a hundred years ago or so and it looks like it's here to stay. At local festivals troupes of dancing men and women can be seen led by an Arabic Pied Piper who darts in and out of the otherwise synchronized dancers in a taunting manner, while the music rises to an ebullient crescendo. Drummers in the background mark the pace in a contagious air of celebration.

Songs and poetry do appear, particularly among the Bedus, who have the same dreams mankind has sought for centuries, songs of love and home and family. Stories woven from the rich tapestry of Arabic life are about confronting the hardships of nature and seeking divine providence and redemption or safe passage and deliverance. Religious themes run strong through all their yearnings. Most of the singing, however, is done by the men as the women are too modest; singing before an audience is contradictory to their comportment.

FINE ARTS

Today as Omanis enter the mainstream of contemporary society, many have taken up applications of fine arts, such as drawing, painting, sculpture, calligraphy, photography, printing, and graphic design. Works by professional and amateurs alike can be seen on display in local galleries and special exhibitions. In these venues women participate in almost equal numbers to men.

A Crash Course in Simple Arabic

The Arabic language is not very familiar to most Westerners but you'd be surprised at the number of words in the English lexicon that are derived from Arabic (algebra and algorithm, genie and ghoul, caravan and shawl). Modern Arabic language derives from the south-central branch of the Semitic family of languages. The Arabic of Oman derives from the colloquial Arabic spoken throughout the Arabian peninsula. Like so many other aspects of Arabic life, the language proceeds from the Qur'an and is more or less uniform throughout the Arab world.

> Very beautiful is the meeting of Arabs in the desert, with their greetings for each other—very formal, very long-drawn-out and repetitive, for each member of each party exchanges the same friendly enquiries and assurances with each member of the other, until all have greeted all, and they part or proceed to any business that may be in hand. "Peace be upon you." " And upon you peace." "How is your state, oh Salih?" "In peace; how are you, oh Ali?" "In peace! May God give you health." "May God improve your condition." "How are you?" "In peace."
> —H. St. John Philby, on the Bedu, *Arabia of the Wahhabis*, 1928

To an Arab, the concept of language is more than just a means of communication, it is a measure for setting a mood. Conversations take on a rhythm through repetition that is a key to determining temperament. Meaning transcends just the definition of words alone. As a result, the spoken language exudes a flamboyant quality. In earlier times, it has been recorded, armies were known to have fled at the barrage of disparaging verbal assaults from their detractors.

The written language is no less florid. Since iconography is banned in Islam, calligraphy has become one of the most visible art forms, and Arabic calligraphy is one of the most beautiful forms of that medium in the world. It is often hard for Westerners to approach written Arabic because the alphabet is so foreign. It is structured quite a bit differently from ours. For starters, in the written language there is no such thing as capitals and lower case. The letters of the Arabic alphabet appear in four different forms depending on whether a letter is at the beginning of a word, in the middle of a word, at the end of a word or standing alone. (There are twenty-eight letters in the Arabic alphabet, which is reproduced below with the initial, medial, final, and singular forms. There is also a listing of the diacritical marks and their counterparts.) Arabic is written and read from right to left (except numbers which are written and read from left to right! Thus a reader must mentally change directions when reading text that is interspersed with numerals.).

Secondly, although there is an almost one to one correspondence to some basic sounds between English and Arabic, particularly among consonants, there are subtle variations that are hard to describe, and there are some sounds represented in Arabic that do not exist in English—and vice-versa. For instance, there is no *p* sound in Arabic; it is usurped by the *b* sound. (If you can imagine, "Beter Biber bicked a beck of bickled bebbers," you've got the gist of that variation.) The hard and soft sounds of the letter *g* in English are commingled and used indiscriminately, probably due to foreign corruption of pronunciation (e.g. the original Arabic word for beautiful, "ga-meel," is also heard as "ja-meel," and "majlis" is also pronounced "maglis" with the hard *g*). Also, there is a set of distinctive guttural sounds produced from the pharyngeal region of the throat, a glottal stop and some velarized consonants (pronounced from the back of the tongue), that are hard for the uninitiated to reproduce. The "zee" pronounced from the back of the throat becomes a transliterated "th" sound. In some cases there are no suitable counterparts in English. There has yet to be determined a uniform definition of these sounds. Finally there are the vowel sounds, which are restricted to three short ("ah," "ih," "uh") and three long ("ay," "ee," "oo") sounds. Sometimes consonants are used in spelling these sounds (like the letter "ya" for the "ee" sound and "waw" for the "oo" sound). Except for the letter "alif," vowels have no letters of their own and are represented by diacritical marks.

The structure of Arabic is quite basic. Verbs are conjugated in two tenses: perfect, which is used to express past tense, and imperfect, which expresses present and future tenses. This is accomplished by attaching suffixes to the root word. In addition there is an imperative form, an active and passive participle, and a verbal noun. Verbs are inflected in three persons: singular, dual (which is hardly ever used), and plural; and two genders. In Classical Arabic nouns were declined in three cases, but in modern spoken Arabic there are none. Pronouns occur as suffixes and independent words. The language also makes use of adjectives, adverbs, prepositions, conjunctions,

Simplified Arabic and Pronounciation Guide

Isolated	Initial	Medial	Final	Name	Approximate Pronounciation
أ	أ	ـا	ـا	alif	*
ب .	بـ	ـبـ	ـب	ba'	boy
ت	تـ	ـتـ	ـت	ta'	tin
ث	ثـ	ـثـ	ـث	tha'	this
ج	جـ	ـجـ	ـج	jim	jet
ح	حـ	ـحـ	ـح	ha'	**
خ	خـ	ـخـ	ـخ	kha'	Bach (Ger.)
د	د	ـد	ـد	dal	do
ذ	ذ	ـذ	ـذ	dhal	then
ر	ر	ـر	ـر	ra'	tree (trill)
ز	ز	ـز	ـز	za'	zoo
س	سـ	ـسـ	ـس	sin	sit
ش	شـ	ـشـ	ـش	shin	shoe
ص	صـ	ـصـ	ـص	sad	***
ض	ضـ	ـضـ	ـض	dad	***
ط	ط	ـطـ	ـط	ta	***
ظ	ظ	ـظـ	ـظ	za	***
ع	عـ	ـعـ	ـع	ayn	#
غ	غـ	ـغـ	ـغ	ghayn	rien (Fr.)
ف	فـ	ـفـ	ـف	fa'	fat
ق	قـ	ـقـ	ـق	qaf	##
ك	كـ	ـكـ	ـك	kaf	kit
ل	لـ	ـلـ	ـل	lam	let
م	مـ	ـمـ	ـم	mim	mate
ن	نـ	ـنـ	ـن	nun	nice
ه	هـ	ـهـ	ـه	ha'	hit
و	و	ـو	ـو	waw	wet
ي	يـ	ـيـ	ـي	ya'	you
ء				hamza	###

* No consonantal value
** A Pharyngeal Fricative
*** The Consonant sound from the back of the tongue (velarized)
# A vowel sound treated as a consonant made by a contraction of the throat
A uvular stop
A glottal stop

´	fathah	*a*t
´	dammah	f*oo*t
─	kasrah	*i*f
لَ	long fathah	f*a*ther
ﹾو	long dammah	f*oo*d
ﹻ ، يـ	long kasrah	*e*ve
وْ	fathah waw sukun	*ou*t
يْ	fathah ya sukun	n*i*ce
ى	alif maqsurah	*a*dd
ة	ta marbutah	(silent *h*)
أ	hamzat al-wasl	(vowel ommited)
آ	alif maddah	*a*dd
وّ	waw shadah, followed by a short vowel	*e*ve
يّ ، ـّ	ya shadah, followed by a short vowel	f*oo*d

and the definite article ("al-") which precedes most nouns and adjectives. (In some words, those beginning in *S, Sh, R, N, T, Z,* and *D*, the preceding article "al-" is assimilated into the word and becomes "As-," "Ash-," "Ar-," "An-," "At-," "Az-,"and "Ad-," respectively.)

It's probably best for the newcomer to just go with what he hears and not worry about all the subtleties, which are glossed over in everyday speech anyway. I find it helpful to read familiar product logos on packaging and billboards and place names on road signs to phonetically familiarize myself with the speech-to-alphabet correlations. For the visitor, Arabic is best pared down to some simple catchwords and phrases which are easily understood; the fewer words you can use in a sentence, the better. Here is a listing of the phrases (in phonetic transliteration) I find most helpful in everyday conversation, some of which may already be familiar.

Arabic Phrase	**Rough Translation**
Sa-laam Al-ay kum.	Peace be upon you. (Customary greeting)
Wah-lay kum sa-laam.	And upon you, peace. (The response)
Ma-harbah.	Hello.
Ah-lan Wah-sahlan	Greetings!
Kaif Halik?	(to a man) How are you?
Kaif Halish?	(to a woman)

Kaif saha?	(Same query)
Zain! Al hamdu lillah.	Fine! Praise be to God. (The response)
Wa inta (intee)?	And you?
Koiz	OK (Another response)
Ta-mam	Good (And another)
Tay-yib	(And another)
Sa-bah Al Kayr.	Good morning.
Sa-bah An-noor	(The response.)
Ma-sa Al Kayr.	Good evening.
Ma-sa An-noor	(The response.)
Ma-salaama.	Good-bye.
Min fadlak	Please
Shu-kran.	Thank you.
Shukran ja-zeelin.	Thank you very much.
Af-wan.	You're welcome. Don't mention it.
Na'am.	Yes.
Iwa.	Yes.
La.	No.
Mafeesh	There is no (general negation)
Mafee Moosh-kalah.	No problem!
In-shal-lah.	If God wills it, or, it will happen at such time as God desires.

    (Omani life-style is very laid back; the use of this expression is quite liberal. It was all put in the proper perspective to me when I was told that the correlated American expression (borrowed from the Spanish), "Mañana," meaning tomorrow, or at some later time, is like "Inshallah." Only Inshallah makes Mañana look urgent.)

Ismi	My name is

Ana Amree-ki
 (*In-gleezi, Fransi,*
  Al-maani, etc.)
	I am an American
	 (Englishman, French,
	  German, etc.)

Ta-takalim In-gleezi?	Do you speak English?
A-tata-kalim Ara-bee *shway-a shway-a.*	I speak a little Arabic.

As-sa'a kam?	What time is it?
Wayn . . . ?	Where is . . . ?
Imta . . . ?	When is . . . ?
Fee	In or at
Al-yom	Today
Bukra	Tomorrow
Bikam?	How much?
Mumkin sura, min fadlak?	May I take your photograph, please? (Literally, "Is a picture possible?" This is very important. Remember it.)
Mo ism had-hi bi-lad?	What is the name of this place?
Hal hadha it-tark ila . . . ?	Is this the road to . . . ?
Mum-kin nab-ni Khay-ma hina?	May we camp here?
Mum-kin ta-dilini al it-arik ila . . . ?	Is it possible to point the way to . . . ?
see-ara	vehicle, usually a four-wheel drive
Wadi	River bed (usually dry)
Jebel	Mountain
Sa-hra	Desert
Ram-la	Sandy desert
Sabkha	Salt flats
Ra's	Point (of land) or cape
Jazira	Island
Bandar	Bay
Khawr	Cove
Khareef	Monsoon
Shalalat	Waterfall
Min wayn ak-dar ash-tari betrol?	Where can we buy gasoline?
Wayn al mus-tash-fah? (ay-ada)	Where is the hospital? (clinic)
Wayn al hammam?	Where is the bathroom (toilet)?
Yassar	(to the) left
Yamin	(to the) right
Sida	Straight ahead

Wara	Behind
Roh	Go
Hena low-sa-maht.	Please stop here.
Bas	Enough
Kabir	Big, great
Mumtaz	Super
Ja-meel	Beautiful
soo-gheer	Small
shwaya-shwaya	A little bit, tiny, or slowly

Numbers

soo-fir	0
wah-heed	1
it-nain	2
ta-lata	3
ar-baa	4
kham-sa	5
si-ta	6
sa-bah	7
ta-maniyah	8
ti-sah	9
ash-ara	10
ihd-ashar	11
itn-ashar	12
ta-lat-ashar	13
ashreen	20
talateen	30
arba'een	40
khamseen	50
mi-yah	100
alf	1000

◆ - 0   ٦ - 6
١ - 1   ٧ - 7
٢ - 2   ٨ - 8
٣ - 3   ٩ - 9
٤ - 4
٥ - 5

A Glossary of Arabic Words

aflaj   (singular *falaj*) network of water channels for irrigation (also called *da'oud*)

Bedouin   Nomadic tribes of the interior Arabian peninsula

bin, also **ibn**   literally "son of"; *bint* means "daughter of"; *bani* means "sons of," hence tribe or clan

caliph	a religious leader, literally, "successor," as in the early days of Islam, a successor to Muhammed
dhow	collective term adapted by the Arabs from the English to mean any large wooden sea-going vessel
dish-dasha	traditional male outer garment worn by Arabs; the Omani variation is usually white, long-sleeved, collarless with a tassel suspended from the neckline to hold fragrance
frankincense	dried gum resin of the genus Boswellia plant used as an aromatic when burned over charcoal; also has purported medicinal properties and is frequently burned after the arrival of newborns
Hajj	pilgrimage to Makkah undertaken by Muslims at least once during their lifetime
halwah	a gooey confection made from sugar, water, spices, nuts, and ghee (clarified butter), served at holidays, gatherings, and festivals
harem	section of the house reserved for the women, wives, sisters, mothers, children, etc.
Ibadhi	small sect of Islam (practiced only in Oman today) that grew out of the Kharajite faction and maintains emphasis on conduct, austerity, and principle
imam	a religious leader, similar to caliph, of the Islamic community. In Shiite, a direct descendant of Muhammed; in Ibadhi, a spiritual leader of the community elected by religious scholars (*ulema*) who fulfills temporal and administrative duties as well
jebalis	mountain people (in Dhofar), in the north, *shuwawi*, nomadic peoples not to be confused with Bedouin who live in the desert, they are pastoralists who prefer to herd goats and sheep
Jihad	defense of Islam from its detractors and conversion, usually associated with radical elements of Islam and frequently interpreted as "Holy War"

jinn or **djinn**   spirit or ghost, genie

khawa   Omani coffee, usually a mixture of roasted beans, cardamom, and rose water

khanjar   a dagger held in an ornate sheath, curved and pointing up

kumma   cap worn by Omani men

majlis   meeting hall or the legislative assembly

Rub' Al Khali   the Empty Quarter, a particularly desolate region covering the lower third of the Arabian peninsula

Salah   prayer; a Muslim is obliged to pray five times a day facing in the direction of Makkah

Sawm   fasting, usually undertaken from dawn to dusk during the month of Ramadân

Shahada   testament of faith ("There is no god but God (Allah) and Muhammed is his prophet.")

Sharia   the law, specifically, Islamic law as defined by the Qur'an; it is the substance of all judicial, legislative, and moral practice

shaykh   tribal leader, usually the most affluent member of a clan

Shiite   the smaller of the two main branches of Islam, claiming descendency from the lineage of Ali (Muhammed's son-in-law) and therefore the presumptive right to the caliphate and leadership of the world Muslim community

sultan   a secular title taken by a leader, as distinguished from imam

Sunni   the larger of the two main branches of Islam, which emphasizes devout performance as the guide to proper behavior and as making them worthy of the office of caliphate regardless of lineage

wali   governor or district leader

wilayat   regional subdivision presided over by a *wali*

Zakat   almsgiving, the belief in Islam that a man is only as rich as
                    his poorest neighbor

Beyond Travel: Business Opportunities in Oman

> The customs house, the palace and its vicinity, the bazars and principal streets,
> were crowded with Arabs of every description and tribe; with Jews, Hindoos,
> Belooches, Turks and Africans.
> —Lt. William Huede, *A Voyage up the Persian Gulf and a Journey Overland from
> India to England, in 1817,* 1819

A 1995 report by the International Republican Institute (a non-parti-
san, non-profit organization based in Washington, D.C.) entitled *OMAN:
Political Development and the Majlis Ash Shura* stated:

> The government [of Oman] supports a free market economy and is making efforts
> to attract foreign investment. There are no restrictions on the flow of capital,
> whether in terms of salaries or repatriation of corporate profits in Oman. Nation-
> alization of foreign enterprises does not occur in Oman, and the government is
> beginning to privatize some state owned companies. Changes in commercial, invest-
> ment and tax laws that rationalize the regulatory environment and equalize the con-
> ditions for competition between domestic and foreign producers/corporations
> are also providing incentives to foreign investors. Oman's primary obstacle to
> attracting foreign investment is the small size of the Omani market.

One of the areas that Oman is keen to promote is the tourism sector. In
a booklet released in May of 1996 at an International Travel and Tourism
Conference held in Muscat, the government outlined plans and incentives
for foreign investors. Indicated were several advantages prospective investors
would have, such as political stability, up to 100 percent foreign ownership,
freedom to repatriate capital and profits, stable currency, no income tax,
interest-free/soft loans, privatization policy, freedom to employ expatriate
personnel (with the condition that certain percentages for Omani labor are
met), a regulated stock exchange, and sound economic policies in a modern
infrastructure. The government would assist investors in coordinating efforts
to provide land for new projects such as hotels, recreational facilities, health
clubs, resorts. etc. Since the country already offers a diversified background
of history, heritage, nature, and environment and an infrastructure (albeit
still growing) in place, they believe that the increase in cultural and eco-
tourism will ease the pressure on the country's limited petroleum industry

and help the move toward diversification. Since the country has grown very rapidly and 52 percent of the population is under seventeen, education and vocational training are going to figure prominently in tourism development (as well as other industries).

A September report in the *Oman Daily Observer* pronounced that 1996 was a fruitful year for the Muscat Securities Market. Foreign investments are up 3 percent over 1995, and two banks, the National Bank of Oman and Bank Muscat Al Ahli Al Omani, are setting up open-ended guaranteed funds for investors totaling over RO 3 million, the first time such funding will be available in Oman. Shell Marketing is offering 40 percent of its capital to the public as well. As a result of all this, the United Nations' Economic and Social Commission for Western Asia has said that Oman's economic growth was the most impressive for any gulf state for the past two years.

For further information regarding tourism development, interested parties should contact The Director General of Tourism, Ministry of Commerce and Industry; Tel.: (country code 968) 796527; Fax: 794238; P.O. Box 550, Muscat 113, Sultanate of Oman.

5

Muscat and the Northern Region

1. The General Picture

> My Journey with the Sultan was to take us through this populous province: now along the golden beaches, past little Arab ports ever associated with Sindbad the Sailor, and little fishing villages whose men go forth to grope under the sea for precious pearls; now through the shady date grove; and now along the hot dazzling plains beyond.
> —Bertram Thomas, *Alarms and Excursions in Arabia*, 1931

When you come to Oman you will most likely fly into Seeb International Airport, which is about 35 kilometers outside of the capital city, Muscat proper. As mentioned before, Muscat takes on three designations (much the same way that the word "Yankee" means different things to different people depending on if you're from England, the old South, or New York): Muscat refers to the old district of Muscat itself; the "tri-borough" area of Muscat, Mutrah, and Ruwi; and the greater area of suburbs referred to as the Muscat Governorate, which stretches beyond the airport to the town of Seeb. This entire region is where the greatest plurality of people reside and where most of the country's growth is taking place. Most of the hotels will be in the Mutrah-Ruwi section of the capital, with some in the suburbs and the farther areas of the Governorate. Check with your hotel to see if

Map Location Guide

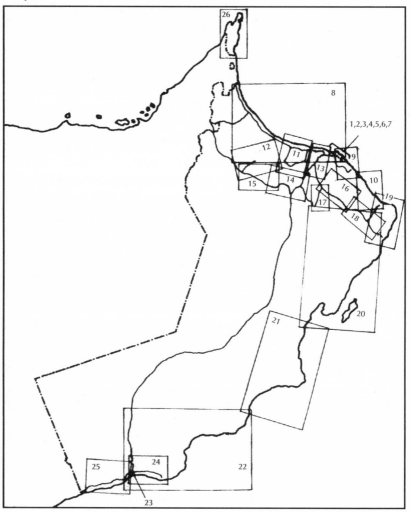

transportation is provided from the airport. Otherwise, you will have to take a cab.

Probably the first feeling you will get when you arrive in Oman, if it is during the day, is cloistered when you step outside and see the string of jebels running southeast-northwest and parallel to the coast. These are, by far, not the tallest mountains in Oman, but you can't help feeling you have arrived in a naturally sheltered haven from the rest of the world. To the north and east extends the Gulf of Oman with beaches running northwest from Muscat all the way to Sohar and beyond, 230 kilometers (140 miles) away. As you move into Ruwi, Mutrah, and Muscat itself, the jebels come right up to the edge of the coast, dissecting the city into natural portions. The feeling is cozy, never cramped, but unchecked over-development could change that in the next few years. Nevertheless, it's no wonder this ancient port was chosen for its seductive seclusive properties.

2. Getting There

Before we can think about cooling our heels in the hotel pool, let's backtrack and talk about what happens before you get there. First, a word about booking. Plan your trip as far in advance as possible, taking into account visa applications and hotel reservations. At the time of this writing, Oman is undergoing a substantial growth in all quarters as people find out about Oman as a destination. In-season booking (October to April) is expected to be a problem until more hotel services come on line. Right now, off-season booking is not a problem as most tourists find conditions in the summer too extreme, but there are those hardy souls who will and do travel to climatic hot spots. An ABC News item in 1994 showed that the number of tourists traveling to Death Valley, California, averaged about 100,000/month in the June-August period when temperatures reached 130 degrees F (54 degrees C), when they could very well have come in December when the temperature is a balmy 53 degrees F (12 degrees C). This is surprising and intriguing because the seasonal weather (and no less, the scenery) in Death Valley and Oman are almost identical. Anyway, European charters are booking large blocks of space in season; this makes it hard for the individual *and* preferential travelers to find accommodations. This guide will try to encompass all of the available lodging, from luxurious to spartan.

When you come to Oman by air, you will arrive at Seeb International Airport (SIA). There are also a number of cruise lines that put in regular and chartered stops into Mutrah at the port of Mina Qaboos. (Check with your travel agent on the availability of cruises if you prefer to come by sea.) Arrivals at SIA have become more and more efficient in the nineties, especially since the 1993 renovations to the arrival and departure terminals. SIA is very orderly with its single strip running east to west, almost parallel to the shoreline. Passengers are bussed from the plane to the arrivals gate. Once inside, there are clear directions to the holding areas for immigration, baggage claim, and customs. There is luggage scanning and spot checks (as previously mentioned, for undesirable materials) but the system is streamlined and much faster than it used to be. (Upon my '96 arrival with several large bags and chests to set up living operations to write this book, from the the time I left the plane to the time I got out to the street was about twenty-five minutes.)

If you arrive during the off season, the first thing you will notice is the heat and humidity. Be prepared to take it in stride and don't get hot under the collar. Courtesy goes a long, long way in all your dealings. Once you have acclimated, you will most likely try to migrate to higher elevations which will afford some relief in temperature, and where the air is considerably drier.

If you are wondering about whether to exchange money at the airport or in town, don't worry too much. Western currencies are fairly stable and the Omani Riyal is fixed to the U.S. dollar. You can "shop around" if you like. Hotels tend to be a bit pricier. The exchange at the airport is at the bank rate. There are numerous exchanges in Ruwi and many banks have branches throughout the capital area. Remember banks close at noon, so get your pecuniary matters taken care of first thing in the morning.

3. Local Transportation

The only mechanized ways to get around the Sultanate are by car, bus, taxi, or boat. There is no rail service in Oman.

Buses. The government offers bus service through its state-owned Oman National Transport Company. This service provides transport to major towns throughout the Sultanate as well as Abu Dhabi and Dubai. In Muscat the main bus stops are opposite the fish market in Mutrah and in downtown Ruwi on Al Jaame St. next to the Sultan Qaboos Mosque. Schedules are published in the local papers or can be obtained from the ONTC office (Tel. 590046 or 590601).

Taxis or Limos. It is very easy to hail a cab in Muscat, or for that matter, anywhere in the Sultanate. (You'd be surprised to see where a taxi turns up in some off-road village in places in the interior best suited for four-wheel drives.) But there they are, you can't miss 'em: orange and white cars. Taxis are unmetered, so you had best decide on a fare before you start. A trip from SIA to downtown Ruwi is about RO 5-6. That's about U.S. $15. The cheapest fare for a short jaunt is about 200 bz (baizas) (52 cents). All the better hire car services (car rental agencies) have limousine services available at competitive rates.

Cars. Once you are in the country, your *modus transitae* is likely to be a hire car. The type of traveling you intend to do will determine the best type of vehicle required. Saloon cars (what Americans call a sedan) are adequate for most areas as tarmac (asphalt) roads network across the country to a good portion of towns with tourist attractions. However, most resident expats living in Oman will tell you that to really see the country, you should take a four-wheel drive (4WD). Saloons and 4WDs are readily available from all the major hire car agencies and most 4WDs are fitted for PDO specs (PDO stands for Petroleum Development of Oman, Oman's national oil company. PDO specs are the specifications for their off-road vehicles, which means they will be quite road worthy under the most extreme conditions.) Drivers must hold a valid international license.

Petrol is not exactly cheap in Oman but the rates are stable. Super unleaded (*mumtaz*) is 118 bz/liter, which comes out to about $1.21 per gallon. Regular is 112 bz/liter ($1.15/gallon).

Major car hire services:

- **Al Maskary Rent A Car** (near Ghubrah roundabout, Tel. 591538)
  Saloon cars and 4WDs, with chauffeurs optional. Special rates on weekends.

- **Al Musafia'a Rent-A-Car** (BP Filling Station, Al Harthy Complex, Tel. 563532)
  Saloon cars and 4WDs

- **Al-Soqoor Al-Omania Rent-A-Car** (Salalah airport, Tel. 294557; Al Muntaza Road; Salalah, Tel. 291600 or 294561)
  Small cars, luxury vehicles, 4WDs, and chauffeur services. Special weekend packages. Tourist services also provided.

- **Avis** (Al Bustan Palace Hotel, Tel. 703242; Sheraton Oman Hotel, Tel. 799899, Ext. 5119; Muscat Inter Continental, Tel. 601226 or 607235; Seeb Airport, Tel. 519176; Salalah c/o Zubair Travel & Service Bureau, Tel. 291145)
  Saloon cars, 4WDs, and luxury cars. Chauffeur services available. Special long- and short-term lease rates.

- **Budget Rent-A-Car** (Ruwi Novotel, Tel. 794721/23; Al Falaj Hotel, Tel. 702311, Ext. 79; Seeb Airport, Tel. 510816, open 24 hours; Salalah Holiday Inn, Tel. 235160 or 235333)
  Saloon cars, 4WDs, and luxury vehicles with chauffeur services. Special weekend tariffs. Mobile phones installed on request.

- **Bustan Rent-A-Car** (near O.C. Centre, Ruwi, Tel. 792804 or 792281)
  Assortment of passenger vehicles and 4WDs at competitive rates. Luxury cars can be arranged. Chauffeur services provided.

- **Deer Orient** (Al Khuwair, Tel. 600750 or 601444)
  Oman's only radio taxi service, available around the clock, throughout the year. Multi-lingual chauffeurs at the wheel. Destinations anywhere in Oman and UAE.

- **Europcar-Interrent** (Mutrah Business District, main office, Tel. 700190/91; Al Khuwair 694093 or 697123)
  Wide range of vehicles available on hire including 4WDs, buses, and vans, on long- and short-term rentals; special long weekend rates. Also luxury cars with professional chauffeurs.

- **Hertz** (Wattayah, Tel. 566208 or 566046)
  Wide selection of passenger cars and commercial vehicles including 4WD station wagons for daily rentals and short/long-term lease.

- **Mark Rent-A-Car** (Seeb Airport, Tel. 510033, 24-hour service; Hatat House, Wattayah, Tel. 562444 or 565567)
  Large fleet with passenger cars and chauffeurs available.

- **Mohd. Taqi Mohsin Trading Est.** (Shell Filling Station, near Sheraton Oman Hotel, Tel. 700728; Mina Al Fahal 563422)
  Passenger vehicles and 4WDs.

- **Rent-A-Car Centre** (near Redan Hotel, Salalah, Tel. 296520)

- **Samoa Oman** (Hamdan Plaza Hotel, Salalah, Tel. 211228; Haffa House, Salalah, Tel. 290088)
  Wide variety of cars for short- or long-term lease.

- **Stag Limousine** (Wadi Kabir, Ruwi, Tel. 703656)
  Oman's first chauffeur-driven limousine service, available 24 hours throughout the week.
  Vehicles equipped with mobile phone and fax on request, chauffeured tours.

- **Suwatco Rent-a-Car** (O.C. Centre, Ruwi, Tel. 707840)
  Vehicles on hire include 4WDs and saloons with limousines either self- or chauffeur-driven.

- **Thrifty Rent-A-Car** (behind Al-Jadeed Supermarket, Al Khuwair, Tel. 604248 or 603648; Seeb Airport, Tel. 521189)
  Round-the-clock service, offering a selection of passenger cars, 4WDs, and coaches. Chauffeurs also available. Special weekend rates.

- **Toyota Rent A Car** (Crowne Plaza Hotel Muscat, Qurum, Tel. 561427 or 561437; Seeb Airport, Tel. 510224 or 510933)
  Saloon cars, 4WDs, buses, and pick-ups, long- and short-term rentals. Chauffeur-driven limousines also available.

- Xpress **Rent a Car** (In the Technique Building in Al Ghubrah next to sister company Sunny Day Tours, Tel. 591244, Fax: 591478)
  Passenger vehicles and 4WDs, service center, and workshop.

Boats. There are a number of ways to explore Oman by boat: fishing, sailing cruises, dhow cruises, whale and dolphin watches, diving excursions. These can be obtained through local tour operators or in direct dealing with private boat owners, marinas, and dive centers (see "Guided Tours" section later in this chapter).

4. The Hotel Scene

Muscat offers hotels for just about everyone in every price range, from the simple to the extravagant. With the economic revival and the formulation of a tourism policy in 1986, the government has paved the way for growth in international development. And grown it has but it still has a long way to go. For a while, bookings will be hard to get in-season until there are more hotels, motels, and resorts. Bookings off-season are a snap but remember the climatic conditions. Only hardy travelers who enjoy the challenge of this type of weather should consider coming to Oman in the summer. Keep in mind that temperatures in Dhofar are milder during the summer and year-round travel is more likely to occur down there (see next section on Dhofar). Hotels in this guide will be described from the top on down in greater Muscat and then outwards into the interior (regardless of rating, because there are so few). All rates are subject to a 5 percent Muscat Municipality tax and a 10 percent service charge. Estimated prices are before tax in Omani Riyals and U.S. dollars. All expensive and medium-price hotels are fully licensed (licensed means they sell beer and wine; fully licensed means they sell beer, wine, and spirits).

Beyond the low end of hotels, there is nothing to speak of in the way of communal bunk houses or the like, even for the most spartan traveler. The outdoor set will most often opt for extended overnight wadi bashes and will find that most tour operators provide necessary camping equipment (check with your operator as to what you need and need not provide). Or you can rough it yourself and bring your own gear, but it is recommended that you travel with a legitimate inbound tour operator to get the most out of your camp-overs in the desert and interior.

The simple and cheap lodgings try to keep up with the rest of the pack by providing TV with satellite coverage, air conditioning, music and in-house movies, refrigerators, and, in almost all cases, private baths. In these places, rooms are generally small to very small and services are streamlined.

EXPENSIVE HOTELS

The **Al Bustan Palace Hotel** (Tel. 968-799666) is the jewel in the crown of Omani hotels. It is truly more like a royal palace than a hotel. The Al Bustan is consistently ranked as one of the world's finest. It is definitely worth a trip to visit it even if you are not staying there. It combines the best of modern and classic Arabian architecture in a stunning setting just five minutes' drive south from Muscat or Ruwi. The hotel was completed in 1985 to host the AGCC (Arabian Gulf Cooperative Council) conference for that year. It is situated near the village of Al Bustan, just south of Muscat, on 200 acres of beachfront property surrounded by the famous Omani ophiolites that frame the lush green setting with ragged warm chocolate brown hues. The central atrium is simply a marvel with its towering columns of beautiful mosaics surrounding a central fountain. There are restaurants, pubs, and coffee shops radiating out from this central area. There are four restaurants throughout the complex, including the Seblat Al Bustan which serves traditional Omani food in a traditional setting: outdoors in Bedouin tents on carpets and cushions accompanied by Omani music and dance (all restaurants are listed in the "Dining and Restaurant" section later in this chapter). There are also 16 banquet and reception halls, a disco, an auditorium, and complete recreation facilities: windsurfing and sailing, game fishing, diving, tennis and squash health club, sauna and Jacuzzi, aerobics and massage services. At the entrance to the hotel, sitting in the middle of the roundabout, is explorer Tim Severin's boat, the *Sohar*, which made the trip from Muscat to Canton, China in 1980. The hotel has 247 rooms starting at RO 113 ($290) a night, suites and grand deluxe suites up to RO 720 ($1860). Reserve through the hotel at P.O. Box 1998, Mutrah 114; Fax: 968-799600.

The **Hyatt Regency Muscat** (Tel. 968-602888) is now fully opened and the results are fabulous. With sweeping designs and elegant workmanship, the Hyatt is fast becoming the center of attention in Muscat There are 280 rooms, 44 executive suites, 3 regency suites, 1 royal suite, and 6 luxury crown suites. All rooms have AC, international direct dialing (IDD) phone service with voice mail, satellite TV, minibar, hair dryers, fax lines, and safes. The Regency Club provides guest rooms and suites with complimentary breakfast, all-day coffee/tea service, predinner drinks, and canapés. Services include a comprehensive business center, banquet and conference facilities, laundry and valet, currency exchange, baby-sitting, specialty shops including florist, jeweler, carpet, and souvenir, beauty salon, car rental, ticketing and sightseeing tours, fitness center, pool, tennis, squash, Jacuzzi, sauna, steam bath, and massage. Dining and entertainment runs the gamut from an African safari pub to a Latin American disco to sunken-ship bar, à la *Titanic* (the legendary *John Barry* frigate, sunk off the Oman coast during World War II with a mysterious payload of silver purportedly earmarked for Joseph Stalin), to elegant fine dining with Mediterranean, Oriental, and Middle Eastern themes. Rooms start at RO 80 ($207) and suites at RO 170 ($439). Reserve through the hotel at P.O. Box 591, Shati Al Qurum 133; Fax: 968-605282.

Muscat Inter-Continental Hotel (Tel. 968-600500). The Intercon, as it is affectionately known, is the next in elegant hotels and owns a very popular spot along the beach in Shati Al-Qurum outside of Muscat, about 20 kilometers from SIA. Surrounded by lush gardens, the Intercon is out in the open away from the surrounding jebels. Like the Al Bustan, it offers a full array of services to the guests including pubs, restaurants, coffee shops, and a nightclub. Of these there are two of note: the OK Corral, an old-fashioned outdoor Western steak house, and an intriguing outdoor Oriental restaurant with the rather pedestrian name of the Car Park. Both serve excellent food and provide entertainment. For recreational facilities there are swimming, sailing, water-skiing, windsurfing, diving, tennis and squash, and a health club. There are 285 rooms including suites and the prices range from RO 51 ($130) to RO 500 ($1290). Reserve through the hotel at P.O. Box 398, Mutrah 114; Fax: 968-600012.

A member of the famous worldwide chain, the **Sheraton Oman Hotel** (Tel. 968-799899) is the "downtown" hotel in the heart of the Central Business District at the intersection of Bait Al Falaj Street and Al Jaame Street, across the street from the Ministry of Commerce and Industry and the Chamber of Commerce. The Sheraton is very elegant and stylish with restaurants, pubs, and cafés serving a variety of international cuisine. The hotel also has recreational facilities including a pool, health club, tennis, table tennis, bowling, and volleyball. Conference and banquet facilities are also available. Rooms run between RO 58 ($150) and RO 75 ($194). Suites are from RO 90 to RO 350 ($232-$903). Group rates and long-stay rates available. Reserve through the hotel at P.O. Box 3260, Ruwi 112; Fax: 968-795791.

The Qurum Beach Tourism Resort (Tel. 968-605945) is a new arrival on the hotel scene and is a first-class resort on the beachfront next to the Intercon in Shati Al Qurum. With only seven suites to offer for overnight guests (RO 50-60, $129-$155) the resort specializes in catering to the banquet and party crowd with an excellent seafood restaurant (diners choose their fare fresh from the resort's own fish market). There is a 350-capacity ballroom, roof terrace, and party halls. Recreational facilities include pool, water sports, gym (members only), and segregated changing rooms with steam baths. Reserve through the hotel at P.O. Box 652, Jibroo 114; Fax: 968-605968.

The **Crowne Plaza Hotel Muscat** (Tel. 968-560100) is one of the older hotels, which is still not very old. It has a prime location on a bluff overlooking the Gulf of Oman in Qurum Heights, one of Muscat's picturesque residential districts, just down the beach from the Intercon. The view of the coast and the surrounding jebels is spectacular. The Crowne has first-class appointments with all the modern comforts, several theme restaurants, pubs, and first-rate recreational facilities: pool, tennis, squash, water sports, fishing. There are complete business and conference facilities available. Renovations are going on now, with tentative completion scheduled for the end of '97, providing 100 additional rooms and services. Rates range from RO 38 to 55 ($98-$140) for rooms and RO 75 to 175 ($194-$452) for suites. Reserve through the hotel at P.O. Box 1455, Ruwi 112; Fax: 968-560650.

MEDIUM-PRICE HOTELS

Another link in the famous chain, the **Muscat Holiday Inn** (Tel. 968-697123) is midway between Muscat and SIA in the center of Al Khuwair, across the Dual Carriageway from the government ministries and diplomatic quarter. It is near the Zawawi Mosque. The hotel features top-notch service and amenities with 123 rooms and suites. Room rates range from RO 39 to 54 ($100-$139) while suites are from RO 80 to 100 ($206-$258). Conference facilities, fitness and health club, tennis, and swimming pool. Reserve through hotel at P.O. Box 1185, CPO Seeb 111; Fax: 968-697789.

A new branch has just opened in the nearby neighborhood of Ghala, the **Holiday Inn Al Madinah** (Tel. 968-596400). While they cater to a largely business crowd, they are fully equipped to handle tourists, with 81 rooms and 6 suites. For dining, there is a coffee shop serving international cuisine, two nightclubs, and a Cheers pub. There is also a pool, gymnasium, and ballroom. Rooms from RO 40 ($104) and suites RO 60 ($155). In Ghala on Way 5221, one kilometer beyond the Royal Hospital. Reserve through hotel at P.O. Box 692, Athaibah 130; Fax: 968-502191.

Just a stone's throw (1 kilometer) from Seeb International Airport (SIA), and next to the Oman Exhibition Centre, the **Seeb Novotel** (Tel. 968-510300) offers creature comforts in a relaxed rural setting away from the bustle of town. It is an excellent spot for getaways to the interior. Another first-rate hotel with business and conference facilities up to 500 capacity, rooms with balconies, sports and recreation including swimming, tennis, bowling, squash, and snooker. Restaurant with theme nights and the Par 19 Club offer a wide variety of culinary tastes. Rates for rooms are RO 36-43 ($93-$111) and for suites, RO 75 ($194). Reserve through hotel at P.O. Box 69, CPO Seeb 111; Fax: 968-510055.

Located on the Shati Al Qurum Beach next to the Hyatt, the new **Laith Howard Johnson** (Tel. 968-692121) opened in the spring of 1999. Bright and stylish with seafaring décor, the Laith offers 32 rooms and suites with central AC, IDD telephones with voice mail, satellite TV, minibars, a 24-hour business center, coffee shop, and the Kann Zaman Restaurant offering fine Mediterranean cuisine. Room rates, RO 35 ($90); suites from RO 60 ($155). Reserve through the hotel at P.O. Box 3951, Ruwi 112; Fax: 968-694404.

Another member of the Novotel group, the **Ruwi Novotel** (Tel. 968-704244) is situated just north of the Ruwi roundabout in downtown Ruwi. Another popular business hotel, it offers 120 rooms and suites, business and conference facilities, sports and recreation (swimming, tennis, squash, and a gym), and a leisure center with beauty salon, car rental, bookshop, laundry, and jewelry store. Room rates, RO 32-37 ($83-95); suites, RO 55 ($142). Reserve through the hotel at P.O. Box 2195, Ruwi 112; Fax: 968-704248.

Downtown Ruwi has a new establishment, the **Haffa House Hotel** (Tel. 968-707207), next to the Ruwi Novotel, with over 80 rooms and 30 suites, an indoor pool, business center, and all the other amenities of an international-class hotel. It is not licensed. Rooms start at RO 35 ($91) and suites at RO 65 ($169). Reserve through the hotel at P.O. Box 1498, Jibroo 114; Fax: 968-707208.

One of the oldest hotels in Muscat, and under new management (it was formerly just the Al Falaj Hotel), the **Mercure Al Falaj** (Tel. 968-702311) is near the Central Business District in a quiet neighborhood. As it is a popular spot for businessmen, the Al Falaj offers complete banquet and conference facilities up to 1,000 and has excellent recreational facilities including a 450-seat glass-walled tournament-level squash court, pool, gyms, sauna, steam, and treatment rooms. On top of the hotel is the Tokyo Taro restaurant serving excellent Japanese cuisine by performing chefs who put on a fantastic display of cooking and juggling cutlery. There are also a British pub, French and Chinese restaurants, coffee shops, a bake shop, and several boutiques and salons. Room rates, RO 32-40 ($83-$103); suites RO 75 ($194). Reserve through the hotel at P.O. Box 5031, Ruwi 112; Fax: 968-795853.

The **Mutrah Hotel** (Tel. 968-798401) is located in a busy area between Ruwi and Mutrah on Mutrah High Street, which is a pass between the mountains that divide the two districts. The street serves as a back entrance to the old Mutrah souq (probably the only advantage of the hotel's location). Mutrah High Street is divided to promote traffic flow, so getting in and out takes a bit of getting used to until you know the (not so) short-cuts. But the hotel itself is nice with decent accommodation at a good price. Rooms range from RO 13 to 24 ($33-$61) and the hotel is complemented by an international restaurant, two pubs, a gym, and a games room. Reserve through the hotel at P.O. Box 1525, Ruwi 112; Fax: 968-790953.

The **White Nile Hotel** (Tel. 968-708989) is a new establishment on Al Iskan

Street across from the Sultan Building and Shopping complex with the Pegasus and Al Dehleez Restaurants. Pleasant and affordable, the White Nile offers its own restaurant and lounge, the Naseem Restaurant and Al Ashjaan Bar. Standard amenities. Rooms go from RO 12 to 25 ($31-$64). Reserve through the hotel at P.O. Box 1028, Al Hamriya 131; Fax: 968-750778.

The **Qurum Beach House** (Tel. 968-564070) is an attractive resort tucked in the residential area of Qurum Heights just before the Crowne Plaza Hotel. The hotel offers rooms and apartments for people on extended trips. Although the single rooms are rather boxy, the larger suites and apartments are comfortable. Rates for the rooms range between RO 16 and RO 38 ($41-$98). Apartments go for RO 52 ($134) for a two-bedroom and RO 65 ($165) for a three-bedroom, with discounts for extended stays. The hotel offers a multi-cuisine restaurant, a luxury yacht, and speed boats for water sports and activities. Reserve through the hotel at P.O. Box 2148, Ruwi 112; Fax: 968-560761.

A scant fifteen-minute ride from the airport will take you to the **Majan Hotel** (Tel. 968-592900), located in Bausher (next to Al Khuwair) on Al Ghubrah Street just beyond the Royal Hospital. It's not a central location, but it's not all that removed either. The hotel offers 68 attractive rooms at good rates and 15 studio apartments. Rooms and suites range between RO 18 and RO 45 ($46-$116). Apartments are RO 125 per week ($322). Conference center and ballroom, banquet facilities, three restaurants, 24-hour café, pub, and disco. Reserve through the hotel at P.O. Box 311, Madinat Al Sultan Qaboos 115; Fax: 968-592979.

BUDGET ACCOMODATIONS

There are several economy hotels in Muscat with one first-class feature: they are situated on the Mutrah Corniche facing the harbor and port of Mina Qaboos, and are in direct proximity to the Old Souq, the fish and vegetable souq, Riyam Park, Mutrah Fort, and a couple of nice restaurants. What more could you ask for in terms of atmosphere in this transformed old world hub?

In the heart of the Corniche, the **Al Nahdha Hotel** (Tel. 968-714196) offers 50 rooms and two junior suites, Oriental restaurant and snack bar, rooftop garden with panoramic view of the harbor, and business services (typing, fax, telex, copies, messengers, currency exchange). Room rates are from RO 8.5 to 14 ($22-$36) with suites at RO 16 ($41). Reserve through the hotel at P.O. Box 1561, Mutrah 114; Fax: 968-714994.

Another delight in the "old quarter" of Mutrah, the **Corniche Hotel** (Tel. 968-714636) has 53 rooms and suites with standard amenities. Rooms go for RO 9.5-14 ($25-$36) and suites, RO 18-25 ($46-$64). International restaurant, catering, group rates. Reserve through the hotel at PO. Box 1800, Mutrah 114; Fax: 968-714770.

Another find on the Corniche, the **Mina Hotel** (Tel. 968-711828) has 28 rooms (RO 12-15, $30-$39) and two restaurants (fully licensed) serving Indian and continental cuisine. Reserve through the hotel at P.O. Box 504, Ruwi 112; Fax. 968-714981.

The **Naseem Hotel** (Tel. 968-712418) has 29 rooms (all with AC, TV, fridge, phone, bath, etc.) and one suite and a large room with partitions. The rooms are RO 11-17 ($28-$43) and the suite is RO 25. Room service (take-out food from nearby establishments), group rates. Reserve through the hotel at P.O. Box 360, Jibroo 114; Fax: 968-712419.

Winding up the Corniche at the far end is the **Seaview Hotel** (Tel. 968-714555), a smallish place. It has only 12 rooms, RO 6 ($15) and RO 12 ($31). The restaurant serves Arabic/Indian food. Reserve through hotel at P.O. Box 974, Mutrah 114; no fax.

The remaining budget hotels in the Central Business District are economical and centrally located but have little or no scenic value.

The **Al Walja Hotel** (Tel. 968-707011) is in downtown Ruwi between Ruwi High Street and Wadi Kabir, close to the Mansoor Shopping Complex in a bustling part of town. There are many electronics repair shops and auto upholsterers surrounding the hotel. If you're driving it's not easy to get to until you have memorized the idiosyncrasies of Ruwi's one-way streets. The rooms (18 in all) are simple with basic amenities, attached baths. Rates RO 9.2-11.5 ($24-$30). Reserve through hotel at P.O. Box 375, Madinat Al Sultan Qaboos 115; Fax: 968-694399.

The **Al Hadow Hotel** (Tel. 968-799329, 708469) is in Mutrah Al Kubra across the street from the Oman House and Mutrah Hotel. It is set back from the street. 36 rooms with basic amenities from RO 7 to RO 13 ($18-$34). Restaurant with Indian/Arabic cuisine and 24-hour room service. Reserve through the hotel at P.O. Box 67, Mutrah 114; Fax: 968-799329.

The **Al Makha Hotel** (Tel. 968-790666) is a good quality trade-off for the price with good services and the standard amenities. For scenic value, it will only appeal to subscribers of *Motor Trend*, as it is located near all the auto repair shops in the Wadi Kabir section of Ruwi off Honda Road. Rooms are larger than others in its class and rates are reasonable: RO 14-21 ($36-54), with special business rate discount. The hotel has three fully licensed restaurants serving Arabic, Continental, Chinese, and Indian cuisine. Reserve through the hotel at P.O. Box 3585, Ruwi 112; Fax: 968-789922.

The **Camilia Hotel** (Tel. 968-799459, 799460) is just off the other end of Honda Road (near the plumbing, hardware, and electrical section of town), just off Ruwi High Street. Straightforward with no frills, it's the only hotel that has both rooms with attached baths (RO 10-14, $26-$36) and rooms with common baths (RO 8.5-12.5, $22-$32). Licensed restaurant with Indian/Arabic cuisine and room service. Reserve through the hotel at P.O. Box 28, Ruwi 112; Fax: 968-799461.

INTERIOR (OUTSIDE MUSCAT)

Lodging in the interior is still sparse considering the country's infrastructure and tourism needs. While some people will want to camp out under the stars (either on their own or through an organized wadi bash) some people will want the comfort of four walls and air conditioning. Because there are so few places at the time of this writing, they will be lumped together under this one heading. Prices and description will be a general indication of quality vs. economy.

The **Istrahat Al Seeb Hotel and Restaurant** (Tel. 968-620916/625512) is on the slip road from Al Hail to Seeb, more precisely, near the Qur'an roundabout. A new establishment with eight rooms ranging from RO 12-20 ($31-$52). Good getaway spot to the interior and away from the capital area hubbub. Rooms with air conditioning, fridge, satellite TV, etc. Restaurant awaiting licensing at time of writing. Reserve through the hotel at P.O. Box 94, Al Hail 132; Fax: 968-624367.

Going away from Muscat towards Nizwa and the interior, the first place you are likely to find is the **Al Rusail Hotel** (Tel. 968-626710), strategically placed near the Rusail Industrial Estate about 20 minutes from SIA and a good place for business travelers. The hotel has 28 rooms and two suites with all amenities, restaurant (fully licensed), coffee shop, pool, health club, gardens, and conference and banquet facilities (up to 400). Rates for rooms are RO 22-25 ($57-$64), suites are RO 45 ($116). Reserve through the hotel at P.O. Box 409, Muscat 113; Fax: 968-694420.

The newly opened (1996) **Nizwa Hotel** (Tel. 968-431616) can be found tucked against the flanks of the Western Hajars about 20 kilometers before Nizwa proper (and a 90-minute drive from SIA). Its central location in the interior makes a good point for many departures. Nearby is a new sports stadium where regional soccer matches are played. The hotel has 40 rooms, RO 30-35 ($77-$90), and one executive suite, RO 120 ($310), fully licensed restaurant, pub, temperature-controlled pool, and gardens. Banquet and conference facilities available. Reserve through the hotel at Nizwa 611; Fax: 968-431619.

Recently refurbished (formerly the Nizwa Motel) the **Falaj Daris Hotel** (Tel. 968-410500) sits only two kilometers away from the center of Nizwa alongside Wadi Ghul. A popular rest stop for travelers to the interior, the hotel offers 25 rooms surrounding a central terrace with a pool. Rooms are RO 21-28 ($54-$72). Restaurant and small banquet hall (75 people). Reserve through the hotel at P.O. Box 312, Nizwa 611; Fax: 968-410537.

Located just past the turnoff to Al Hamra (and Jebel Shams), the **Bahla Motel** (Tel. 968-420211) is a small rest house along the southern flanks of the Western Hajars. Six rooms, RO 17-23 ($44-$60), restaurant, room service. Reserve through the hotel at P.O. Box 375, Madinat Al Sultan Qaboos; Fax: 968-420212.

A 90-kilometer ride up the coast from Muscat will bring you to the **Crowne Plaza Resort Al Sawadi** (Tel. 968-895545), a new installation to draw some of the hotel traffic away from the capital. Perched on the shoreline just opposite the Jazir Sawaidi, a small offshore archipelago, the resort offers a wide variety of services for the vacationers. 100 rooms are available, RO 32-38 ($83-$98), restaurant, pub, snack bar, pool and Jacuzzi, health club and gym, squash and tennis, trips and excursions arranged from diving and water sports to wadi bashing, business and conference facilities. Reserve through the hotel at P.O. Box 747, Barka 320; Fax: 968-895535.

Further up the coast from Sawaidi (120 kilometers from Muscat) is the **Suwaiq Hotel** (Tel. 968-862242), a small rest stop with simple accommodations for interior travelers. Located just two kilometers off the main highway (inland side—keep your eye peeled for a gravel track just past the police station that branches from the main road leading to a royal estate). There are 15 rooms, RO 12-14 ($31-$36), fully licensed restaurant, and pub. Reserve through the hotel at P.O. Box 375, Madinat Al Sultan Qaboos 115; Fax: 968-862243.

The **Sohar Beach Hotel** (Tel. 968-843701) is a new resort in the ancient port city and traditional birthplace of Sindbad. The Sohar boasts luxury class with 40 rooms, chalets, and suites. Rooms go for RO 28-34 ($72-$88), chalets are RO 45 ($116), and suites are RO 62 ($160). Services/facilities include pool and gardens, tennis, gym, Jacuzzi, fully licensed restaurant, snack bar, two pubs, water sports, evening entertainment, treks, and excursions. Reserve through the hotel at P.O. Box 122, Al Tarif 321; Fax: 968-843766.

The **Al Wadi Hotel** (Tel. 968-840058) is in the Al Gassbah section of Sohar. Coming from Muscat, go past the Sohar roundabout and turn back at the next roundabout. The Al Wadi is just off the service road on the inland side. The hotel is a circular structure with 25 rooms and one executive suite facing a central swimming pool and garden. One fully licensed restaurant, two pubs, and conference facilities. A good starting point for those who want to investigate northern Oman on their own. Room rates, RO 23-31 ($54-$80); the suite is RO 52 ($134). Reserve through the hotel at P.O. Box 459, Sohar 311; Fax: 968-841997.

On the interior road to Sur in Mudharib (on your left heading south 175 kilometers from Muscat) the **Al Qabil Rest House** (Tel. 968-481243) is a good stop for exploring places from Ibra to the Wahibah sands, Wadi Tayin (Devil's Gap), and the Jebel Bani Jabir plateau (among others). Simple accommodations, nine rooms, RO 12.6-15.8 ($33-$41). Reserve through the Arab Oryx Rest Houses at P.O. Box 654, Muscat 113; Fax: 968-481119.

Proprietors Said and Abdullah Al Harthy have created a truly memorable experience for their guests at the **Nahar Farm Camp** (Tel. 968-597914 or 957093). For those wanting an authentic Omani experience, a stopover here is a must. It is located just outside Ibra, near Wadi Nahar. Guests stay in palm frond shelters (with modern amenities), are entertained by local singers and dancers at an outdoor barbecue, and are invited to stroll through the farm to see how dates are cultivated. All of this is only RO 15 a night. Reserve through Empty Quarter Tours at P.O. Box 9, Madinat Al Sultan Qaboos 115; Fax: 968-590144.

Home of the shipbuilding center, the **Sur Beach Hotel** (Tel. 968-442031) is located on the beach just northwest of town and near the regions of Ra's Al Hadd (turtle watching), Qalhat, Tiwi, Wadi Shab, Al Kamil, and Al Ashkarah. 52 rooms, RO 25-32 ($65-$83); three suites, RO 51 ($132); and eight executive suites, RO 69 ($178). Fully licensed restaurant, coffee shop, swimming pool, tennis, banquet and conference facilities. Reserve through hotel at P.O. Box 400, Sur 411; Fax: 968-442228.

For the truly adventurous who want to drive to Salalah from Muscat and have time on their hands, there are three **Arab Oryx Rest Houses** along the way, if you don't fancy doing the 10-hour drive in one day. Simple but nice accommodations. There is no other reason to stay at these rest houses other than to be in transit, as the surrounding desert is quite barren and the whole trip is quite monotonous (but the last five minutes of that 10-hour drive is worth the price of admission as you come out of the desert onto the escarpment covered with foliage at 5,000 feet and descend rapidly to Salalah on the coast). All three have 10 rooms, RO 10.5-14.7 ($27-$40), restaurant, and a nearby petrol pump.

Ghaba Rest House. 319 kilometers from Muscat, a 3 1/2-hour drive. Tel./Fax: 968-951385.

Al Ghaftain Resthouse. 626 kilometers from Muscat, a 6 1/2-hour drive. Tel./Fax: 968-956872.

Qitbit Resthouse. 756 kilometers from Muscat, an 8-hour drive. Tel./Fax: 968-951386.

For travelers in transit to or from the UAE or just visiting the northwest section, there is the **Al Buraimi Hotel** (Tel. 968-652010), a luxury class hotel with 36 rooms, RO 43-52 ($111-$134); 20 villas (with kitchenettes) RO 54 ($140) (discount for extended stays, one month or more); and four suites, RO 73 ($188). Facilities include pool, Jacuzzi and sauna, tennis, three restaurants and pub, banquet and conference rooms. Special discounts for groups, business travelers, and corporate. It is located in downtown Buraimi. Reserve through the hotel at P.O. Box 330, Buraimi 512; Fax: 968-652011.

The town of Khasab serves as a home base for travel in the Musandam Peninsula, and the **Khasab Hotel** (Tel. 968-660267) is the only hotel. Transit to Khasab is by plane as the Musandam is separated from the rest of the country by the UAE. Besides offering 13 comfortable rooms, RO 20.8-35.4 ($54-$91), the hotel offers excursions and boat trips to the jebels and fjords of the peninsula. There is a fully licensed restaurant, pub and pool. Reserve through the hotel at P.O. Box 111, Khasab 811; Fax: 968-660989.

5. Dining and Restaurants

It's only natural that Oman's inclination towards cultural diversity is reflected in the variety of cuisine that is available in the country today. Just about any palate can be satisfied and if you like to experiment when you travel, there's no place like Oman. I have eaten at most of the top-name international restaurants and many local cafeterias, cafés, and sidewalk stalls. While most upscale restaurants tend to retain their individual international identity, the smaller bustling shops in the downtown areas tend to merge with types of food predominantly from India, Pakistan, and Sri Lanka. While there is a great opportunity to sample Arabic food (with a mixture of influences from several Middle Eastern countries such as Turkey, Lebanon, etc.), there are few places that serve wholly Omani cuisine, traditional style.

A word about spices, for those who like (or don't like) to walk on the wild side. Omani food is typically very flavorful, owing to Oman's long standing as a hub for the spice trade, but it is *not* the spicy hot food that you find further east in India and Sri Lanka. (Probably Sri Lankan food takes the cake in running off the end of the Scoville unit scale for spiciness. I know because I had a Sri Lankan house boy for two years who cooked for me). If you are in a restaurant or café that serves a spicy rendition of what is presumably Arabic, there's a good chance the cook is Indian or Sri Lankan.

Also a word about pork. Some restaurants *do* sell pork and pork products. For those who have dietary restrictions, these items are marked on menus. If you are unsure, ask a waiter or the maitre d'.

There are a lot of nameless sidewalk cafés and stalls (by that I mean the signs out front usually just say "Restaurant" with the name of the proprietor alongside), particularly in downtown areas and along the highways up the coast and in the interior. Most of them are run by Indians and Pakistanis and they serve sandwiches; falafel (deep fried, ground soy bean patty); samosa (meat or vegetable deep fried in thin-dough pockets); *dhal* (cooked lentils); rice and vegetables; hot drinks (*chai*—tea; coffee); cold drinks (cool, actually, not cold); beef, mutton, or chicken kebabs; whole barbecued chickens (great for picnics if you don't want to cook); and *shwarma,* the Arabic answer to American fast food.

Shwarma is either shaved beef or chicken that is marinated, braised on a spit, then wrapped in a pita pocket with lettuce, tomato, and tahini sauce (made from ground sesame, lemon juice, and spices). Served with optional mixed pickle and chili peppers on the side, for 200 bz (52 cents), McDonald's can't touch 'em.

To complement a shwarma I can't recommend anything better than a glass (served fresh) or container (commercially processed) of *jeera laban.*

Laban (also called *lassi* in the Indian restaurants) is a buttermilk, like yogurt, made from active cultures. *Jeera* is the Arabic word for cumin. Together (mixed with water, salt, and other spices) they make a tantalizingly tasteful drink that I find hard to put down. As you might expect, it is, alas, very rich in calories, so I try to keep it to a minimum, hard as that may be.

One final note about the smaller cafeterias and cafés. They appear rather smoky and dusty from the open fires and the amount of foot traffic. From a decorative standpoint, most of them are pretty plain, with tiled walls and floors, sometimes with a picture or two and colored lights to create a little ambiance in an otherwise pedestrian eatery. But the food is generally well cooked and liberally spiced to satisfy the most demanding, adventurous diner and quell the suspicions of the hygiene-conscious. Also, food is usually served without cutlery as it is common practice in the east—vegetables are mixed with rice and wadded into a ball or wrapped in a piece of bread. Meat is ripped from the bone using one hand. Holding the food on your fingertips, it is then shoved into your mouth using the back of your thumb. When Westerners arrive waiters are only too accommodating as they bring out the knives and forks for you, but if you prefer to join them, feel free: when in Rome, as they say.

If you prefer a more conventional style of service, there are plenty of other places to whet your appetite. Most hotels serve a variety of international cuisine, all of it good. Try as many as you can when you're in town. I think the best way to arrange restaurants is alphabetically by service and ethnic style so it will be easier for the reader to pick his or her fancy. If you don't find a particular style under the specific heading, check the international heading. Average prices are per head, approximation only, drinks and taxes excluded. Directions from the Sultan Qaboos Highway (SQH) are given as required.

Also, some places may be crowded on Wednesday and Thursday nights, so you might want to call ahead.

AFRICAN

Mombasa (Tel. 694340). The Mombasa is a little nook in a block of stores in a back road of Al Khuwair. The Omani owner creates a delightful spread of East African food, but it is difficult to pinpoint as the menu changes from day to day. If you know what you want in advance, order ahead! From the Al Khuwair roundabout (SQH), turn right at the MQ stoplight. This is Dohat Al Adab Street. Follow the road as it bears right after one kilometer and dips down into a steep wadi bed and up again. After the Shell station and around a bend, take your first left and after another two kilometers, the road becomes divided at about the same time you will see a block of shops on your left. The Mombasa is tucked in right next to Golden Threads. You will have to double back at the next roundabout to get there. RO 3 ($7.70)

Maskat Al Miskiria (Zanzibarian/Indian) (Tel. 700950). Behind British

Bank of the Middle East (BBME) and adjacent to Star Cinema on the slip road. This little snack shop has an awful lot of heart poured into it by the proprietress. She currently represents the only Zanzibarian cuisine that I know of served in the country. It is so unpretentious you might miss it, but try not to. Right now, until a better location is found, this shop is sitting behind the big banks in the Central Business District and is only open for breakfast and lunch (hours from 7 A.M. to 2 P.M.). So go early, go often. RO 1 ($2.60).

AMERICAN

Al Inshirah (Arabic, Thai, Indian, American)—see International section
Blue Cactus (Tel. 605979). It's new and it's blue and wow! what a view. Sitting upon the Qurum waterfall hilltop and downstairs from sister restaurant Mumtaz Mahal, the Blue Cactus has a delightful array of foods and drink, live band, and wide-screen TV for sporting-event viewing. RO 8 ($20)
John Barry Bar (Tel. 602888). For those who can't get enough of *Titanic,* the John Barry should fit the bill. Re-creating a sunken ship (that actually sank off the coast of Oman during World War II) and complete with a mysterious legend of a lost cache of silver making its way to the Soviet Union (and Joseph Stalin's coffers), the John Barry gives a sense of life in the briny deep if only you could manage a piano bar. In the Hyatt Regency. RO 8 ($20)
Musandam Café (American, French, Italian)—see International section
Muscateers (Tel. 691014). Good ol'-fashioned steakhouse where you can select your cut and watch it sizzle. Located in the new Zakher Mall in Al Khuwair. RO 10 ($26)
OK Corral (Tel. 600500). Outdoor setting at the Muscat Intercon in Shati Al Qurum, wooden tables, wagon wheels, and other Wild West decor set the scene in this not-quite-so-border town. Extensive menu of Western fare. Select your cut of meat or seafood and see it grilled on the spot. Live Country and Western music round off this round up. Every evening except Tuesday. Closed during the summer. Fully licensed. RO 6 ($15.50)

ARABIAN

Alauddin (Arabian, Indian, Chinese, Continental)—see International section
Al Badiyeh (Arabian, Indian, Chinese)—see International section
Copper Chimney (Arabian Tuesday nights only, Indian)—see Indian section
Ali Baba (Tel. 708515). Located near the Wadi Adai roundabout and across the highway from Al Nahdha Hospital in Al Hamriya. Arabic with a touch of Egyptian fare. Specializes in Lebanese sweetmeats and pastries. Grills, salads, and Arabian-style pizza, too. RO 2 ($5.30)

Al Hamasa (Tel. 652010). At the Buraimi Hotel. Fine Arabic food and live entertainment. Licensed. RO 5 ($12.90)

Al Inshirah (Arabian, Thai, Indian, American)—see International section

Al Shatti'a (Arabian, Indian, Chinese)—see International section

Arabic Oven (Arabian, Indian)—see International section

Layali Zaman (Tel. 684324). Located beneath the new Club Stadium in Al Khuwair. Nice mix of Jordanian and Tunisian dishes. Grills, kebabs, sandwiches, falafel. Good stop for lunch or a late night snack. Follow the Al Khuwair middle road (Dohat Al Adab Street) west to the stadium or east from Bausher roundabout. RO 1.5 ($3.90)

Sadaf Oman (Arabian, Omani, Turkish, Iranian) (Tel. 792860). On the slip road between the Al Hamriya and Ruwi Roundabout. Cheery decoration and ceiling mosaics using the national colors, tiled columns, and a pleasant wait staff greet you at the door. The meals are very moderately priced and the selection is broad. (I like the Turkish Chicken.) Finish off with fresh juices and Omani sweets and you will have one fine evening. They also cater to parties, serving up a plate called "uzzi," which is a whole roasted sheep (mutton) stuffed with rice and nuts and served with salads and sweets. RO 3 ($7.70); uzzi (for parties of 10-20) is RO 55 ($142).

Sindbad Restaurant (Arabian and Chinese) (Tel. 713142). Along the Mutrah Corniche in the Al Nahdha Hotel, Mutrah. RO 3.5 ($9)

BAKERIES

Perhaps a word should be said about the fabulous bakeries that dot the landscape. If you have a sweet tooth, you shouldn't miss out on the tantalizing sweets that they produce. The types range all across Arabia to India. They are all delicious and, unfortunately, incredibly filling. Stop by a bakery and stock up before you take that long trek to the interior.

Al Bustan Bakery, LLC (Tel. 705376), Wadi Kabir

Al Fawaris Bakery (Tel. 705345), Ruwi

Al Lublab Bakery and Sweets (Tel. 703395), Al Hamriya

Al Mina Bakery (Tel. 714084), Mutrah

Cinderella Sweets (Tel. 565419) (and candy, too!), next to SABCO Centre, Qurum

Jenny's Bakery (Tel. 590340), Ghala

Modern Oman Bakery (Tel. 704411/708356), Ruwi; (Tel. 411776), Nizwa; (Tel. 893791), Rumais; (Tel. 622904), Seeb; (Tel. 841398), Sohar

Muscat Bakery (Tel. 590203), Ghala; (Tel. 600517), Al Khuwair, near Zawawi Mosque; (Tel. 697902), Al Khuwair, near Wang Computer

The Patisserie—see Cafés and Coffee Shops section

Star Bakery (Tel. 707691), Ruwi

Zambaq Bakery (Tel. 703814), Ruwi

CAFÉS AND COFFEE SHOPS

Al Bustan Café (Tel. 799666, ext. 4501). At the Al Bustan Palace Hotel, a coffee shop with an à la carte menu, dinner, snacks, and Omani specialties. Casual venue with evening entertainment. Theme nights (call ahead). RO 10 ($26)

Arosa of Switzerland (Tel. 560439). This little shop on the lower level of the new Al Khamis Plaza in Qurum (across from SABCO Centre) has a broad selection of coffees, teas, and fresh juices. Sandwiches and croissants, cakes and pastries. RO 3 ($7.70)

Atrium Tea Lounge (Tel. 799666). At the Al Bustan Palace Hotel. Traditional high tea is served daily with live music. RO 3.9 ($10)

Birkit Al Mawz (Tel. 431616). Casual fare (Oriental and continental cuisine) at the smartly designed coffee shop in the new Nizwa Hotel. Licensed. RO 3 ($7.70)

Le Bistro (Tel. 565358). Across the street from SABCO Centre, Qurum. French café serving sandwiches, crepes, salads, sorbets, desserts, and exotic fruit drinks. RO 4.5 ($11.60)

Le Café De France (Tel. 560337). Located in the Al Harthy Complex in Wattayeh (just across the highway from the SABCO Centre), the café offers a broad variety of imported teas and coffees with delicate pastries and sweets. RO 2 ($5.20)

Café De Muscat (Tel. 602757). In the Oasis by the Sea, Shati Al Qurum, next to the Intercon. A French café with an Arabic touch offering quiches, salads, desserts, international coffees, and teas. Licensed. Turn left from the car park facing the beach. RO 2.5 ($6.50)

Cote Jardin (Tel. 510300 ext. 261). Variety of international cuisines at the Seeb Novotel. Daily specials. Licensed. RO 6 ($15.50)

Le Croissant (Tel. 799899). Coffees, breads, and pastries in the Sheraton Oman Hotel.

Dayvilles (Tel. 563943). In SABCO Centre, Qurum. Ice creams, ices, juices, and plenty of other refreshing drinks to quench one's thirst after a hard day of souvenir shopping. 500 bz ($1.30)

Glacier. Set in the Capital Commercial Centre (CCC) Qurum. Coffees, teas, homemade ice cream, milk shakes, yogurt, Belgian waffles, pancakes, and a raft of snacks. 800 bz ($2)

Hala. Sandwiches, snacks, and juices also in CCC, Qurum. RO 1.5 ($3.90)

Lebanese Roastery (Tel. 686617). Fine blends of coffee and delicious pastries in this new shop in Al Khuwair near the Bombay and SABCO Centre. RO 2 ($5)

The Patisserie (Tel. 698423), Shati Al Qurum; (Tel. 562319), SABCO Centre, Qurum; (Tel. 566137), Wattayeh; (Tel. 521234), Rusail Commercial

Centre; (Tel. 563001), Al Wadi Commercial Centre, Qurum. French pastries and sweets, Arabic sweets, coffees, and teas.

Le Rendezvous (Tel. 567414). Sandwiches, salads, and coffees with that Parisian touch. New in the Alasfoor complex near SABCO Centre. RO 5 ($13)

Sallan Coffee Shop (Tel. 843701). Sohar Beach Hotel, Sohar. Omani dishes, international cuisine, BBQ. Licensed. RO 6 ($15.50)

Sohar Snack Bar (Tel. 600500). At the Muscat Intercon, Shati Al Qurum. Light salads and snacks, outdoor poolside settings, palm gardens. Friday afternoons: Mongolian Barbecue. RO 5 ($12.90)

Vienna Café (Tel. 697123). Teas, coffees, cakes and pastries in the lobby of the Muscat Holiday Inn, Al Khuwair. RO 2 ($5.20)

CHINESE

Al Akhtam (Indian, Chinese, Filipino)—see International section

Alauddin (Arabian, Indian, Chinese, Continental)—see International section

Al Badiyeh (Arabian, Indian, Chinese)—see International section

Al Bashasha (Indian, Chinese)—see International section

Al Dehleez (Indian, Chinese)—see International section

Al Hooti (Indian, Chinese)—see International section

Al Shatti'a (Arabian, Indian, Chinese)—see International section

Arabian Garden (Omani, Indian, Pakistani, Chinese)—see International section

Chinese Garden (Szechwan, Cantonese, Mandarin) (Tel. 605414). Another restaurant that prides itself on authenticity, the Chinese Garden is near the ice skating rink across from the government ministries in Al Khuwair. Take the slip road from the Al Khuwair roundabout past Al Jadeeda Stores. Once inside you'll find a bright and roomy atmosphere with good service. RO 3 ($7.70)

Dragon Chinese Restaurant (Szechwan, Cantonese, Mandarin) (Tel. 702311). Inside the newly renovated Mercure Al Falaj Hotel, excellent food with excellent service (but the Peking Duck must be ordered 24 hours in advance). Licensed. RO 7 ($18)

The Food Corner (Indian, Chinese)—see International section

Four Foods Restaurant (Indian, Chinese, Pakistani, Continental)—see International section

Golden Dragon (Tel. 697374). The Golden Dragon was always a good haunt for me when it was in Qurum, but it moved to Madinat Al Sultan Qaboos (just a few klicks down the road) and still managed to improve on a good thing. Set in the gardens of the Madinat Al Sultan Qaboos Shopping Centre (behind Al Fair Supermarket), the pleasant atmosphere, soft lights, and colors from back-lit aquariums and unusual stained glass in the ceiling set a nice tone. Great food for the price. Nice for a long relaxed evening. Licensed. RO 9 ($23)

Golden Chopsticks (Tel. 697374.) MQ Shopping Centre, Madinat Al Sultan Qaboos. Take out/dine in. Broad selection. RO 1.5 ($3.90)

Golden Oryx—see Mongolian section

Golden Spoon (Indian, Chinese)—see International section

Grand Restaurant (Indian, Chinese)—see International section

Kairaly (Indian, Chinese)—see International section

Omar Khayyam (Indian, Chinese)—see International section

Princes (Indian, Chinese)—see International section

Red Lobster (Indian, Chinese)—see International section

Saj (Arabian, Indian, Chinese)—see International section

Taj (Indian, Chinese)—see International section

Shangri-La (Chinese and Mongolian BBQ) (Tel. 791095). The Shangri-La is hard to get to but it is worth it. If you are coming from Ruwi to Mutrah Al Kubra, you will see the Shangri-La with big circular doors on your left, up the hill only 500 meters in from the highway. But since the street is divided you have to travel on for another kilometer before you find a tricky turn-around (around a block of flats) to make your way back. Or take a cab. Once inside, the food is good and prices reasonable. Licensed. Private rooms available. RO 7 ($18)

Silk Route (Tel. 561741). Behind SABCO Centre, Qurum. If you're trekking to the interior on your own, this might be a good one for take out. Vegetarian and business lunches available. RO 5 ($12.90)

Silver Spoon (Indian, Chinese, Filipino)—see International section

Summer Sands (Indian, Chinese)—see International section

ENGLISH

The sun never sets on the British Empire, as long as there is a pub open nearby. Muscat has three of the finest:

Al Ghazal (Tel. 600500). Muscat Intercon, Shati Al Qurum. RO 3 ($7.70)

Churchill's Pub (Tel. 697123). Muscat Holiday Inn, Al Khuwair. RO 2.5 ($6.40)

Duke's Bar (Tel. 560100). Crowne Hotel, Qurum Heights. RO 3 ($7.70)

Periwinkle's (Tel. 895545). Traditional pub food at the Crowne Plaza Resort Al Sawadi, Sawaidi. RO 8 ($21)

FAST FOOD

What is there to say about fast food except that it is . . . well, fast. The invasion of the franchises has happened in Oman and, just like back home, you don't need to find them, they find you.

2-4-1 Pizza (Tel. 700241). Near Al Falaj roundabout, Ruwi.

Arab World (Tel. 591734), Ghala; (Tel. 637097), Khaburah; (Tel. 785375), Wadi Kabir (Ruwi); (Tel. 798119), Ruwi; (Tel. 411308), Nizwa; (Tel. 297445), Salalah

Baskin and Robbins (Tel. 788984), Ruwi; (Tel. 698721), Madinat Al Sultan Qaboos; (Tel. 563543), CCC, Qurum; (Tel. 698564), Shati Al Qurum; (Tel. 600467), Al Khuwair

BBQ Chicken Tikka (Tel. 798313). Near Ruwi roundabout, Ruwi

Burger King (Tel. 602777), Al Khuwair; (Tel. 565819), Qurum; (Tel. 519049), SIA; (Tel. 563771), Wattayeh

Fuddrucker's (Tel. 568618). A gourmet's fast food. Generous servings in all their dishes. Salad bar with lots of fixin's. Next to the CCC Complex in Qurum. RO 5 ($13)

Golden Chopsticks—See Chinese section

Hardee's (Tel. 564642). Qurum

Kentucky Fried Chicken (Tel. 564641), Qurum; (Tel. 792616), Ruwi; (Tel. 698110), Madinat Al Sultan Qaboos

McDonald's (Tel. 565798), CCC, Qurum; (Tel. 691033), Shati Al Qurum

Penguin (Tel. 701995), Ruwi; (Tel. 601197), Shati Al Qurum; (Tel. 510408), near SIA; (Tel. 622004), Seeb; (Tel. 840585), Sohar; (Tel. 225380), Salalah

Pizza Express (Tel. 603400), MQ Shopping Centre, Madinat Al Sultan Qaboos

Pizza Hut (Tel. 791287), CBD, Mutrah; (Tel. 566533), CCC, Qurum; (Tel. 693564), MQ Shopping Centre, Madinat Al Sultan Qaboos; (Tel. 521122), near SIA; (Tel. 693562), Al Khuwair; (Tel. 542951), Al Khodh; (Tel. 412096), Nizwa; (Tel. 844513), Sohar; (Tel. 737254), Qalboo Park, Mutrah Corniche; (Tel. 290303), Salalah (New branches opening on Ruwi High Street, Ruwi, and Ghala.)

Pizzaland (Tel. 602609), Qurum; also Al Khuwair (Zakher Mall) and Shati Al Qurum

Sajwani (Arabian, Lebanese) (Tel. 562877), behind SABCO Centre, Qurum

Scoops (Tel. 699052). In Jawaharat A'Shati Commercial Complex (near Intercon), Shati Al Qurum. Old-fashioned ice cream parlor serving shakes, sundaes, wild flavors.

Sindbad's (Indian, Chinese) (Tel. 707600), opposite Mansoor Ali Centre, Ruwi

Teejans (Indian, Chinese) (Tel. 510120), near MAM roundabout, Rusail; (Tel. 431694), near Firq roundabout, Nizwa; (Tel. 620604), Seeb

Texas Chicken (Tel. 700175), near Ruwi Roundabout, Ruwi

FILIPINO

Al Akhtam (Indian, Chinese, Filipino)—see International section

Barrio Fiesta (Tel. 592900). Upstairs in the Majan Hotel in Ghala, next to the Royal Hospital. A Filipino splash of color, food, and entertainment. Live band, fixed menu—buffet style, one price (excluding drinks), RO 2.5 ($6.40)

Payalok Restaurant (Tel. 796005). Completely redone and completely Filipino with seafoods and salads and breakfast (on Fridays only). Near the Ruwi roundabout across from the OC Centre. RO 3 ($7.70)

Happy Village Restaurant—see Thai section

Silver Spoon (Indian, Chinese, Filipino)—see International section

FRENCH

Al Madina (Tel. 696515). In the Madinat Al Sultan Qaboos Shopping Center, MQ. Elegant by any standard (no French fries!). À la carte, business menus. Check for outdoor buffet (in season) and other specials (Ladies' night, Sun. and Tues.). Live entertainment. Licensed. RO 10 ($26)

Cork's Bistro (Tel. 702311 ext. 550). In the newly renovated Mercure Al Falaj Hotel, Ruwi. Excellent à la carte or set menu with a good selection of French wines. RO 5.5 ($14.20)

Le Bistro—see Cafés and Coffee Shops section

La Brasserie (Tel. 799899). Fine French cuisine in the Sheraton Oman. à la carte, business menus. Licensed. RO 7 ($18)

Al Marjan (Haute cuisine) (Tel. 799666). Al Bustan Palace Hotel. Luxurious dining at its best. Expensive . . . uh, that should read, extensive wine list. À la carte and "Menu Gastronomique." Live entertainment. RO 15 ($39)

Musandam Café (American, French, Italian)—see International section

Qurm Restaurant (Tel. 600500). At the Muscat Intercon, Shati Al Qurum. À la carte menu and table d'hôte. Business lunch. Piano accompanist. Fully licensed. RO 13 ($33.50)

GREEK/CYPRIOT

Bellapais (Tel. 521100). Just outside the capital area near the MAM roundabout sits a quiet restaurant, unfortunately, the only Greek restaurant in Oman at the present time. The food is wonderful and the atmosphere is straight from the Aegean. It's a nice stop after a long day's trek from the interior. Terrific Greek mezza, flambé, salads, seafoods, grill. Licensed. RO 7 ($18)

INDIAN

Al Akhtam (Indian, Chinese, Filipino)—see International section

Alauddin (Arabian, Indian, Chinese, Continental)—see International section

Al Badiyeh (Arabian, Indian, Chinese)—see International section

Al Bahr (Tel. 711828). In the Mina Hotel, Mutrah Corniche. A variety of Indian styles, vegetarian and non-veg. Continental food as well. Licensed. RO 3 ($7.70)

Al Bashasha (Indian, Chinese)—see International section
Al Dehleez (Indian, Chinese)—see International section
Al Hooti (Indian, Chinese)—see International section
Al Khodh (Tel. 626710). Rusail Hotel, Rusail. South Indian buffet and live entertainment. Licensed. RO 2 ($5.20)
Al Safina (Tel. 711828). In the Mina Hotel, Mutrah Corniche. Fine food and classical Indian entertainment. RO 3 ($7.70)
Al Shatti'a (Arabian, Indian, Chinese)—see International section
Ambassador (Vegetarian) (Tel. 708082), Ruwi; (Tel. 794414) Mutrah Al Kubra, opp. Khimji General Store. Nice selection of Indian vegetarian delights, desserts. RO 1.5 ($3.90)
Arabian Garden (Omani, Indian, Pakistani, Chinese)—see International section
Arabic Oven (Arabian, Indian)—see International section
Bombay—Filmi Gana aur Khana (Tel. 685889). Oman is probably not ready for Planet Hollywood, but that's OK if you've got a Planet Bollywood . . . or the closest thing to it. Fine Indian and Chinese cuisine and nightly entertainment. Live singers and dancers perform your favorite Hindi film classics. Upstairs is the Casablanca Room—same setup but with Arabian themes, music, and dancers. In Al Khuwair on Al Khulliyah Street near the souq. RO 4 ($10)
Copper Chimney (Tel. 706420). Located in the Fairtrade House in the Central Business District, Ruwi. One of my favorite spots, with a warm cozy setting, excellent food, and soft Indian music. The Tandoori is just perfect. Mughlai is also superb. (Tuesday night only—Omani cuisine.) RO 6 ($15.50)
Curry House (Punjabi) (Tel. 564033). Located across from the auto showrooms in Wattayeh (take the turnoff from the highway eastbound and double back). Authentic cuisine and costumes and a budget-conscious price. Note: Please don't touch the elephant. RO 3 ($7.70)
Dalila Restaurant (Tel. 699151). Next to the Shell petrol pump coming into Al Khuwair. Sister to the Kairaly in Ruwi, quick Indian and Chinese fare, good for a late snack or on return from a day's trekking. RO 2 ($5.20)
The Food Corner (Indian, Chinese)—see International section
Four Foods Restaurant (Indian, Chinese, Pakistani, Continental)—see International section
Ghasitaram Halwai (Punjabi) (Tel. 793232), Opposite Makha Business Centre, Ruwi; (Tel. 699880) near Sur Centre, Al Khuwair. North Indian vegetarian cuisine, Indian sweets, snacks, and savories. RO 1.5 ($3.90)
Ghungroo (Tel. 592900). Companion to the Fiesta Barrios in the Majan Hotel (see above), also set menu—buffet style, but the accent is on India with live entertainment straight from the continent. RO 2.5 ($6.40) excluding drinks

Golden Spoon (Indian, Chinese)—see International section
Grand Restaurant (Indian, Chinese)—see International section
Halwan Trading (Vegetarian) (700602). Located in the inner plaza of the Sharp building. Nice selection of vegetarian foods and sweets at this unassuming shop in the middle of Ruwi High Street. RO 1.5 ($3.90)
Kairaly (Indian, Chinese)—see International section
Kalhat (Tel. 790666). Makha Hotel, Wadi Kabir. Live entertainment. Licensed. RO 4 ($10.30)
Moghul (Moghlai, Tandoori) (Tel. 562338). Pleasant Indian venue on the auto showroom slip road, Wattayeh. Licensed. RO 4 ($10.30)
Mumtaz Mahal (Tel. 563850). Recently moved to the waterfall hilltop in Qurum. No less grand than its namesake, the Mumtaz Mahal is a must for Indian food lovers. Authentic decor, terrific food with live music Sunday and Thursday. Tuesday is surprise night with a four-course meal. Licensed. RO 8 ($20.60)
Omar Khayyam (Indian, Chinese)—see International section
Passage to India (Tel. 568480). This could very well be what E. M. Forster had in mind. Elegant dining and fine classical entertainment straight from the Continent. The tandoor kitchen is on display too. Behind the Hatat House in Wattayah. RO 10 ($26)
Pegasus (Indian, Thai)—see International section
Red Lobster (Indian, Chinese)—see International section
Ruwi Restaurant (Tel. 794458). The Ruwi and its offspring, the Kairaly (see International), claim to be one and two on the list of oldest restaurants in the city, going back to the accession of Sultan Qaboos. Still serving up the best of South Indian (and some Chinese) cuisine, these two do a hearty business in the downtown area just off Ruwi High Street near the Sabir Supermarket. RO 2 ($5.20)
Saj (Arabian, Indian, Chinese)—see International section
Samarkand (Tel. 602757). The Indian room attached to the Oasis by the Sea. (See International section). Northwest Frontier cuisine. Licensed. RO 8 ($20.60)
Silver Spoon (Indian, Chinese, Filipino)—see International section
Summer Sands (Indian, Chinese)—see International section
Taj (Indian, Chinese)—see International section
Tandoori Bahar (Tel. 895545). Fine Indian dining at the Crowne Plaza Resort Al Sawadi, Sawaidi. RO 8 ($21)
Venus (Tel. 709035). A quiet retreat amidst the bustle of Ruwi High Street. Curries, biryanis, tandoor, masalas, chattinad . . . the list goes on and you will have trouble making up your mind at this authentic Indian restaurant. Not only is the food great, it is a great buy as well. RO 2.5 ($6.40)

Woodlands (Vegetarian and meat dishes) (Tel. 700192). Central business district alongside Wadi Kabir. The Woodlands changed hands a couple of years ago and added meat dishes to their all-vegetarian menu, probably to entice us carnivores into the shop to see what we were missin'. But I already knew (carnivore that I am) that they have some of the best vegetarian dishes in the Sultanate, and I'm still going back. Licensed. RO 5 ($12.90)

INTERNATIONAL (VARIETY)

Al Akhtam (Indian, Chinese, Filipino) (Tel. 603292). Al Akhtam is a quiet place set back from Dohat Al Adab Street in Al Khuwair. (Take the Al Khuwair roundabout and make a sharp right to Al Jadeeda Stores, where you take a left, then right at the stoplight up ahead. Just a few hundred meters on, you will see Al Akhtam on the left next to a small grocery.) Good variety of food with semi-private booths upstairs. RO 3 ($7.70)

Al Badiyeh (Arabian, Indian, Chinese) (Tel. 736068). Behind the British Bank of the Middle East (BBME) in Muscat proper. There's a bit of mystique at this cozy shop in the heart of the old city near the Royal Palace. Getting there is half the fun, twisting down the winding streets of Muscat. Don't blink, you'll miss it! Small parking lot nearby. RO 4 ($10.32)

Al Bashasha (Indian, Chinese) (Tel. 625314). For a little drive out of town, if you like to explore, there's a nice new stop just along the wadi's edge close to the shore in Seeb. The Al Bashasha is nice and dark inside for deep reflective moods complemented by stirring cuisine. Try the Jade Chicken or Prawn Methi. Licensed. Take the highway to the Seeb roundabout (also called the Qur'an roundabout) and turn right. At the next roundabout turn right again, then left where the wadi crosses the road. Al Bashasha is 100 meters ahead on the right. RO 5 ($12.90)

Al Dehleez (Indian, Chinese) (Tel. 793545). On Al Iskan Street in the Sultan Building. Fine dining and local entertainment highlight this establishment. Choice of Northern Indian foods and delicacies. Licensed. RO 2.5 ($6.40)

Al Falaj Coffee Shop (Tel. 702311). Mercure Al Falaj Hotel, Ruwi. À la carte and daily buffet lunch. Theme nights with live entertainment (Wednesday is Maghrebian Couscous night). RO 6 ($15.48)

Al Hooti (Indian, Chinese) (Tel. 680334). Located on the Dohat Al Adab Street just up the street from Al Akhtam Restaurant and between two closely spaced roundabouts. This is one of my favorite spots, for the shwarma and barbecued chicken. RO 2 ($5.20)

Al Inshirah (Arabian, Thai, Indian, American) (Tel. 714271). An idyllic location on a point overlooking Mutrah Harbor and just below Riyam Park, Al Inshirah offers exotic cuisine, excellent Thai seafood, evening dhow cruises, and a recently opened American West theme ranch. Fully licensed. RO 10 (26)

Al Khiran Terrace (Seafood) (Tel. 799666 ext. 4801). Al Bustan Palace Hotel. Sumptuous daily buffets overlooking the gardens at Al Bustan. Evenings are theme nights (call ahead). Live entertainment. Fully licensed. RO 10 ($26)

Al Maha (International buffet, BBQ) (Tel. 697123). Muscat Holiday Inn. Theme nights, all you can eat BBQ, special offers for families. Licensed. RO 7.5 ($19.40)

Al Rasagh (Indian, Chinese, and Continental) (Tel. 442031). At the Sur Beach Hotel, Sur. RO 3 ($7.70)

Al Sallan (Indian and Chinese) (Tel. 840058). Al Wadi Hotel, Sohar. Live entertainment to complement the meal. RO 5 ($12.90)

Al Shatti'a (Arabian, Indian, Chinese) (Tel. 714636). Located in the Corniche Hotel, Mutrah. Excellent views of the harbor are the backdrop for this fine little restaurant. RO 3 ($7.70)

Al Zafran (Tel. 843701). Sohar Beach Hotel, Sohar. Mixed grill and seafood. À la carte menu. Licensed. ($15.50) RO 6

Alauddin (Arabian, Indian, Chinese, Continental) (Tel. 600667). From the Al Khuwair roundabout, it is half a kilometer to the MQ stoplight. Alauddin is on your right, before the light, but the entrance is 100 meters after a right turn at the light. This is one of the most popular restaurants in Oman. I'm constantly bumping into people I know when I go there. The food is excellent, the variety extensive, and the ambiance pleasant. The owners have taken great effort to give quality food at agreeable prices. (Try the sizzlers!) The same people also operate the Omar Khayyam in Ruwi and the recently opened Golden Spoon in Seeb. All are exceptional. RO 3 ($7.70)

Arabian Garden (Omani, Indian, Pakistani, Chinese) (Tel. 538932). On the slip road between Al Hail and Seeb. An unusual setting, popular among the Omanis, the Arabian Garden features outdoor eating in a palm garden, a zoo full of exotic birds, monkeys, deer, and rabbits, a playground, billiards and snooker parlor, and bingo on Thursday nights. At some point you can get around to the food, which is an international hodgepodge of dishes at reasonable prices. RO 3 ($7.70)

Arabic Oven (Arabian, Indian) (Tel. 797276). Bright outdoor setting next to the Star Cinema in Ruwi, Arabic Oven has many tasty meat and vegetable dishes, burgers and pizzas inside at the Sultan Supermarket, grills and BBQs outside. RO 2 ($5.20)

Beach Pavilion (Seafood and salads) (Tel. 799666). Al Bustan Palace Hotel. Hot and cold snacks, sandwiches, grills, daily specials, dinner (in season only). RO 8 ($20.60)

Blue Marlin (Tel. 737940). On the upper deck . . . excuse me . . . top floor of the Marina Bander Al-Rowdha, just south of Muscat near Al Bustan. Fine choices of French, Asian, and English foods available. RO 10 ($26)

Car Park (International theme nights) (Tel. 600500). At the Muscat Intercon. Outdoor eatery in the Palm Gardens, not the car park itself. Lush setting and exotic foods. RO 10 ($26)

Coral Reef (Tel. 895545). At the Crowne Plaza Resort Al Sawadi, Sawaidi. RO 8 ($21)

Four Foods Restaurant (Indian, Chinese, Pakistani, Continental) (Tel. 709548). Actually, a lot more than four, a good sampling of several cuisines in this cozy walk-down across the street from the Ministry of Commerce and Industry in Ruwi (near the Sheraton Oman). Try the biryanis if you like Indian. Licensed. RO 2.5 ($6.40)

Gazebo (Tel. 798401). Mutrah Hotel, Mutrah Al Kubra. Great surf 'n' turf menu including lobster thermidor and grilled steaks, flambé desserts, and salad bar. Licensed. RO 5 ($13)

Golden Spoon (Indian, Chinese) (Tel. 624214). Run by the owners of Omar Khayyam and Alauddin, with all the highlights of both, in the middle of downtown Seeb, Seeb High Street (watch for the signs on your left!). After dinner visit the souq or stroll on the beach nearby. RO 2.5 ($6.40)

Grand Restaurant (Indian, Chinese) (Tel. 783769, 590951). Two branches: 1) near Wadi Kabir Roundabout next to Modern Oman Bakery; 2) Ghala near the Ghala Roundabout. New entry serving a variety of Indian styles, north and south, with vegetarian and rice dishes, Chinese (Manchurian) too. Eat in or take away. RO 2 ($5.20)

Green Mountain (Tel. 799899). Sheraton Oman Hotel, Ruwi. International specialties. Every night is theme night from vegetarian (RO 5, $12.90) to Thai (RO 7.5, $19.40) to Neptune's Kingdom (RO 10.5 ($27.20). Everything is at its culinary finest. Fully licensed.

Istrahat Al Seeb Restaurant (Indian, Chinese, Arabic) (Tel. 620916). Adjoining a hotel on the slip road between Al Hail and Seeb. Awaiting licensing at time of writing.

Kairaly (Indian, Chinese) (Tel. 703390). Off Ruwi High Street, downtown Ruwi. From my understanding, the second oldest restaurant in Oman, but still fresh with Southern Indian style and Chinese cuisine. RO 2.5 ($6.40)

Khaboura Café (Tel. 592900). Majan Hotel, next to Royal Hospital. À la carte and daily buffet dinner. Live entertainment. Licensed. RO 5 ($12.90)

Musandam Café (American, French, Italian) (Tel. 600500). At the Muscat Intercon, Shati Al Qurum. Specialty nights, good variety, and elegant dining. Licensed. RO 8 ($20.60)

Muscat Par 19 (Continental) (Tel. 510300). Seeb Novotel, near SIA. Exclusive dining and bar, live band, and theme nights: "Cuisine World News," "Break the Can," "Soirée Provencale," etc. RO 8.5 ($21.90)

The Oasis by the Sea (Tel. 602757). In Shati Al Qurum near the Muscat

Intercon. International chefs, radiant beach setting, and an elegant dining experience are all part of the Oasis by the Sea. Catering and parties, live entertainment, kids' specials. RO 6 ($15.50)

Omar Khayyam (Indian, Chinese) (Tel. 703035). The original Alauddin. Tucked into a cozy corner near the Ruwi roundabout. Great variety and great prices. RO 3 ($7.70)

Pegasus (Indian, Thai) (Tel. 786352). Newly opened in the Sultan building on Al Iskan Street, the Pegasus is delightful. A glittering setting with fountains and arbors, excellent service backed by international chefs, tantalizing food, and live music. Good family restaurant. Licensed. RO 3.5 ($9)

Princes (Indian, Chinese) (Tel. 602213). Just off the Al Khuwair slip road adjacent to Zawawi Mosque. One of my most memorable Arabian experiences was to have dinner at the Princes and to hear one of the more accomplished muezzeins call the faithful from the minaret of the Zawawi Mosque next door. The sound echoed rapturously in the distance from the jebels and then dissipated into silence. This is as romantic as it gets, as all the mystiques of the Middle East coalesce and engulf the traveler. Oh . . . and the food is good, too. RO 2.5 ($6.40)

Qurum Beach Tourism Resort (Seafood) (Tel. 605945). Behind the Muscat Intercon. The feature of the restaurant is the fresh fish market where you can select your entree and watch it cooked. Thai chef adds an Oriental touch. Other dishes available. Fully licensed. RO 10 ($26)

Red Lobster (Indian, Chinese) (Tel. 591993). Just off the highway between Ghubrah and Ghala roundabouts, westbound, behind the Al Maha petrol pump. Not the American chain restaurant, this is a comfortable dining spot, softly lit with deep colored woods. Tandoori cuisine, seafood, and continental. Licensed. RO 3.5 ($9)

Regatta (Tel. 895545). At the Crowne Plaza Resort, Sawaidi. RO 8 ($21)

Saj (Arabic, Indian, Chinese) (Tel. 790852). Music and dance. Buffet upstairs, fine dining downstairs. Good selection but hard to find. Take Bait Al Falaj Street from the Sheraton towards the Al Bustan. Turn right at the lights (Honda Road) after the BP petrol pump and your immediate first left. The Saj is almost at the end of the street on your right. Licensed. RO 3 ($7.70)

Salil Restaurant (Tel. 790666). Arabic, continental, Chinese, and Indian fare in the Makha Hotel. Licensed. RO 3 ($7.70)

Seeb Coffee Shop (Tel. 798401). Mutrah Hotel, Mutra Al Kubra. Arabic and international menu. Licensed. RO 4 ($10.30)

Silver Spoon (Indian, Chinese, Filipino) (Tel. 698843). Just off the slip road, near the Shell pump, adjacent to the Sur Centre in Al Khuwair. A bevy of delights in this one, not quite off the beaten path. Take-out is great for picnics. RO 3 ($7.70)

Summer Sands (Indian, Chinese) (Tel. 791175). Behind Sana Fashions in Wadi Kabir. No need to dust your shoes off here, the Summer Sands has a clean, inviting, and pleasant atmosphere. Live entertainment and good food. Licensed. Take Bait Al Falaj Street from the Sheraton to the incense burner roundabout, exit to your left and take your next right. Follow the slip road (Wadi Kabir Street). RO 2.5 ($6.40)

Taj (Indian, Chinese) (Tel. 796880). On Mutrah High Street on your right going towards Mutrah. One of the older establishments in Muscat, the Taj has a long reputation for excellent dining in authentic settings (try the Chinese Room). Facilities for parties, family rooms, take-out. Licensed. RO 7 ($18)

Tropicana (Tel. 560100). International theme nights at the Crowne Plaza Hotel Muscat in Qurum from Arabian and Lebanese to Italian and Indonesian. Buffet lunches. Fully licensed. RO 6 ($15.50)

Tropicana Club (Tel. 652010). Continental, Tandoori, special family lunches at the Buraimi Hotel. Fully licensed. RO 8 ($20)

IRANIAN

Iranian (Tel. 696169). The Iranian is back, in a new home in the food court at the Zakher Mall in Al Khuwair. RO 5 ($13)

Shiraz (Tel. 560100). Crowne Plaza Hotel Muscat, Qurum Heights. Authentic Persian cuisine. Licensed. Closed Friday. For dinner only. RO 4 ($10.32)

ITALIAN

Come Prima (Tel. 560100). At the Crowne Plaza Hotel, Qurum. Traditional dishes served by an Italian chef. For lunch and dinner. RO 5 ($12.90)

La Mamma (Tel. 799899). At the Sheraton Oman, Ruwi. Pizza, pasta, everything Italian. RO 6 ($15.50)

La Pizzeria (Tel. 704244). Ruwi Novotel. Monday is Italian carnival night. À la carte menu. Licensed. RO 6 ($15.50)

Musandam Café (American, French, Italian)—see International section

O Sole Mio (Tel. 601343). Fine Italian cuisine in the Jawaharat A'Shati complex in Shati Al Qurum. RO 10 ($26)

JAPANESE

Tokyo Taro (Tel. 702311). Top floor of the Mercure Al Falaj Hotel in Ruwi. An evening at the Tokyo Taro is well spent. The chefs are the performers. Wonderful mixes of meat, seafood, and vegetables are cooked "Teppan Yaki" style on grills beside the tables. (The fried garlic is great!) Sushi, too. For dessert there's fried ice cream, a real treat. RO 9 ($23)

LEBANESE

Al Pasha (Tel. 708132). Behind Copper Chimney and adjacent to Wadi

Kabir, Central Business District. Authentic food and live entertainment, a complete mezza. Fully licensed. RO 12 ($31)

Automatic (Tel. 561500). The food is fresh, tasty, and straight from the Mediterranean; the service genuinely spontaneous; and the setting pleasant ... so where does the "automatic" come in? Never mind. It's a Lebanese feast. In Qurum behind SABCO Centre and a new branch opening in Al Khuwair. RO 5 ($13)

Fakrudin (Tel. 704244). Lebanese delights in the Ruwi Novotel. RO 8 ($21)

Kargeen (Tel. 692269). This little shop goes a long way with its selection of kebabs and other Lebanese delicacies. In MQ Shopping Centre and the Al Harthy Complex. RO 3 ($8)

Lebanese Roastery—see Cafés and Coffee Shops section.

Mijana (Tel. 601730). Located next to Al Madina in MQ Shopping Centre, Madinat al Sultan Qaboos. Great food and entertainment straight from the shores of the Mediterranean. Licensed. RO 8 ($21)

MEXICAN

Los Amigos (Tel. 687123). Actually Tex-Mex, but who's checking? It's spicy-hot stuff any way you slice it, and that's how it should be. Live entertainment (mostly C&W and pop music). In the Muscat Holiday Inn, Al Khuwair. RO 5 ($13)

Pavo Real (Tel. 602603). In the MQ Shopping Centre, Madinat Al Sultan Qaboos. Nachos, burritos, tacos, fajitas, quesadillas, chimichangas, guacamole, it's all there. Montezuma without the revenge. Go ahead, ask the waiter to spice it up. Fully licensed. RO 9 ($23.20)

MONGOLIAN

Golden Oryx (Tel. 702266). Upstairs at the Golden Oryx is the place to be with the Mongolian BBQ. Choose your own fixings from an array of meats and vegetables and hand it to the chef. He'll prepare it for you on the grill and bring it back to you. Every meal's a masterpiece. Also Chinese and Thai food à la carte downstairs. Fully Licensed. RO 6 ($15.50)

OMANI

Al Bawadi (Tel. 601273). Near Zuwawi Mosque in Al Khuwair, another Omani establishment has come on line and it provides that something-special experience that is wholly Omani. Seating outdoors in a majlis or private rooms. The food is authentic and satisfying. RO 5 ($13)

Arabian Garden (Omani, Indian, Pakistani, Chinese)—see International section

Copper Chimney—see Indian section

Ofair Public Foods Restaurant (Tel. 693695). Located behind the Shell petrol pump coming in to Al Khuwair. Private rooms, floor seating with cushions, authentic down to the TV in the corner (something has to keep Dad preoccupied), this Omani family gathering place serves only Omani food, prepared Omani style, no artificial additives or ingredients. Come in and enjoy a contemporary Arabic setting for very reasonable prices. RO 3 ($7.70)

Sadaf Oman (Arabian, Omani, Turkish, Iranian)—see International section

Sallan Coffee Shop—see Cafés and Coffee Shops section

Seblat Al Bustan (Tel. 799666 ext. 4801). Probably your most memorable impression will be a night at the Seblat Al Bustan, a traditional Omani dinner served under the stars in a (simulated but authentic) Bedouin village. When you arrive at the Al Bustan Palace, you will be bussed (alas, not cameled) a short distance to a date palm grove. Here in this oasis is an enclosure of Bedouin tents with carpets and cushions (parties of 10 will have their own private tent). A network of aflaj burbles underfoot. As you recline, Omani waiters bring breads and crudités with yogurt, mint, and cucumber dip. Green salads and fish salads garnished with Omani limes and green chilis are served. Then comes the *shuwa* on a bed of Mohmar rice surrounded by *meshak,* whole baked *hammour, harees* and *kabuli,* and chicken and vegetable *Salona* (an Arabian curry). As you dine a troupe of Omani dancers performs, reaching a crescendo of revelry. Desserts and fruits are passed about, fresh dates or fried dates with *sim sim* (crushed sesame fried in ghee), halwa, slices of coconut, melons, and citrus. At the conclusion a *megmar* of *bokhur* is passed about (a brazier of hot glowing coals on which frankincense is burned) as guests are invited to take in the rich aroma of the smoky fragrance and let it waft through their hair and clothing, signaling the end of the evening. Open on Wednesday nights only (parties of 100+ can reserve for another night). Reservations in advance. RO 15 ($38.70)

PAKISTANI

Al-Exandria (Tel. 561611). Near SABCO Centre, Qurum. Masalas and biryanis and tikkas, Pakistani style. Convenient and economical. RO 2.5 ($6.40)

SYRIAN

Candles (Tel. 790631). On An-Noor Street in Ruwi shortly past the Sultan Qaboos Mosque, set back from the road. Mixed grills, cutlets, and kebabs. Try the Turkish/Syrian coffee. RO 3 ($7.70)

THAI

Al Inshirah (Arabian, Thai, Indian, American)—see International section
Happy Village Restaurant (Tel. 564995). Behind SABCO Centre in Qurum. This little spot has quite a variety of food for quite a good price. Equally matched by the selection of Filipino food as well. RO 2.5 ($6.40)
Golden Oryx—see Mongolian section

TURKISH

Ibn Al Rodah Traditional Restaurant and Coffee Shop. On Seeb High Street just past the Sports Corner. Grills, kebabs, and coffee made the way coffee is supposed to be made. RO 1.5 ($3.90)
Istanboly Coffee Shop (Tel. 680900). Tasty Turkish treats like kebabs, grills, and superb boneless chicken. Baba ghanouj and hommos too. Try the fruit cocktail! This is fast becoming a favorite of locals and expats. In Al Khuwair near the souq on Street 41. RO 3 ($8)

6. Sightseeing

> Muscat . . . is probably one of the most picturesque places in the world. From a distance, immense granitic masses of rock, with jagged outline of cliff and crag, are seen in gloomy abruptness from the sea . . . its plastered houses glittering against the somber background like a seagull's wing against an angry sky.
> —George Nathaniel Curzon, Marquess of Curzon, *Travels,* 1889

The following is given as a descriptive offering of attractions in the Sultanate. It is highly recommended for maximum satisfaction and enjoyment that you travel in a small group (two vehicles) and employ a reputable Omani guide. It is always better if you travel with somebody who has done the routes before and is aware of all contingencies.

Since most travel proceeds from Muscat it only makes sense to discuss Muscat and environs first of all, then radiate outward covering the coastal areas to the north (the Batinah) and south (Yiti to Quriyat to Sur), followed by the Western Hajars, from the coast and from the interior, the Eastern Hajars from the interior, Dhahirah, and Sharqiyah. If perchance you are traveling directly to Salalah or the Musandam Peninsula, that will be covered separately in the following two chapters.

There's much to see in this country—more than can be covered in an average vacation. The pristine natural setting is more diverse than most people are likely to imagine in a desert locale. I find that there are no two wadi systems alike; they exhibit their own qualities or character. The jebels, although stark, still imbue that mysterious yearning for exploration. The country boasts over five hundred castles, fortresses, towers, and fortified towns liberally scattered throughout. Some have been restored as national treasures or have been turned into museums or historic monuments. Others in various stages of ruin are awaiting restoration. Some, like the UNESCO-sponsored restoration at Bahla, are being tended to and, for the time being, are off limits.

Unless otherwise specified, return routes from specific locales are made by backtracking. Refer to maps in this guide for clarification. Other maps are available in the Sultanate at local bookstores or through the National Survey Authority.

Key: SS=Sightseeing in general
4WD=a four-wheel drive is required
HCP=Hiking, camping, picnicking

MUSCAT GOVERNORATE

> Muscat is a large and populous city. . . . There are orchards, gardens and palm groves with pools for watering them by means of wooden engines. The harbour is small, shaped like a horseshoe and sheltered from every wind. . . . It is a very elegant town with very fine houses and supplied from the interior with much wheat, millet, barley and dates for loading as many vessels as come for them.
>
> —Alfonso de Albuquerque, *Commentaries*, 1506

Muscat, Mutrah, and Ruwi (SS)

When you enter the **capital city** for the first time, you will probably come via the **Mutrah Corniche,** passing the village of **Qalboo** on your left with its resplendent mosque and shoreline promenade (Map 1). As the main road climbs over a saddle between two rocky crags and passes through the bulwarks of the wall that once surrounded the old capital and down into a maze of narrow winding streets, you will get a cozy feeling more akin to that of an old New England fishing village than that of an international capital seat. Apart from the government buildings and the Omani-French Museum, the rest of the city is residential.

When you visit the main gates of **Al Alam Palace,** it is unlike any other capital you will ever visit. The palace itself is elegant but humble in design, unlike the grandiose structures of other capitals. Places like Tien Anmin Square in Beijing have a tendency to intimidate and overwhelm the viewer with their vast control of space. The setting of the Royal Palace in Muscat is welcoming. Its proximity to the residential area is indicative of how closely the Sultan relates to his people; the feeling is, comparatively speaking, downright neighborly; it is one of accessibility.

Flanking the Royal Palace on overlooking ridges are the two forts, **Fort**

1) Muscat, Al Bustan, and Qantab

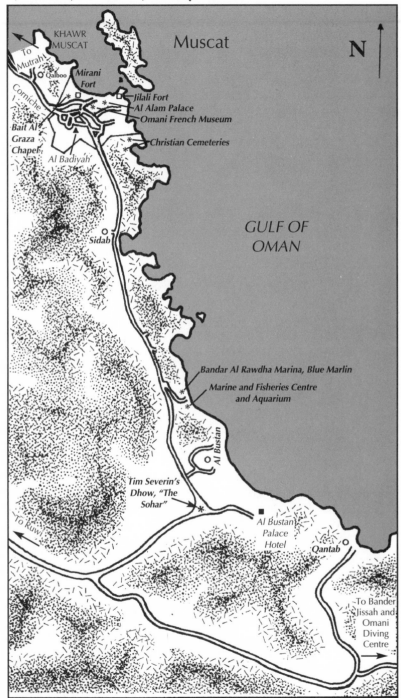

Jalali and **Fort Mirani,** both built by the Portuguese over earlier Omani edifices but refurbished and enhanced by subsequent Omani regimes. Jalali, called Fort Jao by the Portuguese, is quite foreboding sitting atop its perch. Access is by way of a narrow staircase on the harbor side. The towers provide an excellent view of the harbor. The enclosures, surrounded by massive bulwarks, are deceptively cavernous and the maze of stairwells and hallways was designed to confuse the enemy and prevent infiltration. Prior to the 1970s, the fort was used as a prison, but it now is a museum featuring authentic armaments and decoration. Because of its proximity to the Royal Palace, special visitor permits are required.

> A quaint and distinctive feature of Muscat's cove were the names and ships painted on the cliffs of its southern arm. The custom must have been of some antiquity for it was said that when HMS *Seahorse* visited Muscat in 1775, Horatio Nelson was aboard it and as a midshipman, may well have been with the party sent ashore to scale the cliffs to paint the name of their vessel on them. The custom was usually confined to visiting naval vessels, but was later followed by merchant vessels.
>
> —Ronald Codrai, *An Arabian Album: Travels to Oman, 1948-1955*

Across the harbor, atop another precipitous crag, sitting slightly higher, is the sister fort, **Fort Mirani.** Completed before Jalali in 1587 with additions and refurbishments later on in that century, Mirani is an impressive battlement with retaining walls over one meter thick. It is said never to have fallen to outside attackers, but rather by deception of a crafty Indian merchant who served as the fort's accountant during the Portuguese occupation. Faced with a "shotgun marriage" of his comely daughter to the Portuguese commander, he managed to buy some time and deplete the fortress's stores. He did this by insisting to the quartermaster that older stores, food, and gunpowder had spoiled and needed replacement. Once the stores were removed, he informed the Omanis of the fort's vulnerability. After a siege, rather than face an embarrassing surrender, the humiliated governor threw himself over the ramparts to be dashed on the rocks below.

Facing the fort and adjacent to Jalali is a small islet, another rocky outcrop that is festooned with graffiti from merchant vessels of bygone times who claimed Muscat as a port of call.

Close by the Royal Palace is the **Omani-French Museum,** former residence and French consulate from 1894 to 1920. The museum holds over two hundred years of diplomatic documents and cultural artifacts.

If you wish to visit the old **Christian cemeteries,** it would have to be by boat as they face the sea in a tiny secluded inlet below Muscat Harbor. Of the three churches built by the Portuguese, remnants of one still stand—that is the **chapel of Bait Graiza** near Fort Mirani.

Continuing out of the city, heading south over a small rise, you will come upon the quaint fishing village of **Sidab** nestled in between the rocks. Further on is the **Marine Science and Fisheries Centre,** the **Oman Aquarium,** and the newly opened **Marina Bander Al-Rowdha.** The Centre and Aquarium offer a landlubber's view of the diversity of marine life of Omani waters. But if you are not satisfied with that and want a first-hand accounting, you may proceed to the Marina, where boating and diving excursions are offered.

Further on, beyond the next rise, the **Al Bustan Palace Hotel** comes into view. An awesome spectacle, it rests majestically in green groves of palms along a sandy beach shrouded by the dark ophiolites of Eastern Hajar Mountains as they reach down and kiss the sea. Sitting in the roundabout at the entrance to the Al Bustan is explorer/researcher **Tim Severin's dhow, the** *Sohar,* built in 1980 to retrace the path of ancient Omani mariners from Muscat to Canton, China.

Taking the right at the roundabout will bring you over a mountain pass and back to Ruwi, but not before passing an intersection that leads just a few klicks over the hills to **Bander Jissah** and **Qantab.** Qantab is an old fishing village where you can hire an outboard and skipper from the village for fishing in the coastal waters. Or you can just saunter along the beach and outcrops, enjoy the scenery, and watch the marine life scurry in and out of the tidal flats. Back at Bander Jissah is a public beach area if you're just up for sunning (but not too much!) and swimming. Bander Jissah is also home of the **Oman Diving Centre,** where you can engage in diving and snorkeling ventures or take lessons, if you are a novice.

We backtrack a little bit to the port of **Mutrah,** which is just outside Muscat, slightly to the northwest. Here is the main container facility of **Mina Qaboos** on the northwest side of the bay. Mutrah has been an important center for centuries dealing with India, Africa, and the Far East. As such it was named by UNESCO as a focal point in the Silk Road Project begun in 1990. (This project promotes international unity using the old silk routes to the Far East.) Perchance you might spy His Majesty Sultan Qaboos's **royal yacht Fulk Al-Salamah,** which was placed at the disposal of the Silk Road Project in 1991. As you enter Mutrah from the main highway, at this point called **Al Mina'a Street,** you will come to the **Al Corniche roundabout** at the edge of the waterfront (Map 2). To the left are the fish, fruit, and vegetable souqs where you can idly spend a whole morning watching business transactions, old world style. Further on is the entrance to the container facility, and just across the street from the souqs are the **Al Nahdha, Corniche,** and **Mina Hotels.**

Taking a right at the roundabout will put you on the **Mutrah Corniche,** skirting the harbor past the **old mercantile buildings,** the **Naseem Hotel,**

2) Mutrah

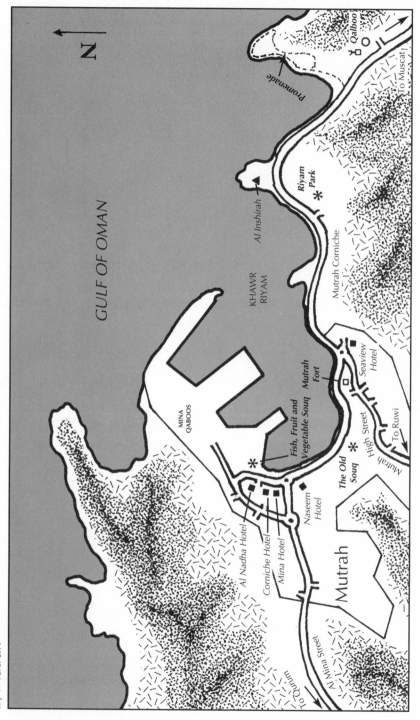

and at the stoplight the entrance to the **Mutrah souq.** Here is the spot where time has stood still (almost). Here you can wander through alley after alley in search of that long-sought bauble or artifact. Buy some frankincense or *bokhur,* a mixture of aromas collected in jars and canisters, sold by Bedouin women. Don't forget—you need to buy a ceramic burner and the specially treated charcoal briquettes. Wander through the gold and silver souqs or the antiquities section (shops of a kind tend to cluster in one area)—or is it textiles and clothing you want? or sandals? a khanjar or a dish-dasha with a kumma? Will that be MasterCard or Visa, sir?

As the Corniche winds away from the center you will pass underneath **Mutrah Fort.** Overlooking Mutrah harbor and the port of Mina Qaboos, Mutrah Fort is an impressive sight perched upon a rocky crag. Its location can only attest to the importance of Omani commerce during its long and noble history. Built during the time of the Portuguese occupation of Muscat (and the construction of the two sister forts in Muscat harbor, Jilali and Mirani), the fort is often called the Makara as it distinguishes the port as a seat of commerce. Many additions were made to the original edifice over a period of time, including several towers and a curtain wall. The design of the eight towers is such that if an enemy invader succeeded in breaching any part of the fortress, it could be shelled from any one of the towers to prevent capture. The fall of Mutrah Fort to the Omanis was instrumental in ousting the Portuguese in 1654. Since that time the fort has been regularly maintained. In 1980 a complete restoration took place using original materials and techniques to maintain the fort's original appearance.

Shortly beyond is the **Seaview Hotel.** Around another bend is **Riyam Park,** a pleasant garden and promenade with picnic areas, a children's amusement park, and a huge replica **incense burner** perched atop a crag from which you have an excellent view of the harbor. At a point jutting out across from the park is the **Al Inshirah Restaurant** and dock for **dhow cruises.** Around that final bend Qalboo and the gateway to Muscat come in sight.

Another way into Mutrah is through **Mutrah Street,** which leads from Bait Al Falaj Street in Ruwi past the rear entrance of the old souq and comes out at the Corniche by the Seaview Hotel. Along Mutrah Street you will find the **Mutrah Hotel,** the **Al-Hadow Hotel,** and **Shangri-La** and **Taj** restaurants.

The commercial center of the capital is **Ruwi** which in 1970 was a cluster of thatched huts along **Wadi Kabir** ("Great River"). The first modern airstrip ran parallel to the wadi before it was replaced by the international airport at Seeb. Remnants of that strip, several hundred meters long, can be seen behind the Ministry of Commerce and Industry and the Muscat Security Exchange on Al Jaame Street. The layout of Ruwi is generally

3) Ruwi

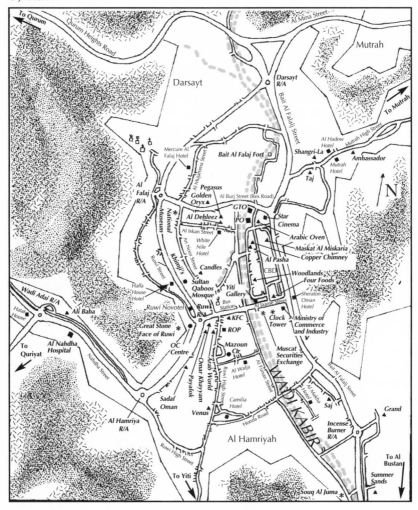

1 km

north/south on either side of the wadi as it runs north to the mouth in the Gulf of Oman through the village of **Darsayt** (Map 3). Servicing the city from the west is the closed loop extending from the Sultan Qaboos Highway in Qurum. At the north end of the city this loop splits into the main thoroughfares that enter Mutrah: the previously mentioned Al Mina Street and **Bait Al Falaj Street,** which runs south along the eastern side of Ruwi, past the **incense burner roundabout** in the Wadi Kabir section of town. It continues on to meet up with the already mentioned road that leads from the Al Bustan Palace Hotel, Qantab, and Bander Jissah.

There are two main connectors and to a lesser extent, a third, running east/west between the loop and Bait Al Falaj Street. The first of the two is **Al Burj Street,** called **Rex Road,** running from the **Al Falaj roundabout** to the intersection on Bait Al Falaj Street next to the **Star Cinema.** Midway along Rex Road is the wonderful **Golden Oryx Restaurant** where you can enjoy Mongolian BBQ. From the roundabout you can easily spot the nine-story **Mercure Al Falaj Hotel,** which can be reached by taking Al Mujamma Street off Rex Road. Further on down Al Mujamma Street and close to the wadi is the entrance to the **Fort Bait Al Falaj.** Built as a summer country home by Sayyid Said, the fort served as a staging ground for Omani and British troops during the Wahhabi incursions. It last saw action in the 1915 interior rebellion and was restored by Sultan Qaboos in 1988. It is now the Armed Forces Museum depicting Oman's (sometimes) turbulent and glorious military past.

Clustered on a side road just north of the Al Falaj roundabout are several places of worship including the **Catholic Church of Saints Peter and Paul,** the **Protestant Church of Oman,** the **Shree Govindrayji Temple,** and the **Shree Ganesh and Devi Kalaka Temples.**

It should be noted here that side streets and lesser alleys in any urban or suburban area in Oman are not named but are identified by a four-digit way number. These are usually posted on green signs at intersections.

The next main thoroughfare is **Al Jaame Street,** which runs from the Ruwi roundabout over Wadi Kabir to the intersection with Bait Al Falaj Street, where sit the **Sheraton Oman Hotel** and the **Ministry of Commerce and Industry.** Next to the ministry is the **Clock Tower Park** and the **Muscat Security Exchange.** Going over the wadi to the westward side is the **bus station** and **Sultan Qaboos Mosque** to your right, and Ruwi High Street (one way, coming out) to the left before coming to the roundabout. The **Ruwi Novotel** is just to the north of the roundabout. Behind the roundabout is the **OCC** (**Oman Commercial Complex,** also called the **OK Centre**). Above and behind the OCC sits one of the more unusual formations in Oman, a naturally shaped head and face of a man looking south, in profile—the **Great Stone Face of Ruwi.** A work completely done by the hand of nature, this face is filled with astounding detail: lips and nostrils, eyebrows and iris, and perhaps a vestigial ear. Not nearly as well known as New Hampshire's Old Man of the Mountain or Switzerland's Sphinx of the Alps, he sits implacably staring off into space, keeping a watchful eye over the city.

Ruwi High Street is a bustling center of activity with shops and stalls of every kind, restaurants and cafés, and mini-souqs all along its two-kilometer stretch. The street actually starts (from the other end) at the Al-Hamriyah round-about on the main highway loop and loops itself around to exit onto Al Jaame Street. Ruwi High Street is two-way from the Al Hamriyah roundabout to Honda Road and one-way, heading out, from Honda Road to Al Jaame Street. Note: at the bottom of this loop (where the street is still two-way) in the center of **Al Hamriyah** is an intersection that runs through some back alleys and out of the wadi course into the mountains. This is the main road to Yiti, Bander Khayran, and other points south that we will take up further on.

Midway along Ruwi High Street is the juncture of the third connector which runs to Bait Al-Falaj Street, **Al Baladiyah Street,** better known as **Honda Road.** This street passes through the hardware, plumbing, and electrical shops before it takes a swipe at the auto repair centers. The **Camilia Hotel** can be found near the Ruwi High Street end and the **Makha Hotel** can be found at the Bait Al Falaj Street end close to the wadi.

Back at the Clock Tower is the juncture with **Markaz Mutrah Al Tijari Street** (next to the **Chamber of Commerce**), which runs north to join Rex Road by a building shaped like a series of cylinders placed on end, **GTO** (the **Telephone Company of Oman**). Next to GTO is the **Ruwi Post Office** and the **Philatelic Society.** This street is known generally as the **Central Business District (CBD),** where almost all the major banking institutions and several major travel agencies can be found. There are also several nice restaurants in the area, including **Woodlands, Copper Chimney, Al Pasha, Arabic Oven, Four Foods,** and the **Maskat al Miskiria Snack Shop.** Close to the Chamber of Commerce in the Sony building is the **Yiti Gallery,** a fine establishment for art collectors and artifact hunters. The gallery sells a wide variety of originals, prints, and reprints, with a framing service offered as well.

Other connectors are **Al Fursan Street** which runs north/south along the west bank of Wadi Kabir. Just one block in from this street you can find the **Walja Hotel** near the **Mansour Ali Centre** south of Al Jaame Street. If you happen to be traveling south on Al Fursan Street and it happens to be Friday morning you are in for a treat. Continue south past the Honda Road intersection and the auto upholsterers' shops until you come to another souq area, a **fruit and vegetable souq** that is open all the time, and the **Souq Al Juma,** the Friday Flea Market selling everything from kitchen utensils and bric-a-brac to used cars. Hagglers, loosen your tongues and get ready to hone your technique, because here is where it's done.

A' Noor Street runs north/south from the Sultan Qaboos Mosque to Rex Road, where you can find the **National Museum** next to the Abdulridha Mosque near Rex Road. **Al Iskan Street** runs east/west from A'Noor Street to Al-Fursan Street. Here you can find the **White Nile Hotel, Al Dehleez,** and the **Pegasus.**

Qurum and Shati Al Qurum (SS)

The northern end of the loop out of the city from the **Darsayt round-about** is by far the most picturesque part of the loop, but it offers only one vantage point for stopping. As you climb over the ridge and descend you will see ahead and off to your right **Mina Al Fahal,** where lies Oman's oil refinery and repository, otherwise known as **PDO (Petroleum Development of Oman)** (Map 4). In the distance offshore is **Jazir Fahal,** Fahal Island, a popular spot for divers. After a few quick kilometers the road joins the southern end of the loop at Qurum.

The southern end of the loop departs Ruwi through the suburb of **Al Hamriyah** and intersects with the main highway heading to **Quriyat,** and other locales further south, at the **Wadi Adai roundabout.** On your left you will see a landmark building called **Hatat House.** Nearby is the **Ali Baba Restaurant** (across from **Al Nahda Hospital**) and farther along are the **Moghul** and **Curry House** restaurants as the automobile dealerships loom into view. At the **Wattayah roundabout** there are signs to the right for **Khoula Hospital,** and a unique mosque on the left with spheres balancing atop the minarets. Shortly after you will see two sports stadiums on your right, the **ROP Stadium** and **Maiden Al Fateh Stadium.** Then the posh **Al Harthy Shopping Complex** comes into view on your left followed by the **SABCO** et al. complexes on your right, before the road meets up with the northern loop and continues on as the **Sultan Qaboos Highway,** often referred to as the **Dual Carriageway.**

If you get off the highway at this juncture and head north toward **Qurum,** take your first right after the underpass beneath the northern end loop. This will take you to PDO, which for the most part is off limits, except for the **Oil Exhibition Centre** nearly two klicks down the road on your right just before the main entrance to PDO. Here you will see informative displays and presentations on the discovery and processing of petroleum.

Coming back to the main road into Qurum you will see the **Qurum Park and Nature Reserve,** where you can take a casual stroll down lanes amongst trees and flowers and over a sparkling cascade that is lit up at night. As you drive further into Qurum, keep to the main road, as winding as it gets, and you will eventually reach **Qurum Beach, Qurum Beach House,** and up above on a bluff, the **Gulf Forum Hotel.** Qurum is a quiet and elegant residential neighborhood with many villas adorned with bougainvillea and flame trees.

4) Qurum

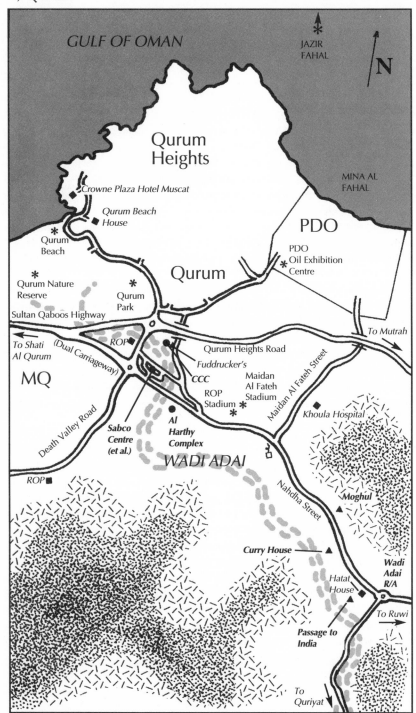

GULF OF OMAN

JAZIR FAHAL

N

Qurum
Heights

MINA AL
FAHAL

Crowne Plaza Hotel Muscat

Qurum Beach
House

PDO

Qurum Beach

PDO
Oil Exhibition
Centre

Qurum Nature
Reserve

Qurum

Qurum
Park

Sultan Qaboos Highway

To Mutrah

To Shati
Al Qurum

(Dual Carriageway)

ROP

Qurum Heights Road

Fuddrucker's

Maidan Al Fateh Street

MQ

CCC

Maidan
Al Fateh
Stadium

ROP
Stadium

Khoula Hospital

Sabco
Centre
(et al.)

Al
Harthy
Complex

Death Valley Road

WADI ADAI

ROP

Nahdha Street

Moghul

Curry House

Wadi
Adai
R/A

Hatat
House

To Ruwi

Passage to
India

To
Quriyat

1 km

As you journey west on the Dual Carriageway past Qurum you will be passing the area on your right known as **Shati Al Qurum** (Map 5). Almost the first thing you will see past the waterfall cascade outcrop is a low-lying domed building on your right, which is the **Children's Museum.** Like many modern museums, this one adopts a hands-on policy for inquisitive minds that allows youngsters to observe and participate in various types of natural physical phenomena. You can access the museum by taking the first exit on your right, proceeding halfway through the roundabout, and taking the slip road past the **Oman Women's Association.** There is also access from this roundabout to the beach that skirts the **Qurum Nature Reserve,** a tidal flat and wetlands for marine life and migratory birds. A three-quarters turn from this roundabout will put you onto **Al Kharajiyah Street,** which runs past the **Ministry of Foreign Affairs.** The next right-hand turn from Al Kharajiyah Street will take you to the entrance of the **Muscat Inter-Continental Hotel** (quite visible from the main highway) and the new **Jawaharat A'Shati Shopping Complex,** the **Qurum Beach Tourism Resort,** and the **Oasis by the Sea** restaurant.

Further along the slip road there is the new **Sarooj Shopping Complex** next to the well-established rest stop and **Shell petrol pump.** It is a very busy spot on weekends with many wadi bashers stopping to have their vehicles cleaned at the car wash—you can be fined for driving a dirty car in Oman. There are a couple of fast food joints and a wonderful coffee shop that sells all kinds of nuts and snacks and sweets. The rest of Shati Al Qurum is residential except for the new Hyatt Regency under construction and due to be finished sometime in 1997.

Madinat Al Sultan Qaboos and Al Khuwair (SS)

The next main intersection on the highway is the **Al Khuwair roundabout.** Exiting to your right will take you to the far end of Shati Al Qurum, **Embassy Road** leading to some, although not all, of the consular offices, including the United States and Great Britain, and **Al Wazarat Street** which houses most of the country's government ministries. Tucked in between these ministries at the far end is the **Natural History Museum** adjacent to the **Ministry of Heritage and Culture.** All of the ministries face the highway and the suburb of **Al Khuwair** across the way.

Backtracking a little bit to the Al Khuwair roundabout, a three quarter turn on the roundabout (left) will take you up the road to a stoplight (about five hundred meters). On your right in a building complex is the **Alauddin Restaurant.** A right-hand turn from this stoplight will take you to the back way of Al Khuwair via Dohat Al Adab Street. Straight ahead through the stoplight is **Madinat Al Sultan Qaboos Street** (also called **Death Valley Road** because of the terrain's resemblance to the American national park), which

5) Shati Al Qurum, Madinat Al Sultan Qaboos, and Al Khuwair

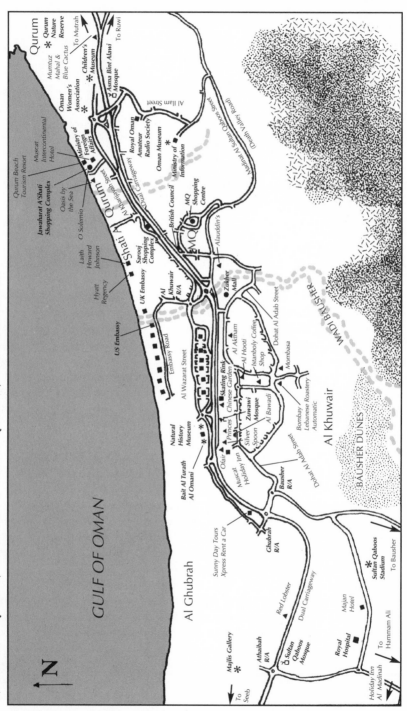

1 km

eventually meets up at the SABCO Centre back in Qurum. This was the main road before the highway was built. A left-hand turn at the stoplight will take you into the residential area of **Madinat Al Sultan Qaboos,** still referred to as **MQ.** MQ is a very attractive neighborhood that surrounds a central shopping plaza with several stores and restaurants including the **Golden Dragon,** the **Al Madina, Mijana,** and **Pavo Real.** To get there, follow the road (known as **Al Bashair Street,** or just plain **Road One**) from the stoplight and take a right at the **British Council.** This is still Road One. Follow it as it snakes around and up a hill until you see the shopping complex on your right. The complex is accessible from all sides. A drive around MQ will take you past many villas and estates bedecked with bougainvillea and shade trees. Several embassies can also be found here.

If you return to the British Council, take the slip road (**Al Inshirah Street**) back towards Muscat until you come to a flyover just before the **Asma bint Alawi Mosque** with a beautiful gold dome and clock tower minaret. (This flyover will take you to the previously mentioned roundabout in Shati Al Qurum and you can also re-enter the highway in front of the mosque.) But take a right turn to beyond the mosque where the road ends in a T-junction. Turn right on **Al Ilam Street** and proceed up the hill. Turn left at the **Royal Oman Amateur Radio Society** (this is still Al Ilam Street) and make your way to the top of the hill where you will see the **Ministry of Information** complex. Turn right before the entrance on the road that skirts the perimeter of the complex and follow the signs to the **Oman Museum,** which is behind the MOI complex on a bluff overlooking the whole coastline.

Back at the highway, the suburb of Al Khuwair lies just beyond Madinat Al Sultan Qaboos and is directly opposite the government ministries section. It is mostly residential but there are still a few places to shop, mostly along the slip road facing the highway. There are also several restaurants sprinkled about including **Al Hooti, Al Akhtam, Mombasa, Princes, Silver Spoon,** and **Chinese Garden,** as well as the **Muscat Holiday Inn.** If you are in Oman and happen to have the uncontrollable urge to go ice skating, you are certainly in luck because the **ice skating rink** is located on the slip road near the **Zuwawi Mosque.**

Bausher (SS, HP)

Continuing on the highway past Al Khuwair, the next turnoff is the **Ghubrah roundabout** where a quarter turn (right) will take you to the residential neighborhood of **Al Ghubrah.** Three quarters around (left) and you will head up a hill to another roundabout, **Bausher roundabout.** Halfway around this roundabout (straight) will take you back to Al Khuwair via Dohat Al Adab Street. But a quarter turn (right) will take you out to the village of **Bausher** and the famed **Bausher dunes.** Just a few kilometers down the road you will see on your left a rise of sand dunes a couple of kilometers from the base of the jebels. This is where just about every expatriate resident who comes to Oman for the first time and is issued a 4WD will come to cut his teeth—on the Bausher dunes. It's a great place to practice your 4WD sand-driving technique and if you get stuck, you're not far from home and a tow. Just beyond the dunes on your right is the **Ghala-Wentworth Golf Club,** where the greens are browns and emerald fairways have given way to the soft beige hues of the desert.

Just past the dunes is the village of **Bausher,** where you can see a perfect example of a society in transition. The old village is still kept up with crisscrossing aflaj. Old and dilapidated buildings are left behind to crumble beside more modern structures. Date palms fill the area with shade. Livestock roam the streets. If you drive through the narrow alleyways, go slow and keep your eyes peeled for children who are always playing about. Men and women come and go doing their daily chores. If you can trace the falaj back to the jebels you will find the hot springs from whence it emerges. Near the center of town there is the recently restored **Bait Al Mahqam Fort,** built 300 years ago by Albusaidis and occupied as recently as 1970 by a local shaykh. Its sad state of disrepair made it a prime target for renovation and now the fort is completely restored and open to the public. The fort is easy to find in the center of town as it is clearly marked.

There is a cluster of 65 ancient burial chambers in Wadi Bausher only 100 meters from the roundabout at the entrance of the village. These chambers predate the Christian era and they are quite different from other remains. They are small in comparison, indeed a body would have to be stowed in fetal position, but when they were discovered, they yielded a good number of artifacts: pottery, weapons, and beads. Look carefully as they are easy to miss, but they are not too far from the road and the wadi bed. Further out on the outskirts of town to the east behind the dunes are remnants of some forts of bygone eras. The **Fateh Fort Castle** and the nearby **Sur Jal Fort,** made of mud brick and mortar, are slowly but surely slipping away due to the ravages of time. But enough remains to give the viewer an impression of these once majestic structures and the reliance the people put on them to protect their towns, homes, and families. Slightly beyond Fateh Fort on the crest of an outcrop are vestigial remains of tombs that are similar, and most probably concurrent, to the beehive tombs found in the interior near Bat and Al Ayn. Bausher serves as an interesting point of departure and a good way for the traveler to "get your feet wet," as it were. Bausher is a nice half-day excursion at the most; its proximity to Muscat makes it an easy venture that can be combined with other local ramblings in the capital area.

Meanwhile, from the Bausher roundabout (Map 5), there is a right turn intersection barely one kilometer along the road which will take you to the **Sultan Qaboos Sports Complex,** where international-level football (soccer) is played. Just beyond the sports complex on your right is the **Majan Hotel,** followed by the **Royal Hospital.** Down the hill to the **Ghala roundabout** and a quarter turn (right) will take you back to the highway and the **Athaibah roundabout** (see below). Three quarters (left) will take you out past the **PAMAP Centre (Public Authority for the Marketing of Agricultural Produce)**, which is a food co-op where you can get locally grown fruits and vegetables.

> The water gushes with much violence from the aperture at the base of a hill of clay ironstone. Veins of crystallized quartz run in a diagonal direction through the rock and large fragments have been dislodged from it. The local people will drink no other water.
> —Lt. James Raymond Wellstead, *Travels in Arabia*, 1838, describing the Hammam Ali Spring

Ghala (Sanub and Hammam Ali) (SS, HP)

Turning left will take you out toward the jebels and a short trip to a town with hot springs. Follow the tarmac for three kilometers and take a right at the Ansab sign. A few kilometers on you will see signs for the village of **Sanub**

Row of towers near Hammam Ali.

off to your left. At the village there is a ruined fort. Here you can park and walk through the village, tracing your way to the source of the springs: a high enclosure that may be locked. If so the villagers will unlock it for you. Past the gate you can descend some steps to a bubbling source emanating from the rock. The water is hot to the touch.

Further on from Sanub is where **Hammam Ali** can be found, which may sound funny as "hammam" is the Arabic word for "bathroom" (making this Ali's bathroom). But although there may be a bath in the sense of the springs that are there, it is believed the name has been corrupted from Imam Ali, a religious leader for whom the spring had been named. Follow the signs to the village (left from the tarmac road onto a well-kept track). It's signposted at 5 kilometers but I found it to be more like 3.5 kilometers. Take a right at the next junction and drive until you pass some ruined towers on your left followed by a village with farm plots on your right. Park at a small square tower and follow the falaj to the source. The mineral content of this water is evident by the remains of the old falaj, which is encrusted thickly with laminated material. The water still flows hot (scalding hot) out of the spring, but these days it is assisted by a pump. You can take note of the effectiveness of this particular spring by the number of farm plots it supports in this cozy country village.

SIA and vicinity (SS)

Back to the highway, the next roundabout encountered is the **Athaibah roundabout,** also called the **Caterpillar roundabout** (because of its proximity to the Oman office of the famous bulldozer manufacturer). However, these names will probably be eclipsed with the completion of the new **Sultan Qaboos Mosque,** which is under construction by the roundabout (Map 5). When finished it will be the largest mosque in the Arabian peninsula (outside of Makkah) and an outstanding landmark. This roundabout provides the most direct access to the **Royal Hospital** as well as the residential/commercial district of **Athaibah** (sometimes spelled Azaiba).

From this point onward the highway enters into open territory, a slip of oasis-green cutting through parched barren landscapes until it reaches the next developed area, **Seeb,** which includes the residential areas of **Al Hail** and **Al Khoudh.** But before you reach these there are still a few more points along the way. Beyond Athaibah (Map 6) you will see on your left, going westbound, the **Motor Sports Club** complete with go-cart track, followed by the **ROP office** for traffic control, the **Majlis Ash Shura,** the **Oman Exhibition Centre,** and the **Seeb Novotel.** These places can only be accessed by traveling the slip road eastbound from the **SIA roundabout** or taking the same slip road from Athaibah. As you pass them on the highway **Seeb International Airport (SIA)** will be looming on your right. Also close to the

6) Seeb International Airport

GULF OF OMAN

N

Al Hail

Al Mawalah R/A

To Seeb

Sultan Qaboos Highway
Dual Carriageway

Sahwa Tower
(MAM R/A)

Bellapais

To Nizwa

Seeb International Airport (SIA)

Sultan Qaboos Highway

Dual Carriageway

CPO Seeb
(Central Post Office)

Seeb Novotel

Oman Exhibition Centre

ROP (Traffic Control)

Majlis Ash Shura

Motor Sports Club

To Muscat

1 km

roundabout is the **Central Post Office (CPO Seeb),** the central artery for incoming and outgoing mail.

The Oman Exhibition Centre is a vast hall used for commercial exhibitions, public functions, and entertainments. It is the site of the Eid festivals, which are akin to county fairs where everyone comes to browse among booths selling crafts and commercial items. It's a time for celebration when Omani families come en masse, proudly showing off their new holiday clothes. There are snack bars, dance exhibitions, fashion shows, raffles, and other amusements.

Just beyond the airport is the intersection of the coastal highway with the main road to the interior. The juncture is at the **Muaskar Al Murtafa'a roundabout,** commonly known as the **MAM roundabout,** but properly it is the **Sahwa Tower** and is used as a key landmark for orientation. In recent years traffic up the coast has increased to the extent that the highway department constructed a shunt that bypasses the roundabout to ease traffic flow along the coastal corridor. The roundabout is nevertheless striking and a good place to pause after a long day's journey. You can park in the nearby parking lot just off the southeast side of the roundabout and enter via the walkway underpass. In the center is a huge clock tower over a central fountain surrounded by a maze of paths. Situated about the perimeter of this tower are eight murals. The arrangement of the maze is that of four interior murals nested and offset at oblique angles to four exterior murals. All are visible from the roadway but none are in sight of each other. The murals consist of intricate ceramic relief/mosaics depicting Omani settings. The roundabout was presented as a gift to His Majesty Sultan Qaboos from his people and is one of the more elegant structures in the Sultanate. You will directly engage the roundabout on your way to Nizwa and the interior but you will slightly bypass it when going up the coast.

Al Hail and Seeb (SS)

Taking the coastal road will bring you first to the community of **Al Hail,** which is identified by the **Al Mawaleh roundabout** with a replica fort sitting resplendently four kilometers past the MAM roundabout (Map 7). The slip roads on either side offer access to small shops and cafés, **Arabian Gardens Restaurant,** and the **Istrahat Al-Seeb Hotel.** The next intersection, six kilometers on, is the **Al Khoudh roundabout,** which features an open Qur'an and where a right turn will take you to Seeb proper.

Seeb is a busy coastal town with a modern souq, old souq, and plenty of fish markets. From the Qur'an roundabout (right), follow through to the next roundabout and continue straight (a right-hand turn will take you to the **Al Bashasha Restaurant** along the nearby wadi). You will then bypass the **Royal Stables** and race course on your right before coming to a T-junction.

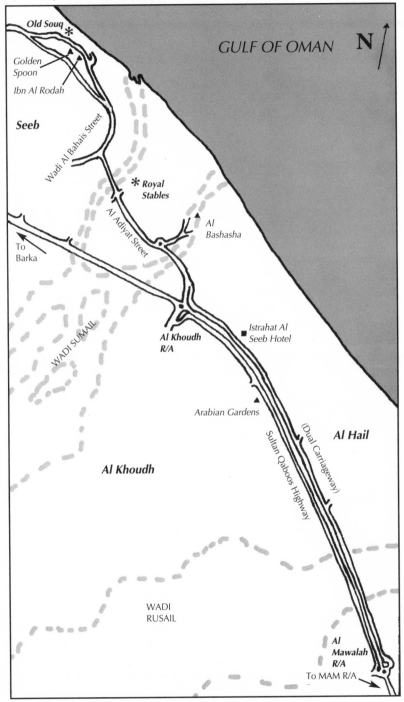

Old Souq

Golden
Spoon

Ibn Al Rodah

Seeb

Wadi Al Bahais Street

GULF OF OMAN

N

* Royal
Stables

Al Adiyat Street

Al
Bashasha

To
Barka

WADI SUMAIL

Istrahat Al
Seeb Hotel

**Al Khoudh
R/A**

Arabian Gardens

Al Hail

Sultan Qaboos Highway

(Dual Carriageway)

Al Khoudh

WADI
RUSAIL

**Al
Mawalah
R/A**

To MAM R/A

1 km

Turn right and you will be on **Wadi Al Bahais Street,** which is the main thoroughfare into Seeb. The street becomes one-way in (don't worry, a parallel street becomes the one way out) and in the center of town you will come across the old souq. The **Seeb old souq** provides a similar charm to that of the Mutrah souq and a good opportunity to see old world traditions still in practice. Side streets to the right will take you to the shore where, depending on the time of day, fishermen will be hauling in their boats and nets and displaying their catch for immediate sale.

THE BATINAH COAST

From Seeb to Barka (SS)

Continuing on the highway for another 4 kilometers, there is the beautiful **Al Zulfa Mosque** on the left side of the highway (Map 8). Further along there is **Rumais Prison,** which is Oman's primary correctional facility. Beyond that about 18 kilometers from Seeb on the right is **Naseem Garden,** one of the largest public gardens in Oman and a favorite spot for taking an evening stroll. Five kilometers past the gardens on the left is a sign post to the Al Falaij dam. This road leads to the newly constructed **Al Falaij camel racetrack** which is several kilometers up the road, set back from the road to the right in the open plain. You'll have to check with newspapers or locals as to when races take place.

The next major roundabout will be at the city of **Barka,** approximately 38 kilometers from Seeb. A right turn off the roundabout will bring you into the center of Barka, a seaside town with small souqs, a fort along the shoreline, and home of a favorite Omani pastime: **bullfighting.** This is not the Spanish variety; compared to the running of the bulls at Pamplona, this is quite orderly . . . and civilized. On alternate Fridays, farmers will bring their prize bulls to face one another in a showdown where the bulls are pitted against each other in an open arena and try to shove each other to the ground. No blood is drawn and the worst damage any bull suffers is maybe wounded pride and a bad headache. Half the fun is watching the cheering partisan onlookers, who have taken sides with their favorite performers and fill the air with revelry and friendly chiding.

The Fort at Barka was restored in 1986 and serves as a reminder of the many times Oman had to protect itself from outside invaders. Barka is the site of the famous ousting of the Persians by Ahmed bin Said in 1747. The fort is quite impressive when seen from offshore with four tall towers rising above the surrounding palm plantations. Today the wali uses the great hall of the fort to receive visitors and dignitaries.

If you travel through the environs of Barka, you might come across some abandoned plantations that appear like little ghost towns. Nothing survives

8) The Batinah Coast

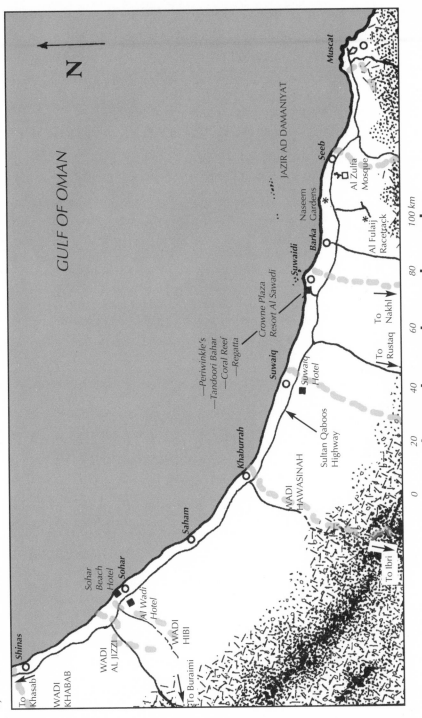

here any more as over-pumping of the wells has caused salt water from the sea to creep into the water supply. The date palms are probably the hardiest of vegetation in these parts; if the date trees have died, nothing can survive. The saline intrusion problem is something that can only be corrected by nature as water levels adjust, with time, to pre-pumping levels as fresh water aquifers are replenished by groundwater from the jebels.

Just west of Barka is the huge plantation and **Castle Bait Al Nu'man.** This is one of the castles that is testament to the success of the early Ya'rubas. It was a common rest stop for traveling officials and was the scene of the death of Badr bin Saif at the hands of the young Said bin Sultan, who went on to become the longest lived of the Albusaidis.

Suwaidi (SS, HCP)

Continue up the coast on the main highway beyond Barka. At 10 kilometers you will pass the left turnoff to Wadi Abyadh (see below) and continue on. The next area of interest is the coastal area of **Suwaidi.** The right turnoff is 18 kilometers past Barka and from there it is a short drive to the coast passing through the town of Suwaidi. Just before the beach is the new **Suwaidi Beach Resort** (see previous hotel section), where you can center your activities.

The beach itself is long and wide in both directions, great for casual strolls and beachcombing. The chief point of interest is the **near-shore archipelago, Jazir Suwaidi,** which can be accessed by hiring a boat from the local fishermen. (Don't get taken for a ride, haggle for the fare.) They will take you on fishing or diving jaunts or just a curiosity excursion. If you get dropped off, establish a time for a return. The islands are small but filled with nooks and crannies, ridges, and peaks for investigating. It is a nice way to spend an afternoon. The largest one (visible from several spots along the coast and further inland, see Wadi Abyadh) is nearest to the shore and can be waded to at low tide. Some of the islets are just rocky crags and others have beaches in tiny coves. All are fun to explore.

> Go back to those who sent you, and tell them that I shall defend the fort to the utmost of my power; and if they choose to cut [my husband] to pieces before me, they will find no alteration in my resolution.
> —Wife of Sayyid Hilal bin Muhammed Al Bu Said, wali of Suwaiq, in response to empty threats that her husband was overthrown

Suwaiq (SS)

The road continues up the coast passing the Masana'ah roundabout (which leads up to Al Hazm and Rustaq) at 35 kilometers from Barka. Shortly after this you will be passing the town of **Wudam** where the country's major naval station and training base is located. At 51 kilometers you will come to the **Suwaiq roundabout.** Nearby (follow the signs inland) is the **Suwaiq Motel,** a good spot for an overnight respite. Suwaiq is a quiet fishing village but the fort there was witness to many turbulent times. During the 1800s there was a denounced assassination attempt of the sultan and subsequent foiled assassination of the wali. Later the fort, under siege from dissident tribes, was ably defended by the wali's wife while her husband was away on business in Muscat.

Khaburrah (SS)

From Suwaiq to Khabburah is about 38 kilometers. **Khaburrah** is the traditional center of weaving in the Sultanate. Here rugs, bags, baskets, and tapestries are made. Other handicrafts such as pottery can be purchased. Prices here are very reasonable as the craftwork is subsidized by the government (so there's no need to haggle). These items can also be purchased at outlets back in Muscat: one in the Ministry of Social Affairs and Labour Shop in SABCO Centre, and the Ministry of Heritage and Culture Shop in Al Ghubrah (see map 5, Bait Al Tarath Al Omani).

After Khabburah you will come to **Suwairah roundabout,** which is distinguished by the eight artificial palm trees arranged in the center. A detour around the roundabout and back in the direction of Muscat will bring you to the **Oman Sun Farms Dairy** where you can quench your thirst with a variety of flavored milk, laban, and yogurt drinks.

Sohar (SS, HP)

> Sohar is the capital and is on the sea. Its traders and commerce cannot be enumerated. It is the most developed and wealthy town in Oman. The rest of Islam hardly knows that a town such as Sohar, with its wealth and development, exists.
>
> —ibn Hawqal, tenth century

Sohar is quite a distance along, 68 kilometers from Khaburrah and 300 kilometers from Muscat. But once you arrive you have the pleasure of staying at one of two resorts while you can take the time to explore the town and environs. **Sohar** goes back to antiquity, although there is little left to see of the old, old Sohar. Still, there is an **old souq,** a fort (**Sohar Fort**) along the beach—singularly conspicuous with its whitewashed walls and towers, a stadium and bullfighting arena, long sunny beaches, and enclaves of village fishermen.

Outside of town on the next turnoff to Buraimi is **Wadi Al Jizzi,** a nice off-road romp with villages, running water from gushing springs, and, to make it complete, an impressive **recharge dam,** a feat of modern engineering.

Further on up the road is the **Lusail Copper Mine** where copper ore has been extracted for several thousand years. Outside of Sohar on the main highway there are signs to **Wadi Hibi,** which runs parallel to the east of Wadi Al Jizzi. You will find a turnoff, a tarmac road which goes into the jebels for a stretch before it turns to gravel. But there are many quaint villages with neatly painted walls and decorated windows situated in bright green oases. After you pass the foothills, the oases start popping up and the road will dip into the wadi at intervals. There could be water at times. This track, if pursued, will cross through the jebels and come out somewhere between Dank and Ibri, although I have not followed it all the way through.

Wadi Khabab (SS, HCP, 4WD)

Continuing on past Sohar for about 70 kilometers you will come to a roundabout that is signposted to Dubai and Al Wajaja. Turn left toward the interior and follow the wadi bed. After 21 kilometers an intersection to your left reads Tumait; here you turn onto a dirt track. There may be running water in the wadi, but press on. After 1 kilometer take a left fork; after another 4 kilometers, a right fork. You will pass through terraced plantations fed by aflaj. Shortly after are the **blue pools of Wadi Khabab.** These mineral pools are similar to the ones found in Wadi Abyadh but the color is a remarkable resilient hue of aquamarine. Nearby water and gases seep to the surface. A dam constructed by the locals holds back water for the farms below. Wadi Khabab is a nice day trip out of Sohar or a good overnight camp with lots of little pockets to explore along the wadi.

Shinas (SS, HP)

Further up the coast is **Shinas,** the last major town along the Batinah before you reach the UAE border. Here is another coastal city with a restored fort, which saw action in the 1800s when combined Omani and British forces stormed it to oust Wahhabi infiltrators backed by Persian support. A three-day siege of the fort from the coast was necessary to dislodge the defenders, another testament to the original Omani architects and engineers.

THE COAST FROM YITI TO QURIYAT TO SUR

Yiti, Bander Khayran, and As Seifah (SS, HCP, 4WD)

There are two approaches to **Yiti,** the small coastal village southeast of Muscat, second in proximity to the capital next to Bander Jissah (Map 9). The first, and most direct way, is as previously mentioned, from a side road off Ruwi High Street. From the Al Hamriyah roundabout turn right off Ruwi High Street at roughly 0.8 kilometers. After twisting through a dense

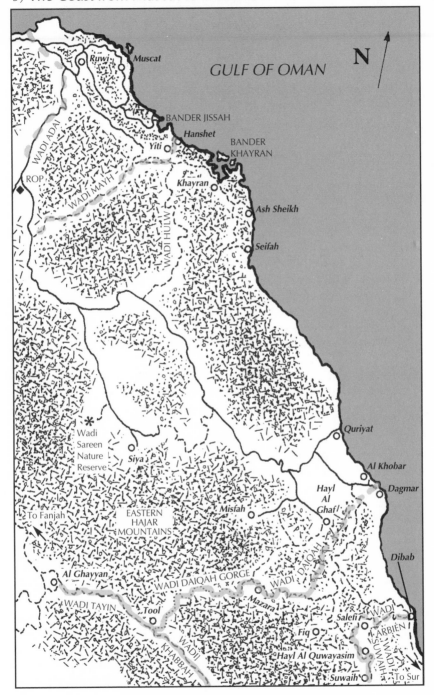

GULF OF OMAN

N

Ruwi Muscat

BANDER JISSAH

Hanshet

Yiti

BANDER KHAYRAN

ROP

WADI ADAI

WADI MAYH

WADI HULW

Khayran

Ash Sheikh

Seifah

Quriyat

Al Khobar

*
Wadi Sareen Nature Reserve

Siya

Hayl Al Ghaf

Dagmar

To Fanjah

EASTERN HAJAR MOUNTAINS

Misfah

Dibab

Al Ghayyan

WADI DAIQAH GORGE

WADI DAIQAH

Mazara

Salefi

WADI ARBIEN

WADI TAYIN

Tool

Fiq

WADI SUWAIH

WADI KHABBAH

Hayl Al Quwayasim

Suwaih

To Sur

10 km

neighborhood (the road narrows the further you get) it reaches the end of the housing and passes between two buildings and up out of the wadi over a ridge. Now paved, the section of road is easily traversed with saloon cars. Yiti is signposted ahead. The road is fairly flat for a while until it takes some dips to the wadi bed (Wadi Qanu) and finally over one large rise, down onto the floor of a broad flood plain (at 15.6 kilometers). The pavement ends just before an intersection, entering from right, which is the other way to Yiti, a gravel track that has run 20 kilometers through Wadi Mayh from the main road to Quriyat.

Keeping to the left, pass through a local plantation and at 16 kilometers the road narrows to one-way. (The return one-way skirts the far side of the farm to the north and meets up with the main track.) The one-way split rejoins after about 1 kilometer. Up ahead is another intersection with a signpost. Yiti is on the road bearing left. 300 meters after this there is another triangular intersection with Yiti still off to the left. The road to the right will eventually reach the Quriyat road through Wadi Hulw, but just a few meters past this intersection there is a left-hand turnoff between a sharp ridge and some houses. There is also a government building which looks to be a GTO relay station. We'll return to this turnoff in a few minutes.

Continuing on to the left, pass through the village of Yiti and through the gap toward the beach. There are several football field boundaries scratched into the ground and usually lots of kids around playing football or milling about. The beach is about 2 kilometers from Yiti and here is a nice spot for swimming, snorkeling, fishing, and camping as long as you don't get too near the shoreline village of **Hanshet.** The people welcome you, but a little space will afford you and them some privacy. If you don't care to fish you might haggle for your dinner with the local fishermen as they come in with the daily catch. There are some nicely windblown and waterswept spires close to the shore that are home to many species of tidal fauna, and the beach itself is fun to explore for shells.

Back at the intersection before Yiti, take the road between the ridge and the houses with the GTO building on your right. After 4.8 kilometers you will pass by a small village called **Yenkit** that has its own snug little harbor off to the left as you climb over a saddle. At 5.4 kilometers there is a left-hand turnoff by an encampment of huts. This is the main entrance to **Bander Khayran** picnic area which is just a short drive ahead. When you arrive at the shoreline you will find a number of places to hide away for an afternoon or overnight. There is a lot of boating activity in the bay. Snorkeling is excellent along the ridges that meet the water and swimming is great along the many shallow sandy bottom coves. At night sometimes, particularly in the summer, the phosphorescence in the water is tremendous, giving the swimmer a veritable underwater light show.

There is an overlook of the entire bay that is about a 25-minute hike from the main beach and picnic area. Facing the beach, turn right and walk to the ridge as far right as possible and find the goat paths that lead up the side of what looks to be a fairly steep ridge (but looks are deceiving, it's not that hard). The climb is hardest at the outset when you break from the goat path to scramble over some loose rocks until you reach a point two-thirds of the way up, where some clambering over the outcrop is required. Just beyond this, the trail levels out and you can proceed to any number of vantage points several hundred feet above the bay for some magnificent photo ops. Although this is the best vantage point, many of the ridges on either side of the bay are accessible and provide great views and secluded inlets for exploring. If you come to Bander Khayran by boat, there are several islands with isolated beaches and trails for idle rambling and exploring. It is a favorite spot among Omanis and expats alike.

Back out at the entrance to the picnic area by the encampment, the road continues on and eventually runs along the shore of the bander (bay) for several kilometers, first along mangrove trees, then rising above the water around a narrow spit and past a fisherman's enclave, eventually coming onto the village of **Khayran.** Here the local children will try to sell seashells that they have collected, decorated, and scented to passersby. After the village the road turns into the jebels and climbs and falls along a narrow graded track. At about 5 klicks past the village there is a left-hand turnoff to the village of **Ash Sheikh.** This is a short road but a steep one as you will climb a very high ridge and descend very quickly. You will soon pass through the village which is situated near a small but beautiful cove that is excellent for picnicking, swimming, and exploring.

Beyond the turnoff, it is another 12 kilometers to the village of **Seifah,** one of the best spots to spend an idyllic weekend on the Omani coast. The road is rocky and steep and the last descent to the coast is breathtaking, but once you have reached sea level (and started breathing again) there is a turnoff on the floor of the wadi to your left that will bring you to Seifah. At the village you can turn left or right and follow the tracks out of town to any remote locale along the beach. The right-hand turn past the school, the hospital and across a ragged stretch runs for quite a distance down the coast to some excellent dunes along the shore; this is the favored option. The road continues beyond a point that I have yet to explore but I perceive it is more of same until you reach Quriyat: long stretches of white sand beaches at the base of the jebels. Pick your spot. They're all beautiful.

From Muscat to Quriyat (SS, HCP)

The primary link to the eastern seaboard is a road that starts from the Wadi Adai roundabout in Watayah (Route 17 on NSA country maps), just outside of Ruwi. As you head south you will go through a narrow pass (8 kilometers) and come out onto a broad plain which has been developed into a suburban area servicing the capital district. You will see right away a major telecommunications installation off to your right with huge dishes pointed to the sky. The highway is divided at this point and remains so for the next few kilometers as you continue on straight through a series of 4 roundabouts, the last one near the ROP station at 16.5 kilometers from the Wadi Adai roundabout. The main highway is now off to the left (10 o'clock on the roundabout).

The road is now undivided but paved. At 24 kilometers there is the other turnoff to Yiti through Wadi Mayh (see above). The villages are now spread out and removed from the road for the most part. The scenery is striking with outcrops and escarpments being the predominant features. Off to the right the Eastern Hajars run to the southeast. At 38 kilometers there is a right intersection which will take you to the village of **Siya** and, in passing, the **Wadi Sareen Nature Reserve** which is land set aside for the Arabian Tahr (see chapter 3). At this time there is no mechanism in place to observe the tahr, as they tend to stick to the higher slopes of the jebels. Siya, on the other hand, is quite accessible and is a charming little village with well-established plots and aflaj. For the most part the streets in the village are paved and it serves as a nice diversion for travelers who don't wish to go too far afield. At the far end of town there is a dirt track which leads down an embankment and over a ridge to an older set of ruins, through which a path leads to the source of the aflaj.

Back on the Quriyat road, you will wind in and out of some narrow passes, cross a flood plain or two, and rise to a plateau (72 kilometers) before descending very steeply into the wilayat of Quriyat. From the top there is a breathtaking vista as you are several hundred meters above the flood plain ahead. Down at the bottom there is a right turnoff next to a BP station which will take you to the lush village of **Hayl Al Ghaf** and Wadi Daiqah Gorge. Turn right here and proceed in. This road will take you straight to the village, but after 3.5 klicks turn right again. This road is paved and it will take you over a ridge and on down toward the village of **Misfah.** (This is one of several villages named Misfah. The Misfah of considerable attraction is the one situated in Jebel Akhdar behind the town of Al Hamra on the way to the Grand Canyon.) After 2.8 kilometers turn left onto a well-traveled dirt track.

> We found ourselves at the entrance of a cleft, which is as sharp and abrupt as if we were entering the portals of some monstrous castle and stood immured within its massive walls. Towering loftily, sheer and perpendicular above the narrow floor, the huge walls of rock give the appearance as if the mountain range had suddenly been split in twain from the base to the summit by some convulsion of nature, exhibiting a singular illustration of impressive grandeur.
> —Lt. Colonel Samuel Barrett Miles, on Wadi Daiqah, 1884

Wadi Daiqah (SS, HCP, 4WD)

This track is generally in pretty good shape. After 8 kilometers the road branches right by a blue sign. If you continue on straight you can work your way back to Hayl Al Ghaf through some interesting scenic spots along the canyon floor, but this is not Wadi Daiqah proper. Take the right turn by the blue sign offering valuable tourist information and follow the road as it winds through a narrow stretch along the wadi floor, then climbs to the plateau. Continuing on you will eventually descend into the mouth of the gorge, a breathtaking spectacle. At 15 kilometers from the tarmac there is another track turning off right by a soccer pitch. Turn right here and follow past an encampment of Shuwawi and you should see the wadi up ahead through a stand of trees. The track approaches this stand and crosses through over a narrow concrete slab covering the falaj. The track is now on the floor of **Wadi Daiqah Gorge** and you can wend your way up the track for several kilometers, past glittering streams, shimmering pools, burbling cascades, and waterfalls until you can go no further (by vehicle, that is). Here you can get out and stretch, walk around, and find that perfect retreat. There's lots of places to have a picnic and a swim. Wadi Daiqah flows year-round.

And then there's the hike. If you are of such inclination you can walk through Wadi Daiqah to its entrance point on the other side of the jebels, 8 miles away, where Wadis Tayin and Khabbah converge at a point called **Devil's Gap,** the start of the ravine. In between there is an incredible display of geology and nature and lots of scenery. Most folks are content with an idle ramble of a mile or two. But some just have to get to the other side. The best way for this is to have two teams start at either end for a combined hike and overnight, meet in the middle, and exchange car keys before continuing on. (Details of Devil's Gap are explained further on.)

If you are just passing through without doing the cross, you will probably want to go back to the turnoff by the soccer pitch and head for the town of **Mazara,** just 3 klicks off to your right, an old and still thriving oasis town. As you pass through the town keep to the left of the buildings on the main track until you see a track running through a stand of palms to your right. This track is only one car-width and has stone walls on either side for 20 meters. At the far end it opens out onto the wadi and one of the most scenic, picture-postcard areas in Oman. As you splash through the wadi and head up the far bank to the far end of town, everywhere is a sight to behold. Just before an old majestic fort-like building on a ridge (3.8 kilometers), the road turns right, up through the trees and into another part of the village. The road winds left around a cemetery and down a slope. The track, almost imperceptible on the glare rocks, crosses the wadi one more time before leaving all the lush greenery behind. The track then climbs a steep plateau,

Wadi Daiqah from below Mazara.

dips down into another valley, and climbs another steep wall to the top of the plateau. Here you will see a spot to pull over (about 3 kilometers past Mazara) and marvel at the canyon from above, looking back at the town and ahead out to the flood plains and the sea.

Another 5 kilometers on and you will be at an intersection with the right turn going to Al Ya. The left continues toward the coast and is the route you want to take. Throughout this area of the plateau there are beautiful abstract sculptures of windblown rock as outcrops decorate the landscape.

Wadi Suwaih (SS, HCP, 4WD)

In another 5.3 kilometers there is an intersection with the right turnoff going to **Wadi Suwaih.** The track into Suwaih runs along the rim of the plateau before descending and rising in a roller-coaster ride over ridges and wadis with several switchbacks. At 9 kilometers there is a turnoff to the village of **Fiq,** which provides a fairly interesting diversion, a close encounter of the jebel kind. At 11.4 klicks there is a turnoff to the left that runs through **Wadi Arbien** through the village of **Salefi.** (We will come back to this route presently.) At 13 kilometers you will descend a steep track past the village of **Hayl Al Quwaysim** on your left. There is usually running water in the wadi off to your left that services the local farms. A lone tower stands up ahead above the village as the road winds down past the village first and the tower next as it goes further on up the far ridge. The ride at this point gets a little more bumpy and the track narrows, if that is physically possible. The end of your ride, though, is only a few klicks up ahead.

Once over the rise you will descend again and run parallel to the wadi. The road is extremely narrow and if someone is coming the other way, someone will have to back off as there are few spots for pulling over. As you descend you will pass some beautiful pools, one with a perennial waterfall near the village. Finally you descend to the wadi floor and cross to a short but particularly steep and winding track up into the village of **Suwaih.** (Lombard Street in San Francisco never had it so good!) Here there is some space to park although a better option is down by the wadi floor. There are several paths that lead alongside the village and through burbling cascades that invariably have kids swimming in them. The kids in this town especially like treats, so be prepared. You can follow the paths up the wadi in two directions, as there is a confluence near the village, as far as your wanderlust will take you. The locals know trails to the top of the jebels here, but that is a particularly long haul, meaning you'll have to do it as an overnight and return the next day. If you do camp in this area try to remove yourself as far as possible from the village so as not to disturb the locals.

If you want to return by a slightly different route you can return to the turnoff to **Wadi Arbien** and follow it as it snakes its way out to the coast, passing some interesting geology in the canyon and some remote settlements cum plantations. The trip out to the coast and the town of **Dibab** is about 13.5 kilometers; from here you can either backtrack to Quriyat or continue on down the coast to **Tiwi.**

Quriyat (SS, P)

The following description starts back on the main road by the BP station and the turnoff to Hayl al Ghaf and Wadi Daiqah. If you continue past this road you will come upon a Shell petrol pump on your right, a hospital on your left, and a roundabout. Continuing through the roundabout will take you into **Quriyat** proper. Upon entering the town you will see two Omani mainstays: a fort that is over a hundred and fifty years old and a spreading *Shareesh* tree said to be much older. These days it is just a fishing and agricultural town, but it was a teeming port of call before the Portuguese invasion. No doubt you will run across many fishermen here and along the shore as they repair their nets or make ready for the next cast-off.

Along the coast outside of town are stands of mangroves that harbor any number of birds. Here and in Hayl Al Ghaf are two prime spots for bird watching because of the abundance of foliage and ground cover in an otherwise open plain.

Besides fishermen and farmers, there are a variety of crafts people in Quriyat, from weavers and basket makers to silversmiths to musicians and instrument makers to creators of the gooey confection halwa. To celebrate National Day a few years back, a collective of these folks put on a three-day craft show to celebrate their heritage. As tourism continues to grow, seasonal events will be scheduled to show off their wares and skills. It is hoped that a permanent venue will be established in the town. Check with local newspapers or the *Oman Today* publication, which carries listings for events throughout the Sultanate.

The Coast Road to Sur (SS, HCP, 4WD)

From the roundabout in Quriyat you can take a right and proceed down the tarmac toward the village of **Dagmar** and a beach area called **Al Khobar.** Before you reach these places, just a few klicks from the roundabout you will see a turnoff to the right, a well-traveled track that heads through some scrub and across the flood plain to the mouth of a large canyon. This is the extreme lower extremity of Wadi Daiqah. At the time of this writing, there was extensive quarrying being done to the right side of the mouth, facing in. However, no amount of quarrying could remove the steep rock face that forms the walls of the canyon. Turning right into the mouth, you will be driving over gravel beds of the outwash plain. Daiqah is flowing at further points upstream; at this point the flow has gone underground and the surface does

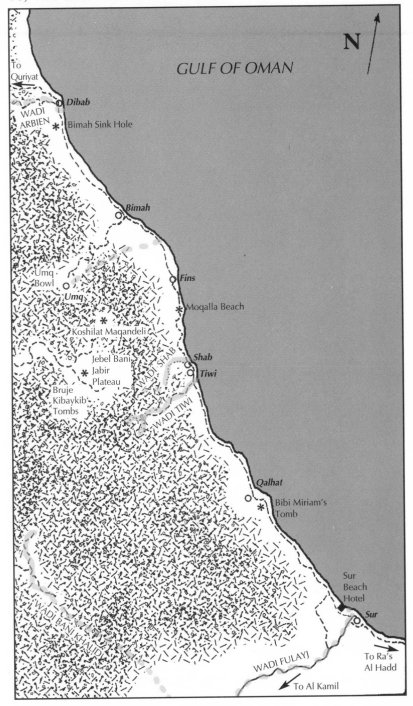

N

GULF OF OMAN

To
Quriyat

Dibab

WADI
ARBIEN ✳ Bimah Sink Hole

Bimah

Umq
Bowl   Fins
Umq
          ✳ Moqalla Beach
    ✳
Koshilat Maqandeli

Jebel Bani   Shab
   ✳ Jabir   Tiwi
Plateau
Bruje
Kibaykib
Tombs

Qalhat
       ✳ Bibi Miriam's
           Tomb

WADI SHAB

WADI TIWI

WADI BANI KHALID

Sur
Beach
Hotel
         Sur

WADI FULAYJ
                To Ra's
                Al Hadd
        ← To Al Kamil

10 km

not usually see water except in flood season (early spring). After a few kilometers, the track climbs out of the wadi and rises to a plateau.

The road is in generally good condition, with small rises and dips for the next 10 klicks or so. The view of the escarpment of the Eastern Hajars and the Wadi Daiqah Canyon running towards Devil's Gap is breathtaking. After 8 kilometers you will meet up with the intersection off to the right that will take you back towards Mazara and the road that leads to Wadi Suwaih (see above). Continue on straight over the plateau as the road gets windier, steeper, and bumpier. It's not that hard traveling and pretty soon (16 kilometers past the last intersection) you will descend quite precipitously to the coast (the view down the coast before you descend is superb). At the bottom you will pass through the village of **Dibab** and the outlet of Wadi Arbien (if you chose to exit Wadi Suwaih this way you will know where you are).

The road now stays on the coastal shelf from here to Tiwi (Map 10). The sea is rich aqua and there are places up and down the coast that are excellent stopping-off points for swimming, beachcombing, snorkeling, etc. At about 5.7 kilometers past Dibab there is a turnoff to your right on a particularly flat section of track. It is not signposted as of this writing and if you blink, you'll miss it. But if you look off to your right just a hundred meters or so and see some shelters for picnickers, you are at the right spot. Turn in here and drive up to these shelters and stop. You have arrived at the **Bimah Sink Hole** (more properly, *Al Faqa'ah* in Arabic). The sink hole itself is not visible until you are directly upon it.

The sink hole is a fine example of karst activity: underground water dissolves limestone bedrock until the expanse is too wide to support the weight of the overlying rock and the roof caves in. This particular sink hole is about 40 meters across and 20 meters deep. At the bottom the dark emerald brackish water (mixture of sea water and fresh water) is in stark contrast to the bright aqua of the sea just a few hundred meters away. Water activity continues to hollow out underground areas and divers have gone in to find a network of submerged caves. The life forms in the pool lead a separate existence from the tidal shelf environment just across the way. This stop is a fine diversion and a good place for some exploring. Note: a concrete stairwell has recently been put into place to prevent visitors from damaging the fragile walls of the hole in descending, plus there is a modest retaining wall around the perimeter, enough to prevent the unwary from accidentally falling in.

Umq Bowl (SS, HP, 4WD)

Continuing on the main track, the road stays fairly flat, dipping into a wadi or two and weaving in and out between the shoreline and the base of the scarp. The next village you will encounter is Bimah and just after Bimah is a turnoff to the right. This track will take you to the spectacular area known as **Umq.** You can see the track ahead as it rises into the hills and disappears into the jebels. This track is only 17 klicks to the end and the first part of the drive is fairly easy, but as you go deeper in you will have to engage in four-low as the road is awfully steep, rutted, and loose, with chunks of debris that have slid down into the path. The drive to the end is worth the effort as you will come into a vast box canyon hollowed out by immeasurable forces. At the bottom is a well-established village with aflaj, trees, running water, and stunning scenery in every direction. The people in this village are very friendly and may very well ask your party to take khawa with them.

The shaykh lives in a settlement above the village, which gives him a great vantage point. He told us of trails that lead up the jebels and further in to the interior and of one path that will lead to the Khoshilat Maqandeli Cave (which I don't doubt, but I know that access to the cave from the interior is much easier, especially if you plan any serious exploration of the cave). The canyon is haunted by the spirit of a young village girl who roams about, they say. Many years ago she climbed the trail to collect grasses at the summit for her goats and fell off the edge into the canyon. She fell to a ledge where her body was unrecoverable.

Further on down the coast is the village of **Fins.** From Fins on to Tiwi the shoreline is known as **Mokallah Beach.** There are many great spots for overnights. There are even shelters constructed at various points along the way at the beachfront before and after Fins. After Fins, the coastal shelf overlaps the shoreline in some spots, leaving secluded coves and inlets. The marine life in the tidal flats is abundant. Beaches vary from fine sand to pebbly. Outcrops display a wide variety of fossils and at one point, there are bi-valve shells in the rock wider than an outstretched hand. There are many spots to camp and picnic. At night, the stargazing is excellent because of the remoteness from built-up areas—there is no light pollution. During the day you might even catch sight of cavorting dolphins playing along the coast or sand gazelles coming out to lap the morning dew on the plain.

Tiwi and Shab (SS, HCP, 4WD)

From Fins to Shab is about 14 kilometers. You can easily spot the sister towns of Tiwi and Shab up ahead in the distance. These are two fishing and agricultural villages that go back to antiquity and it is easy to see why. They have the best of both worlds, between food cultivation and fishing. And both Wadis Shab and Tiwi offer spectacular hikes through stunning scenic gorges.

Wadi Shab is the first you will come to as you enter the town and descend to the floor, with houses perched on the rim on the opposite side. There are boats lined up on the beach to your left and sometimes fish spread over the beach to dry in the sun. To your right you will see a lagoon and a grassy area beyond. You can drive along the far bank and park off to the side by the rope ferry, which you will need to cross the wadi at this point. The ferry is invariably attended and if there is no one there, you can let yourself across. But if there are kids hanging around (there usually are) they will want to take you across (for a gratuity). The path up the wadi is easy to follow and you will soon be in a steep gorge with sparkling pools, lush greenery, and nothing but silence and bird calls (that is, if the diesel pump upstream is turned off). As you move into the wadi you will eventually leave the date plots behind, but the scenery is still green and attractive. Follow the wadi as it bears to the left and soon you will have to negotiate a series of pools by swimming or wading across. Rocks close to the waterline can be slippery with algae, so watch your step.

The last pool appears to come to a dead end but the best is yet to come. Depending on the water level you will see a narrow cleft in the rocks. If the water level is too high you will have to take a breath and swim underwater through the cleft for about 10 feet. If the water is low enough you can tread your way through a very narrow (and deep!) channel for the same distance until it opens up into a fantastic little grotto with a tumbling waterfall and several "shelves" to clamber up onto to sit, relax, and take it all in. If you look around you can find footholds next to the waterfall to climb further, but it is tricky. Most people are satisfied with this as their destination point. The wadi up above is not quite so interesting. If you take this hike give yourself plenty of time. The round trip takes several hours.

"[Tiwi is] one of the loveliest of villages and most striking in beauty with flowing streams and abundant orchards," wrote Ibn Battuta in *Travels* in the fourteenth century.

Wadi Tiwi is just about as nice, with the added feature that you can drive in for at least 10 to 12 kilometers (something you can't do at Wadi Shab). Take the road through Shab and Tiwi (it's hard to tell them apart because they abut one another) and at the far side of Tiwi you will see a broad flood plain that runs to the beach. Just off to your right you will see tracks heading up the wadi. For those not ambitious enough to take the Wadi Shab hike, Wadi Tiwi is a nice alternative. You can find many quiet and bucolic spots with running water, lots of shade, friendly locals, and some nice spots to picnic. However, for the hale and hardy, if you want to hike Wadi Tiwi, you can do that too. You can also drive to the end and hike further on into the jebels if you want to.

> Qalhat has many fine bazaars and a very beautiful mosque, the walls are tiled with qashani tiles which resemble enamel. It stands on an eminence overlooking the sea and anchorage and was built by a holy woman, Bibi Maryam. The inhabitants are traders and live entirely on what comes to them from the Indian Ocean. Whenever a vessel arrives at the town, they show the greatest joy.
>
> —Ibn Battuta, *Travels*, 1368

Wadi Tiwi.

Qalhat (SS, 4WD)

The coast road continues on hugging the beach for a while and then slowly works its way back to the jebels, but not too far. The sea always stays close at hand. Twenty klicks or so past Tiwi you will come upon a forlorn sight just on a rise past another village. A lone ruin (and fragment of another) stands looking out over the ocean. This is known as **Bibi Miriam's Tomb** and it is the only building remaining from the ancient port of **Qalhat,** which was razed by the Portuguese in 1507. Sadly, the tomb is in desperate need of repair and it is hoped that it will soon reach the top of the list of priorities of the Ministry of Heritage and Culture's reclamation projects.

The road continues on down the coast rising above the sea (maybe 100 meters) for some beautiful overlooks up and down the coast. Ahead is the coastal town (and boat building center) of **Sur.** The road winds down to the beach again and the last leg of this route is across flat sweeping plains into the city. The description of Sur and points east is taken up in the section on Sharqiyah.

WESTERN HAJARS, FROM THE COAST

The roundabout at Barka is the leading intersection that will take you to the northern flanks of Jebel Akhdar. In a nutshell, the tarmac road leads from the coastal plains of the Batinah to the foothills and along the base of the jebels. It loops back out to the coastal highway just west of Masana'ah.

The simple loop is about 132 kilometers with another 35 kilometers back to Barka. On the way you will pass through the two major wilayats of Nakhl and Rustaq, as well as the entrances to several wadi systems that will be discussed here in detail, those of Wadi Mistal, Wadi Abyadh, Wadi Bani Kharus, Wadi Bani Awf, Wadi Sahtan, Wadi Hoquein, and Wadi Bani Ghafir. Wadi Hawasina is further up the coast and can be reached from Khabburah on the coast or from the far end of the Wadi Bani Ghafir track to the interior. Nakhl, Awabi, and Rustaq can be approached with saloon cars. The wadis require 4WD.

Nakhl (SS, HP)

The road to **Nakhl** is a simple leisurely drive from Muscat. Once you have turned off the main highway at Barka you will come directly face-to-face with the Jebel Akhdar off in the distance (Map 11). They may appear hazy at first but will come into focus as you approach. Nakhl is 32 kilometers from Barka and the road is flat crossing a stretch of savanna until you reach the foothills. As you approach Nakhl (clearly marked), keep an eye out for the fortress that sits on a hillock outside of the town. The **fortress at Nakhl** will look quite imposing as you get near. Take the left-hand turn off of the main road; the entrance to the fort is just beyond. Once you step inside and take a view from the watchtower you will see just how strategically located the fort is. The fort's origin is pre-Islamic with major contributions by the Ya'ruba and Al Bu Said dynasties. The fort underwent a major restoration in 1990 and is open to the public.

If you continue past the fort on the road into the town you will pass by the modern commercial center and then immediately pass through date plantations dissected by many aflaj. The road becomes winding and narrow, but if you press on you will see water up ahead tumbling across the road in a broad stream. Beyond, there usually will be a gathering of people as they come to spend a relaxing afternoon in the public garden and enjoy the source of the running water, the **Nakhl Hot Springs**. Here you can park, walk along the wadi course, and explore the valley that runs into the jebel. There are many shady spots for a picnic and it is fun to go wading in the everflowing stream. (Keep your clothes on, please.)

Wadi Mistal (SS, HCP, 4WD)

Coming back to the main road, you can take a left as you leave Nakhl and drive into the foothills of the jebels. The road dips through several wadi beds. Outwash plains are quite in evidence. The area is sprinkled with acacia trees and other small scrub. After about 13 kilometers you will leave the flood plains behind and be in the foothills proper. You will perhaps recognize these foothills as the same ophiolites that surround Muscat. In another

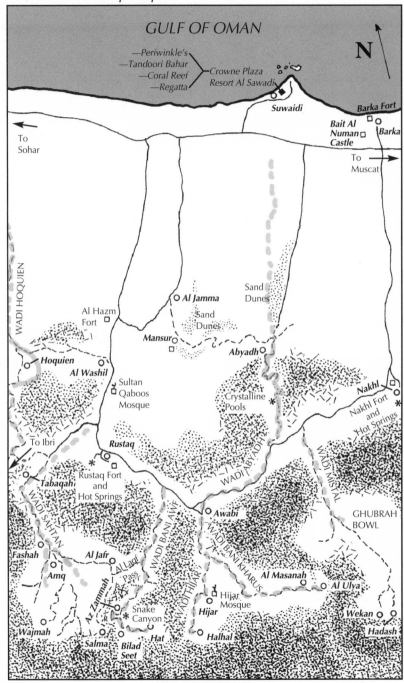

GULF OF OMAN

N

—Periwinkle's
—Tandoori Bahar
—Coral Reef
—Regatta

Crowne Plaza
Resort Al Sawadi

Suwaidi

Barka Fort

Bait Al
Numan
Castle

Barka

To
Sohar

To
Muscat

WADI HOQUIEN

Sand
Dunes

Al Jamma

Sand
Dunes

Al Hazm
Fort

Mansur

Abyadh

Hoquien

Al Washil

Sultan
Qaboos
Mosque

Crystalline
Pools

Nakhl

Nakhl Fort
and
Hot Springs

To Ibri

Rustaq

WADI ABYADH

WADI MISTAL

Tabaqah

Rustaq Fort
and
Hot Springs

Awabi

GHUBRAH
BOWL

WADI SAHTAN

Fashah

Al Jafr

Amq

Al Laqi

Pass

WADI BANI AWF

WADI BANI KHARUS

Al Masanah

Al Ulya

Az Zammah

Snake
Canyon

WADI HIJAR

Hijar

Hijar
Mosque

Wekan

Wajmah

Salma

Bilad
Seet

Hat

Halhal

Hadash

10 km

3 kilometers you will see the turnoff to the left for **Wadi Mistal** and the **Ghubrah Bowl.** The road is a graded track that enters into the bowl at 6.6 kilometers. At this point, the road for a while is narrow as it crosses the wadi floor and winds around huge boulders, and, for a short stretch, ascends slightly above the floor. After a few kilometers the floor opens out to give some elbow room. The walls of the canyon are thrust faults with a steep pitch. At 12 kilometers there is a small plantation and some ruins on the left. Now the bowl widens dramatically and the walls of the surrounding jebels can be seen on all sides. From the middle of the bowl the feeling is quite insular.

There are several side tracks that lead from the main track. Among them there is a track to the right (about 13 kilometers from the entrance of the wadi) with a sign to **Wadi Hirras.** A drive up this road will take you to some rare glacial deposits about 5 kilometers along the way. Other tracks invariably lead to small villages perched on the side of the jebel walls, some obscured, some in plain sight but still hard to spot. If you follow these tracks they will more than likely bring you to a new horizon: a village of pastoral people tending their vegetables and livestock. I will tell you about two in particular that are worth pursuing but there are at least seven or eight that I know of in this region. At 25 kilometers the road splits with the right track going to the village of **Wekan** and the left going to **Hadash.** Both of these villages are halfway up the jebel face and the only way up is to drive on through some perilous-looking hairpin turns and steep ascents until you reach the edge of town. Try to park as unobtrusively as possible. The people are generally friendly but shy and it is best to tread lightly when walking through the villages. I do encourage conversation and open gestures. Children will be more curious and if you wish you can offer them candy or treats. Please *don't* take photos of people without asking for and obtaining permission first. As a rule you probably will get a direct refusal if you ask at first. However, a friendly conversation for a while with your acquaintance might ameliorate the situation and you may find them amenable.

Both towns show excellent examples of the **falaj network** as it taps water from aquifers in the jebels behind the village and distributes it to plots, cisterns, and reservoirs. If you are lucky you might spot a falaj clock near a critical juncture. This is nothing more than a simple sundial with markings that tell the water magistrate when to divert the flow of water to another plot. If properly managed, the water will be available all year round, even in times of drought.

Wadi Abyadh (SS, HCP, 4WD)

On the tarmac road again from the turnoff to Wadi Mistal heading west, the foothills start to get a little more crowded and the road winds above a wadi course. At 6 kilometers there is a turnoff to the right into the wadi by a sign for the village of Al Mahaleel. Turn here and turn right again immediately as you follow a track on the wadi floor that runs parallel to the main road you were just using. This track hugs the main road for about a couple of klicks until it starts to bear left away from the road. You will see a broad wadi course with a plantation to your left. And soon you will be seeing running water. You are in the upper reaches of **Wadi Abyadh** ("White River"). The track veers back and forth across the floor and through the streams until you reach a point at 9.6 kilometers from the main road where you can go no further by vehicle (unless you have a Hummer). At any rate it is advantageous to park here and explore the wadi course from here on in by foot. This is the northerly approach to Wadi Abyadh.

The wadi cuts through various types of strata, leaving its singular mark on the jebels. Shortly after you begin your hike you will see an area off to the left of the running stream where there are standing pools that are in the process of depositing minerals in crystal laminations along the rock surface. The hues range from white to soft grays and blues. The water itself is stagnant and fetid due to the high mineral content, but these **crystalline pools,** which occur in several places in Oman, show a unique display of the mineral-forming chemical processes that have carried on above (and below) the surface for millennia. Small hot springs can be found by detecting gas bubbles (probably methane) escaping from the pools. It is interesting to note that a walk through Wadi Abyadh is a walk through a former contact point between the crust and the mantle, better known as the Moho.

Back along the wadi course, there are pools, shallows, and gentle cascades that have cut through soft beds of sandstones, conglomerates, and limestones. In some places the sides of the valley have a moderate slope where you can climb for better vantage points. There are several date oases with wild grasses and flowering oleander along the course. In season these attract a broad variety of insects, butterflies, and birds. After about 3 kilometers you will meet up with the southerly approach to Wadi Abyadh, which can be accessed from the main highway outside of Barka. That description is included further on in this section.

Wadi Bani Kharus (SS, HCP, 4WD)

From the Al Mahaleel signpost the main road continues to parallel the wadi, snaking through the foothills until it opens out onto an open stretch in front of the imposing jebels. At 15 kilometers you will be in the town of **Awabi,** perched at the entrance to **Wadi Bani Kharus.** Turn left and drive through the village. Near the old fort you will find the gravel track that leads into the wadi. The entrance to the wadi is not as narrow as some but is nevertheless imposing, as you are quickly enshrouded by steep canyon walls.

After a couple of klicks you will see a tall, rusty, upright, metallic object on your left. This is a wadi gauge used for measuring various parameters of water flow. If you step out here and traverse the floor where it meets the wall to your left, you will find rock art that predates the Islamic era. Further along and up the canyon walls are fossils of bivalves and gastropods (okay, okay, just clams and snails, but "bivalves and gastropods" sounds better).

Wadi Bani Kharus has some of the oldest rocks found anywhere in Oman. A trip through Wadi Bani Kharus will take you back about 600 million years in geological time. As you drive into the wadi you will be generally moving from the younger rocks to the older.

Along the way you will come to a major split in the track (at about 7 kilometers). The right track takes you up the tributary of **Wadi Hijar,** where in the village of **Hijar** (8 klicks on), you can find one of the oldest mosques in the country, built about 900 A.D. (278 A.H.). A very humble mud brick structure sitting at the back of the village next to the plantations, it has been continually restored over the centuries. At the far end of Wadi Hijar is the village of **Halhal,** another isolated farming community at the base of Jebel Akhdar.

The main track of Wadi Bani Kharus will take you to some beautiful farming villages at the far reaches of the wadi. There are farms sprinkled liberally about the wadi, all connected by aflaj to supply their water needs. Two villages of note near the end of the wadi track: **Al Masanah,** which has built some striking houses along the steep wall of the ravine above the wadi floor, and **Al Ulya,** a pleasant farming community. If you drive past the village from below and park your vehicle, follow the watercourse above the farms and you will find trails that lead to scenic overlooks of the villages as well as some burbling streams that lead to a source in the jebel wall. The sound of gentle cascades will guide your hunt for the source. Above the level of the plantations there is a very old falaj that still carries water to the plots down below. Polished rocks from centuries of traversing will also steer you along. There are many places to picnic or bivouac, just as long as you keep some distance between you, the locals, and their farm plots so as not to disturb their privacy. Whether you stay for an afternoon or overnight, be sure to cart out all your refuse.

Wadi Bani Awf (SS, HCP, 4WD)

This is one of my favorite wadis. I love to come back here time and again because of new things to discover, or just to visit the old haunts. I never get tired of them. **Wadi Bani Awf** is beyond the village of Awabi back on the Nakhl/Rustaq loop. The turnoff is easily spotted to the left just 5 kilometers after Awabi. A short ride across the plain (2 kilometers) will take you into the wadi that emerges as a narrow cleft in the jebel face. Off to the right at the entrance is a new establishment just getting under way, a rest stop called **the Sheikh's Lodge,** offering overnight accommodations in an authentic Omani setting. The track into the wadi is relatively narrow for the first 10 kilometers. A couple of villages are pressed up against the wadi floor. At times there is running water, so your wadi bash becomes a wadi splash! The track winds back and forth and you'll have to maneuver around large boulders in the wadi floor. In some parts it can be a rough drive, especially after a flood when the graded tracks have been washed away.

After 10 klicks or so the wadi opens out to give you some breathing room; the floor is now 100 feet across. At 13.2 kilometers there is an intersection with a track that goes off to the right and leads through a pass known as **Al Laqf** into Wadi Sahtan by way of the village of Al Jafr. This is convenient to know, coming from either side, if you plan to take on more sightseeing before going back to the main road. The description of Wadi Sahtan will be taken up further on.

The left track narrows again and begins to climb, gradually at first, eventually leaving the wadi floor and climbing over a ridge (at 15 kilometers) to the other side where the track once again meanders along a broad wadi floor to the left of a broad steep scarp. Barely 1 kilometer on the other side of the ridge there is an intersection with a track going left into the jebels. (This track I have only explored for 5 klicks or so; it deserves further attention.) Immediately on the right there is a very narrow cleft in the scarp which leads through to the other side of a ridge but not before some very interesting spots are encountered along the way. There is plenty of room to park your vehicles and venture into the cleft.

First of all, this narrow trail into the cleft leads to a huge valley of boulders the size of small cabins strewn about the floor between two steep canyon walls. But first you may encounter a small pool of water which can be negotiated in two ways: swimming or a fairly easy clamber over the ledge to the left. If you backtrack slightly you will find footholds and stepped inclines to take you over to the boulder field. Here, water gurgles in and around the boulders and finding your way through (there are several) will definitely get your feet wet if they aren't wet already. Past the boulders, the valley remains open for several hundred meters before it narrows to a paper-thin cleft again. Above the valley floor you will see a huge concave impression about 30 meters above the floor and 50 meters across. This impression was carved by water action of an earlier period of geologic time. It looks like a giant ice-cream scoop has taken a chunk out of the wall.

Where the wadi narrows there are more pools and here you will have to swim. It's deep in some spots (15-20 feet) but the water is nice, fresh, and cool and there are a few ledges above that are great for high diving. After you finish your sequence of hiking and swimming, the cleft opens out again;

you have reached the far side of the cleft. Follow the water off to the right. At the furthest point of visible water there is a pool where the water is standing, slightly murky, and gives off a mild odor. Nearby there is a spot where there appears to be some human activity. A tree looking very festive is shrouded in clothing and another is draped with goatskins. Earthenware pots and incense burners litter the ground and small pits are dug near the pool's edge. This site was described to me by a local shepherd as a holy place where the people perform rituals and bathe in the murky water to either cure or ward off disease. It appears to be more of a pagan practice although the locals insist it is Islamic in origin (but the shepherd thought not). After their ritual they sacrifice a goat (hence the skins on one tree) and hang a personal article of clothing on the other. The scenery beyond this point is not so dramatic and a return at this point is recommended. Round trip is about 2 hours back to the vehicles.

Continuing on the main track, the next landmark is the village of **Az Zammah** at 22 kilometers. A small but prosperous village, the people are generally friendly, but increased popularity and the influx of visitors to the next attraction has left them a bit wary. That attraction is known by the expats as **Snake Canyon,** a small tributary from Wadi Bani Awf that provides an exhilarating day in some of the best scenery in Oman. The track through the village breaks off to the right and climbs up a twisty steep grade leading to the top of the canyon. (The left track has been closed off by the villagers, who didn't care for the influx of traffic, and it now prevents wadi bashers from parking at a strategic spot. This is the lower end of the canyon, where your wadi bash concludes.)

The right track which climbs up the jebel runs parallel to the canyon. At one point you can step out and view the narrow gorge from above. Indeed it looks snakelike, but I believe its moniker is given for the several varieties of reptiles that inhabit the canyon. Up ahead the track descends in a convoluted fashion before rising again on the far wall of the jebels. It is midway in this dip (3.6 kilometers from Zammah) where you can turn off, disembark, and begin your 2+ kilometers trek through the canyon. Snake Canyon is nature's little water park. An extremely narrow gorge for much of its run, it is negotiated by hiking, jumping, diving, swimming, and sliding through pools in a stairstep configuration until you reach the bottom. Average time of traversal is about 3 hours at a slow to moderate pace. The jumps into deep wadi pools will be from 2 to 10 meters in height. Some places afford different levels (or degree of difficulty, if you will) and at one point you have to swim through a cave. Travel light: shorts, T-shirt, and sneakers. *Everything* gets wet. The only way to record pictures of your trek is to have a waterproof camera or a waterproof container for it. Midway down the gorge there is another tributary entering from the right but this one can only be negotiated with ropes and climbing gear going from top to bottom. When you get to the bottom at Az Zammah you should have someone wait for you to pick you up, or find an unobtrusive spot to park your vehicle away from the village.

A word of caution: Because of the narrowness of the canyon, coupled with its depth, it is very difficult to keep an eye on the sky. At some points only a sliver is visible. There are isolated occasions of flash floods and people have drowned. If the weather looks even slightly foreboding, put off your trip to another day and visit some other part of the wadi instead. Once you are past the first jump, there's no turning back. Also, the wet rocks can be treacherous themselves and falls can occur. Cautious clambering is the key here to having a terrific bash. Make sure you have brought a nice picnic lunch for that appetite you just worked up.

Continue on the track as it winds its way up the opposite side of Snake Canyon and around a point where, 2 kilometers later, it forks. Continue on the lower fork to the left. The road drops steeply to the wadi floor and winds around some terraces. Some that have gone fallow make excellent campsites, as they are quite removed from the rest of the plantations. Just a few klicks along the bottom of the wadi before it starts to rise again there is a series of terraces off to the right. If you follow the sound of a trickling brook you will spot a small waterfall tumbling out of a very narrow cleft. The fall itself is about 30 feet high. If you walk along the canyon wall to the right you will find paths that run along the falaj, up beyond the waterfall and past a small holding reservoir on your right. The path disappears into the cleft where you will see a well-worn path on the rock as it criss-crosses the stream. After twenty minutes of walking through this narrow chasm, the chasm branches left and right. Follow the right track and you will shortly come out upon one of the most charming villages ever tucked away in a world of its own. The town is called **Bilad Seet.** (Of course if you'd rather, you can also enter the town by vehicle on the right turnoff at the last junction, mentioned at the beginning of this paragraph, but this entry by foot is far more dramatic.)

The town takes its name from the fact that during an occupation of earlier times, the Moghul commander swept through the valley sacking villages all the way to the end village of Hat. Upon returning, they discovered one secluded village, and the chroniclers asked the general what they should call this one. He replied, "Call it the town that I forgot."

The track beyond the waterfall continues past a couple of small villages tucked into the wadi floor and proceeds up some steep inclines and on to the village of **Hat,** which is centrally located in a broad bowl. Here is essentially the end of the road (at about 30 kilometers from the beginning). However, there are trails that lead up into the jebels, even to the summit of the higher peaks, that provide an excellent vantage point of the entire region (see the description under the Sharfat Al Alamayn overlook). You might find a local inhabitant who will point out the trails to the summit. There are also several tributary wadis that empty out into this bowl before it plunges down into Snake Canyon. All provide some interesting explorations for those inclined to serendipity. If you look due west you will see the summit of Jebel Shams, Oman's tallest peak.

> Your might spread all over the world as a good omen
> that brought prosperity to land and sea.
> You are a roaring boat that delivered niceties to man
> bringing peace and security.
> The great, mighty fort surrounded by majestic magnificence
> like a beautiful girl enbosomed with fine gold.
> If Al Hadieth Tower shines with light,
> then the wind tower will roar with thunder.
> —Mohammed bin Sheikhan Al-Saliemi, from an ode to Rustaq Fort, from a
> collection of poems, 1914

Rustaq (SS)

The main road continues on past Wadi Bani Awf for another 12 kilometers until an intersection puts you near the center of town. You probably noted the towers of the fort sticking out over the broad fields of date palms. Another fort predating the Islamic era, the **castle at Rustaq** has seen many occupants, including the Persian invaders who were probably responsible for the original construction. You can reach it by taking the left turn on the roundabout and heading through the center of town. (There is another turn at this roundabout that will take you to the far side of town; we will come back to that.) Like many other forts, it was constantly refurbished, redesigned, and improved with additional towers, ramparts, and other structures. The overall effect is grand. For a time Rustaq enjoyed the privilege of being a capital seat and the fort was used as a residence by Imam Saif bin Sultan ("the Chain of the Earth") of the Ya'ruba dynasty. His addition to the fort was the Burj al Riah wind tower and it is here where Imam Saif is interred. Ahmed bin Said Al-Said, founder of the Albusaidi dynasty, is buried here as well, within the walls of the fort. Witness to many tumultuous events in Oman's past, the fort was a brief center of attention during the jebel conflict of the 1950s.

Outside the fort there is an old souq where you can find antiquities, artifacts, and other collectible items. Not as busy as older days (the newer business center has taken some of the old clientele), the old souq is a fine place for a casual stroll amidst tantalizing Arabian settings.

After the fort and souq you can proceed out of town. Now take the road mentioned above to the outskirts of town where there lies an enclosed hot spring next to a mosque. The springs empty into a series of segregated bath-houses for men and women before following the falaj into the living quarter. The springs are at a constant 42 degrees C and the waters are a deep aquamarine color.

Out at the main roundabout the road leads north back to the coast. From this road you can proceed on to Wadi Sahtan (via the Ibri road), Wadi Bani Ghafir (via the same road), Al Hazm Fort, or Wadi Hoquien, or just continue on to the coast road (35 kilometers).

Wadi Sahtan (SS, HCP, 4WD)

If you don't choose to enter **Wadi Sahtan** through the back door (see Wadi Bani Awf), the direct route is from a road that leads from a roundabout just north of Rustaq (heading back to the coast). This road is a connector with the interior town of Ibri via Wadi Bani Ghafir, Wadi Mabrah, and Wadi Hidaq. Follow the signs to Ibri but at 9 kilometers from the roundabout you will see the turnoff to Wadi Sahtan on your left. At this point you leave the tarmac behind and start on a graded track that dips down to the wadi floor and passes a village called **Tabaqah.** Two kilometers later the track still parallels the wadi floor and heads directly into a narrow ravine. This is the entrance to the wadi. For the next 8 kilometers you will be driving in and out of narrow tracks and dodging boulders. The walls to the right in some places have more examples of primitive (but not too early) rock art and at times there may be running water. In times of flood, the locals upstream have sent goods and supplies downstream on the raging torrents to the flooded victims below. Date palms appear in profusion and aflaj can be traced to perennially gushing springs along the jebel walls.

Old time residents call the Sahtan Bowl *mandoos,* the "chest of Oman," because it is so secluded. The 2,500-meter wall of Jebels Shams towers over everything and sundown in the bowl occurs rather early in the afternoon in some spots. Wadi Sahtan retains its rustic charm, although modern machines and technology have made it a bit more accessible and productive. Between the dates, limes, fodder crops, vegetables, and livestock the more than 40 villages in the bowl manage to stay prosperous.

The main track in Wadi Sahtan eventually opens out into the bowl proper. Once you pass the villages of **Fashah** and **Amq,** you can make your way to many of the signposted villages along the base of the bowl. One prosperous village of note is **Wajmah,** which is about 10 kilometers from Amq, along a steep winding drive up the jebel wall. It is marked. You will arrive at the village from a ridge slightly above that will provide an excellent view of the town, the terraces, and plots. There are always people passing to and fro with their day-to-day routines, and children are always on the lookout for visitors (with sweets to give away!) in a very genial pastoral environment.

The cutoff from Wadi Bani Awf to Wadi Sahtan runs about 6 kilometers to the town of **Al Jafr,** cutting through the Al Laqf pass, a very narrow pass between the wadis. On the way just before Al Jafr there is a left turnoff that goes deep into the jebels and requires some clever driving skills over the rocky terrain. There are several nice places to camp along the way and the endpoint, 16 kilometers from Al Jafr, is a village called **Salma,** another mystery tucked away in the jebels that demands exploration. Perched on the side of jebels with sawtooth peaks, these plucky people carry on with their farming of dates and limes on terraces hewn from the jebel wall. Guides in Salma will take you over the top of the rim to the interior side. Best done as a two-day hike, it is meant for the hale and hardy who enjoy a good overnight trek through the high reaches.

Back at Al Jafr there is one of the few apiaries found in the country. If you can find beekeeper Nasser bin Khalfan Al Auf, he will show you how he keeps his hives and bees and possibly sell you a jar of honey. The bees take their nectar from the *sidr* tree, a mountain shrub, and build their combs in hollowed-out date palm logs at the farm. On Nasser's farm, the bees nest about three times a year, yielding about 100 bottles of honey each time— barring blight and other natural difficulties.

Beyond Al Jafr the road winds through Wadi Sahtan until it reaches the main track at **Fashah** at 14 kilometers. A left will carry you deep into the wadi, past the village of **Amq** where the roads lead up the walls of the jebels to more secluded villages with terrace farms that cling to the side of the canyons. This track through Al Jafr can be used as an option to leave Wadi Sahtan if you happened to enter from Rustaq.

Wadi Hoquein (SS, HCP, 4WD)

This is simply a splendid wadi with a little bit of everything and a lot of greenery, although you would never know until you are right on top of it. To get there is fairly easy although it sounds harder. If you take the road out of Rustaq to the coast you will pass the beautiful new Sultan Qaboos mosque on your right. After 5 kilometers you will come to a roundabout with a sign to Al Woshil. A left (three-quarter) turn on the roundabout will put you on a road that has a school on the right. Just past a culvert the road bears right, but you should continue straight off the main road toward a cluster of buildings ahead. Work your way behind these buildings and you will see the track running between two fairly large trees near the end of a local soccer pitch (football field). Drive around the pitch and continue out of the village until you see a plantation looming up ahead on your right (less than one klick away). A left-hand turn here puts you onto a fairly good track. After 3 klicks, pass a battered and beaten black and white sign. After 15 kilometers of rather boring terrain you might wonder if it's all worth it. Don't worry, it is.

After traveling over a rise you will see a beautiful green plantation guarded by a majestic-looking though ruined fortress off to your left. This vista is best seen in morning light. You are entering the town of **Hoquein** along a plateau on the upper rim of the wadi. Some of the town is perched on the upper rim, but you will bypass this and head beyond, where after a volleyball court you will see a track to your left dip down into the wadi floor. The floor is very wide with several parallel tracks depending on how much water is running. Turn left up the wadi and drive as far as you can, as far as the water will let you. Midway on your right you will notice a road that turns out of the wadi through a date plantation. This road will take you to the fort on the far side that was visible when you entered the valley. A little way up this road you will see a decorative sign with a horse on your right (alas, the horse has been replaced by wrought iron designs). Shortly past you will be in the town and the fort will be on a promontory on your left. It is quite dilapidated, so tread carefully. Also be on the lookout for an open well inside the premises that is quite deep and not the kind you would want to lose your footing around. From the bus station by the fort it is easier to access Al Khabah A' Zarqa and Umm Falaj Al Bishman (see below).

Back on the wadi floor, continue as far as you can, park, and hike/wade

Wadi Hoquein.

the rest of the way up the wadi through some well-eroded boulders and tumbling cascades. You will come to an **old stone weir** that stretches across the wadi floor. In full flood this looks quite impressive, dumping sheets of water across the wadi. Off to your right are some beautiful terraces and more gardens and plantations. This is a marvelous spot for walking around and exploring. Many shady spots along the wadi afford a nice area for picnics, but if you stay overnight, remove yourself to a remote area so as not to bother the locals; this is an area with many people passing about.

Behind the town near the fort there is thick growth of sidr trees which hides the **Al Khabah A' Zarqa** ("blue pool"), fed by a beautiful waterfall that plummets from 10 meters above. Further beyond the town is the **Umm Falaj Al Bishman,** one of the many sources for the village farms. It is here that you are sufficiently removed from the town and can find places to camp near the springs and a pretty little canyon with falls and cascades. Near Umm Falaj Al Bashman there is an ancient settlement; legend has it that the men of this community were renowned for their strength (and no less, their pride). However, one night they slept in the dry wadi watercourse, shrugging off warnings from their families that they would be inundated by spring floods. Their vanity led to their downfall as the wadi flooded that night and washed them away, after which the village never recovered.

Throughout Wadi Hoquein there is other evidence of early settlements. Rock art appears on cliff walls near Wadi Ma'aidin and evidence of early mining can be found that dates back to Persian occupations. Tailings and shafts can be found as well as some small caves. In Harat Al Ail near Tawi al Bedu is an archeological site of oval-shaped gravesites (similar to the ones in Bausher, but larger) up to 4 meters long. There are also some observation posts similar in construction to the beehive tombs in Al Ayn that seem to pre-date Islamic times.

Al Hazm (SS)

If you retrace your tracks back out to the main road from Rustaq and continue north to the coast, you will eventually see on your left, shrouded by dates, the impressive **Al Hazm Fort,** built by Imam Sultan bin Saif in 1711. For a brief period the castle was also a capital seat. A masterfully designed structure, its pattern was imitated in subsequent forts and castles throughout the country. It was complete with living quarters and stores for prolonged occupations; a falaj ran through it (concealed by a network of phony aflaj), giving a constant water supply. The castle employed an economy of space, making the most of confined areas and maximizing its defensive capabilities. The fort also contained three dungeons and two escape tunnels. One presumably went all the way to Rustaq, 32 kilometers away.

One of the last members of the Ya'ruba dynasty, the beleaguered and beset Imam Saif bin Sultan II, spent his last days here, dying in 1743. It is tribute to the designers of the fort that it did not fall out of Ya'ruba hands for another 120 years.

Wadi Abyadh from the Coast (SS, HCP, 4WD)

On the coastal highway proceeding toward Sohar, you will see a left turnoff on the highway 10 kilometers past the Barka roundabout. There is no roundabout here, just an access way to turn left across the highway. The road in is paved for a while as you pass farmland and savanna until you get to the foothills again. At 14 kilometers from the main road there is a stretch of dunes just off the road to the right; this is a good spot for a small romp.

If you return by this stretch to the main highway you will be able to see, up ahead in the distance beyond the trees, the most prominent peak of the small islets that make up the **Jazir Suwaidi archipelago,** which you can reach by traveling to Suwaidi (see index).

At 28 kilometers the road turns into a graded track and dips below a hill. Ahead you can see the mouth of Wadi Abyadh, a gravelly bed of out-wash plain. The loose gravel of the wadi bed is harder to traverse if you are out of practice in driving a 4WD. But the track is clear and should be in good condition if it hasn't flooded recently. Several klicks in you will see the village of **Abyadh** perched on a cliff wall to the right. The people here are friendly, though more retiring than most. You will see adjacent date plantations and aflaj as you proceed up the wadi. You will also begin to see running water. First a little, then more. And here is where Wadi Abyadh takes on the character of a true bash. Water flows briskly over loose gravel beds. Get up a good head of steam to maneuver through these. Continue on for as long as you can, round corners and through pools studded with oases. Where the rocks and boulders impede your progress, here is a good spot to get out, walk around, and explore. You can continue heading upstream until you reach the northerly approach. Or you can climb the surrounding walls for scenic vistas or study the variety of flora and fauna that abounds in this idyllic spot.

Mansur (SS, HCP, 4WD)

This is a neat little side trip on a rough little road leading from the village of Abyadh. The road is quite rough and tough to follow in some spots, but it makes for some good diversion with a chance for dune bashing and a glimpse of an old estate that was built by Albusaidis. At the mouth of Wadi Abyadh, where the gravel track meets the road, there is a sign posted for the village of Al Hesain. Follow this track as it climbs up a hill, skirts the village of Abyadh, and heads deeper into the foothills. After 5.5 kilometers you will

Interior of ruined estate at Mansur.

be running parallel to a dry wadi on your right. After 1 1/2 klicks the track crosses the wadi, but you should turn hard right and travel up the wadi for a very short distance until you see a track that emerges from the wadi on the left. The track becomes apparent again and soon you will be skirting some dunes incongruously placed (it seems) next to the foothills. Here is a good spot to camp and explore.

Continuing on past the dunes you will find a right track rising out of the wadi bed which follows the wadi, occasionally dipping to the wadi floor. After 2.5 kilometers turn right out of the wadi bed; 2 kilometers later, turn left. This track will go past a small village, over a falaj bridge, and through some rough wadi bed. Near a small settlement the road veers right and then turns right up a steep embankment and out of the wadi bed. A "give way" sign with its back to you will be the landmark to a fairly even graded track ahead. Now you can motor for the next 10 klicks and you will be in the village of **Mansur.** Next to the mosque in the village are the remains of an old estate built by a descendant of the Albusaidis. Abandoned and fallen into ruin, the main building still retains a bit of majesty to it. However, if ruination is allowed to continue, another relic will be lost to the sands. The track remains flat and fast as it continues on past Mansur and eventually reaches **Al Jamma.** Here the road is tarmac once again and you can proceed either north to the coast or south to Al Hazm and Rustaq. (If you want to skip the dunes and the wadi, you can always come to Mansur via Al Jamma, obviously a quicker route.)

Wadi Hawasinah and the Chains (SS, HCP, 4WD)

The Khabburah roundabout is about 50 kilometers from the Rustaq cutoff on the coast road. If you take the left and move inland you will be traveling up **Wadi Hawasinah.** This road is paved for 20 kilometers or so as it runs across the plain, occasionally dipping into wadi beds, but gradually climbing to the foothills. At 22 kilometers you will approach the town of **Al Ghezayn** (Map 12), where the road forks, running into the wadi and across to the village (right) or above the wadi (left). Take the left track. This track will quickly cross the wadi up ahead and run alongside the village. At a signpost up ahead take a left fork again away from the village. You will cross the wadi again back to the left and still run parallel to the village. Climbing a rise you will come to a signposted triangular intersection (at 23 kilometers) where the right turnoff will take you to Wadi Hawasinah. A falaj runs across the road and up ahead you will see a photogenic ruin: a single tower sitting off to the side of the road. A couple of side tracks look like they lead back to Al Ghezayn, but stay on the main track as the foothills get deeper and give way to steeper jebel faces.

The track continues to run in and out of the wadi. Depending on the time

12) Wadi Hawasinah and Wadi Bani Ghafir

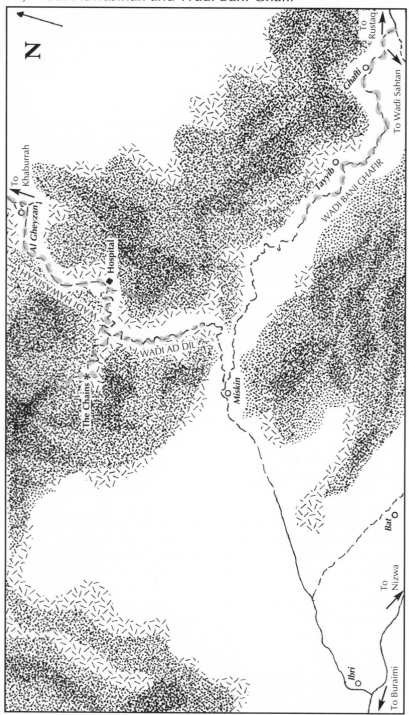

of year there may be running water. At 35 klicks from the coast you will be in the jebels proper and you will pass by several settlements. At 39 kilometers there is a nice area for stopping off to reconnoiter with plantations, ruins, and aflaj. The plantations are continually denser as you move inland, with abandoned villages replaced by newer settlements. At 44 kilometers you will come to a rural hospital on your left and the wadi track splits off to the right down a bank and onto the wadi floor. Follow this track for exactly half a kilometer where the road splits again. Take the right track. This is the tributary of Wadi Ad Dil. (The left track will continue into Wadi Hawasinah.)

The road now winds through the wadi floor for the next 11.5 kilometers. At 57 kilometers from the coast road you will see an outcrop straight ahead with a white water tank resting on it. As you approach it you will see the back side of a sign, "Qarib—1 km." Continuing on straight for another half kilometer you will see a turnoff on your right through a small stand of trees. Take that right. The rest of the way is rather rough going as the track is rough and strewn with boulders that could do a number on your undercarriage if you don't look out. But in just a few klicks you will pass a village on your right and around a bend there is a plantation on your left. The track will soon end up against a steep rock face with a sharp cleft in it and a falaj running out of it. You have reached the place known as **the Chains.**

This part of the wadi is an excellent invigorating trek similar to that of Snake Canyon in Wadi Bani Awf. Here, however, you will be traveling up the wadi instead of down. There is constant running water, deep and shallow pools, and lots of boulders to clamber over. The chains in question are regular flexible metal couplings (with stirrups) that have been embedded in the rock face a short distance along and dangle down to aid people into the further reaches of the wadi. At some point last century, the chains replaced ropes that had hung for who knows how long. They had been there for as long as anybody can remember. (They were noted by Captain G. J. Eccles in the *Journal of the Royal Central Asian Society* in 1927.) It's a nice energetic climb and the trekker is rewarded with a pool and waterfall at the top for a nice refreshing dip. (Which is as far as most people care to go. However, for the adventurous, the wadi does go further on . . .)

It is a nice day trip in itself. You might consider bringing some extra rope to facilitate the vertical climbs. If you want to take pictures, you'll need a dry box for your camera. The return trip is made descending the wadi in reverse direction. From your vehicle just reverse the way you came out to the clump of trees.

Back out at the clump of trees (where you hung a right to get in), you can take a right to continue further inland. (A left now would bring you out of Wadi Hawasinah past that rural hospital above the embankment.) However, if you follow this track inland through the winding wadi floor, you can cross

Wadi Hawasinah.

through the Western Hajars and in 45 kilometers or so be on the interior side. The jebels will give way to foothills and you will eventually come to tarmac again with signs directing you to **Miskin** and, further beyond, **Ibri**.

Wadi Bani Ghafir (SS, HCP, 4WD)

About 35 kilometers from the Chains on this same track, you will pass through a broad valley and come to an intersection off to your left. This is the Rustaq cutoff that leads through Wadi Bani Ghafir and Wadi Mabrah, 83 kilometers to Rustaq. (This is the track that meets with the entrance to Wadi Sahtan. See above.)

From either approach the road is a pleasant ramble through villages deep in the jebels. There is some spectacular scenery of the main scarp of the Western Hajars and several villages with ruins. **Ghafti, Se'a**, and **Tayyib** are notably good for scouting around. The road dips in and out of the wadis, and there are many side tracks, but the main track is fairly clear—in spite of the lack of long-range directional signs to Rustaq and Ibri for the entire length of the run.

WESTERN HAJARS, FROM THE INTERIOR

Fanjah (SS, HP)

Fanjah is the first major town you will come across when you head into the interior on the **Nizwa Road** from Muscat (Map 13). It is 33 kilometers

13) Sumail Gap

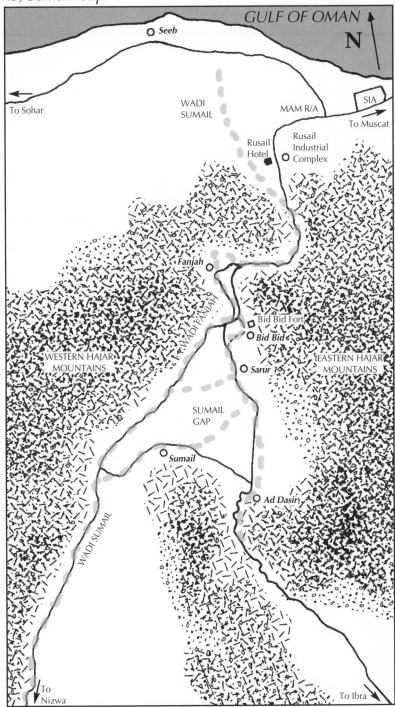

GULF OF OMAN

N

Seeb

To Sohar

WADI
SUMAIL

MAM R/A

SIA

To Muscat

Rusail
Hotel

Rusail
Industrial
Complex

Fanjah

WADI FANJAH

Bid Bid Fort

Bid Bid

Sarur

WESTERN HAJAR
MOUNTAINS

EASTERN HAJAR
MOUNTAINS

SUMAIL
GAP

Sumail

Ad Dasir

WADI SUMAIL

To
Nizwa

To Ibra

10 km

from the MAM roundabout, all divided highway, completed in 1995. This
new highway parallels the old road in some spots, which is still in use. The
old road heads off directly into **Fanjah,** but now the highway diverges and
bypasses the town through a man-made gap in the jebels. But if you wish,
Fanjah is a welcome detour at any time. Because of its location along the
major pass to the coast, much of the country's merchandise passed through
Fanjah on the way to and from the ports. Today Fanjah is still a thriving town
(noted for its successful football team). The modern quarter is close by the
old road while the **old section** sits back on a rise across the wadi (Wadi Fanjah). If you leave the highway for the old road that goes through town, you
will cross the long overpass over the wadi. Turn right onto a track past the
sign for Al Trahoom Clinic. Travel slowly through the village: the streets
are narrow and there are always children. At less than one kilometer turn
left up a tiny lane in front of the Al Harthy Foodstuff store. Presently you
will see the old village in front of you. There is a space to park outside the
walls past the gate. You can enter through the gate and explore this mostly
abandoned village. (The views from the towers of the town of the date plantations and the surrounding jebels are terrific!)

Returning to the tarmac road just past the bridge, turn right. This road
eventually meets up with the highway again but not before it passes a series
of **roadside shops** with clothing, some antiquities, and Bahla pots. The
road eventually meets up with the highway (which abruptly ends just after
Fanjah, but is due to be extended all the way to Nizwa) just before a Shell
petrol pump and a rest stop with convenience stores and a restaurant. This
is a good spot for a break in your journeys either for a snack or to heed
nature's call (the rest rooms here are better than some). It was usually a
good stop off on return trips but the divided highway has made access difficult and coming back, you have to go all the way to Fanjah to double back
to the stopover. Hopefully this situation will be addressed because the station is losing half its business due to the divided highway.

Southwest from the Sumail Gap (SS, HP)

There is a major intersection just beyond the Shell station where the
divided highway ends and the road splits. To the left, the road goes towards
Bid Bid, Mudharib, Al Kamil, and eventually Sur (take the exit ramp *off to the
right* which crosses back over the highway). The other choice is straight on
to Nizwa. The village of **Sumail** with its cozy atmosphere and old souq is also
straight ahead (20 kilometers). You are in the heart of the **Sumail Gap.**As
you drive along the gap the jebels rise sharply to your right. They look quite
imposing and it will be like that all the way to Nizwa. But the road stays low,
passing through small villages and settlements, dipping in and out of wadi
courses. There are many places to pull over and survey the countryside

and grab a snap or two. There are date palm oases, old towers, roadside vegetable stands, and the ever-present Hajars.

Wadi Halfayn and the Persian Steps (SS, HCP, 4WD)

Thirty kilometers past Sumail is the village of **Al Afiah; 2.**8 kilometers after that there is a turnoff to a gorge off to your right a short distance from the main road (Map 14). Drive as far as you can up to the gorge and park. This is **Wadi Halfayn.** You can then either pick your way through the wadi (which is strewn with rubble and boulders) or find the old falaj channel running 20 feet above the wadi on your right, climb up to it, and follow it. The latter is much easier. When you reach the end of the gorge you will find steps cut into the cliff wall. These will eventually lead along an invigorating path to the top of the ridge where the view is tremendous. I have not been able to ascertain why these steps are called the **Persian Steps** but undoubtedly they were created during the years of the Persian occupations of Oman. The hike is rather long and a round trip in one day is about twelve hours, so you might want to make this one an overnight stay on the plateau. Just remember, you've got to carry your gear for this one. Curiously enough, Wadi Halfayn is the country's longest wadi. From its departure from the jebels it winds along the western edge of the Wahibah Sands for 200 kilometers before running to the Indian Ocean at Barr Al Hikman.

Once at the top there are tracks that lead across to the **Saiq Plateau** (which I have not taken), one of the most verdant of interior reaches and the heart of the *jebel akhdar* (see below). It's not called the "green mountain" for nothing. If you take in the Saiq plateau from Wadi Halfayn, it had best be done in more than one day, returning by the way you came, because the main entrance to the Saiq Plateau from the Birkit Al Mawz side is a road that requires a special road pass at a military checkpoint. You can also reach the Saiq Plateau by hiking Wadi Muaydin (see below), another difficult day hike (but thereby circumventing the checkpoint).

Birkit Al Mawz (SS, HP)

Back on the Nizwa Road the next major town is **Izki,** where the gap begins to open out to the eastern reaches of the Empty Quarter. But it isn't quite empty yet. There are a number of towns in the low-lying foothills that spread to the south. In Izki the road splits again. The turn right goes toward Nizwa while straight ahead leads to Sinaw (see below). The road to the right now bends around and follows the base of the jebels and soon you will come over a rise to the town of **Birkit Al Mawz.** This pretty oasis has much to offer for sheer scenic value. The town is abutted up to the jebels and the anticlinal strata directly behind give the town its nickname, "the rainbow city." There are ruins on a ledge and palm trees

14) Jebel Akhdar

To Muscat
Afiah
Hamma
Persian Steps
WADI HALFAYN
Izki
To Sinaw
Checkpoint
Birkit
Al Mawz
Bait Al
Rudaidah Fort
Nizwa
Hotel
Manah Fort
Manah
To Salalah
SAIQ PLATEAU
Gisha'al
Sharijah
WADI MUAYDIN
Falaj
Daris
Nizwa
Stadium
WADI BANI KHARUS
Wadi Bani
Habib
Al Far
Sharfat Al Alamayn
WADI QASHAH
Nizwa Mosque
and Fort
Falaj Daris
Motel
Tanuf
Tanuf Water
Bottling Plant
Hoti Cave
Wadi
Bani
Awf
Misfah
Wadi
Bahla
Motel
Bahla Fort
Hasat
bin Sult
Jebel
Shams
WADI SAHTAN
Wadi
Nakhr
Gorge
Recharge Dam
Nakhr
Al
Hamra
Bahla
Jabrin Fort
Checkpoint
Al Khateem
Ghul

10 km

N

To Ibri

all around. A world apart, Birkit Al Mawz is a pleasant place to spend an hour or two just walking around in the quiet and seclusion of an interior hideaway.

At the far end of town near the entrance to Wadi Muaydin, there is the reconstructed **Bait Al Rudaidah Fort,** which saw some activity during a 1954 conflict. The castle was refurbished in the 1980s and turned into a historical site/museum. Its history goes back much further. The only other time it fell was to a Persian invasion in 973 A.D.

Wadi Muaydin (SS, HCP, 4WD)

This is a terrific wadi for hikes and camping. The entrance is just beyond the fort at Birkit Al Mawz. Follow the track in but turn off to the left just before the military checkpoint. You can continue driving for a few more klicks, but at some point you will have to start walking. From there you can follow the wadi as far as you wish, and if you push all the way, you just might make the summit of the Saiq Plateau—a good six to seven-hour hike *in*. My first trip up the wadi was not quite so long. There was plenty of running water along the 7-8 kilometer drive in from the turnoff and we had to leave our vehicles a little further back than in dry times. On the hike in we passed an army camp bivouacked by the wadi. We traded caps and T-shirts and posed for the camera with the Omani foot-soldiers. Continuing on, we waded through running water and maneuvered around sharp boulders. An hour and a half into the hike the sky turned overcast and then it started raining, only a drop or two, but up in the jebels we could see cascades forming where there were none before. We decided to turn back, owing to the uncertainty of the weather. As we returned we were met by Army scouts who were concerned and set out to fetch us. We got back to our vehicles and drove out of the wadi and back onto the main road. When we looked back, high in the jebels a veritable sheet of water tumbled over a precipice 20 meters wide and tumbled into an unseen gorge 100 meters below. We were so awestruck, we didn't notice that the road we stood on (a good 2 klicks from the jebel wall) was beginning to fill up with water. We then beat a hasty retreat and settled for a picnic lunch back home. And the whole time, it never really rained *overhead.*

Saiq Plateau (SS, HCP, 4WD)

The **Saiq Plateau** is not easy to get into for two reasons: 1) you need a road pass to get through the checkpoint, and 2) the road up to the top is very demanding and you must have a 4WD. The next 12 kilometers past the checkpoint are fairly steep and you will have to engage low ratio. The road ends 33 kilometers on at the village of Saiq. There are about

30 villages scattered about the plateau. The area is one of the most agriculturally productive (outside the Batinah and Dhofar). Terraces extend down steep valleys growing an assortment of fruits and vegetables. The villages that are noteworthy in one respect or another are **Sharijah, Wadi Bani Habib,** and **Gisha'a,** and they can all be reached from the main track that leads to Saiq. From here you can see communities in transition as modern technologies assist age-old farming traditions to work the land.

To obtain a road pass is rather difficult as you will need a sponsor and a letter of intent, stating the exact date and time of your visit and other details such as vehicle numbers and registrations, names, addresses, visas, and photos of all attendees. You will need to contact the Office of His Honor, the Deputy Prime Minister for Security and Defense, at the Ministry of Defense office in Bait Al Falaj, Ruwi. Contact Mr. Halfan Salim Al Roshidi at 312605/08.

Manah (SS, HCP)

Continuing on the main road you will pass the new **Nizwa Hotel** on your right tucked up against the jebels a few klicks out of Birkit Al Mawz. Just beyond on your left there is a new sports stadium close to the road. The jebels to your right are just as imposing as before but to your left the foothills give way to rolling plains of parched dry land. Up ahead is the intersection with the main road to Salalah (a mere 900 kilometers away). There is a roundabout and if you turn right you will be continuing on to Nizwa. But just for the moment there is a suitable diversion not far from here. If you take the Salalah road and follow the signs to a town called **Manah,** 13 kilometers from the roundabout, you will find an intriguing abandoned village and fort just behind the current village. While it is certainly safe to walk the maze of streets and alleys in this one-time center, it might not be wise to climb into any ruins above ground level, as dilapidation is rampant. But you will get a flavor for the structure and function of these old towns; you can almost predict which building housed what establishment. It is hoped that places like these can be restored to serve as living relics of the long-lived Omani culture.

> Oman flourished under [Imam Sultan's] rule and the people had respite from their wearisome problems. The roads were safe, goods were cheap, profits high and crops plentiful. The Imam was . . . kind to his subjects [and] he was not distant or haughty with his people. He used to walk the streets without guards, sit with the people and talk to them without any constraint.
> —Hamid bin Muhammed, Omani historian, on Sultan bin Saif Al Ya'ruba

Nizwa (SS, HP)

Back at the roundabout you will head toward **Nizwa** along a broad wadi with rushes and reeds and the surrounding oasis. This is the old capital, sitting 160 kilometers from Muscat. Here is the splendid **Nizwa Fort,** going back to the twelfth century, with the latest edifice built by Sultan bin Saif Al Yarubi and refurbished in 1991. The current structure, completed in 1680 by Sultan bin Saif, was built over an earlier fort that had been constructed from remnants of smaller forts. The huge citadel tower hovers 30 meters over the modern-day souq like a watchful giant. The fort is a maze of vaults, stairwells, and breastworks designed to confound enemy invaders. The 360-degree parapet with crenellations offered soldiers a superb view of the surrounding area from which to defend. The fort was near impregnable.

Imam Sultan bin Saif also built the **Falaj Daris,** the largest single falaj in Oman, and raised the many farms in the surrounding region. The town is still a bustling center for crafts and the **silver souq** is the best in Oman. During the Eid festivities the farmers bring out their livestock for sale in preparation for the holiday feasts. They gather in the shade of tall palms. The holiday begins with the sale of cows and goats for the upcoming feast and the souq is alive and festive.

You can bypass Nizwa by taking a right at the roundabout just as you come into view of the fort and the souq. This road leads through some residential areas. Before it departs Nizwa altogether, you will pass a small park built around the Falaj Daris that is nice for a quiet evening stroll. The road moves out into the open and onto a broad section of wadi floor between the jebels, the more imposing Jebel Akhdar to your right. Now and then you will see tracks that run off to the right and snake up the sloping jebels or disappear into a yawning cleft.

Tanuf (SS, HP)

One of the tracks you will see is marked. This is the village of **Tanuf.** Today Tanuf is famous for its **mineral water springs** and **water bottling plant.** You can follow the signs to the plant and take a walk-through visit. You can also take the track past the old village (that was bombed in the 1954 clashes) and follow the track down into the wadi past a picnic area, then up and over the Wadi Tanuf Recharge Dam and on through the wadi bed. The main track sticks to the right. Follow it as far as you can. This track is quite rough at times, especially after a flood, as boulders are strewn randomly. After 8 kilometers or so you will see a village up ahead on your left. Here you should find a place to park in such a way as to not block the track. The village is **Al Far** and you are in the lower reaches of **Wadi Qashah.**

Wadi Qashah (SS, HCP, 4WD)

The wadi is easy enough to follow for the first half of your trek, although you will have to pick your way around some massive boulders as you skirt the village above. The path will widen just past the village and then narrow very suddenly. You will be passing into a very narrow chasm. (Keep one eye to the sky and watch for rain.) As you hike further in you will pass aflaj, pools, and running water (possibly) from the ledges above. At one point you will see a solitary pinnacle rising out of the far jebel walls as you pass beneath a plantation high up on a ledge to your left. After a few klicks the wadi makes a dog leg to the right (but don't even think about playing golf here). Remember this spot. We'll come back to it. As the walls become narrow again you will find more and more running water. At some point you will have to leave your packs (and everything you want to remain dry) behind. There is a series of long pools to cross. At the far ends you can find footholds to clamber up and continue on. The second pool looks impossible to extricate yourself from but if you are clever and resourceful there are several ways out.

Follow the path upstream. You will eventually come to a convergence. The left side takes you to a series of more pools until there are some boulders that block your path and further climbing is prohibited. The right side takes you up a series of cascades for about 50 meters until you come upon the most secluded moss-draped pool that you have ever set eyes upon, with a gentle waterfall flowing into it from the cliff above. Here is the spot to relax and have a great swim before you return.

After a careful survey, it is possible to continue on. I have climbed up to the right of the pool for a couple hundred meters to take some dramatic shots of the pool and waterfall from above. I reckon with a little more clambering you could push on to the source of the wadi . . .

The walk/swim back is easy to retrace. At the corner (mentioned above) it is possible to scramble up the side of the cliff wall, pass through an old metal gate, and go upwards to a plateau where you can gain a great view of the wadi from above. If you pick your way along the rim back to the starting point you will come across an abandoned village as well as the plantations on the ledge mentioned earlier. From the abandoned village there is a trail which leads back to Al Far, taking you along the rim of the canyon. Although there is much traversing to get around the several tributaries, the entire path is level for most of the journey back owing to the flatness of the undisturbed layers of strata you will be walking on. By the time you reach Al Far, you will start to make a descent. The path leads through the heart of the village, which because it is perched on the cliffside is narrow and cramped. The villagers are friendly but shy and sometimes wary. The children always run after you and if you come prepared with some sweets to offer them, you should have a pleasant transit. You may be invited to take khawa with the men in the majlis. From this point it is just a short haul back to your vehicle; all in all, this makes for an exhilarating day hike.

Hoti Cave, Al Hamra, and Misfah (SS, HCP, 4WD)

From the turnoff at Tanuf you should continue on the main road in the direction of Bahla. After 15 kilometers you will see a BP petrol pump to your right and a tarmac road. Turn right here and head to Al Hamra. At 4 kilometers you can turn right (signposted Qal'at Al Masalha) onto a track that cuts to the other side of the ridge. On the far side you will see an open area of well developed farms before another ridge just beyond. Turn right and make your way to that far ridge and run with it. You should not have to travel more than 5 or 6 kilometers when you will see on your left a small ridge. You can drive up to the top of this ridge (over solid rocky ground) and there at the top you will look across a ravine to a huge overhang in the far wall. You are standing before the entrance to **Hoti Cave.**

A path leads from this ridge down into the ravine and up the far wall to the mouth of the cave, or what looks to be the mouth of the cave, which appears to be a huge gaping maw. Actually, when you get there you will find that the recess is not that deep and you will be staring at a blank wall.

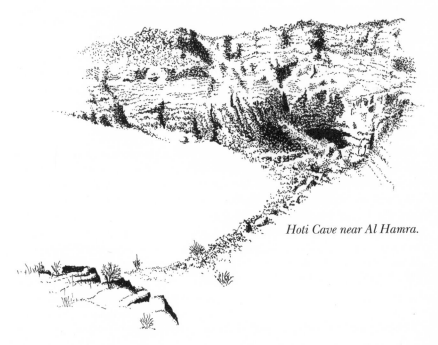

Hoti Cave near Al Hamra.

The actual entrance is a small crevice between some rocks in the floor where you can see a rope hanging down. This is one of the entrances to Hoti Cave.

It should be noted that you should not enter the cave without proper gear for spelunking activity—torches (flashlights), hard hats, etc. You can let yourself down, dropping onto shelf after shelf for 20 meters until you reach the bottom and what appear to be two small and unimpressive rooms (with water). It is at this point you will realize that you have climbed down too far. Halfway down there is a path around a boulder that is hard to discern. Once around this you will pass into the deeper reaches of Hoti Cave. The Hoti Cave system is a wadi that enters the ground several kilometers upstream (where the other entrance lies). This entrance (or should I say exit) is at the downstream side. There are several rooms and chambers with typical (but not exceptional) flowstone activity: travertine stalactites, stalagmites, curtains, etc. There is a lake that separates the lower chambers from the upper chambers and can be crossed at low water. However, there are very delicate eco-systems in the cave, including a species of blind fish. If you go into Hoti Cave, it is advisable to disturb the area as little as possible.

The entrance to the upper level of the cave can be found by taking the nearby track over the ridge 4 kilometers on, but this entrance is the harder of the two and should only be attempted by serious spelunkers/climbers.

Back on the tarmac road leading from the BP station, you will soon come upon a turnoff left onto a track, this time by a Shell petrol pump. This track leads on to the village of Ghul and eventually Wadi Nakhr Gorge, the Grand Canyon of Oman. But first continue on into the town of **Al Hamra,** a busy agricultural center (the above-mentioned farms near Hoti Cave are part of the Al Hamra network). The town is not as prominent as in older days. The construction of the Nizwa-Ibri Road has shifted the main focus of trading to Bahla. But there are several points of interest in Al Hamra. One of them is **Bait Assfah,** a three-story 400-year-old mud house very popular to visitors which is being contemplated for the honor of being declared a national monument. The house, in spite of its component parts, is rock solid and still occupied. It serves as a repository for antiques. It sits in the old quarter, a fine conglomeration of old-style mud buildings.

Outside of town there sits **Hasat bin Sult,** a rock about 20 feet high with engravings and graffiti, some of which date back to antiquity. The relief of these figures of men, women, and children is striking for its depth and clarity. Probably the most interesting story revolves around three figures whose origins stem from slightly above the mundane, but the story serves as a worthy parable. A man and his wife gave birth to a child who was less than perfect—he was deformed. The parents (the father's name is the one given to the rock) were so distraught and confused that they dashed the baby against the rock. But lo, the impression of the baby was stamped on the surface forever, and more importantly, the parents were not to outlive their infamy. Not only was an impression of the babe formed, but of the parents, Hasat bin Sult and his wife, as well. (Many thanks to David Insall at the Ministry of Municipalities and Environment for providing this and several other intriguing bits of Omani folklore.) The relief is best observed in the morning hours around 9 A.M., when the detail is most prominent. You can see the rock by taking a right track on the outskirts of Al Hamra in front of a garden. The rock is near a wadi bed and out in the open less than one klick in from the main road.

At the back of the town against the jebel slope there is a winding track that is traversed easily enough by saloon cars. This track climbs above Al Hamra for several kilometers before it dips behind a ridge and eventually stops at the town of **Misfah,** one of the most picturesque villages that ever strapped itself to the side of a mountain. Unfortunately, the locals have been edgy, owing to the number of European bus tours that have inundated this little hamlet. They are beginning to feel, and rightfully so, that their privacy is being violated as large groups are pressed upon them. They are not really used to all this attention. It is a remarkably quaint and beautiful spot, however, with old clusters of buildings, aflaj, and date palms. If you go to Misfah, go easy on the home folks.

Wadi Nakhr Gorge/Jebel Shams (SS, HCP, 4WD)

The turnoff left before Al Hamra used to be adorned with the most marvelous sign. It was in Arabic, so most foreign visitors could not read it anyway, but there were arrows extending from a main trunk in about twenty directions pointing to twenty different locations. I wish I knew what those locations were 'cause it sure looked interesting from the sign. I didn't think there were twenty locations out there. Alas, the sign is gone, so use the Shell station as your landmark. This road immediately turns into a well-graded track that follows the course of a wadi, sometimes dipping into gravel beds, but mostly running parallel to the wadi. At one point you will pass a recharge dam on your right.

After 8 kilometers you will round a bend in the wadi and up ahead see an abandoned village on a ledge of an outcrop where two wadis now converge. You have been following the track of **Wadi Ghul** and the village is, or was, that of **Ghul.** Up on a plateau on your right is where the current village stands. The old village goes back to antiquity; there are three distinct periods that have been determined. The youngest (most recent) is the low-lying string of buildings nearest you just beyond the palms. The older sections are removed further up the ridge with the oldest near the top of the ridge, identified only by a string of stone walls. If you hike to the top you can look over the edge to see cisterns built into the cliff wall that stored water that was lifted to the top from the falaj in Wadi Nakhr.

Wadi Nakhr is the bed that comes out of a canyon alongside the village, separating it from the newer inhabited village on the right. This is the start of the **Wadi Nakhr Gorge** and it winds for several kilometers into the jebels to become the Grand Canyon of Oman. From this point it is possible to drive/hike into the wadi (mostly hiking). But if you start early in the day you can wend your way to the village of **Nakhr,** several kilometers in on the wadi floor. (The village can be viewed when you visit the upper rim of the gorge—almost 2 kilometers straight down! . . . but first things first.) There is water in the wadi at times and it does flood. Bring your lunch and bask at the bottom of a prehistoric sea, the lowermost levels of which have not seen the light of day since the Jurassic era.

The other wadi is the continuation of Wadi Ghul, which runs in front of the falaj-fed plots at the base of the ridge and the old village. Follow this track. It is only 30 kilometers to the summit from Ghul. For the first 8-10 kilometers you will still be tracing the wadi floor until it appears that you will run into the wall of Jebel Misfa up ahead. The track now climbs to the right, switching back along a steep course. At 16 kilometers from Ghul there is a Y-junction. Keep to the right. You will start to descend and cross a broad valley. You will climb the opposite wall. As you descend you might just be able to make out the communications installation on the peak of **Jebel Shams** ahead, the tallest peak in Oman at 10,000 feet. As you approach it from the next ridge it will ultimately be your best view of the summit: further access is restricted at a military checkpoint and you'll have to turn back. (Passes beyond this point to the summit are available if you follow the same procedures outlined above for Saiq Plateau.) But wait! Only a short distance back from the checkpoint (only 1 kilometer) there is a right turnoff (heading up), left, if you're coming back down. This turnoff runs down an embankment and across another ridge on a steep, bumpy, but well-traveled track. It is well traveled because this is the entrance to the gorge from above, and its proximity to the summit of Jebel Shams compensates for missing the summit. It is only a few klicks from here when you round a bend and come across a very flat section. I'm surprised that no one has turned it into a soccer pitch. Just beyond is the rim of the canyon . . . and the Shuwawis (mountain people).

You might have seen one or two of them on your way up, hawking their blankets and carpets by the roadside. They are very nice folks but they could give the founder of Amway lessons in giving sales pitches. They pop up out of nowhere with carpets, trinkets, and sandals, and, oh yes, fossils to sell. I remember one particular lady trying to sell me carpets. She was one-legged, on crutches, blind from cataracts, and holding an infant in her arms. These have got to be the most resilient people I have ever met. Anyway, you can haggle for just about anything ("Photo snap—1 riyal!"). And the rugs they make are quite nice. But they always like to make a sale. You haven't seen the last of them. Wait till you get up next morning from your tent and see who's waiting outside. They are friendly as any of the rural folk go, and I try to appease them (or at least the kids) with candy or sodas. By the way, in the morning, the men like their coffee black. You'll want to befriend them, actually, so they can show you the trail that leads down into the canyon.

From the rim at the first approach of the canyon (**Bir Dakhiliyah**), you can look down (if you can do it without vertigo) and see one kilometer below you some abandoned terraces on a ledge. What you can't see from this vantage point is the cliff dwellings set back into the ledge, and the overhang, 20 meters thick. The terraces are resting upon this overhang, which forms a concave depression about 50 meters deep. There is nothing between the shelf, suspended another kilometer above the canyon floor, and the wadi below. Amazingly enough this terrace is easily reached by a path (remember the Shuwawis) that starts in the village at the end of the road/track at the far end of the canyon, just a couple klicks' drive from the first vantage point as it skirts the rim heading south. The track passes by some looms stretched on the ground under a tree where the weavers make their rugs and ends in a little stand of huts. From the Shuwawi village of **Al Khateem** it is possible to see the mouth of Wadi Nakhr where it enters Wadi Ghul by the old abandoned village at the bottom.

The trail here from the village is very safe as it hugs the rim ledge and descends roughly halfway down the canyon. The round trip to the terraces is four-plus hours. Also, I understand there is a cave that goes into the cliff wall from the short falaj that extends from a source in the wall to the terraces. I have been to the cliff dwellings and the terraces but not to the cave, which supposedly has at least one large room. It is easier to climb to the falaj at the far end of the terraces and make your way past some boulders to a pond in front of the mouth of the cave. The terraces have gone fallow as the result of recent drought. The cliff dwellings appear unoccupied, but a spate of good weather and rain could change that.

> This is life, my sons. When I was young I did my best. I herded goats and walked around these mountains and life was very tough. When you are old you accept what you get. But I have no regrets. Thank God for everything.
> —Old blind man from Jebel Akhdar, reputedly over 120 years old

From your campsite near the gorge (pick your spot—there's lots of them) it is possible to walk around and survey the area. If you look from a rise westward over the route you just drove (the return to the bottom is made by retracing the same route), you will see a singular mountain with a broad gentle slope on one side and precipitous cliffs on the others. This is **Jebel Misht** from the eastern side. The western flanks are those that frame the beehive tombs in Al Ayn (see below). Jebel Misht, Jebel Kawr, and Jebel Misfa make up the exotics along the southern jebels, so called because their strata cannot be identified or matched with any of the surrounding mountains.

If you would like to catch a glimpse of the northern face of the Hajars near the summit of Jebel Shams (one of the most spectacular scenes in Oman), you can, on your return trip down, make a detour through Al Hamra and follow the road to Qalat Al Masalha. After 8.3 kilometers, take a right fork, and at 8.7 kilometers, a sharp right. One kilometer later you will see a mountain road to your left climbing up the sides of the jebel. Take this track for 30 clicks or so and you will arrive at the **Sharfat Al Alamayn Viewpoint** at the edge of the escarpment for a stunning view of the region.

DHAHIRAH

Bahla (SS)

On the road from Nizwa (Route 21), the first town you will come to is **Bahla,** one of the oldest recorded regions of civilization in Oman. Artifacts

Bahla souq.

found here date back to the third millennium B.C. There is the enormous **Bahla Fort** here (it is currently off limits for restoration and will likely be so for two or three years from this printing). The town is one of the few that has a surrounding wall, which runs for 12 kilometers. The cultural value of the town and fort has earned it a place on UNESCO's World Heritage list of monuments. Today Bahla is the **pottery capital of Oman** and you can find the potters busy at work deep in the heart of the town past narrow alleys, overhanging palms, and gurgling aflaj. The **old souq,** which can be found running off a main track across the street from the fort, is filled with crafts and antiquities. There is also a fair amount of weaving and one of the last indigo dyers in Oman can be found here. Like many other towns, Bahla is growing again and new buildings are sweeping out into the plains past the old city limits. There is a motel, the **Bahla Motel,** just on the outskirts of town as you enter from Nizwa.

Jabrin (SS)

After Bahla, just a few klicks on, there is a left-hand turn to the famous **Fortress at Jabrin.** Built by Ya'ruba Imam Bil' arub bin Sultan in 1688, the style and architecture of this impressive fort have been marveled at by archeologists and onlookers alike. Built as a fortress and domicile for the imam, it was established as a college, using the many partitioned areas and courtyard for Islamic studies. The fort contains a maze of rooms with painted ceilings, staunch breastworks and impressive towers, courtyards, dungeons, vaulted chambers, secret passages, hidden corners, false floors, tunnels, and escape routes. (The imam even had a stable on the second floor for his favorite horse.) Unfortunately, these were not enough to protect Bil'arub as he was eventually overthrown by his brother Saif bin Sultan in a siege of the castle in 1692. There he died and there he is buried. The capital was then removed to Rustaq and the fort saw little activity (apart from its use as a headquarters during the Civil War of 1822-24) until its restoration in 1983.

The main road to Ibri is flat and progress is swift along the back of Jebel Kawr to your right (Map 15). This is among a group of mountains, mentioned above, known to the geologists as the exotics for their unusual composition and structure. After 45 kilometers there is a turnoff to the right to the village of **Amlah,** 14 klicks hence. The graded track is in good condition and well traveled. After passing through Amlah the road continues straight. Shortly after there is a turnoff to the left toward Bat.

Al Ayn/Bat (SS, HP)

If you ignore this turnoff for the time being and continue straight you will see up ahead, looming in the distance, the western flanks of Jebel Misht, an imposing piece of rock 2,500 meters high. Sufficeth to say it is also a rock

15) Jabrin to Ibri

To Khaburrah

Araqi Cave ✱
○ Araqi
○ Ibri
○ Sulaif
To Buraimi

Beehive Tombs ✱
○ Bat

Beehive Tombs ✱
○ Al Ayn

Jebel Misht

○ Sint

Amlah ○

Wadi Nakhr Gorge

To Nizwa
Jabrin Fort □

10 km

N

climber's delight. (An excellent guide to rock climbing in Oman is published by Apex Publishers; it covers a lot of trails for Jebel Misht and other cliffs to scale.)

Just 7 kilometers past the road to Bat you will see in front of Jebel Misht off to your left a small rise with about 20 of the best examples of **beehive tombs** from the third millennium B.C., near the village of Al Ayn. If you circumnavigate the farm nearby and park in the wadi bed it is then a short climb up the hill. The sturdy construction of these tombs has allowed them to stand all these years without so much as a drop of mortar. Only the roofs on some have caved in. Whatever artifacts were there have since been removed, but you can examine the tombs, even crawl into one if you like, and see the unique structure from, well . . . a corpse's-eye view.

The road beyond continues in to the remote town of **Sint.** I have not been there but I understand it is an interesting diversion and a good look at real interior village life.

The road to Bat is not very distinctive. It is a good track, but not much scenery. After 24 kilometers you will be in an area of ridges that are peppered with **more beehive tombs,** more than the cluster in Al Ayn. These tombs, however, are in a worse state of ruination; some have collapsed into just piles of stones. A tomb or temple of sorts by the roadside has been roped off for restoration/renovation. The surrounding area can be approached and observed but nothing should be removed from these sites.

This track will eventually connect with tarmac at **Dariz** and from there it is a short drive to Ibri. A right turn here toward Miskin will take you through the Wadi Hawasina Pass to the coast.

Ibri/Al Sulaif (SS)

Ibri is a busy modern-day town that is currently experiencing growing pains. There is lots of new construction as the city starts to encroach on the surrounding plains. There are some beautiful new mosques by the main road, a nice mix of old and contemporary Arabic styles. The palms make a pleasant backdrop for this otherwise urban scenery. On the main road running east/west, which is the same road we left to hop/skip up to Al Ayn, there is a fascinating ruined fortified village outside Ibri called **Al Sulaif** that sits on an outcrop next to a modern settlement. The souq to this village is still used from time to time, but mostly for storage. If you enter the old souq (near the new quarter) you will pass into a lost time. Here the walls of the village bear inscriptions on rocks and unusual raised reliefs of hands and faces appear on walls and doorway arches. Further into the maze of alleys there is room after room of crumbling antiquity. The open court area sits askew on a gentle slope; the watchtowers seem to be the only structures that are still plumb, or was that tall one leaning just a little bit . . .

The road out of Ibri continues up past the town of **Dank** and on for 150 kilometers to the outpost/border town of Buraimi. If you want to continue this way you will have to procure a road pass from the ROP in Muscat.

> El-Bereymi is the appellation usually applied to a collection of seven villages or settlements, of which the one, specially bearing that name is the largest and most important. . . . From the outside the appearance of these settlements is very pretty and refreshing, the date palms and orchards forming a green setting to the low palm-leaf huts, which are seated throughout, and which just peep through the foliage.
>
> —Lt. Colonel Samuel Barrett Miles, on Buraimi, 1877

Buraimi (SS)

The **Buraimi oasis** was always a prosperous cluster of villages, one worth fighting for over the course of time. Today it is divided by the Oman/UAE border and the two cities are Buraimi, in Oman, and Al Ayn, in the UAE (see Map 1).

Buraimi still retains its quality as an oasis, as the aflaj which feed the city and the surrounding villages keep it productive. Being on the fringe of the Rub' Al Khali, temperatures are a little more extreme than in the rest of the country (hotter in summer, cooler in winter). The fort, **Husn Al Khandaq,** which played a key role in the Wahhabi occupation, occupies an area on an open plain and was restored in the 1980s. It features a 24-foot-wide dry ditch moat surrounding an 8-foot wall, an inner wall 14 feet height and 5 feet thick at the base, and 4 towers. It holds cannons purchased from America in 1840 for the sultan's fleet and subsequently transferred to the fort. A nearby watchtower can be entered via rope dangling from a doorway near the top.

EASTERN HAJARS FROM THE INTERIOR

South from the Sumail Gap (SS, HP)

The highway from the Shell petrol pump after Fanjah splits (as mentioned above), and the crossover heads for points south (Route 23) (Map 13). Very shortly you will see a turnoff and signs to **Bid Bid,** a prosperous community with plantations and a **restored fort.** Bid Bid, like Fanjah, was an important stop-over on the trade routes to the coast. The town has a very strategic location on the Sumail Gap as it intersected with the road to Nizwa. The fort is on the far side of town next to the plantation and the falaj.

Further on the main road you will pass between a wadi on your right and oasis on your left, hiding the village of **Sarur.** After crossing over a plain, the road enters a narrow gap by the village of Ad Dasir that runs south through the jebels for the next 24 kilometers. In this stretch, the road winds

Portal to the walled village of Al Sulaif.

around ledges and promontories and through wadi courses (Wadi Seigani). (It's in stretches like these where you will find that drivers use a language of signals with their vehicle lights. Slow-moving trucks ahead of you will signal their left blinker when it is not good to pass, and their right blinker when it is. Oncoming traffic will flash their headlights as a courtesy of awareness, even in daylight.) There are some **farm stands** at the near end of the pass that sell their produce by the roadside: dates, mangoes, limes, and sweet lemons! in season. It's a good idea to keep an eye on the weather as you make your way through this pass, as rare flash floods could cause traffic delays.

Wadi Tayin/Devil's Gap/Wadi Khabbah (SS, HCP, 4WD)

After 24 kilometers the road opens out into foothills again and after a while you will begin to see open plains to the south. After another 10 kilometers you will approach a BP station on your right followed by a turnoff 100 meters to your left that heads into the mountains (Map 16). It is signposted **Wadi Tayin.** This is a rugged little track that takes you through some off-the-beaten-path villages guarded by old watchtowers, with aflaj, crops, and flowing wadis. Eventually the track will wander along a broad gravelly wadi floor with water flowing intermittently. This is Wadi Tayin. There are many places to stop between villages and in villages to reconnoiter.

After 60 kilometers from the main road you will come to an intersection in the village of **Al Ghayyan.** A right turnoff here will take you back to the main road through an equally impressive segment of interior interspersed with wadis, plantations, and villages. Continue to follow Wadi Tayin as it is now running south, parallel to the base of the jebels to your left. Several villages crop up on either side, making use of the water which is now flowing abundantly. In another 18 kilometers you will be approaching the village of **Tool** and a side track that splits off from the main track and leads to the village. It also leads over a couple of hillocks of dunes and stops at the opening of a deep crevasse. Another wadi, **Wadi Khabbah,** running north, has converged with Wadi Tayin and here they both disappear into the crevasse. This spot is known as **Devil's Gap** and is the start of the **Wadi Daiqah Gorge,** which wends its way through spectacular mountain scenery for 8 miles before it comes out at Mazara and eventually runs into the sea. If you are doing a Wadi Daiqah cross, you should park your vehicle high on the bank, near, but not in, the village. Again, if you choose, you can hike into the canyon as far as you wish and return.

The main track continues on but now instead of going with the downstream flow of Wadi Tayin, you are tracking against the flow of Wadi Kahbbah. It is not hard to maneuver and makes for a splendid wadi bash. There are many groves along the wadi and great spots for a rest stop or a picnic.

16) Ibra and Wadi Tayin

N

Karan
Bruje
Kibaykib Tombs
Koshilat Maqandeli
Jebel Bani Jabir Plateau
Al Maktah
Devil's Gap
WADI DAIQAH
WADI KHABBAH
WADI TAYIN
Al Ghayyan

To Sur
Mintirib
WAHIBAH SANDS
Al Qamil Rest House
Mudharib
WADI NAM
Nahar Farm Camp
Ibra
Mansfah

To Sinaw
To Fanjah

10 km

After a while the track breaks from the wadi and climbs into the jebels before coming out onto a plain some 50 klicks from Devil's Gap. Keep to your right and the track will eventually come to the main road via Wadi Naam. You will be in the town of **Ibra** (not to be confused with Ibri which is further to the north after Bahla).

Mudaybi and Sinaw (SS)

Mudaybi and **Sinaw** are two outpost towns between the Wahibah Sands and the Empty Quarter. Both are sprawling and expansive and the souq at Sinaw is quite impressive, especially when you attend the morning session when all the local farmers have brought in fresh produce and livestock. (Try to get there as early as possible . . . eightish.) The road to these two is a right turnoff on the Muscat-Sur road, 17 klicks after the Wadi Tayin turnoff (Map 17). The tarmac road (Route 27) heads due south, passing several items that deserve note. These are three villages that appear in rapid-fire sequence near the beginning of your turnoff toward Sinaw.

The first village you come to 5 kilometers along the road, is **Ar Rowdah.** You will see signs to Ar Rowdah off to your right. If you turn in here you will find a couple of forts, one that has been restored, one that has not. Both are visible from the main road. The first is just 1 kilometer up ahead on the left and the second is reached by a left track through the plantation half a kilometer beyond the first fort. Both afford good views of the village, the plantations, and the surrounding plains.

The second is the village of **Al Akdar.** The village is, once again, just off the main road and can be identified by some ruins and a lone tower. The tower can be entered and climbed. (You must enter through the big wooden double doors in the wall to the left of the tower. Find your way through a small alley and up some well-worn steps, turn right onto a roof, and climb an archway into the tower.) Inside there reside vestiges of decaying ordnance: rusty cannons and stone cannonballs. The view from the roof, accessed by a narrow stairwell, is superb. Down below, the village is the typical maze of alleys and at the far end next to the falaj an old pit weaver can be found. The pit weavers construct their looms on the ground with pits dug beneath them to provide mobility for the weaver and the treadles. (If you get lost, there are many helpful hands in the town to guide you there.) The cloth produced has distinctive colors and textures and items are for sale.

The third village is that of **Samad Ash Shaan,** where you can find more forts, towers, and an abandoned walled city in various stages of ruination. Some, like the walled city, are so far gone as to be beyond reclamation. It will only be a matter of time until it crumbles into dust and is lost to time, but there are enough remains at present to give a feel for lives past. As you enter Samad Ash Shaan, turn left and follow the road as it turns to gravel

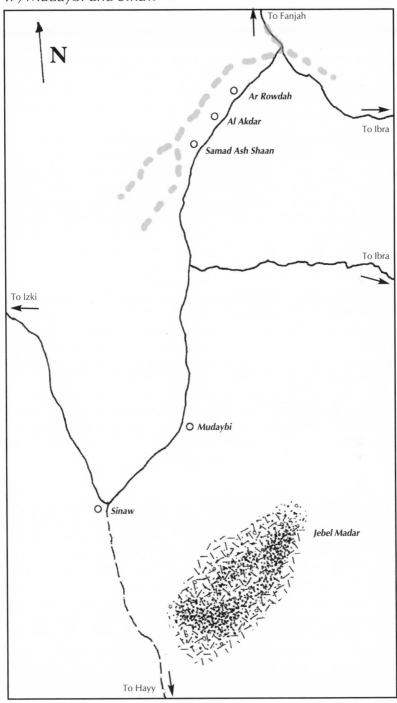

and leads up a wadi between plantations. After a short distance the first ruin can be spotted on a rise to your left. Shortly after (200 meters), a right turnoff will take you into the plantation past another fort, through the current village, and if you keep to your right, the towers and the abandoned walled city.

After Samad Ash Shaan on the road to Sinaw, there is a road (Route 28) left to Ibra (which is 64 kilometers further on).

Mudaybi is 45 klicks along from the Muscat/Sur road, off to your left. Although it is thriving quite well, there is an old quarter that is nearly abandoned, including an old souq. This section is contained by walls and can be entered from any number of archways around it. When you go inside, you can't escape that sheltered, cloistered feel. There are carved doors and windows, arches, aflaj, and a few old residents wandering about. The people are friendly, especially the children, and will enjoin in conversation in their own modest fashion. The children are a bit more direct, however.

Sinaw is just another 18 kilometers beyond Mudaybi. The road is rather flat with only one jebel protruding in the distance beyond Mudaybi (Jebel Madhr). The souq is toward the center of town and it is a large walled area with green gates. There's lots of things for sale here, not just produce and livestock. If you can be tempted away from purchasing that fine specimen of a racing camel, you'll find dealers of more manageable items such as antiquities and jewelry (including khanjars). You may even strike a deal better than anything you could get in Muscat. Give it your best shot.

A few hundred meters beyond the souq on a rise above the town is an old walled village that is great for exploring. Outside you may find a falaj clock (still working! but not on rainy days). If you drive to the village be sure not to park in the cemetery nearby. There is also an old abandoned souq not too far from the current one.

Ibra (SS)

Like so many other interior towns, **Ibra** is expanding by the minute (Map 16). New houses are sprouting like mushrooms and businesses are coming into the city. You will most likely just use Ibra as a rest stop or to tank up, but there are a couple of places of note.

Wednesday at the souq in Ibra is an all-ladies affair. Independent craft women come from all over the Sultanate to the **Souq Al Arba'h ("Wednesday's Market")** to sell their wares: clothing and textiles, woven goods, bokhur (incense). Zuweina bint Hashim Al Maskari, a leading social worker and past president of the Oman Women's Association, has been instrumental in organizing the Wednesday Market, which started in 1986. She has proclaimed the souq an instant success because it has given poorer families a chance to earn some extra cash and to practice a trade. The men have to sit this one out, so if your significant other has ditched you in Ibra, you know where to find her. Traders average about 150, while there are as many as 1,000 customers. It is open from 7:30 A.M. to 11 A.M.

On the far side of Ibra there is an old abandoned village worth examining called **Al Mansfah.** If you travel through Ibra on the main road, take a right at 1.7 kilometers south of the Shell petrol pump. (It's tarmac all the way.) After 1.1 kilometers turn left. This road winds through a village and at 1.7 kilometers crosses a wadi. Up ahead at the next intersection turn right. Al Mansfah is straight ahead, 1 kilometer, beneath the old stone archway (and a hundred years into the past). Much of the charm and character of this old mercantile village has not washed away and it is hoped that this place will receive due attention for restoration as have forts and towers. At any rate, a casual careful stroll down its alleys and ways reveals more than enough atmosphere for this bygone trading center, with homes of some grand old merchant families.

Jebel Bani Jabir Plateau (SS, HCP, 4WD)

The road to the **Jebel Bani Jabir Plateau** is not an easy one but it is rewarding. The region boasts centuries-old **Bruje Kibaykib Tombs** and the **Khoshilat Maqandeli,** which up until recently has been known as the Majlis Al Jinn Cave. When you have gone there and back you will feel like you have

The tombs of Kibaykib on the Jebel Bani Jabir plateau.

really accomplished something, because the area is quite remote and has a lot to offer. Be sure you have enough petrol and your spares and tool kit are in order, etc.

Description of this trek will start from the turnoff in Ibra that is the same track that comes from Wadi Khabbah/Devil's Gap (see above) tracing Wadi Naam. Three kilometers in on your right is **Nahar Farm Camp,** operated by Empty Quarter Tours, which provides overnight accommodations for guests in an all-Omani environment. For a modest sum (RO 15) you can have Omani food and entertainment before you retire in charming rustic palm frond huts. Further on, the tarmac road leads in for 17 kilometers before stopping at a plantation. There is a short track skirting the plantation to the right. Abruptly this track forks into a broad wadi where the track to the left is thickly packed gravel as it travels over the wadi bed. Follow this left track. After another 17 kilometers the road, which is fairly flat and straight, now bends sharply to the left. As you approach the jebels the road stays flat, but eventually the hills close around you and the track climbs and dips. At 55 kilometers from the main road the track forks right. Up ahead is a tower on a hill. Take the right fork (signposted to Al Maktah) and continue driving toward the sheer face ahead of you. After another kilometer, turn right again and bypass a village on your left. After 69 kilometers the road forks again by a sign to Al Gayla and Habenah. Take the left fork up the wadi past an earthen wall and 1 kilometer later take a right fork that climbs out of the wadi. After another kilometer take a left fork again. Now you should be heading into the steepest part of your ascent (use low ratio).

After 6 kilometers you will climb over a rim onto a plateau where up ahead there are a few huts, goat pens, sporadic vegetation, and other signs of life. About halfway across this hanging valley, about 1 kilometer, take a left and begin to climb again. Once again the road is steep. At roughly 78 kilometers from the main road back in Ibra you will be on top of the plateau, but there is a bit of driving yet to do. The track here is very rocky with stone shards lying about. If you look across the plateau you will see up ahead **tombs,** similar to the beehive tombs near Al Ayn, spread across the skyline. Although there are up to 50 tombs in this region, they are much more dispersed across the plateau. Some of these tombs are several meters high and in surprisingly good condition, considering that they date back to the Bronze Age.

The track meanders across the plateau, linking up the clusters of tombs. At 86 kilometers you will come to **Green Can Fork.** I don't know how long this has been called Green Can Fork, but the green can is still resting on a post by the fork, although now it is a bit rusty. Perhaps some do-good trekker with a can of Krylon on his next visit . . . just a thought. If you go right at Green Can Fork the track leads to more tombs, including a dramatic cluster by the edge of the plateau where the view is tremendous. (You are over 1,500 meters in altitude.) This track continues on past some remote settlements and appears to head eastward toward the coast but I don't know if it reaches there. If it does, I believe it would come out somewhere near Shab and Tiwi.

The left fork from the green can leads over a rough 5 kilometers to the remote village of **Karan,** built into a cliff side. The people here are friendly but very traditional. Please observe the "no photography without permission" rule explicitly. If you do manage to start up a chat, ask the folks to show you the trail to the cave of **Khoshilat Maqandeli.** The koshilat was revealed to Westerners (and given the fanciful title of Majlis Al Jinn) by an American, the late W. Don Davison, Jr. (He was affectionately known by his friends as D^2.) Don was a long-time resident of Oman and an employee of the Ministry of Water Resources when I met him late in his career. He was an excellent field geologist, mountain climber, and explorer. Shortly after his retirement from MWR in 1994, D^2 went on a climb in the Andes. He was attempting to be the first person to do a solo climb of Volcan Llullaillaco, the world's second tallest volcano, on the Chilean/Argentine border. After filing his trek with authorities and embarking, he failed to return to his checkpoint. A search and rescue mission only found his rental truck buried in the snow. He is presumed dead . . . and sorely missed by the many friends and colleagues he left behind in Oman.

The legend behind the cave goes as follows: A *qandaleh,* in the local dialect, is a term for an enclosure for keeping goats. And it was in one such qandaleh that a long time ago a shepherd girl named Salma penned her goats and went off to find food. While she was gone, a leopard stalked the enclosure and consumed some of the kids. It then fell asleep guarding its hoard. Salma returned late that afternoon and found the leopard sleeping. She then wrapped her cloak around her head along with a spiky thistle for protection, and with her axe attacked the leopard, crying, "You despicable thing!" The leopard jumped up and raked her with its claws, blinding her, while she swung down with her axe and split the leopard's skull. When the members of the tribe later came onto the scene, both Salma and the leopard were dead, locked in each other's embrace.

To honor her bravery, God sent seven stars down from the sky where they crashed into the earth. The first two created the *khoshilat,* or sinkholes, to what is now cataloged as the world's second largest cave chamber in the world. The others are lesser ones scattered about the region.

The Khoshilat Maqandeli is valuable for its speleological content as well as for being a repository for organic matter (namely seeds and skeletal remains). The cave itself is a single chamber, 310 meters long and 225 meters wide (1,018 feet by 740 feet), which means it is large enough to place several Boeing 747s end to end on the floor. The volume of the cave is about 4,000,000 cubic meters. The only access to the cave is via 3 breakdowns in the roof of the chamber, allowing for vertical free descent for 160 meters. These entrances are known as First Drop, the Asterisk, and Cheryl's Drop, names given by Davison's team in 1983. The roof is free-standing with no central support. There are no lower exits or passages.

The cave contains stalactites and stalagmites, draperies, heligmites, rim-stone dams, and cave pearls. It is part of a very active region, geologically speaking, with particular emphasis on karst terrain. The surrounding area of the cave is fairly accessible and contains other karst features, interesting geological structures, and fossil-rich limestone. Because of the nature of the cave and its remoteness, entering the cave should only be attempted by those who are interested in geo-and speleo-research and are *seasoned experts in climbing.*

This trek from Ibra can be done in one day if you just plan to visit the mouth of the cave without going in. However, it seems that two days would be better to afford more time to take in the surroundings. There are ample places to camp on the plateau. Remember, it's a little cooler at these alti-tudes. Don't remove anything from the area, particularly from around the tombs, but please remember to cart out all your refuse. The return trip is made by the same way you came in. If you are just taking a day trip, allow yourself plenty of time before sundown to get off the scarp. It's 90 klicks of rugged off-road from the cave to Ibra and no lighting in between. And the hike from Karan to the cave is at least one hour.

Mudharib (SS)

Traveling south on the Muscat/Sur Road, the next town is **Mudharib,** another thriving oasis. After Ibra if you look off to the southwest you will begin to see rolling stretches of the **Wahibah Sands.** From here to the south-ern coast, 200 kilometers away, these longitudinal dunes rise up above 100 meters in an undulating sea of sand. Interspersed throughout are prosopsis stands which serve as the only vegetated spots in the desert. Here the Bedouins carry on with their old established ways of seasonal migration through the desert, from waterhole to waterhole, where enclaves reside. Camel treks can be obtained in Muscat through local tour operators. If you have never been to the desert and want to know how it's done, seek out the operator that provides a trek adjusted to your needs and capabilities.

Just beyond Mudharib on the left is the **Al Qabil Resthouse,** a good stopover for those who want to take in more of the region and not be exposed to the elements.

There are many entrances to the sands from Mudarhib on down through **Mintirib** and **Al Kamil** (Map 18). Eight kilometers past Mintirib is

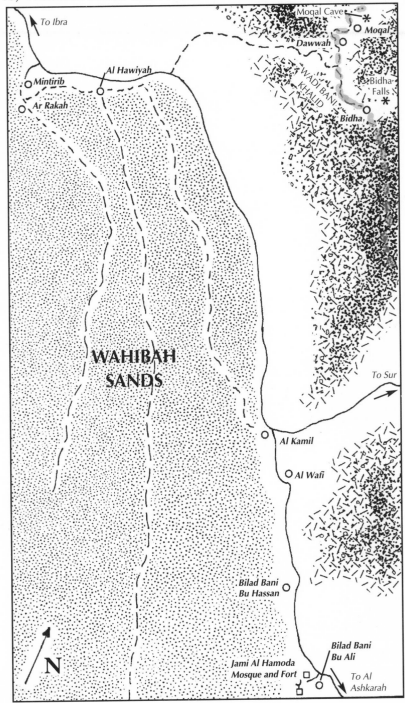

To Ibra

Moqal Cave

Moqal

Dawwah

WADI BANI KHALID

Al Hawiyah

Mintirib

Bidha Falls

Ar Rakah

Bidha

WAHIBAH SANDS

To Sur

Al Kamil

Al Wafi

Bilad Bani Bu Hassan

Bilad Bani Bu Ali

N

Jami Al Hamoda Mosque and Fort

To Al Ashkarah

10 km

the settlement of Al Hawiyah, which has a track leading into the desert running 170 kilometers to the coast. If you are not familiar with desert driving and the conditions, it might be best to hire a guide. But short forays of a few kilometers into the Wahibah from these spots will be enough to satisfy the inquisitive, as the scenery doesn't change much until you reach the ocean 200 kilometers away. Minitrib is 20 kilometers past the Al Qabil Resthouse. This town has a rebuilt fort and a souq where many Bedouins come to trade. From here it is easy to find tracks that lead from town past the settlement of Ar Rakah into the Wahibah. At Al Kamil, the track into the desert leads through some **prosopsis oases** and several **Bedu encampments.**

Wadi Bani Khalid (SS, HCP, 4WD)

The road after Minitrib starts to bend away from the Wahibah. In another 15 kilometers you will see a turnoff to the left, signposted to **Wadi Bani Khalid,** one of the most picturesque wadis in the interior. In older days it was one of the harder wadis to get to, as the track went over a very steep ridge. However, a newer graded track has been completed with several switchbacks, making access to the wadi a bit easier. It is still quite steep on the downside into the wadi. From the main road it is about 25 kilometers to the main juncture in the wadi. The first part of the track is flat. Keep to the right and soon the level ground gives way to greenish-tinged foothills before finally yielding to a steep mountain ridge. From the top of this ridge the view back to the Wahibah is spectacular. Down into the valley you . . . is *plummet* too strong a word here? . . . until you reach the main junction in Wadi Bani Khalid.

If you take a right, you will wind up and down, in and out of the wadi past lush plantations and an old tower or two before ending up in the remote village of **Bidh'a,** several kilometers in. Behind the village of Bidh'a you can clamber over some rocks on a fairly rough trail that leads to a beautiful series of waterfalls and cascades into pools. These are the **Shalalaat Al Hawer,** or "waterfalls at Hawer." There are numerous places to stop and have a picnic and chat with the locals (the kids are always curious in a tentative sort of way). The season will determine how much water is in the wadi, but you can always count on one or two pools to create an idyllic spot.

The left turn will take you through a string of villages alongside the wadi. A number of tracks break away, but stick to the track near the wadi floor and you will pass through Amq, Dawwah, and eventually Moqal. The last part of this drive, 5 kilometers from the junction, is a winding, grueling course around boulders and over falaj crossings. Sometimes the road seems no wider than your vehicle as you instinctively hold your arms to your side. After a low-lying dam across the wadi, the wadi floor widens, running between two dense groves of date palms. At one point you will have to stop and continue your trek on foot. But here, it is recommended that you have a nice picnic lunch first to work out the cramps of a long drive from Muscat and prepare you for what's ahead.

Trek up the wadi, and in a short time you will hear children cavorting. Water is running abundantly now, and soon rush-lined pools grow into a sprawling old-fashioned **swimmin' hole.** Here the pools are very deep with ample ledges of varying heights to jump off of. The town has fashioned some shaded sitting areas for the older folks. If you wish, join the youngsters, who never get tired of showing you ways of entering the water from the rocks.

The pools continue beyond the main swimming area and now streams and rivulets can be seen winding along the floor of the wadi. The pools are just as attractive and deep here as downstream and just as accessible. The canyon walls close in and flowering oleander permeates the air with its gentle scent. Water action over the millennia has carved the pools into intriguing abstract sculptures. You will have to do a bit of clambering. You might pass a goatherd or two tending their flocks. These folk are rather shy, so warm smiles and waves will allay their trepidation. Further on up the wadi you will come to another aspect of time and water: on the right-hand side of the wall where a set of concrete steps has been built up to a ledge 20 feet off the ground, there is a slim crevice in the rock. This is the entrance to **Moqal Cave.**

The entrance is rather narrow, which makes hard hats or protective gear recommended and torches a necessity. Once inside there are several large chambers, some with running water. In times of flood, the cave is not accessible. The length of the cave extends over 450 meters.

The mountains, cave, water, plants, and teeming life of this region are a stunning example of a mini-ecosystem that has developed in contrast to the harsh desert immediately to the west. Wadi Bani Khalid is one of the most agriculturally productive regions. They even have their own variety of red peel banana that doesn't seem to grow anywhere else in the Sultanate. If you come to Wadi Bani Khalid, be sure to pay Mother Nature her due respect for keeping this vibrant community alive and well.

SHARQIYAH

Sur (SS, HCP)

From the border of the Wahibah Sands the main road, Route 23, sweeps to the twin towns of Al Kamil and Al Wafi, where another route (Route 35) diverges to the coast. Route 23 then swings to the north around the southern tip of **Jebel Khader** and the furthest extremity of the Eastern Hajars. It is then a 54-kilometer drive to **Sur** along **Wadi Fulayj.** As you approach the

19) The Eastern Tip from Sur to Al Ashkarah

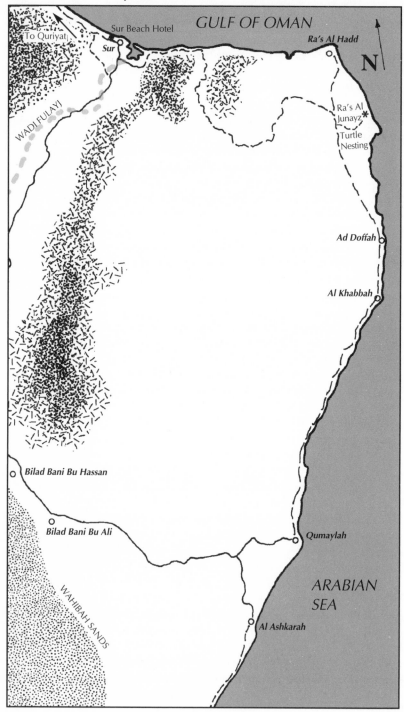

GULF OF OMAN

To Quriyat

Sur Beach Hotel

Sur

Ra's Al Hadd

N

WADI FULAYJ

Ra's Al Junayz
Turtle Nesting

Ad Doffah

Al Khabbah

Bilad Bani Bu Hassan

Bilad Bani Bu Ali

Qumaylah

WAHIBAH SANDS

ARABIAN SEA

Al Ashkarah

10 km

town (which is also undergoing rapid growth like many other Omani commercial centers), you will see the Gulf of Oman spreading beyond to the horizon. Here is the last vestige of the old mercantile days, the fabled **Shipyards of Sur** (Map 19).

As you approach the town you will pass through a series of roundabouts until you are just about in the city center. A right turn at the T-junction will take you through a winding course of shops and markets until you reach the bay. The road skirts the shore of the bay, winding along until you see the shipyards ahead. Dhows rest in the bay or are beached. Some of them are retired and waiting to wither away. Others are careened for scraping the hulls free of barnacles. A number of sambuks and shuis are in various stages of construction. These are the only boats made today. The old baglahs and booms are long extinct in this world. Still you can manage to see some of the boat builders' craft. Imported timbers are hewn to size and placed in line. Only recently have they employed modern tools to expedite the labor. All the work is done by eye. There are no plans or blueprints for these boats . . . there haven't been for generations. Some of the craftsmen have taken to building scale models, which can be seen at some of the hotels and museums in Muscat. Even the smaller ones can be ordered and purchased. (Hold on to your hat when you hear these prices. Don't worry. You'll definitely get what you pay for. This priceless skill is becoming a lost art.)

As you cruise past the shipyards and out to the mouth of the bay, there is a long beach and promenade. Slightly up the coast towards Tiwi you will come to the **Sur Beach Hotel.** Beyond the hotel, the sandy beach extends up the coast toward Qalhat and Tiwi.

Ra's Al Hadd and Ra's Al Junayz (SS, HCP, 4WD)

On the approach to Sur from Al Kamil, as you enter city limits, you will see a right turnoff that is signposted to **Ra's Al Hadd** from the second roundabout near the mosque. This road is tarmac for a short distance as it skirts the far side of the bay, then turns into the hills. You will reach a small coastal settlement of Ayja as the road now skirts the ocean across some rocky terrain. After 20 kilometers the track turns inland and snakes through a ravine for 18 kilometers before emerging on a broad plain. Keep to the left and after another 12 kilometers you will be at Khawr Al Jaramah lagoon. You will then come upon a junction that leads left to the village at Ra's Al Hadd and right to the **government campground at Ra's Al Junayz.** If you have obtained your permit from the Ministry of Regional Municipalities and Environment, you can go to this campground for the express purpose of observing the green turtle nesting season (from September to early December). You can do this by applying several days in advance to the Directorate General of Nature Protectorates. The office is in the ministry building in

Al Khuwair, next to the Ministry of Housing, and you can fill out an application there or call 696442. You will have to pick up the permit in person during government hours (before 2:30 P.M.).

You will also be given some informative material about the turtle nesting habits as well as a list of dos and don'ts while you are at the campground. When using this campground, please obey the caveats to insure that you (and the turtles) have a pleasant visit. Fires and lights are only permitted at certain spots away from the beach. There are attendants who will escort your group to the beach at night to watch the turtles come ashore to lay their clutches of eggs. If you feel like having a kip (taking a nap) before you venture down to the beach, it would be advisable, as the best viewing hours are after midnight.

By the way, you are at the easternmost extremity of the Arabian peninsula.

Al Ashkharah (SS, HCP)

The track south from Ra's Al Junayz runs down the coast, threading its way between desert and coast with some exciting scenery between **Ad Daffah** and **Al Khabbah.** Here the track runs the rim of a bluff over the ocean. On the beaches below you will see tracks left by nesting turtles during the nesting season. After 60 kilometers you will come to the town of **Qumaylah,** and, lo and behold, tarmac. Give your 4WD gears a rest and cruise on down to **Al Ashkharah,** another 20 klicks along. Here is a beautiful coastal town where the residents have plied the waters for fish for as long as anyone can remember. There are beaches and more sand than you could possibly want to see in your shoes in a lifetime. It is here that the Ramlat Al Wahibah meets up with the coast. There are places along the shore or further in amidst the dunes for camping. Follow established tracks and you shouldn't get stuck. The surrounding hills give great vistas. But if you plan to rough it, there is not a better place than Al Ashkarah. Come to think of it, this might be a good opportunity to rough it out here before they start to dig for the new resort planned for this region.

Bilad Bani Bu Hassan and Bilad Bani Bu Ali (SS, HCP)

The tarmac road that connects Qumaylah and Al Ashkarah is the one that runs from Route 23 in Al Kamil. This connector is numbered Route 35 and passes through the two enchanting villages of **Bilad Bani Bu Hassan** and **Bilad Bani Bu Ali.** Both towns are overflowing with buildings, forts, and mosques from bygone times. The main feature is the **Jami Al Hamoda Mosque** in Bilad Bani Bu Ali, built in the eleventh century A.H. by Shaykh Rashid bin Salim Al Hamoda. The mosque has 52 domes supported on a network of pillars, a falaj flowing through bathing rooms for ablutions, a huge portico, and a main entrance with studded wooden doors. You can reach there by turning off the main road to Al Ashkarah and heading toward the fort. The fort was also built by the shaykh and both mosque and fort have undergone extensive restoration. The fort has several walls, towers, and dungeons, and an escape passage 4 kilometers long. After the fort, make your way through a cluster of houses to the left and you shortly come upon the mosque. A nearby mosque, over 250 years old, with 6 domes, sits in a stand of trees (although I have not visited this spot).

Make your way back to the fort, but instead of heading out, drive behind the fort and through a cluster of partial ruins, past a newer mosque and out into an open plain. Ahead you will see the old entrance to the wilayat, an archway, a 2-domed mosque, and a wall from a single tower. To the right extending for several hundred meters are remnants of the old city wall. This is said to have been the inspiration for Shaykh Rashid to build his mosque.

Bilad Bani Bu Hassan next door is a sightseers' delight with 13 castles, 20 forts, 60 towers, 30 fortified houses, and 6 walled enclosures, including a prominent stretch from Dawazah to Al Mahyawal graveyard. The region is fed by Wadi Batha, one of the region's biggest wadis. There are aflaj running throughout and the town retains its quaintness, not to mention the sand that blows in from the Wahibah. The region is known for raising horses and camels for racing. Both of these towns are easily accessed by the road from Al Kamil and Al Wafi.

7. Guided Tours

Touring offers a multiplicity of ways to see the country: across, through, from above, and from below. No doubt if you are an off-the-beaten-path sort, you will want to take up the favorite pastime of Omanis and expatriate residents (expats) alike, that is, wadi bashing, an activity that allows one to come as close to Indiana Jones as one would care to. The previous section was written for those who would like to wadi bash on their own, but for those who would like a more supervised atmosphere, here is the list of local operators that can provide these services.

Al Inshirah Cruise Service
P.O. Box 3940
Ruwi 112
Tel. 714271
Fax: 712642
Half/full-day cruise, sunset cruise, leisure cruise, Tom Cruise (just kidding!); lunches, BBQs

Al Nahdha Tourism
P.O. Box 2031
Mercure Al Falaj Hotel
Ruwi 112
Tel. 799928/702311/795206
Fax: 799928
E-mail: hbt123@gto.net.om
Custom tours, desert and wadi trips, boating, diving and water sports, game safaris, hot air balloon flights

Arabian Sands Tour Services
Tel./Fax: 566147 (Muscat) or 256421 (Salalah)
Pager: 911-7262 (Muscat) or 919-5410 (Salalah)
Day treks, overnights, extended camping tours, camel treks with authentic Bedouin experience

Arabian Sea Safaris
P.O. Box 2785
CPO Seeb 111
Tel. 693223
Fax: 693224
Boating excursions, game fishing, diving, anything to do with water

Bahwan Travel Agencies
P.O. Box 282
Muscat 113
Tel. 780559
Fax: 700483
Inbound tours, day trips, wadi bashing, desert trips, historical tours, cultural tours, snorkeling and diving, dhow trips, etc.

Desert Discovery
P.O. Box 99
Madinat Al Sultan Qaboos 115
Tel. 597914
Fax: 590144
The team that brought you Nahar Farm Camp split up and Said Al Harthy has his own camp in the Wahibah Sands. He also does tours to anywhere in the Sultanate.

Eihab Travels
P.O. Box 839

Muscat 113
Tel. 796387/786282
Fax: 793849
Half/full-day city tours, overnight camping excursions to the interior (wadi bashes), extended desert treks, cruises

Empty Quarter Tours
P.O. Box 9
Madinat Al Sultan Qaboos 115
Tel. 957093/911-5514 (pager)/597914 (office)
Fax: 590144
Desert treks, wadi bashes, cultural and heritage tours, overnight facilities in a totally Omani setting near Ibra

Explorer Tourism Co.
P.O. Box 2440
CPO Seeb 111
Tel. 706654/211908 (Salalah)
Fax: 706654/211907 (Salalah)
Half/full-day city tours, overnight camping excursions to the interior (wadi bashes), extended desert treks, fishing and boating cruises

Gulf Ventures
OUA Travel Centre
P.O. Box 985
Ruwi 112
Tel. 700326
Fax: 795237
City tours, cultural tours, wadi trips, nature safaris, desert excursions

Khasab Travels and Tours/Oman Discovery
P.O. Box 3932
Ruwi 112
Tel. 706424
Fax: 706463
Complete coverage of the Musandam Peninsula: day trips, boating and diving, cultural tours, custom tours

Marina Bander Al-Rowdha
P.O. Box 940
Muscat 113
Tel. 737288

Fax: 737285
Dhow cruises, game fishing charters, diving, snorkeling and instruction
(PADI), sailboarding, water sports. Charter a cruise (contact 968-953309 or
607721, or Fax: 605117). Club membership, berthing, boat hire—cruiser, catamaran, jet ski, windsurfer, water skiing, banana boat, doughnut ride

Mezoon Travels
P.O. Box 629
Muscat 113
Tel. 796680
Fax: 795721
Half/full-day tours, dhow cruises, nature tours, cultural tours, wadi bashes,
diving

Midland Tourism
P.O. Box 426
Muscat 113
Tel./Fax: 566524
E-mail: alwosta@gto.net.om
Half/full-day city tours, wadi bashing, cultural tours, hang gliding

Moon Travels
P.O. Box 2534
Ruwi 112
Tel. 706217/793551
Fax: 706418
Half/full-day tours, cultural tours, wadi bashes, desert excursions

National Travel and Tourism
P.O. Box 962
Muscat 113
Tel. 566046
Fax: 566125
Half/full-day tours, heritage and cultural tours, adventure tours, wadi
bashes, desert excursions, camel safaris, dhow cruises, diving and snorkeling

Oman Dive Centre
P.O. Box 199
Madinat Al Sultan Qaboos 115
Tel. 950261
Fax: 950261
Boat hire, diving and snorkeling, beginner and advanced instruction (PADI)

Oman Geo Tours
P.O. Box 194
Shati Al Qurum 134
Tel. 600914
Fax: 600917
See the country from the natural point of view. Specializes in geo-tours and natural history tours with a liberal dash of culture and history for academics, scientists, and all inquisitive minds. Owner and chief tour guide is a PDO field geologist, Salim Al Maskary, with rapt regard for accuracy, detail, safety, and conservation.

Oman National Transport Company
P.O. Box 620
Muscat 113
Tel. 590046
Fax: 590152
Government-run bus line, coach services, half/full-day tours, transfers

Oman United Agencies (Travel Centre)
P.O. Box 985
Ruwi 112
Tel. 700362/291132 (Salalah)
Fax: 796998/290770
Half/full-day tours, heritage and cultural tours, wadi bashes, desert excursions

Orient Holidays
P.O. Box 198
Mutrah 114
Tel. 604902
Fax: 692681
Groups, package tours, desert treks, and wadi bashes

Orient Tours
P.O. Box 409
Muscat 113
Tel. 605066/235333 (Salalah)
Fax: 698898
Half/full-day tours, cultural tours, wadi bashes, desert excursions

Sand and Sea Tours
P.O. Box 76

Al Hamra 131
Tel. 595083
Private tours and treks to the interior

Shanfari Travels
P.O. Box 783
Muscat 113
Tel. 786916
Fax: 785371
Half/full-day tours, cultural tours, wadi bashes, desert excursions

Sunny Day Tours
P.O. Box 375
Madinat Al Sultan Qaboos 115
Tel. 591244
Fax: 591478
E-mail: sunnyday@gto.net.om
This is my company and we will design tours for your group any way you
like. We can provide rental cars too if you want to travel on your own. See
Xpress listing under Local Transportation section.

Ubar Tourism
P.O. Box 754
CPO Seeb 111
Tel. 932-9185
Fax: 694433
E-mail: ubartour@gto.net.om
Interior treks and wadi bashes

United Tours
P.O. Box 599
Mutrah 114
Tel. 703303/787648
Fax: 799502
Half/full-day tours, heritage and cultural tours, wadi bashes, desert excur-
sions, dhow cruises

Z Tours by MDS (Marine Development Services)
P.O. Box 1775
Jibroo 114
Tel. 737614
Fax: 737612
Game fishing, dolphin/whale watches, dhow cruise, scenic tours

Zubair Tours
P.O. Box 833
Ruwi 112
Tel. 708081/708071
Fax: 787560
Cultural and heritage tours, wadi bashes, desert excursions, dhow cruises,
custom tours

If you would like to arrange a customized tour, you can contact the
author of this book through Faye Sell, Martinelli Travel, Apple Tree Mall,
Londonderry, NH 03053; Tel. 603-434-4989, 800-324-4989; Fax: 603-434-
1696; or Paradise Holidays Pte. Ltd., 111 North Bridge Road, #03-24, Peninsula Plaza, Singapore 179098; Tel. 65-733-1877; Fax: 65-336-7115.

8. Shopping

> The bazaar, filling a large area, consists of covered partly vaulted streets, running
> at right angles to each other. One could buy there silk, linen, spices, incense, cof-
> fee and among the foodstuffs the best and most delicious mangoes I ever tasted.
> I bought 100 mangoes for one mamudi, but when other foreigners arrived, they
> soon put up their prices.
> —Engelbert Kaempfer, *Travels*, 1688

There is no doubt that things can get tough in Oman, and when the goin'
gets tough, the tough go shopping. Oman displays a variety of stores from
the old world souqs to the trendy upscale malls. You can go bargain hunting
or sink a fortune and anything in between on just about any kind of commodity, from Japanese hi-tech cameras and stereo components to elegant textiles and clothing to handmade local crafts. Lots of opportunity for the
souvenir buyers among us. Note that there is always the opportunity for kitsch
to rear its ugly head. Be sure to investigate and know what you are buying.

Also, a word about haggling. In the old souqs you can try your hand at
this venerated custom which approaches an art form. It is not as widely in
use as in other parts of the Middle East, but it is still considered an honor to
the shopkeeper if you bicker over price, the longer the better. (Personally, I
find that one of the best—and funniest—descriptions of haggling in a Middle
Eastern bazaar comes from the 1978 film *Monty Python's Life of Brian*. The haggling scene is priceless and not too far from accurate. Watch it a couple of
times and you'll get the gist of it.) In the old souqs you will find the best
opportunity to haggle, as well as among the craft dealers in the interior; however, the recent influx of tourists who are ignorant of this old practice and
whip out their wallets at the slightest provocation has given the shopkeepers
impetus to hang on to a higher price. Give it your best shot. Hang in there.

Keep up the conversation. Raise your tone and inflection. Throw up your arms in mock disgust. Turn and walk away. Seek out another item for comparison. Feign impending bankruptcy. If it's worth it to you, you'll get your price, or close to it. Traditional souqs are places where you can haggle almost indefinitely, but don't waste your time haggling for cheap items (1-2 riyals).

In the gold souqs, items are sold by weight, so there is no need to haggle. But you can, if you have the time, keep an eye on the fluctuations of the international gold market in order to get the best price.

In the more modern shops, particularly on Ruwi High Street, you can get away with a modified haggle. After selecting an item, ask for "best price?" or "after discount?" and you will usually get 5-10 percent shaved off the listed price (which has been marked up anyway). In the upscale malls you can't haggle at all. Everything is fixed price. But you can try anyway. The worst they can say is "no."

> Caravans overland brought ostrich feathers, cattle hides, sheep and skins, honey, beeswax, taking back with them cutlery, toys, spices, rice sugar, coffee and tobacco. The trade with Mocha was enormous: Muscat sent 20,000 bales of coffee every year to Basra, intended for Constantinople. . . . Goods so greatly exceeded in volume the warehouse space available that they lay in the streets, but were never stolen.
> —Abraham Parsons, *Travels in Asia and Africa,* 1808

The highest concentration of malls is just after the split of the Sultan Qaboos Highway in Qurum. (This split eventually turns into a loop that skirts downtown Ruwi and diverges once again towards Mutrah, Muscat, and the Al Bustan.) Back at the split several new complexes cluster around the original complex called **SABCO Centre** (Tel. 563949). These are **Al Araimi Complex** (Tel. 564787); **Al Khamis Plaza** (Tel. 562791); **Alasfoor Plaza** (Tel. 566217); and **Al Wadi Commercial Centre** (Tel. 566180).

A few hundred meters away on the far side of a wadi sits the **Capital Commercial Centre (CCC)** (Tel. 563672), which has undergone a recent expansion.

Further down the right-hand split of the highway on your right is the impressive **Al Harthy Complex** (Tel. 564481), which opened in 1992.

Other recent arrivals are the **Sarooj Commercial Centre** (Tel. 691311) (along the highway in Shati Al Qurum) and the **Jawaharat A'Shati** (Tel. 564250) (next to the Intercon), also in Shati Al Qurum.

Khimji Ramdas have opened a chain called **Khimji's Megastores.** They have showrooms near the Ruwi Novotel, on Ruwi High Street in the Makha Centre, Qurum, Nizwa, Sohar, and Salalah.

In Ruwi there is the new **Mazoun Complex** just off Ruwi High Street, and there is **Ruwi High Street** itself, a bustling center of shops and stalls. Some stores are removed from the street in alcoves and courtyards. There are street vendors and cafés. Jewelry, textiles, appliances, stereos and recorded music, fine arts, cameras, watches, shoes, and clothing are all sold in a busy atmosphere that's fun just to stroll around and observe.

There is also the new **Zakher Mall** (Tel. 707147) near the Al Jadeeda Stores on Dohat Al Adab Street in Al Khuwair. It promises to be the largest mall in the country to date.

SPECIALTY SHOPS (ARABIAN ANTIQUITIES) IN THE CAPITAL AREA

If you are not up to haggling or just want to pay full price and get it over with, there are several specialty shops worth investigating.

Antique World (Tel./Fax: 566503). Proprietor Samir bin Salim Al Harthy has scoured the Arabian peninsula for exquisite examples of antiquities—woodwork: doors and chests; ordnance: cannons, rifles, swords, and sabres; navigational instruments: astrolabes and sextants; decorative trays and utensils. Samir operates a small shop in the Al Harthy complex filled with rare books, stamps, prints, and coins. He also has a floating exhibition with the finest examples of Arabian craftwork.

Al Joori Trading (Tel. 703748). Close to the ROP on Ruwi High Street and across the street from Al Yafour Shop 'n' Save (Way. No. 3711, Building No. 845) there is a building materials supply house selling bathroom appointments and tiles, *but,* if you go into a side room there are a number of antiques (tables, bookstands, clothing, bric-a-brac) of varying age and condition. Prices here are probably negotiable.

Bait Al Turath Al Omani (Tel. 593719). This is a craft shop sponsored by the Ministry of Heritage and Culture to support traditional crafts in Oman such as weaving and pottery, etc. You can find good products at fair values. It is located next to the Natural History Museum in Al Khuwair Note: This shop is only open during government hours—7:30 A.M. to 2:30 P.M.

Handicraft Centre (Tel. 791454). Manufacturers of pottery, gifts, and special orders. Suppliers of raw materials and equipment. On Al Noor Street in Ruwi next to Zubair Furnishing.

Majlis Gallery (Tel. 697014, office; 501057, showroom). This is a great shop for connoisseurs of fine furnishings and stylish decorations: doors and shutters converted into beautiful tables, wooden chests from the old trading days, traditional weavings made into pillows and carpets, jewelry mounted into old window frames. It is in Al Ghubrah. Take the Dual Carriageway to the Ghala roundabout and a quarter turn (right) down Street 44. Three hundred meters on you will see a white villa on your left, No. 57. Turn in here.

Omani Heritage Gallery (Tel. 696165, 696974). Trendiest of the lot, but you can still get authentic crafts, clothing, and jewelry as well as up-scale market items. In the Jawaharat A' Shati Complex next to the Intercon in Shati Al Qurum.

Yiti Gallery (Tel. 713723, Ruwi; 564297, Qurum). Fine arts, prints, antiquities, and jewelry. The main showroom is in Ruwi in the Sony building across from the securities market and adjacent to the Chamber of Commerce and Industry. The new showroom is on the lower level of the new Al Khamis Plaza in Qurum.

6

The South:
The Eastern
Seaboard, Al Wusta
and the Nejd, and Dhofar

1. The General Picture

> Mr. Smith, an officer of the vessel which I commanded, was deputed by me to examine the whole of the [southern scarp]. He traversed it entirely in perfect safety, and, under the name of Ahmed, became a great favourite of the mountaineers. He was everywhere hospitably entertained by them, and they would not even permit him to drink water from the numerous clear mountain streams that were meandering in every direction. "No," they said, "do not return, Ahmed, and say we gave you water while our children drank nothing but milk." In every instance they gave him the warmest place at the fire, and invariably appointed some one to attend his wants. They even extended their generosity so far as to offer him a wife and some sheep, if he would only stay and reside among them.
> —Captain Stansford Bettesworth Haines, *Memoir of the South and East Coasts of Africa,* 1845

In terms of area, the southern expanses of Oman ranging from the Hajars southward constitute the bulk of the land mass. For the most part it is the most barren and desolate region of the country. Except for the shoreline strip, there is little or no livelihood in this the central region except for roving Bedouins and the petroleum interests. That is not to say that this is devoid of any tourist attractions. You can have tours organized, either 4WD or camel treks, to some very remote isolated regions.

Tour operators such as **Gulf Explorers** (Tel. 799928/702311) and **Al Taie Travel** (Tel. 795087/708179/705389) cater to the more exotic tastes. Heide Beal and her husband Chris (Gulf Explorers) have been organizing and customizing tours for as long as anybody and they have explored some of the deeper reaches of the Sultanate, including treks into the Empty Quarter and the Umm As Samim.

Further south the terrain doesn't get any better as you cross Al Wusta into the region known as the Nejd. If you happen to be driving through this region you begin to wonder if there is some goal on the opposite side. Here the desert seems to be at its harshest. Just remember that the trip from Muscat to Salalah, which takes 10 hours to do today, once took 10 days by camel. Only the more intrepid traveler goes off road here, and only when armed with satellite photographs, a GPS, and a Bedu.

But the drive to Salalah from Muscat is elucidating, if only to give the feel for the emptiness of the open expanse beyond the Hajars and Muscat. And certainly the first 9 hours and 55 minutes of the 10-hour drive is a monotonous exercise. But it's the last 5 minutes that are worth the price of admission, as the road climbs the slope of the escarpment and plunges 4,000 feet through the lush green forested region surrounding Salalah to the coastline. If this trek is taken in September after the khareef has lifted you will see Dhofar dressed in its finest, bedecked in greens as green as any Irish drumlin.

The name "Salalah" comes from Arabic, meaning "the place where animals are tethered." And it is no surprise that Salalah is teeming with animal life. What is surprising is that there don't seem to be any tethers. Herds of camels by the hundreds wander across the plains, loping toward nowhere in particular with a predisposed disregard for traffic signs. (They are quite fond of telephone poles, however, which make excellent scratching posts.)

The city itself is spread along the coast around the old plantations that still produce a broad selection of fruits and vegetables. Fruit stands do a brisk business well into the hours of night after all the stores have closed. The layout of the city is east/west. It is contained in a 15-kilometer span with 5 major thoroughfares, once again running east/west. The airport is close by, just 2 kilometers from the center of town. From the edge of town to the base of the escarpment are cultivated fields and open plains.

The cultural aspects of Salalah are slightly different from those found up north. Salalah is a bit more conservative than Muscat. Undoubtedly there is a larger concentration of Sunni Muslims in Salalah, but this conservatism is only a reflection of their moral code and not necessarily representative of politics (on a larger scale). They are Omani first and foremost. The Holiday Inn is the only licensed establishment in the region. You will see a higher percentage of veils in Salalah, although the dress styles are no less extravagant. Travelers should be on their best behavior (see "Social Customs and Courtesies" in chapter 2) toward the locals and should respect their sensibilities. I was once politely asked to circumvent a picnic area occupied by an extended family because I might come into contact with the harem. But nevertheless, the people still have that distinctive brand of open Omani hospitality that you will find everywhere.

In the interior you should be aware that the jebalis speak a dialect of Arabic that is almost incomprehensible. Towns and villages are more clannish and protective than those in the north. In older days, if you were traveling through a number of wilayats, you would usually have in your party a member from each and every tribe for every town you passed through so as to allay suspicions from that particular tribe and let them know your intentions were friendly (i.e., not hostile). Today, you will see a higher percentage of armed men in the jebels. This harkens back to the 1970s conflict and, very likely, earlier times. But even though they are very protective of their families and life-style, on the whole the people are still courteous.

2. Getting There

As mentioned above, Salalah can be done in a 10-to-12-hour drive from Muscat. This can be accomplished in one day, if you have a mind to, or broken up into two days with a stopover at one of the three rest houses along the way (see "The Hotel Scene," following).

Of course, if you opt for the softies' approach, you can take the Oman Air shuttle to Salalah for RO 50 ($130) round trip. The flight is just over an hour and flights run continually.

There is also the possibility of chartering boat trips to Salalah. Check a local tour operator or the marina at Bander Ar Rowdha.

3. Local Transportation

Many of the hire car services in Muscat maintain branch offices in Salalah. Check the listings in the previous chapter for branch offices and independent companies in Salalah.

4. The Hotel Scene

Your choices for accommodation are fairly simple in Salalah. At this time there are five hotels offering excellent lodging, food, and entertainment. All of them are of better than average rating. All offer the usual package of amenities: AC, cable and satellite TV, business services, conference facilities. Once again rates are per person and do not reflect service charge and tax.

Arab Oryx Rest Houses. (For convenience, this listing is repeated from the previous chapter.) Simple but nice accommodations. There is no other reason to stay at these rest houses other than to be in transit to or from Salalah, as the surrounding desert is quite barren and the whole trip is quite monotonous. All three have ten rooms, RO 10.5-14.7 ($27-$40), restaurant, and a nearby petrol pump.

Qitbit Resthouse. 278 kilometers from Salalah, a 3-hour drive. Tel./Fax: 968-951385.

Al Ghaftain Resthouse. 408 kilometers from Salalah, a 4 1/2-hour drive. Tel./Fax: 968-956872.

Ghaba Rest House. 715 kilometers from Salalah, a 7 1/2-hour drive. Tel./Fax: 968-951386.

The **Dhofar Hotel** (Tel. 968-292300/290484) is the most recent entry to the growing list of Salalah hotels. Just a few minutes from the airport on Al Matar Street in downtown Salalah, the Dhofar has 66 rooms and 12 suites and, due to open in early '97, an annex with 20 two-bedroom flats. Spacious restaurant and coffee shop. Banquet hall, conference facilities, and business center. Rooms are RO 21-27 ($54-$70); suites, RO 33 ($85) Reserve through the hotel at P.O. Box 2539, Salalah 211; Fax: 968-294358.

At 11 stories, the **Haffa House** (Tel. 968-295444/294755) is the predominant landmark in Salalah; no other building is taller. Just a stone's throw from the airport, on Burj Al Nahdah Roundabout, the Haffa House offers 107 rooms and suites decorated in rich Italian marbles. The complex houses a shopping area and the hotel has a health club, recreational facilities, pool, and tennis. The Salalah branch of Omar Khayyam Restaurant is here, too. Rooms RO 25-28 ($64-$72); suites RO 35-50 ($90-$130). Group rates and long term available. Reserve through the hotel at P.O. Box 427, Salalah 211; Fax: 968-294873.

On the northwest side of Salalah, situated in the Hamdan Commercial Complex near the Industrial Workshop area, the **Hamdan Plaza Hotel** (Tel. 968-211025) boasts 200 rooms, suites, and villas with beautiful appointments. On Robat Street. Squash, tennis, pool, and health club. Ballroom, conference and business facilities. Restaurant and coffee shop. Rooms RO 28-50 ($72-$129); suites RO 65 ($168); villas RO 85 ($219). Reserve through the hotel at P.O. Box 2498, Salalah 211; Fax: 968-211187.

The **Redan Hotel** (Tel. 968-292266) is in the central downtown area on Al Salaam Street. It has 27 rooms, 3 suites, 10 flats, and a restaurant. This hotel is the best choice for the budget-minded, but offers the same amenities as other hotels. The room rates are RO 14-17 ($36-$43); suites are RO 23 ($60); and flats are RO 25 ($65). Reserve through the hotel at P.O. Box 957, Salalah 211; Fax: 968-290491.

Salalah's own beach resort, the **Salalah Holiday Inn** (Tel. 968-235333) is located in an exotic setting east of town amidst coconut plantations and wooded groves. It is on Al Khandaque Street in Al Dahariz. Spread out along the waterfront, the hotel offers over 120 rooms, suites, and villas in a lush tropical setting. During the khareef, the thundering surf lulls you to sleep. The beautiful white sand beach extends for miles along the coast. There is a first-class restaurant, lounge and beach café, pool, tennis, mini-golf, snooker, cycle track, diving, horse riding, squash, health club with gym, Jacuzzi, steam bath, sauna, and massage. Fully licensed. Rooms RO 33-41.5 ($85-$107); suites RO 70 ($180); and villas RO 84 ($217). Reserve through the hotel at P.O. Box 870, Salalah 211; Fax: 968-235137.

5. Dining and Restaurants

Salalah has a fair choice of eateries but not the diversity that Muscat has to offer. Most of the good restaurants are in the hotels or located in the downtown area (with one exception, the Al Muhit). Most of the fare is the standard Chinese/Indian/Arabic breakdown that follows the style of many of the restaurants in Muscat (if you hadn't noticed already). There's also quick food to be had and there are always the strings of nameless cafés, sidewalk eateries, and shwarma stands. Don't forget the bake shops either. They have the same delightful array of sweetmeats that you can find up north.

Al Kharif Coffee Shop and Lounge (Arabian, Indian, Chinese, Continental) (Tel. 235333). At the Salalah Holiday Inn. Serving breakfast, lunch, and dinner, stylish buffets and the laid-back atmosphere of Salalah's coastline add up to a tasteful gastronomic outing. Fully licensed. RO 8 ($21)

Al Lou' Lou'a Restaurant (Continental and seafood) (Tel. 211025). At the Hamdan Plaza Hotel, Salalah. RO 3.5 ($9)

Al Luban (Lebanese) (Tel. 235333). At the Salalah Holiday Inn. Arabian Nights come alive in this swanky night spot. Lebanese specialties, kebabs, and salads are prepared to perfection. The temperature rises with live entertainment, singers, and belly dancers to set your mood for an exclusive evening Al Arabiya. Fully licensed. RO 10 ($26)

Al Muhit Restaurant (Arabian, Indian, Chinese) (Tel. 211243). Out of town, 5 kilometers west toward Raysut on Sultan Qaboos Street. This place has got it all (except the license)—elegant dining, beach-side patios, fountains, pool, recreation halls with snooker and bowling, party and conference facilities; the only thing missing is the beach-side cabanas and this could be a fantastic resort. But for now the food will have to suffice, and it's enough. Highly talented chefs are behind this one for a variety of international cuisine. RO 7 ($18)

Al Sultana Coffee Shop (Coffee and pastries) (Tel. 211025). At the Hamdan Plaza Hotel, Salalah.

Arab World (Tel. 297445). Fast food.

Bin Atique (Arabic) (Tel. 292384). On 23rd July Street near the center of town and Sultan Qaboos Road, Al Hafa. Traditional Arabic foods—meat, rice, and vegetable dishes—at very reasonable prices. RO 2 ($5.20)

Chopsticks (Tel. 291400). Cozy Chinese restaurant on 23rd July Street. RO 2 ($5.20)

Dhofar Hotel Restaurant (Arabian, Indian, Chinese, continental) (Tel. 292272). On Al Matar Street. The Dhofar offers choice and exotic cuisine and excellent buffets in a stately setting of marble and stone. RO 4 ($10)

Hassan bin Thabit Restaurant (Indian, Chinese) (Tel. 291010). On 23rd July Street. A nice and quiet eatery near the center of town with the usual selection of Chinese and Indian fare. RO 1.5 ($3.90)

Imperial Dragon Restaurant (Chinese) (Tel. 211025). At the Hamdan Plaza Hotel, Salalah. Opened in December, 1996.

Omar Khayyam (Arabic, Indian, Chinese) (Tel. 295444). Terrific setting in the Haffa House Building. The original Alauddin, now a new branch in Salalah. Great variety and great prices. RO 4 ($10)

Penguin (Tel. 225380). Fast food.

Pizza Hut (Tel. 290303). Fast food.

6. Sightseeing

> After another day spent in sketching, photography and measurements, we felt that we had thoroughly explored the neighborhood . . . the ancient sites, the abyss, and above all the surprising fertility of the valleys and mountains, the delicious health-giving air, and the immunity from actual danger which we had enjoyed combined in making us feel that our sojourn in Dhofar had been one of the most enjoyable and productive of any expedition we had hitherto undertaken, and that we had discovered a real paradise in the wilderness, which will be a rich prize for the civilized nation which is enterprising enough to appropriate it.
>
> —J. Theodore Bent, *Exploration of the Frankincense Country, Southern Arabia,*
> 1895

Salalah is undoubtedly a pleasant surprise, especially to expats who live in the north. But before I can begin to describe Salalah, there remain a few items to be described along the way.

Adam (SS)

As mentioned in the previous chapter, the road to Salalah (Route 31) begins at the roundabout in Izki and runs past the town of Manah. From Izki to the town of Adam is a 54-kilometer ride where the terrain becomes increasingly flat with the jebels receding in the rear view mirror and only an occasional rise or outcrop looming in the distance. The last ridges appear after **Adam** and then . . . nothing. Nothing but open expanse of desert. Before you embark on this leg it might be worth your while to take a cruise around Adam to see how a town on the edge of the desert manages to get along. There is a souq and some local industry here.

After Adam you will pass **Jebel Medhmar,** the last vestige of the Hajars before the desert. After 120 kilometers you will pass near some mounds in the area known as **Qarit Kirbit.** Take a right turn-off from Route 31 onto a track signposted for Ghaba North. This is a PDO oilfield. Keep left on the wider track and after 22 kilometers on this track (keep the gas flare in sight), follow the sign to Qarit Kirbit from the roundabout. In 14 kilometers you will arrive at a **salt dome** (unique geological formation) in the desert. This low-rising hill is about 1 kilometer across and the salt structure has broken through to the surface. In the center there is a recess that leads to a cave. Here salt, as well as sulfur, was mined in older days by Bedouins.

AL WUSTA AND THE NEJD

You will also pass, close to the main road, a beautiful spot of high rolling dunes, a mini-ramlat, if you will, where you can cruise around and step out to climb over, if it's not too hot.

At about 320 kilometers from Muscat you will pass the **Ghaba Rest House.**

Fifty kilometers past the Ghaba Rest House you will see a turn-off left to Saiwan, which is about 40 kilometers in from the main road. The Saiwan area is good for rock, mineral, and fossil hunting. Beyond Ghaba the trip gets increasingly monotonous. The surrounding desert is less than beckoning for any but the most obdurate explorer. Your only respite will be the **Al Ghaftain Resthouse** 100 kilometers after Hayma and the **Qitbit Resthouse** 130 kilometers beyond Al Ghaftain.

The road bends southward and at 80 kilometers past Qitbit you will come to the village of **Dawkah.** There is nothing except the turn-off to notify you that this is the northern approach to the village of **Shisr.** The track will take you 80 kilometers into the village, which is the site of the archeological dig to discover the **lost city of Ubar,** trading center and frankincense capital of the ancient world. Ubar has long been the stuff of legend. Described as a be-jeweled capital with towering spires, a center for commerce for thousands of years until God saw fit to destroy it for its iniquities and transgressions, it has been swallowed up by the sands and lost to obscurity. Historically, Ubar has been mentioned in annals by Claudius Ptolemy, who described an Omanum Emporum somewhere in the southern desert of

Arabia. References to the city of Irem in the Qur'an are believed to be synonymous with Ubar. T. E. Lawrence (of Arabia) and Bertram Thomas were no less interested in discovering the whereabouts of this fabled place.

An Arabist and a documentary filmmaker, using some high-tech hunches, collaborated to dig up what they believe to be the remains of Ubar. With infrared photos taken from the NASA space shuttle, along with other satellite imagery, they were able to trace ancient trade routes that were buried in the sand, some up to a depth of 10 meters. These tracks converged on a point which is now the modern-day village of Shisr, a small Bedu enclave. What they found may not be conclusive, nor is it the jewel-encrusted paradise in the oasis that was alluded to. They did find remnants of a fortification with towers with a commanding view of a central area, where they believe tented settlements provided the background for the main commercial exchange. More than 4,000 artifacts were discovered— cloth, bone fragments, iron, coins, pieces from a chess set over 1,500 years old, Roman pots, Egyptian jars, Chinese stoneware, and an Arabian lamp from 200 B.C., the oldest of artifacts related to the incense trade.

Beyond Shisr, to the west in **Wadis Ghadun and Haluf,** geodes can be found lying on the ground. To the north, another sandy region, the **Ramlat Fasad,** is the southern extremity of the Rub' Al Khali. Here the dunes rise several hundred feet like mountains and stretch well beyond the horizon.

The main road continues south from Dawkah and eventually reaches Thumrait. Here you will begin to climb, very gradually, the back side of the Jebel Qara escarpment. The landscape here is particularly barren and takes on the appearance of **Mountains of the Moon.** You wind through water courses, slowly rising higher and higher. As you reach the peak, the scenery will change abruptly. Scrub gives way to grasses which, in season, become greener and greener. Bushes and trees start to fill out the area and the next thing you know you begin the deep descent into the lush green domain of Salalah.

THE EASTERN SEABOARD

The Coast Southward from Al Ashkarah (SS, HCP, 4WD)

Before we enter into a description of Salalah, a word or two will be spent on the eastern seaboard, which is an alternative route to the southern reaches. It has its own attraction, but is not necessarily the choice of the more casual tourist. There are many natural sights and settings along the way, but this is the least inhabited and least developed region of the country. This venue is recommended for experienced travelers as there are few services and many hazards along the way.

It is possible to run the coast south from Al Ashkarah where the Wahibah

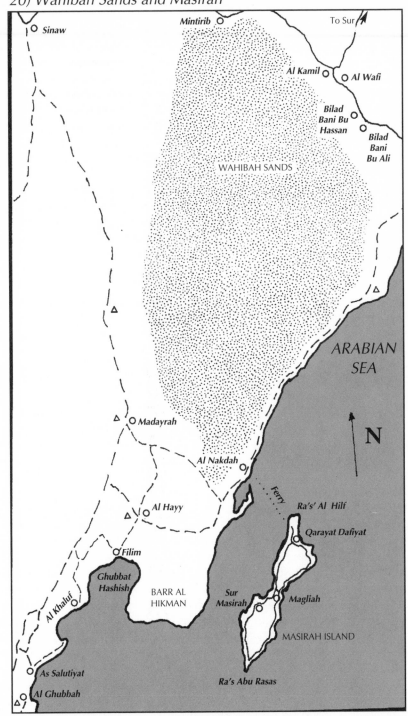

Sinaw

Mintirib

To Sur

Al Kamil

Al Wafi

Bilad
Bani Bu
Hassan

Bilad
Bani
Bu Ali

WAHIBAH SANDS

ARABIAN
SEA

Madayrah

N

Al Nakdah

Al Hayy

Ferry

Ra's' Al Hilf

Qarayat Dafiyat

Filim

Ghubbat
Hashish

BARR AL
HIKMAN

Sur
Masirah

Magliah

Al Khaluf

MASIRAH ISLAND

As Salutiyat

Al Ghubbah

Ra's Abu Rasas

100 km

Sands meet the ocean (Map 20). The seascapes are breathtaking but they can get monotonous. Of geological note are the exposed layers of **aeolianite,** which is compressed and cemented wind-blown sand derived from quartzitic, sedimentary, and ophiolitic sources. The trek along the coast is over 175 kilometers. There are a couple of strategically placed petrol pumps but it would be wise to take along a jerry can or two. At the southern tip of the Wahibah is the coastal town of Al Nakdah. From here it is possible to take a ferry to **Masirah Island.**

Masirah (SS, HCP, 4WD)

Masirah is not everybody's cup of tea, unless you *really* want to get away from it all or you happen to be a loggerhead turtle. This island, 60 kilometers long, is about 15 kilometers off the coast. It is south of the Wahibah Sands near Barr Al Hikman, a smallish barren peninsula jutting south into the Arabian Sea. There are a few settlements, an air strip and flight training school for the Royal Air Force, beaches and points, some varied topography and wadi channels, and for a real change in scenery, no fortresses or castles. The people are predominantly fishers and remain somewhat isolated from the rest of the country. You can reach Masirah by puddle jumper from Muscat or you can drive down the coast and take the ferry, mentioned above, which runs daily.

The Coast from Barr Al Hikman to Ra's Madrakah (SS, HCP, 4WD)

The first town of any importance is the settlement of **Al Hayy** near the southern extremity of the Wahibah. The easiest way to reach Al Hayy is to drive from Al Mudaybi or Sinaw along the western border of the Wahibah. From Muscat this is a six-hour proposition. When you reach the southern end of the Wahibah at Madrayah, take a right fork. About 20 kilometers before Hayy is a juncture where you can decide to go left (to Al Hayy) or right, which eventually reaches the coast at Duqm, another three hours on. From Al Hayy you can proceed to **Filim,** where there is a desalination plant at the shore of the bay Ghubbat Hashish. The hashish referred to here are a variety of sedges along the coast used as fodder for goats. Beyond Filim, the track winds around a tract of sabkha before rejoining the main track to Duqm. This juncture also leads to the shoreline village of **Al Khaluf** where the locals will sell you fresh fish. Campsites along the beaches to the south are some of the finest in Oman.

South from Al Khaluf, the main track runs by **Salutiyat,** another coastal village and the entrance to **Wadi Shuram.** Several tracks lead into the wadi and a drive inland will take you to the borders of the **Jiddat Al Harasis** and the Arabian Oryx Sanctuary, a 16,000-square-kilometer reserve also declared by UNESCO as a world natural heritage site. There is no formal infrastructure as yet for interfacing with the oryx, but there is a chance, if

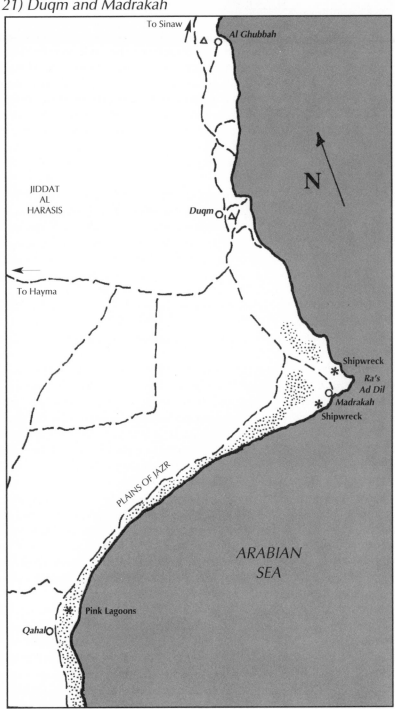

To Sinaw

Al Ghubbah

JIDDAT
AL
HARASIS

Duqm

N

To Hayma

Shipwreck

Ra's
Ad Dil

Madrakah

Shipwreck

PLAINS OF JAZR

ARABIAN
SEA

Pink Lagoons

Qahal

100 km

you are cautious, to spot them roaming the wild plains of the reserve.

The road to Duqm (Map 21) continues through wadis and through sabhka. Another coastal town, **As Sidrah,** offers spectacular and isolated settings along the coast. Here is a paradise with secluded beaches to hide away and watch the show put on by Mother Nature between the sea, the tidal flats, and the coast. In season, this is an ideal spot to watch migratory birds. At **Duqm** there is a beautiful bay, with beaches, and more beaches. A track that leads through the Jiddat Al Harasis for 160 kilometers eventually meets up with the Salalah Road at Hayma.

From Duqm to **Madrakah** the setting is particularly unspoiled. The beaches are filled with wildlife and the scenery sports some of the oldest rocks in Oman, volcanic basoliths, uplifted and exposed, that have been sculpted by the sea. Several **shipwrecks** can be spotted off the coast, one near **Ra's Ad Dil.** Another pair near Madrahkah involved a ship that sank as well as its rescuer, a salvage vessel. In the village there is another de-sal plant and several tracks that lead up and down the coast where local fishermen launch their boats, haul in their catch and stow their nets.

From Ra's Madrakah to Shuwaymiyah (SS, HCP, 4WD)

Following Madrakah are the **Plains of Jazr,** which run inland behind a long stretch of beaches (over 100 kilometers). One spot, 45 kilometers after Madrakah, is the **Three Palm Tree Lagoon,** which I have not visited, but I have good word that there are three palm trees there . . . and thousands of birds. Further along and interspersed here are **pink lagoons** that are an eerie sight. The best of these can be seen near **Qahal.** Cut off from the fresher waters of the ocean, these highly saline ponds breed a type of algae that gives the waters its pinkish hue. The largest and most scenic lagoon is the Khawr Ghawi, near Qahal, which is temporary home to thousands of migratory birds.

From Qahal to Ash Shuwaymiyah is another 200 kilometers where the track moves away from the shore and crosses some headland. It is quite possible that you might spot some oryx or gazelle in this tract.

Soqra (Map 22), a village on the coast some 60 klicks past Qahal, is filled with a remote charm. Many ruins of stone houses dot the landscape. The people here fish for oysters, crustaceans, and other species. The views of the surrounding jebels from the coast are exhilarating, the beaches are sprinkled liberally with shells, and wrecks and abandoned boats punctuate the landscape.

As you move inland, there are tracks to the left that lead to settlements on the coast and more secluded beaches. You will find that one of the chief industries in these villages is basket weaving; like anything else, these baskets can be haggled for. Outside the village of **Shuwaymiyah** is **Wadi Shuwaymiyah,** which is unique for its white limestone cliffs and freshwater pools. The cliffs

22) Soqra to Salalah

To Madrakah

Soqra

Amal

Shalim

Ash Shuwaymah

To Muscat

Marmul

Thumrait

JEBEL SAMHAM PLATEAU

Hadbin

Sadh

Al Yofa

Mirbat

Salalah

JAZIR AL HALAANIYAT

ARABIAN SEA

N

100 km

are overlaid with layers of travertine. Plantations abound and wildlife is ubiquitous. The entire wadi is great for camping and one can easily become attached to this remote but idyllic spot.

At 100 kilometers from Shuwaymiyah is the **oilfield at Marmul.** If you can make it this far and then across the labyrinth of pipelines to the PDO camp, you have accomplished something. Ironically there are no petrol pumps here; you'll have to backtrack to **Shalim.** From here you can see signposts to Salalah. But if it is summer you might miss the signs in the mist, as now you will be well within the reaches of the khareef, or summer monsoon. The trek will be inland now as the track heads to Thumrait, 160 kilometers away. There is no petrol on this leg of the route. You can expect to spend six hours driving from Shuwaymiyah to Salalah.

Alternatively you can take tracks that skirt the coast all the way down through extremely remote areas to Hadbin and Sadh and from there on to Mirbat and Salalah. These locales will be taken up below. The tracks here are not clearly defined and local NSA maps have not been updated. The terrain is extremely rough and lack of use may allow tracks to disappear. This particular segment is up a couple of notches in difficulty from the rest of the off-road trekking that can be accomplished in Oman. If you really haven't found that perfect beach yet, it just might be around that next bend in the wadi, or you missed it somewhere back along the coast above.

SALALAH AND ENVIRONS

Salala (sic) is a small town, little more than a village. It lies on the edge of the sea and has no harbour. . . . The Sultan's palace, white and dazzling in the strong sunlight, was the most conspicuous building, and clustered around it was the small suq or market, a number of flat-roofed mud-houses, and a labyrinth of mat shelters, fences and narrow lanes. The market consisted of only a dozen shops, but it was the best shopping centre between Sur and the Hadramaut (Yemen), a distance of 800 miles.

—Wilfred Thesiger, 1945

Salalah (SS)

Whether driving down off the jebel or taking a plane from Muscat, Salalah is a sight to behold, especially in September after the khareef has lifted. Either way you will descend to a broad plain that surrounds the city. The change in scenery is quite a contrast from the browns and ochres up north. The road enters the city at the **Umm Al Ghawarif Roundabout,** which intersects with **Robat Street,** the northernmost thoroughfare, running east/west. Three kilometers west is the **Burj Al Nhadhah Roundabout,** which intersects with **Al Matar Street** and will take you to the airport, one

23) Salalah

To Muscat

Thumrait Road

Umm Al Ghawarif R/A

Robat Street

Salalah Civil Airport

Al Matar Street

Burj Al Nahdah R/A

Al Nahdah R/A

The Old Souq *

Robat Street

23rd July Street

Mazin Al Ghadubah Street

To Ayn Jarziz

Hamdan Plaza Hotel

Sultan Qaboos Hospital

KHAWR SALALAH

Al Awodayn R/A

To Raysut

Al Dhariz R/A

To Mirbat

Umm Al Ghawarif Street

Sultan Qaboos Street

Al Faradhi Street

Al Mansurah Street

Salalah Holiday Inn

Mamura Palace

Al Khandaque Street

Fruit Vendors *

KHAWR AL BALEED

Al Haseelah St.

Haffa House

Dhofar Hotel

Al Salaam Street

Redan Hotel

Al Muntazah Street

Sultan Qaboos Street

ARABIAN SEA

N

1 km

klick along. Adjacent to the roundabout is the **Haffa House.** To the north of
Robat Street are open fields and cultivated areas. To the northwest side of
town about 6 kilometers beyond the **Al Nahdhah Roundabout** is the Hamdan Commercial Centre, which houses the **Hamdan Plaza Hotel.** Just
beyond the industrial park is the **Al Awodayn Roundabout,** where all the
main thoroughfares through Salalah eventually meet and converge into one
road out of town heading west.

From the Al Awodayn Roundabout **Sultan Qaboos Street** emerges and
heads east. This street is the coast road that skirts the south side of Salalah
before it ends at the **Al Dhariz Roundabout** 14 kilometers across town. Sultan Qaboos Street runs past the Sultan Qaboos Hospital, over a creek—
Khawr Salalah, which serves as a bird sanctuary—into some cultivated
groves, and through a residential district before returning to some thick
palm groves. After passing another enclosed cove, **Khawr Al Baleed,** the
road crosses first **Al Mansurah Street** and then **Al Faradhi Street,** which both
access the **Salalah Holiday Inn** on the shoreline on **Al Khandaque Street.**
Al Mansurah Street runs north through **Mamura Palace** complex (the
southern residence of the Royal Family) to the **Robat Roundabout,** where it
eventually meets up with the **Thumrait Road** (Route 31) coming south.

Shortly before Al Mansurah Street, heading east on Sultan Qaboos
Street, there is a left turn onto **Al Muntazah Street,** which doubles back

Roadside fruit stands in Salalah.

west through some thick groves and plantations. Here are many fruit stands which sell everything that the gardens can produce: fresh coconut, bananas, mangoes, citrus, other fruits, and vegetables. These groves run for the entire length of the street (on the south side) until the street ends at a small cut-off, **Mazin Al Ghadoobah Street,** near the Khawr Salalah. This cutoff will take you to Sultan Qaboos Street to the south and Al Salaam Street to the north. **Al Salaam Street** is the next major east/west thoroughfare which runs through the heart of downtown Salalah. It starts from the Sultan Qaboos Hospital and runs west until it ends at **Al Haseelah Street** just before the Royal Palace on the east side of town. In the center of town the **Redan Hotel** can be found.

The last main thoroughfare through town is **23rd July Street.** The 23rd of July is a date which commemorates Sultan Qaboos's assumption of power in 1970. 23rd July Street runs through residential and commercial areas where you will come across the **main souq/municipal market,** a modern open-air structure where "business as usual" takes on a much older, deeper meaning. Besides meats, fruits, and vegetables, you can purchase bokhur and frankincense and related paraphernalia. There is also a gold and silver souq. Other venues such as textile markets are liberally scattered throughout town. 23rd July Street eventually runs into Robat Street east of the Burj Al Nahdhah Roundabout.

The two main thoroughfares running north/south are the previously mentioned Al Matar Street running from the airport on which you can find the **Dhofar Hotel,** and Al Nahdah Street, which runs from the Al Nahdah Roundabout and the Royal Farms down to Sultan Qaboos Street.

EAST OF SALALAH

Dhofar and the Gara Mountains which encircle it form a quite abnormal feature in this otherwise arid coast. This plain is never more than nine miles wide and at the eastern end, where the mountains come down nearer to the sea, it is reduced to an exceedingly narrow strip. Water is here very near the surface. Streams making their way to the sea are of constant occurrence; consequently the plain is very fertile and capable of producing almost anything.

—J. Theodore Bent, *Exploration of the Frankincense Country, Southern Arabia,*
1895

Taqah (SS)

From the Al Dhariz Roundabout it is about 24 kilometers to **Taqah,** a small fishing village east of Salalah, one whose history is tied to the old trading empires of ages past. Taqah has a reconstituted fort in the center of town overlooking the stores and residences .

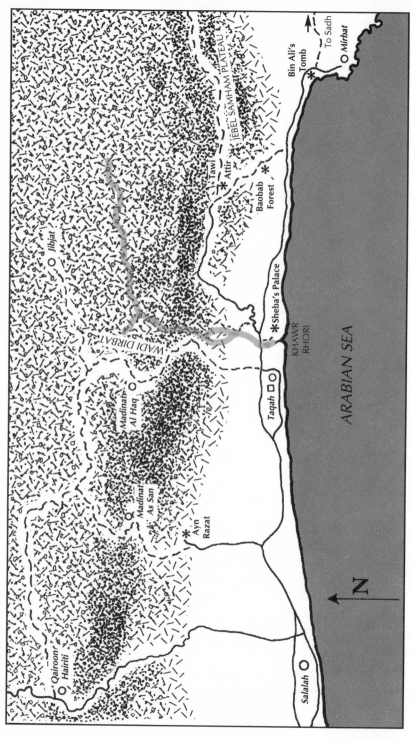

24) East of Salalah

Bin Ali's tomb and cemetery near Mirbat.

As the road winds east, there is a beautiful vantage point near Khawr Rhori, from which to view the hanging valley of Wadi Dirbat (see below). From the side of the road on a bridge that crosses the wadi, you can get a marvelous panorama of the wadi, which looks like Niagara Falls in full flood (but is dry most of the season). Just up ahead there is a turn-off left (4 kilometers from Taqah) on a paved road that leads to the track to enter Wadi Dirbat and further on to Tawi Attir (see below).

Khawr Rhori (SS, HP)

From Taqah it is only 4.9 kilometers east until you see signs to **Khawr Rhori**. At 7 kilometers, a graded track leads over a rise and down to a ruin situated by a pleasant cove. This ruin is the remains of **Samhuram,** or **Sheba's Palace.** The legendary Queen of Sheba was known for her wealth, judging from the many gifts of frankincense she gave to Solomon. Now all that remains is the crumbling ruin of her castle. Access inside the site is restricted because it is an archeological dig that is still revealing secrets of the past. The promontory upon which the castle sits overlooking the cove and the tall bluffs flanking the entrance to the cove give the area a regal touch. The cove is one of many which shelters many birds in their peregrinations.

The road continues east, dipping in and out of wadis and running along the crest of a shelf. After 25 kilometers from Taqah there is another signpost to Tawi Attir. This time it is a graded track that leads straight up the jebel. We'll come back to this track presently. Shortly after this track, the road bends down to the shore past a long stretch of beachfront with picnic shelters before curving inland slightly around a small ridge and heading into the ancient seacoast town of **Mirbat.**

Mirbat (SS, HP)

At 35 kilometers from Taqah there is a new paved entrance to **Bin Ali's Tomb** and cemetery. This holy shrine bears the remains of an early Islamic scholar and seer. The twin onion-shaped domes are typical for the region. Surrounding the tomb is an old cemetery with headstones that appear similar to Christian design. Many of the headstones have inscriptions (all in Arabic).

Shortly past Bin Ali's Tomb is a graded track to the left that leads to Sadh.

Mirbat is a picturesque town with whitewashed buildings, a refurbished castle, and a rugged coast with pounding surf. An inlet with a man-made jetty protects the local fishing vessels which ply the waters every day for the myriad species of fish. There are many spots along the shoreline suitable for casual exploration. Mirbat is an enchanting place to spend a relaxing afternoon.

Seacoast mosque in Mirbat.

Sadh and Hadbin (SS, HCP, 4WD)

The graded track opposite Bin Ali's Tomb reaches across the plain and disappears into the ridges ahead. The trip out to Sadh is rather monotonous, but a newly graded track makes it worthwhile. At 50 kilometers there is a small outpost called **Yofa** and the track here takes a more southerly run. It is another 14 kilometers to **Sadh,** where the track dips into and out of wadis on a very twisting course. At one point you will switch back to a small plantation in the bottom of a wadi and move out and up to the ridge beyond. Shortly thereafter there is a juncture. The right turn will take you into Sadh and the left will wind along the coarse shoreline to some fantastic isolated campsites on the beach. I followed the road for 10 or 15 kilometers or so before I realized there's more than enough to suit anyone's outdoor fancy. A few kilometers beyond is the remote town of **Hadbin.**

The village of **Sadh,** meanwhile, is a surprising turnaround from the usual Omani village. The first distinction is probably Main Street. The town lies along the wadi course between two steep ridges. The wadi is straight as an arrow and the street runs just as straight for about 2 kilometers to the beach. In the middle there is a fort, remodeled and renovated. There are lots of little shops and scads of kids running about. It's quite bustling for such a remote area. I gave an old fisherman a lift out of town to one of the points, where he took his nets slung over his side and cast them into the surly waters.

The coast beyond Sadh and Hadbin gets more and more rugged. I have not ventured beyond but hope to one day make the excursion up the coast to Ash Shuwaymiyah.

THE SOUTHERN ESCARPMENT: JEBEL QARA AND JEBEL SAMHAM

> We found the Gara women exceedingly shy and retiring, they fled if we approached them, like timid gazelles—so different from the bold hussies in the Hadramaut, who tormented us with staring into our tent. They have but poor jewelry—silver necklaces, armlets, and nose and toe rings; they love to join their eyebrows with antimony, and stick some black sticky stuff like cobbler's wax over their noses and foreheads; they are very small . . . they do not cover their faces, and are very lightly clad in dark blue homespun cotton garments.
> —J. Theodore Bent, *Exploration of the Frankincense Country, Southern Arabia,*
> 1895

Ayn Jarziz (SS, HCP)

The range of mountains behind Salalah is officially called **Jebel Qara.** There are several routes into the jebels including the main road from Muscat which bisects the region. To the west of the main road there is another road leading from the Hamdan Plaza Complex (Map 25). If you take this road out of town you will see that the foliage starts to thicken as soon as you reach the base of the jebel and climb the ridge. At 9 kilometers you will see off to the right a track that will take you down a steep embankment to **Ayn Jarziz.** This is a pleasant spot with flowing water, and in season, some of the nicest greenery you have set eyes upon. There are many tracks leading into the hills and spots to have a fine picnic. During the khareef, water is abundant, and the thick veil of clouds from the ocean enshrouds the area with a thick mist. One can almost expect Heathcliff to emerge from the fog looking for his Catherine.

Job's Tomb (SS, HP)

Further up the main road, 13 kilometers along, there is the turn-off to the left signposted to **Nabi Ayoub.** A short drive in and you will come across a mosque and tomb. This tomb is said to house the remains of the Prophet Job. The tomb is a humble dwelling where people come to offer prayers and visit the site. There is a restaurant located at the entrance of the property that provides lunches and snacks.

Twenty kilometers past Job's Tomb there is a right turn-off by the town of **Teetam.** The road is paved. Soon you will be climbing over the rim of the jebel and the scenery reverts, very quickly, to arid desert. The land gets parched in a hurry and the only vegetation you will find is small scrubs and some tall green bushes. The taller ones with gnarled trunks and bright green leaves are the *boswellia sacra* that produce the sap for **frankincense.** Another 18 kilometers from Teetam there is a signpost for Ayun to the left. You can see the settlement from several kilometers back perched upon a ridge above a broad canyon, that of **Wadi Ayun.** Turn left toward the town, but only a few hundred meters in, turn left again and follow the track for 3.8 kilometers. You will descend to a ridge above the canyon where there is a water trough. You can park here and climb down onto the wadi which is a narrow strip of green in the otherwise parched region. At the bottom there are pools and flowing water around sedges and grass. The surrounding rocks are a chalky brilliant white.

The road past Ayun eventually loops back and meets up with Highway 31 to Salalah.

Ayn Razat (SS, HP)

The Gardens of Ayn Razat are just a short jaunt out of town heading east toward Taqah (Map 24). Seven kilometers after the Al Dhariz Roundabout another roundabout has signs posted to Ayn Razat to the left. After another seven klicks is the entrance to the park at the base of the jebels. Inside there are gardens, springs, shallow caves, walkways, and barbecue pits; in other words, a great spot for a picnic and a stroll. Also a great spot for people watching if you happen to be a bird.

The road to Ayn Razat continues beyond and runs up into the jebels. After another 20 kilometers you will reach the edge of the plateau and an intersection which runs the breadth of the plateau from **Qairoon Hairitti** on the main route to Salalah, to **Madinat Al Haq** and **Jibjat,** two villages that live on the fringe of the khareef. There is also a track from Taqah that leads to Madinat Al Haq. All along this route there are excellent vantage points for viewing the coast, that is, if you are not visiting during the monsoon when you can barely see your hand in front of your face.

Wadi Dirbat (SS, HCP, 4WD)

> It occurred to us that this must be the site of the town which is alluded to by Claudius Ptolemy and Arrian as Abyssopolis—it is the harbor for the town Zufar . . . the harbor is good and is often mentioned by traders. . . . A ride of 4 or 5 miles brought us to . . . one of the most stupendous natural phenomena we have ever seen . . . an isolated hill in the middle of the valley and a perfectly straight and precipitous wall 550 feet in height and 3/4 of a mile long on the eastern side of the hill and about a quarter mile long and 300 feet high on the western side. Over these walls feathery waterfalls precipitate themselves. . . . During the rains the falls must be magnificent, but it was the height of the dry season when we visited it.
>
> —J. Theodore Bent, *Exploration of the Frankincense Country, Southern Arabia,*
> 1895

The track to **Wadi Dirbat** runs from the main road to Tawi Attir midway up the side of the jebel wall. Although it is a particularly rugged track, it is relatively short as it drops to the wadi floor several hundred feet above the coastal shelf. This scenic hanging valley is spectacular in full flood. In drier times, it is possible to traverse the wadi for several kilometers up where smaller tributaries tumble down from the jebel wall in burbling cascades. There is a lot of water up here, with caves; some are yet to be found as this is a very active karst region. If the weather is dry you can drive/walk to the precipice for a tremendous view of the valley.

Tawi Attir ("Hole of the Birds") (SS, HP, 4WD)

If you continue on the paved road beyond Wadi Dirbat you will eventually come to a town where the tarmac ends. There is a juncture of several tracks in this farming community of jebalis. One track off to the left is sign-posted to Kisais Adeen. Take this track for about 1 kilometer, pull over, and park by a water trough. Beyond is an open field strewn with rocks. Follow the water pipeline toward the village and about 200 meters on you will come across the **Tawi Attir Sinkhole** off to your right. This is a massive sink over 100 meters long and 200 meters deep. There is a trail that leads to a shelf midway down. At the bottom of the main shaft there is a cave system which should only be accessed by experienced spelunkers/divers as there is continual water activity at the lowest levels. Some of the lower shafts can only be reached by diving through siphons that extend another 35 meters (so far). The hole is an obvious source of water for the surrounding farms. In older days of tribal conflicts, the women were sent to fetch water from the hole because they couldn't afford to lose a valuable fighting man to the treacherous depths. As the name implies, Tawi Attir is home to many species of birds that nest in the walls and can be seen swooping in and out of the sinkhole.

Jebel Samham Plateau (SS, HCP, 4WD)

Continue on the same track past Tawi Attir. After 16 kilometers you will approach the summit of **Jebel Samham,** where the plateau rises 1,300 meters above the coast. Along this stretch you will reach the highest point in Dhofar (5,000 feet). The view is nothing less than magnificent and here you can find tracks along the edge that will lead to some splendid spots to camp.

Baobab Forest (SS, HCP, 4WD)

Another approach to Tawi Attir is the graded track from the Mirbat Road about 22 kilometers from Taqah. The track is signposted to Tawi Attir just before the long stretch of beach leading into Mirbat. This route has a number of interesting experiences to offer. First of all the track heads out over a fairly flat surface before it passes over a promontory and then rises up the jebel wall. If you stop your vehicle in the saddle between the promontory and the jebel wall, release the brake, and throw the shift into neutral, you will experience what appears to be in defiance of the law of gravity as your vehicle will roll backwards *up* the hill. Dubbed as the anti-gravity point by the locals, I have to say it does feel like you are defying gravity, but I have a tendency to think that the combination of angles and perspective lies at the heart of the explanation to this illusion. If you return to the main road by this track you can also stop your vehicle on the apparently flat surface about 1 kilometer from the entrance. A tree 10 feet from the road serves as a marker. Once again shift into neutral and release the brake. From a standing stop, the car will move over seemingly flat ground and reach a speed of 65 kph (40 mph) before you have to hit the brake to keep from spilling out onto the main road (and possible oncoming traffic).

If you continue up the track there is a turn-off to the left exactly 3 kilometers from the main road. This is a small track that stops after 50 meters. There is plenty of space to park on a ledge overlooking the valley. From here you will find two paths. One leads down a hill to the sound of gurgling water. A small wadi and falaj can be found beneath the dense growth.

There are many species of wildflowers growing here and the forest is rife with birds and wildlife. The second path is just to the right of the first one and leads up through a patch of rocks sticking out of the hillside. Follow this path for about 100 meters and you will find yourself in a forest of Baobab trees with bulbous trunks and bloated limbs. At the center of this forest there is one tree with a diameter of about 30 feet; it is most likely over 2,000 years old. Some of the branches from the main trunk are over 6 feet thick. The area is almost Tolkienesque. There are many boulders to clamber over and some very shady spots by the stream for a picnic.

The track continues up the side of the jebel and in 14 kilometers reaches the intersection at Tawi Attir (see above).

WEST OF SALALAH

Raysut (SS, HCP, 4WD)

The road west from Salalah leaves town at the Al Wodayn Roundabout (Map 25). From here it is about 10 kilometers to the roundabout for **Port Raysut**. Here is the southern container facility for the Sultanate. On your way to Raysut, you will pass the **Al Muhit Restaurant** on your left at about 4 kilometers. At the roundabout the road to the left leads into the port. Just to the right you will see many tracks that lead into gravel quarries behind the port facility. Many of these tracks continue on through the hills and eventually come to some very remote scenic spots along the beach. The furthest and southernmost extremity is the point known as **Donkey's Head.** Before Donkey's Head there are windswept cliffs plunging to the ocean with tracks running along the upper rim. One vantage point hangs vertiginously out over the water and is a great spot for photos. Somewhere in here is one beach which I understand is known as **Beer Can Beach.** I can only guess as to how it got this moniker. Beyond Donkey's Head there are bluffs that extend for the next 30 kilometers to Mughsail, hiding many secluded beaches. Although the tracks down to the beaches and the bluffs are not long, they are extremely rugged and you should have a roadworthy vehicle to get you there.

There are other tracks leading to the bluffs. As you proceed along the main road to Mughsail you will see them off to your left criss-crossing first arid, then fertile plain and disappearing over the rise. There is no set way to go. Just follow a well-established track until you run out of real estate. These tracks are no more than 8-10 kilometers long as the crow flies, and they lead to some very nice shoreline scenery. Drive along the bluffs until you can find trails down to the beaches below. You will spot many camp-sites used by the locals. Also, you will find just about any kind of domestic animal grazing in the fields en route. Don't try to rout them or otherwise upset their grazing habits.

25) West of Salalah

N

Salalah O
Ayn Jarziz *
Job's Tomb *
JEBEL QARA
Al Mahit
Raysut
Donkey's Head *
Ayun
WADI AYUN
Teetam
Mughsail
WADI AFAWI
ARABIAN SEA
To Yemen
Rakhyut

10 km

Southern coast west of Salalah.

Mughsail (SS, HCP)

If you keep to your right at the roundabout at Raysut and continue on the main road through countryside that looks like the Badlands of the Dakotas, you will eventually come to one of the most popular spots on the coast. This is **Mughsail Beach.** There are beach shelters constructed the entire length of the shoreline and at the far end is the main parking area. Just beyond the parking lot a trail leads up the hill to some dramatic sculpted bluffs overhanging the path. The recesses underneath are shallow but no less impressive and the kids will love to clamber over them. Shortly beyond, the path leads to one of Oman's most popular sites. Perched on the shelf over the ocean are several **thundering blowholes** that give out a deafening roar and spew sea foam 50 feet into the air with each passing wave. The holes were carved by wave action beneath the shelf, which eroded the limestone. The surrounding jebels and bluffs that meet the sea are no less spectacular. There is a picture-postcard shot in every direction.

Wadi Afawi (SS, HCP)

Just beyond Mughsail, the road turns into a marvelous feat of engineering as it slices down through a series of hairpin turns to the base of **Wadi Afawi.** It then climbs over 3,000 feet to the opposite side in another series of hairpins, each succeeding one providing another level of panorama. Over the rim and onto the plateau, the road now skirts the rim along the coast, sometimes turning inland and winding along the rims of wadis snaking to the coast. The views from here, if the monsoon is past, are breathtaking.

Rakhyut (SS, HCP, 4WD)

You are now in the **Jebel Qamr** range and you will want to look for signs to **Rakhyut** after about 60 kilometers. There is no point in going further; you'll be coming upon the border to Yemen. Rakhyut is one shore town I have visited and it is worth the time to take the drive out there. There are a number of villages in between and if you find the tracks that lead left from the main road you may find some spots just as worthy. Throughout this region there are scenic villages that look more like the New England countryside (except for the camels) than anything else. The road to Rakhyut is typical. It is a graded track, very steep at some points, that loops over hill and dale through farm after farm before dipping to the coast and the major coastal community. You can skirt the town and drive along some very nice beachfront, and if the waves are not too choppy, go for a swim. A trip from Salalah to Mughsail to Rakhyut is a long haul but it makes for a nice day's outing. I recollect that the track from the main road to Rakhyut is about 15-20 kilometers. Make sure that you start your trip with a full tank of gas since there are no petrol pumps on the scarp.

7. Guided Tours

Many of the tour operators up north operate offices in Salalah. In addition there are a few independents. See listings in previous chapter.

8. Shopping

The stores in Salalah are all congregated in the downtown area on 23rd July Street and Al Salaam Street. Just as in the rest of the country, store types tend to clump together. An exception in Salalah is that textile stores are everywhere. The Hamdan Plaza Hotel and Haffa House are themselves commercial complexes with a number of specialty and department stores. The main souq is on 23rd July Street near the Oman Arab Bank. Here is where you will no doubt want to buy frankincense, bokhur, and related paraphernalia. There are many fresh fruit stands along the plantation roads.

7

Far North:
The Musandam
Peninsula

1. The General Picture

> High on a throne of royal state, which far
> Outshone the wealth of Ormuz and of Ind
> Or where the gorgeous East with richest hand
> Showers on her Kings barbaric pearl and gold.

—John Milton, *Paradise Lost*

When it came time to write about the Musandam, I decided that it deserved a chapter of its own. Not necessarily for the quantity of information I needed to include, but because I felt the Musandam experience is significantly different from the rest of the country, just as Salalah is different from Muscat.

For starters, the terrain is *a lot* more rugged than the interior and points south. If the surrounding jebels made you feel cozy in Muscat, it's even cozier when you reach Khasab, the local capital. Steep walls crop up in every direction. Jebels rise to about 2,000 meters. Sheer faces and dizzying cliffs block the horizon. The sun disappears by four o'clock. (In the words of baseball legend, Yogi Berra "It gets late early out here,"—and conversely, it gets early late.) In spite of that, the roads, or graded tracks, are in generally good shape with broad lanes and sweeping turns, even in the jebels. There is a new section of road being constructed from Khasab to Bukha which has already greatly improved the condition of the track.

341

One of the first things I noticed was that the ophiolites of Muscat are nowhere to be found in Musandam (the last of them can be seen just south of Diba). Instead, what we have is strata, strata, and more strata. The rocks are predominantly carbonates from deep oceanic deposits stacked in sheets like reams of paper in a warehouse. In some places it is flat as a table. In others, it is steeply pitched, rumpled, wrinkled, twisted, and contorted. The forces of nature at work on these layers were massive. The result is some very eye-catching, pleasant formations. It appears that the Musandam represents the fulcrum upon which the anticline was brought to bear. Strata on the eastern side tend to dip to the east, and on the west, they dip to the west.

Last but not least, after many periods of upheaval and submergence, we have the feature for which the Musandam is famous for: the **fjords.** If you are not sure of this, just ask some ship's mate on an oil tanker heading through the Strait of Hormuz. From the sea, or from any angle, the fjords are a truly majestic sight. In older days they were havens to pirates and marauders. The outer borders are massive gates to some lost domain. The inner reaches are placid and as calm as a pond. The wildlife, particularly marine life, abounds: flying fish skip out of the water, dolphins play tag with your boat. Sea turtles meander about.

But in spite of all this natural beauty, the Musandam is a harsh environment. The population in the region is sparse. Temperatures reach extremes as the mountains conspire to trap hot air masses. In season, the temperatures are more forgiving during the day, but it does get cold in the jebels at night.

There is some history connected with the Musandam. As mentioned before, it was an important commercial center in older times. It has always been an important strategic locale for its owners, fought over by the Portuguese and Persians. In the nineteenth century there was a British telegraph station; it serviced the line stretching from Bahrain to India.

The locals are very private and in some ways more austere than Omanis to the south. They lead quiet lives as fishers. Many of the villages are only accessible by boat as there are no roads north of Khasab. Birqas among the women are more frequent but they are not the same style as the Bedu variety. They have larger eye holes and cover only a small portion of the face.

You can probably spend a couple of days to see what there is to see in the Musandam before moving along to other parts of the country, but for some, you just might want to stay a little longer . . .

2. Getting There

Here, your options are simple. The easiest way to the Musandam is to fly from Muscat to Khasab via puddle-jumper. Actually it's a Twin Otter turbo prop De Havilland (the safest plane in the air, the pilot captain assured me). Round trip is RO 40 ($103) and you don't need any special passes or additional visas, but bring your passport anyway. The flight is about an hour and a half and there is one flight daily except on weekends (at the time of publication). For the best scenery en route, do it the posh way—port out, starboard home. You'll catch some great shots of the fjords from above.

The other alternative is to drive there, but here you will need special permits from the ROP in Qurum as well as a visa for the UAE (from the embassy in Muscat). If you do apply for one, make sure you get endorsements for all the checkpoints at Wajaja, Khatmat, Milalah, Wadi Al Bih, and Tibat. Car insurance for the UAE is also required.

3. Local Transportation

If you haven't already driven in, you might want to rent a car or 4WD. This can be done from the desk at the **Khasab Hotel,** the *only* show in town. The other mode of transportation of any concern here is by boat. Once again the hotel will be able to accommodate your boating needs, as most of the sightseeing in the Musandam is done by boat. Diving and fishing excursions are arranged as well.

4. The Hotel Scene

If you drive to Musandam it is possible to break up your trip into two days, as it is about four hours from Muscat to Diba and another three hours to Khasab. And if you want to take your time there are several hotels along the eastern seaboard from Fujayrah to Diba Al Hasn in the UAE. Beyond that in the Musandam there is only one hotel.

The town of Khasab serves as a home base for travel in the Musandam Peninsula and the **Khasab Hotel** (Tel. 968-660267) is the only hotel. Besides offering fifteen comfortable rooms, RO 16.5-28 ($43-$72), the hotel offers excursions to the jebels (day trips and overnight camps) and boat trips to the fjords of the peninsula. There is a fully licensed restaurant serving continental and Indian dishes, pub, and pool. Reserve through the hotel at P.O. Box 111, Khasab 811; Fax: 968-660989.

5. Dining and Restaurants

Apart from the usual cafés (**The Musandam Restaurant** and **The Shark,** among others) and shwarma stands, there is a restaurant and a pub in the **Khasab Hotel.**

6. Sightseeing

FROM DIBA TO KHASAB

Once you have crossed the border, traveled through the Emirates, and re-entered Oman at **Diba,** it is a simple matter to get to Khasab (Map 26). It is impossible to get lost in the Musandam, as long as you stay on the main track. You will also note that there is no checkpoint until you reach the station in Wadi Al Bih tucked away beyond Diba. But while you are in Diba, it is worth your while to explore this section of seacoast on the Gulf of Oman side. There are several nice white sand beaches that make good camping locales and you can always rent a boat for fishing or diving excursions along the coast. Just go down to the *mina* ("port") and find yourself a seaworthy vessel cum skipper and haggle for their services.

When you leave Diba for Khasab, you will pass a Shell petrol pump (be sure to tank up, it's the last one before Khasab) and the signs will lead you ahead to Khasab. The track is in generally good shape as it winds through **Wadi Khabb Shamsi** and into the mountains. The great scenery indicator light in your mental dashboard should be clicking into overdrive as you wind higher and higher into the jebels. From Wadi Khabb Shamsi you will switch to **Wadi Al Bih,** and here you will come to the only intersection of great concern. A right turn will take you on your way to Khasab. The left will take you to Ra's Al Khaymah on the Arabian Gulf side of the UAE. Shortly after this turn-off is the checkpoint where you will need to produce your passport, road permit and driver's license. (There is no checkpoint on the road to Ra's Al Khaymah.)

Just beyond the checkpoint the road will start to wind up into the jebels once again but you will notice a turn-off to the right. This track immediately bifurcates, left and right, and although both tracks are worth exploring for desert delights such as abandoned villages, remote oases, and unique strata formations, the right one is the better of the two. It is not very long and pretty soon you will notice that the track has gotten very wide, very flat, and very straight. When you see the wind sock off to your right you will realize that you are on an airstrip in the middle of the plateau in the jebels. Off to your right there is a field of grasses and acacia trees which provide good shade. This is a nice spot for a camp. You are in the **Rawdah Bowl.**

Once again, the main track to Khasab starts to ascend a winding course to another plateau and then on to **Jebel Harim,** the tallest point in the Musandam. When you reach the plateau, gaze around at the surrounding valleys and you will spy isolated enclaves along the steep walls. Some are prospering, some are fallow. Sometimes it hard to imagine how these enclaves ever got started because the terrain is so steep. The road winds

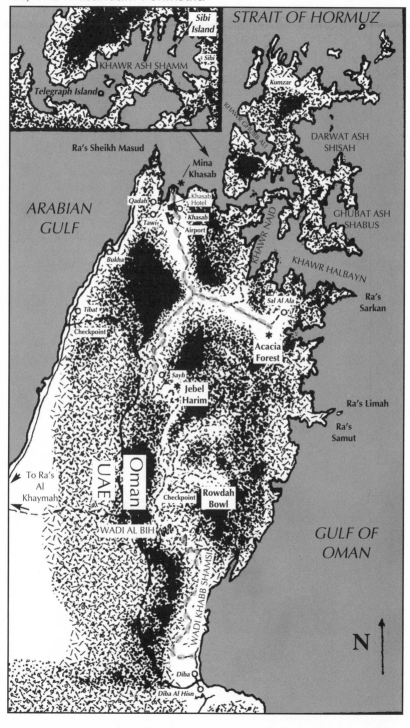

STRAIT OF HORMUZ

Sibi Island

Sibi

KHAWR ASH SHAMM

Telegraph Island

Kumzar

KHAWR GHUBB ALI

DARWAT ASH SHISAH

Ra's Sheikh Masud

Mina Khasab

GHUBAT ASH SHABUS

ARABIAN GULF

Qadah

Khasab Hotel

Khasab

Tawi

Airport

KHAWR NAJD

Bukha

KHAWR HALBAYN

Sal Al Ala

Ra's Sarkan

Tibat

Checkpoint

Acacia Forest

Sayh

Jebel Harim

Ra's Limah

Ra's Samut

To Ra's Al Khaymah

UAE

Oman

Checkpoint

Rowdah Bowl

GULF OF OMAN

WADI AL BIH

WADI KHABB SHAMSI

Diba

Diba Al Hisn

N

Isolated farm plot near Jebel Harim, Musandam.

higher and higher amidst beautiful strata and then skirts the summit of Jebel Harim. Alas, the summit is not accessible because of sensitive communications installations at the peak. But the views are still terrific.

Now you start to descend to the coast. Partway down you will pass through a particularly fertile area on a plateau, the village of **Sayh.** The people here harvest a number of vegetables and grass crops as well as some dates. There are many shady spots here to take a lunch break if you wish. You will find the local people cordial, but don't try to impose too much. You may also find that the dialect of Arabic they speak is unfamiliar. Another point of note is the absence of aflaj. Water in this region is collected in cisterns, and it is probably just as well, as the terrain is much too steep to accommodate the age-old aflaj network. The final descent to the coast (1,700 meters) is a steep, winding, breathtaking course that takes about thirty minutes, but the road is well traveled and in pretty good shape. At the bottom the road is flat until you reach Khasab, with the exception being that you will pass over the recharge dam which runs across the wadi floor.

There is one more intersection of note and that is before you reach the dam. Signposts to the right will point to Khawr Najd (see below), **Wadi Sal al A'la,** and **Birkit Khaldiyah.** Birkit Khaldiyah is another beautiful acacia forest just before the quiet town of Sal al A'la. It is a popular spot for campers and picnickers and there is even a small playground constructed in the middle of the woods.

As you approach Khasab, you will pass by the airport as the road bends right. When you get to city limits, *voila!* tarmac. Up ahead is the Shell petrol pump on your right and the **Khasab Hotel** on your left before the center of town. The wadi floor, you will note, is quite broad but the walls surrounding are precipitous. The feeling here is much more cloistered than Muscat.

KHASAB AND ENVIRONS

Khasab gets as busy as any town of 5,000 people gets. There are extensive date plantations that separate the commercial center from the coast proper. The shoreline traces the inner limits of a small bay. The **mina** does a bustling business with local traders; dhows are lined up along the docks, bringing in the daily catch. It is from this point that you will embark on your sea ventures. A souq in the center of town is like other souqs you will see in Oman, only on a smaller scale. At the head of the bay before the mudflats is the **Khasab Fort** which has been restored and beckons the traveler to take a look inside.

There is only one road leading out of town past the mina. It runs along a winding coastline around a point, past the villages of **Qadah** and **Tawi** (a few kilometers inland from the road through Qadah). Just before the village of Tawi itself, there are some prehistoric rock drawings opposite a well. They depict men on horseback, boats and houses. Qadah has some very photogenic houses and huts perched on the walls of the wadi opposite the date plantations.

The road from Khasab to Bukha was under reconstruction at the time of writing and is due to be completed in 1997. However, the conditions were quite good, the road passable, and the only delays experienced were to accommodate the trucks, bulldozers, levelers, and road crews. The trip from Khasab to Bukha is about forty minutes, barring delays. From the coast the road climbs up a steep cliff wall, over the top, and down to the Arabian Gulf side. From the top the views of the Musandam are some of the best in Oman. Looking due east you will see the entrance to **Khawr Ash Shamm,** the main fjord on the western side of the peninsula. If you haven't already, you will want to take the dhow cruise into the fjord.

The road comes down to the coast and now winds along very narrow passes between cliff and shore. Some shallow inlets provide small sandy beaches. In other spots where wadis reach the coast there is a considerable buildup of dunes. One town just before Bukha, **Al Jadi,** is striking for its whitewashed buildings, some in ruins, framed by bright green trees that I have yet to identify but were the most striking of any I have seen in Oman. This town is photo-op central. The same can be said for **Bukha,** just beyond, with its forts and towers and dhows and barks perched on the shore. From

Dhows resting in Khawr Ash Shamm.

here it is only a twenty-minute ride to Tibat, which is on the border of the UAE. Once again, you will have to produce the proper papers to pass through. Between Bukha and Tibat are a few more isolated towns and small sandy beaches looking west into the gulf.

THE FJORDS

The principal fjords of the Musandam are **Khawr Habalayn,** with its off-shoot **Khawr Najd,** on the eastern side, and **Khawr Ash Shamm** from the west. They almost, but not quite, separate the peninsula from the mainland. You will get good views of Khawr Habalayn if you are coming from Muscat by plane. One of the innermost inlets is Khawr Najd, which is the only khawr accessible by road. On the track to Wadi Sal al A'la, you will see the sign-post for Khawr Najd about 5 klicks in from the main track. From here it is another 5 klicks over a ridge and down a steep winding course to a landing where many local fishermen push off. You can hire boats here for excursions and fishing. There is also a campsite at the far left of the landing, but the swimming and diving here are not as good as other places. The views from the ridge, though, are stunning.

There is no way to enter Khawr Ash Shamm except by dhow (unless you really want to tough it out and hoof it from Khasab). Cruises are obtained from Khasab Tours at the Khasab Hotel desk if you haven't booked before-hand. There are half- and full-day tours as well as overnight camping. Need I tell you what I prefer? The dhows (shuis, actually) skirt the coastline past remote beaches, isolated villages, towering cliffs, and hidden bays. There are many spots for picnics and swimming, diving and snorkeling. As stated above, the marine life is abundant. Midway into the khawr is **Telegraph Island.** A way-station maintained by the British for the telegraph lines to India, it was installed in the 1860s. Now only a few bricks and foundations remain, but the commanding view is the best in the khawr.

At the far end of the khawr is the small fishing village of **Sibi.** Here, as in many other places in the khawr, the only contact with Khasab is by boat, and some of the towns are seasonal as villagers have migrated to Khasab and only come back for the fishing season. Beyond Khawr Ash Shamm, heading to the northernmost tip of Oman, are smaller khawrs, spindly capes, rocky outcrops, barren islands, and treacherous passes. Around the northern tip and tucked away in a small khawr lies the fishing village of **Kumzar,** perched 200 feet above the shoreline. Old houses cluster about, watched over by a fort on a nearby ridge. Just north is the Strait of Hormuz. From here it is possible to see why this land, so desolate, was craved by kings. Although little remains from those times and life goes by slowly and qui-etly today, the Musandam retains a wonderful mystique that many have known but few have fathomed.

Telegraph Island, Musandam.

7. Guided Tours

Khasab Travels and Tours/Oman Discovery
P.O. Box 28050
Khasab 811
Musandam
Tel. 660464
Fax: 660364
Complete coverage of the Musandam Peninsula: day trips, boating and diving, cultural tours, custom tours

8. Shopping

There is no real shopping to speak of in the Musandam.

8

Zanzibar

Zanzibar is no longer the trading center it used to be. Although there is still demand for cinnamon, clove, and pepper, time and change have shifted the trade winds away from this tiny port. For those wishing to pursue the Zanzibar connection either as a separate trip or in conjunction with a trip to Oman, the following information is made available.

The former colony of Zanzibar consists of a group of islands. The two most prominent are **Unguja,** which is usually referred to as Zanzibar proper, and **Pemba**. The name comes from the Persian *Zenj Bar,* meaning "land of the black people." The islands are located about 35 kilometers off the coast of Tanzania, about 6 degrees south of the equator in the Indian Ocean. Unguja is the larger of the two at about 1,464 square kilometers. The population is about 750,000.

Swahili is the national language but English and Arabic are widely spoken.

Because Zanzibar is still principally a Muslim community, though not necessarily Arabic, many of the strictures that apply to Oman also apply to Zanzibar. Skimpy clothes are frowned upon. Permission should be obtained before photographing the locals. PDA (public displays of affection) and consumption of alcohol in public are also not appreciated. About 90 percent of the population is Muslim but the remainder is made up of Christian, Hindu, and other religious minorities.

How to Get There

Gulf Air offers a direct flight to Zanzibar from Muscat. **Oman Air** is scheduled to begin service from the Middle East. You may also fly to Dar es Salaam, the capital of Tanzania, first. Many major airlines fly to Tanzania, including **Air France, Alliance Airline, British Airways, KLM, Swiss Air,** and **Egypt Air.** The national carrier, **Air Tanzania,** offers service to many cities throughout Africa, Europe, and the Middle East. Connections to Zanzibar can also be made through Kilimanjaro, Nairobi, or Mombasa.

Once in Dar es Salaam, you have the option of travelling to Zanzibar by shuttle flight or a 75-minute ride via catamaran or hydrofoil. There are many local travel agents in Dar es Salaam to give you a leg up on this part of your journey.

Travel Facts and Figures

Weather and Climate. The climate in Zanzibar is almost constant, with temperatures only ranging between 20 and 30 degrees C. As you might expect, it is a bit wetter than Oman; the islands are almost constantly influenced by the Indian Ocean monsoons, with the most rainfall coming in March to May and lesser amounts falling from October to November.

Packing and Wearing. Casual, light clothing with minimum exposure is best (this *is* a predominantly Muslim country).

Mail and Telephone Service. The country code for Tanzania is 255 and the city code for Zanzibar is 54. Zanzibar is in the East African time zone and is three hours ahead of Greenwich Mean Time.

Business Hours. Hours in Zanzibar are roughly the same as Oman, with shops opening for morning sessions before closing at 1 P.M. and reopening at 4 P.M., running into the evening hours. Most offices operate from 7:30 A.M. to 3:30 P.M., Monday through Friday. On Friday, there is a break for prayers between 12 noon and 2 P.M.

Tipping. Feel free to tip your waiters, guides, and porters at your discretion.

Metrics and Electrics

Metrics apply as in Oman. Electrical current is 220 volts, using the three-pronged, triangular African outlet.

Money and Prices

The unit of currency is the Tanzanian shilling. There are roughly 450 shillings to the U.S. dollar. Visitors are advised to pay for their hotel bills in foreign currency and change to shillings only what you need for food, shopping, and entertainment. Most stores will accept U.S. dollars.

Driving

Traffic in Zanzibar is British style, i.e., on the left and all cars are right-side drive. An international license is required to drive a car or motorbike in Zanzibar.

Health

The requirements for vaccination are the same as in Oman. You need not get a Yellow Fever vaccination unless you are coming from a zone of contagion. Malaria prophylaxis, however, is strongly recommended.

Governmental Fiddle-Faddle

Visa. Preparations are under way for visitors to obtain visas upon entry to Zanzibar and other Tanzanian borders, but as of this writing, it is not known when this will go into effect. Your best bet is to obtain a visa from your home country through any Tanzanian Embassy, High Commission or Consulate. Visas are required from all visitors except members of the British Commonwealth and other specified countries. Once again, check with an embassy to be sure.

Fees. There is an international departure fee, U.S. $20, and a local domestic departure fee, 1,000 shillings. There is a port departure tax of U.S. $5.

The Hotel Scene

As Zanzibar realizes more and more its potential for up-scale tourism, there will be an influx of business to create trendy resorts. At present there is a variety of accommodations available, ranging from the simple and quaint to the stylishly modern. You can stay in town houses in Stone Town or hide away at bungalows and villas in isolated reaches of the island. Prices range from U.S. $10 to $100 a night. The resorts offer many amenities: pool, bar, restaurant. If languishing about along a placid tropical waterfront is your cup of tea, there are some ideal locales. Swimming, snorkeling, and diving are offered. The underwater scenery is just as splendid as the above-ground. Your travel agent will be able to assist you in choosing the right setting for your travel and recreational needs. A few places of note here are the **Dhow Palace** in Stone Town, where you will immediately step into a bygone time of Arab kings and merchants; the trendy **Mwaimbini Club Village** on the west coast; and the remote **Tamarind Beach Hotel** at Uroa on the east coast.

Note: there is a 15 percent hotel levy, so be sure to enquire if the price quote includes the tax.

Dining

Zanzibar reflects a good cultural mix when it comes to choices for eating out. Besides the liberal styles of African food available, you can sample Arabic, Indian, and continental cuisine.

Sightseeing

The old center of Zanzibar is called **Stone Town** (Map 27). Over the years it has retained its Arabic quality with old whitewashed stone buildings. Places of interest in Stone Town are the **House of Wonders,** the **National Museum,** the **house of Tippu Tip** (the notorious slave trader), and the **Anglican Cathedral,** which stands on the site of the old slave market. Of interest here is the crucifix in the cathedral made from wood from a tree planted in Chitambo, Zambia, at the spot where explorer Dr. David Livingstone died. The **Jamitive Gardens** offer a relaxing excursion and the **Forodhani Promenade** provides an exotic array of foods to try, from fish fritters and grilled squid to spicy kebabs and exotic fruits.

Outside of Stone Town there are the remains of **Maruhubi Palace** from the days of the Omani sultans, the **Mmangapwani Slave Caves, Persian Baths,** and the **Jozani Forest.** Here many indigenous species of animals can be found including Kirk's red colobus monkey. Further out on the island there are **spice plantations** with still-flourishing groves of clove, cinnamon, nutmeg, and pepper, the medicinal iodine plant, and a plant that produces bright red berries that local women use for lipstick. The roads are lined with tall coconut palms and mango while banana trees hug closer to the ground. Cassava, chilies, and vegetables grow wherever they can find room. Needless to say, your olfactory senses will be tantalized. Local domiciles are made out of coral, mud, mangrove, and palm leaves. You can have a spice tour arranged in town.

If you want to go farther afield, that is, beyond the limits of the shore line, boating charters can be arranged to go on deep-sea fishing expeditions to the Pemba or Mnemba Channels, or you can investigate the string of smaller islands that surround Zanzibar. Of interest here is **Prison Island**, the site of an old-time . . . you guessed it! . . . jail. **Grave Island** is the site of an old cemetery and **Chumbe Island** is where a marine park and resort are being built.

27) Zanzibar

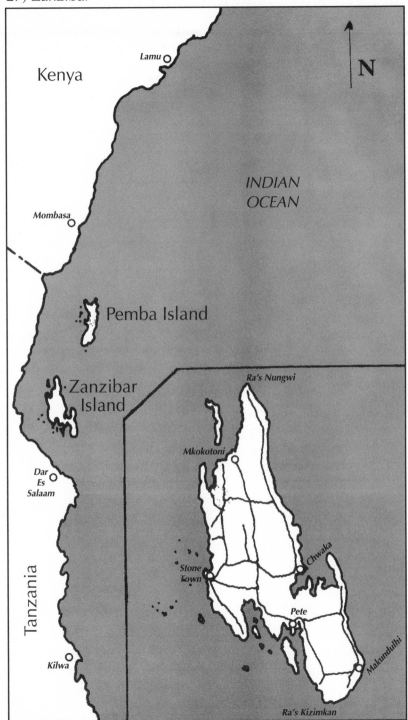

Kenya

Lamu ○

INDIAN
OCEAN

N

Mombasa ○

Pemba Island

Zanzibar Island

Ra's Nungwi

Mkokotoni ○

Dar Es Salaam ○

Chwaka ○

Tanzania

Stone Town ○

Pete ○

Makundulhi ○

Kilwa ○

Ra's Kizimkan

10 km

Guided Tours

I have it on good word that the best person to contact in Zanzibar is Mr. Fabian Fernandes of **Fernandes Tours.** Not only will he see to all your travel logistics while on the island, he is the local expert and authority on the culture and history of Zanzibar, particularly when it comes to describing the days of the old Omani empire and the time of Sultan Said the Great. Mr. Fernandes can be reached at his office in Zanzibar, Tel. 255-54-33102 or 355-54-30666.

For further information you can also contact:
The Commission for Tourism
P.O. Box 1410
Zanzibar, Tanzania
Tel. 255-54-33485/86/87
Fax: 255-54-33448

Shopping

There's not much in the way of malls but you can go dizzy from all the local shops which produce a profundity of local arts and crafts: wood carvings, embroidering, colorful printed textiles, carved shell and bone, jewelry, and woven baskets, to name just a few. And feel free to haggle for all your purchases.

List of Towers and Fortresses Maintained by the Ministry of National Heritage and Culture

Name	Region	Wilayat	Remarks
Nizwa Tower	Dakhiliya	Nizwa	Open for visitors
Bait-Radida	Dakhiliya	Nizwa	Under maintenance; temporarily closed
Jabrin Fort	Dakhiliya	Bahla	Open for visitors
Bahla Tower	Dakhiliya	Bahla	Under renovations; closed for the next 2-3 years
Bidbid Fort	Dakhiliya	Bidbid	Not open for visitors
Hazm Fort	Batinah	Rustaq	Under maintenance; temporarily closed
Rustaq Fort	Batinah	Rustaq	Open for visitors
Nakhal Fort	Batinah	Nakhal	Open for visitors
Tharmid Fort	Batinah	Suwaiq	Open for visitors
Suwaiq Fort	Batinah	Suwaiq	Open for visitors
A'al Hilal Wall	Batinah	Suwaiq	Open for visitors
Al-Maghabishah Wall	Batinah	Suwaiq	Open for visitors
Saham Fort	Batinah	Saham	Open for visitors

Ruined fortress on a promontory that overlooks Wadi Hoquein.

A lone tower overlooks a plantation in Fiq.

Sohar Fort	Batinah	Sohar	Open for visitors
Barka Fort	Batinah	Barka	Open for visitors
Bait-Numan	Batinah	Barka	Open for visitors
Majid Wall	Muscat	Seeb	Open for visitors
Bait Magham	Muscat	Bausher	Open for visitors
Ibri Fort	Dhariah	Ibri	Open for visitors
Khandaq Fort	Dhariah	Buraimi	Open for visitors
Hilah Fort	Dhariah	Buraimi	Open for visitors
A-Rawda Fort	Sharqiya	Mudaibi	Open for visitors
Gaalan Bani Bu Hassan Fort	Sharqiya	Gaalan Bani	Open for visitors
Sunaisila Fort	Shariqiya	Sur	Open for visitors
Bilad Sur Fort	Shariqiya	Sur	Open for visitors
Al-Eiga Fort	Shariqiya	Sur	Open for visitors
Ras Al-Hadd Fort	Shariqiya	Sur	Open for visitors
Al-Muntarib Fort	Shariqiya	Badiya	Open for visitors
Bait Al-Yahmadi Fort	Shariqiya	Ibra	Open for visitors
Khasab Fort	Musandam	Khasab	Open for visitors
Diba Fort	Musandam	Diba	Open for visitors
Bakka Fort	Musandam	Bakka	Open for visitors
Mirbat Fort	Southern Region	Marbat	Open for visitors
Sadah Fort	Southern Region	Sadah	Open for visitors
Taqah Fort	Southern Region	Taqah	Open for visitors

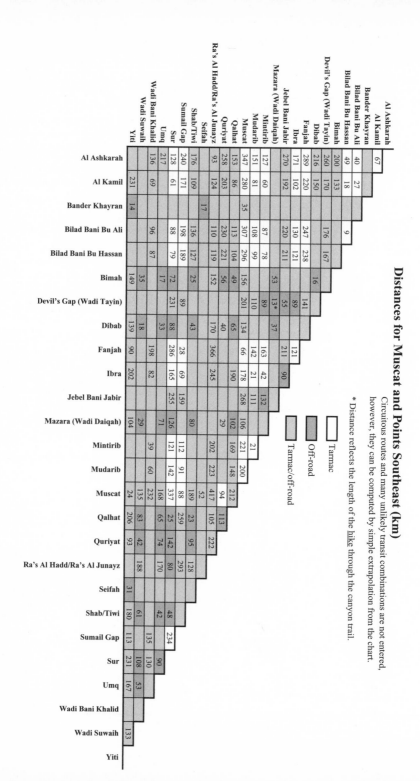

Distances for Muscat and Points Southeast (km)

Circuitous routes and many unlikely transit combinations are not entered, however, they can be computed by simple extrapolation from the chart.

* Distance reflects the length of the hike through the canyon trail.

Legend: ☐ Tarmac ■ Off-road ▨ Tarmac/off-road

Distances for Muscat and Points Northwest (km)

Circuitous routes and many unlikely transit combinations are not entered, however, they can be computed by simple extrapolation from the chart.

Legend:
- ☐ Tarmac
- ▦ Off-road
- ▨ Tarmac/off-road

* Distance reflects the length of the hike through the canyon trail.

From \ To	Awabi	Barka	Buraimi	Gubrah Bowl (Wekan)	Ibri	Jazir Suwaidi	Khaburah	Khasab (Musandam)	MAM Roundabout	Masna'ah	Muscat	Nakhl	Rustaq	Salalah	Shinas	Sohar	Suwaiq	W. Abyadh (coast)	W. Abyadh (Mahaleel)	W. Bani Awf (Bilad Sayt)	Wadi Bani Ghafir (Ghafti)	W. B. Kharus (Musayna'ah)	W. Hawasinah (The Chains)	Wadi Hoqein	Wadi Sahtan (Al Jatr)
Al Hazm	38	60	273	99	152	53	87	362	114	25	144	75	20		214	152	39	77	62	64	34	68	149	27	52
Awabi		68	283	88	225	93	109	372	122	64	152	36	19		234	174	61	26	35	39	22	43	26		
Barka				152	277	30	97	372	54	35	84	32	87	1088	222	162	49	45	64	104	94	99	159	93	95
Buraimi				152	217	118	186	396	337	248	346	315	293	1201	161	121	234								
Gubrah Bowl (Wekan)					206	118	186		142	124	172	56	79	1049	310	250	87								
Ibri						126	206		177	302	302	138	195	1118	255	174	118				118	84	156	161	
Jazir Suwaidi							91	340	84	84	84	29	62	74	1185	216	156	43	47	115	91	122	153	85	106
Khaburah								340	151	62	181	129	107	1185	125	65	48	114	148	121	155	62	118	139
Khasab (Musandam)									470	337	500	404	382		215	275	388								
MAM Roundabout										89	119	67	45	134	1034	284	216	103	93	118	156	161	152	213	145	147
Masna'ah											116	67	45	1123	187	127	14	52	88	100	73	107	124	56	77
Muscat												55	116	171	1064	314	236	133	123	148	188	191	184	243	175	179
Nakhl													55	171	254	194	81	71	32	72	75	68	80	63
Rustaq														1310	232	172	59	97	43	41	20	132	25	32
Salalah															1310	1250	1133	1133	1250	1310					
Shinas																62	173	179	239	275	287	294	246	187	243	264
Sohar																	113	179	215	227	234	186	127	183	204
Suwaiq																		52	102	100	73	107	110	70	91
W. Abyadh (from the coast)																			3*						
W. Abyadh (from Mahaleel)																				60	63	56	68	51	
W. Bani Awf (Bilad Sayt)																					61	65	66	21	
Wadi Bani Ghafir (Ghafti)																						59	112	39	37
W. B. Kharus (Musayna'ah)																								73	56
W. Hawasinah (The Chains)																									
Wadi Hoqein																									57
Wadi Sahtan (Al Jatr)																									

Distances for Muscat and Points West (km)

Circuitous routes and many unlikely transit combinations are not entered, however, they can be computed by simple extrapolation from the chart.

Legend: ☐ Tarmac ▓ Off-road ▒ Tarmac/off-road

From \ To	Al Hamra/Hoti Cave	Al Ayn-Beehive Tombs	Bahla	Birkit Al Mawz	Buraimi	Fanjah	Ibri	Izki	Jabrin	MAM Roundabout	Manah	Misfah	Mudaybi	Muscat	Nizwa	Salalah	Sharfat Al Alamayn	Sinaw	Tanuf/Wadi Qashah	Wadi Nakhr Gorge
Adam	110	178	105	71	348	148	196	72	114	178	60	120	65	223	63	800	47	157	50	150
Al Hamra/Hoti Cave		94	24	74	273	156	121	83	33	194	71	10	177	191	47			160	35	43
Al Ayn-Beehive Tombs			73	139	215	223	63	148	72	254	136	104	242	279	115		141	227	103	126
Bahla				66	249		75	101	9	181	63	34	169	206	42	952	71	154	30	61
Birkit Al Mawz					315		167		75	115		29	84	140	24	918	121	88	52	114
Buraimi						399	152		252	434	312		283	418	291	1201		403	279	302
Fanjah							247		159		114		166	145	108	1003	203	160	137	196
Ibri								75	100	282	160		131	307	139	1049		251	127	150
Izki									75	106	38		93	131	32	927	130	79	61	123
Jabrin										190			72	215	51		80	154	39	70
MAM Roundabout											81		204	30	139	1034	241	205	167	234
Manah												187		169	21	907	118		49	111
Misfah													220	201	57		57		45	53
Mudaybi														127				224	155	214
Muscat															174	1064	235	238	202	264
Nizwa																909	112	94	28	90
Salalah																				
Sharfat Al Alamayn																			209	90
Sinaw																			140	199
Tanuf/Wadi Qashah																				78
Wadi Nakhr Gorge																				

Distances for Muscat and Points South (km)

Circuitous routes and many unlikely transit combinations are not entered, however, they can be computed by simple extrapolation from the chart.

Legend:
- ☐ Tarmac
- ▨ Off-road
- ▦ Tarmac/off-road

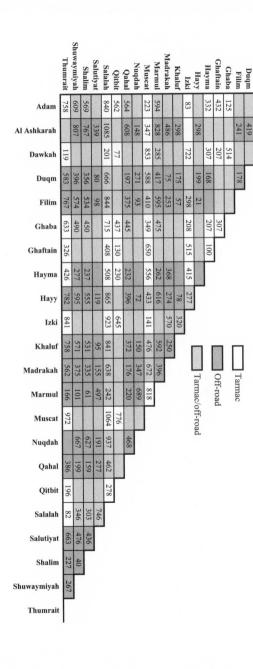

From \ To	Al Ashkarah	Dawkah	Duqm	Filim	Ghaba	Ghaftain	Hayma	Hayy	Izki	Khaluf	Madrakah	Marmul	Muscat	Nuqdah	Qahal	Qitbit	Salalah	Salutiyat	Shalim	Shuwaymiyah	Thumrait
Adam	639	419	514	125	432		332	298	83		486	594		594	223	564	562	840	569	609	758
Al Ashkarah		241	207		307		298	722	298			285	828	347	148		608	1085	339	767	807
Dawkah			178	168	307		722	199	175	75	285	417	853	197	271	77		201	356	396	119
Duqm				21	208		199	57		93	595	417	588	271		375	844	666	534	574	583
Filim					208			298	57	57	253	475	349	93		437	445	715	450	490	767
Ghaba						100	415	277	208		253	475	349	445	437	715		450		490	633
Ghaftain							515	78	274	368	262	556	650	232	230	408	508	237	277	326	
Hayma								72	78	274	368	262	556	230	232	508		237	277	426	
Hayy									78	320	570	274	616	433	396	865		555	595	782	
Izki										141	476	592	141	72	645	923		119	555	841	
Khaluf											150	347	592	250	372	841	645	531	571	758	
Madrakah												176	672	396	347	638	841	335	375	562	
Marmul													689	818	220	242	638	155	101	166	
Muscat														468	776	1064	937	627	462	972	
Nuqdah															468	776	937	627	667		
Qahal																278	462	277	159	199	386
Qitbit																	278				196
Salalah																		746	303	346	82
Salutiyat																			436	476	663
Shalim																				40	227
Shuwaymiyah																					267
Thumrait																					

Distances for Salalah and Environs (km)

Circuitous routes and many unlikely transit combinations are not entered, however, they can be computed by simple extrapolation from the chart.

Legend: □ Tarmac ■ Off-road ▨ Tarmac/off-road

	Ayun	Jebel Samham	Mirbat	Mughsail	Rakhyut	Raysut	Sadh	Salalah	Shisr	Taqah	Tawi Attir	Thumrait
Jebel Samham	124											
Mirbat	40	116										
Mughsail	91	120	75									
Rakhyut	170	195	195	106								
Raysut	64	89	90	32	145							
Sadh	176	104	64	171	259	125						
Salalah	51	73	70	46	122	20	178					
Shisr	167	249	243	226	298	200	298	213				
Taqah	86	38	38	78	157	52	93	32	22			
Tawi Attir	108	16	52	96	179	74	88	57	233	133		
Thumrait	67	149	143	126	198	100	198	78	100	105	121	
Wadi Dirbat	94	28	38	90	165	59	102	43	221	8	14	

References and Further Reading

Books

Al Lawati, Malallah bin Ali Habib. *Outline of the History of Oman: 5th Edition.* Muscat: Self-published, 1993.

American Women's Group. *An Introductory Guide to Life in the Sultanate of Oman: 5th Edition.* Muscat: 1995.

Bhacker, M. Reda. *Trade and Empire in Muscat and Zanzibar—Roots of British Domination.* London: Routledge, 1992.

Codrai, Ronald. *Travels to Oman—An Arabian Album.* Dubai, UAE: Motivate Publishing, 1994.

Dinteman, Walter. *Forts of Oman.* Dubai, UAE: Motivate Publishing, 1993.

Discovering Oman, An Apex Explorer's Guide: 2nd Edition. Muscat: Apex Publishing Company, 1992.

Dorr, Marcia Stegath. *A Taste of Oman—Traditional Omani Food.* Muscat: Self-published, n.d.

Hanna, Samir S. *Field Guide to the Geology of Oman, Volume 1.* Muscat: Historical Association of Oman, 1995.

Hawley, Sir Donald. *Oman and Its Renaissance.* London: Stacey International, 1977, revised edition 1990.

Hourani, Albert. *A History of the Arab Peoples.* New York: Warner Books, Inc., 1992.

Jones, Gigi Crocker. *Traditional Spinning and Weaving in the Sultanate of Oman.* Muscat: Historical Association of Oman, 1987.

Kay, Shirley. *Enchanting Oman.* Dubai, UAE: Motivate Publishing, 1988.

Klein, Heiner, and Brickson, Rebecca. *Off-Road in Oman.* Dubai, UAE: Motivate Publishing, 1992.

Metz, Helen Chapin et. al. *Persian Gulf States, Country Studies: 3rd Edition.* Washington, D.C.: Federal Research Division, Library of Congress, 1994.

Miller, Anthony G., and Morris, Miranda. *Plants of Dhofar—The Southern Region of Oman, Traditional, Economic and Medicinal Uses.* Muscat: The Office of the Advisor for Conservation of the Environment, Diwan of the Royal Court, 1988.

Oman '95. Muscat: Ministry of Information, 1995.

Oman People and Heritage. Ruwi: Oman Newspaper House, 1994.

Oman Today. Muscat: Apex Publishing, 1986-1996.

Parfitt, Joanna, and Velentine, Susan. *Dates.* Muscat, Oman: Summertime Publishing, 1995.

Pride, In the Year of Omani Heritage. Muscat: Al Roya Publishing, 1994.

Progress, A Silver Jubilee Special. Muscat: United Media Services, 1995.

The Promise and the Fulfillment: The Sultanate of Oman Throughout 20 Years. Muscat: Ministry of Information, 1990.

Shaw Reade, S. N. et. al., eds. *The Scientific Results of the Oman Flora and Fauna Survey 1977 (Dhofar)*. *Journal of Oman Studies, Special Report Number 2,* 1980.

Sheriff, Abdul. *Slaves, Spices and Ivory in Zanzibar.* London: James Currey Publishers, 1987.

The Speeches of H. M. Sultan Qaboos bin Said, 1970-1990. Muscat: Ministry of Information, 1991.

Thesiger, Wilfred. *Arabian Sands.* London: Longmans, 1959.

A Tribute to Oman. Muscat: Apex Publishing, vols. 1989-95.

Vine, Peter, et. al. *Oman in History.* London: Immel Publishing Ltd., 1995.

Ward, Philip. *Travels in Oman.* Cambridge, England: Oleander Press, 1987.

Water Resources of the Sultanate of Oman. Muscat: Ministry of Water Resources, 1995.

Articles

Curtiss, Richard H. "Oman: A Model for All Developing Nations." *Washington Report on Middle East Affairs,* July/August, 1995.

Davison, W. Donald, Jr. "Majlis Al Jinn Cave, Sultanate of Oman." Public Authority for Water Resources, October, 1985.

Ellis, Hermann Frederick. "A Friendship Two Centuries Old: The United States and the Sultanate of Oman." Boston University, 1990.

"Exploiting Omani Tourism Potential." *Al Markazi,* Nov.-Dec., 1994.

International Republican Institute. "Oman: Political Development and the Majlis Ash Shura." Washington, D.C., 1995.

Joyce, Anne. "Interview with Sultan Qaboos bin Said Al Said." *Middle East Policy Journal,* April, 1995.

Mais, Karl, et. al. "Show Caves in Oman—Feasibility Study 1995."

"The Scientific Results of the Oman Flora and Fauna Survey 1975." *Journal of Oman Studies,* vol. 1, 1975.

Severin, Tim. "In the Wake of Sindbad." *National Geographic Magazine,* 1982.

Simarski, Lynn Teo. "Fortified Oman." *Aramco World,* Jan.-Feb., 1991.

Simarski, Lynn Teo. "Oman's 'Unfailing Springs'." *Aramco World,* Nov.-Dec., 1992.

Sultan, H.E. Maqbool bin Ali. "Economic Diversification in the Sultanate of Oman." *Middle East Insight,* Fall, 1992.

Winser, Nigel de N. et. al. "The Scientific Results of the Royal Geographical Society's Oman Wahiba Sands Project 1985-1987," *Journal of Oman Studies,* vol. 10, 1989.

Index

THE MAVERICK GUIDE TO HONG KONG, MACAU, AND SOUTH CHINA

By Len Rutledge

A land of contrasts—traditions and modern ambitions, Eastern and Western influences, skyscrapers and mountain monasteries—the Hong Kong, Macau, and South China area is one of the world's most fascinating regions and the new China's most dynamic area.

As with all Maverick Guides, the culture, people, and geography of this land as well as the main points of interest for visitors are described. You will find everything from Hong Kong Island's double-decker trams to the Happy Valley racecourse, from the ferry to Lantau Island to Macau's A-Ma Temple. Covering transportation, hotels, dining, sightseeing, events, shopping, and entertainment, Rutledge has created a pleasant-to-read guide designed to get you ready for a trip as well as act as a handy reference during your stay. An excellent aid for those traveling on business.

296 pp. 5½ x 8½ Photos Maps Index
ISBN: 1-56554-071-9

THE MAVERICK GUIDE TO AUSTRALIA: 11th Edition

By Robert W. Bone
Edited by Kevin Voltz

For fifteen years one of the best guides to take down under, with current information on lodging, food, sightseeing, the language, getting on and off the continent, and more. Cities dazzle with shopping, dining, and the arts. Natural wonders such as the Great Barrier Reef abound.

416 pp. 5½ x 8½
Maps Index
ISBN: 1-56554-151-0

THE MAVERICK GUIDE TO NEW ZEALAND: 10th Edition

By Robert W. Bone
Edited by Susan Buckland

Accurate and detailed information on every aspect of this explorer's wonderland. Includes a glossary of indigenous terms, current prices for attractions, restaurants, and hotels, as well as ideas for activities such as safari tours with Maori guides and bungee-cord jumping.

368 pp. 5½ x 8½
Maps Index
ISBN: 1-56554-140-5

THE MAVERICK GUIDE TO SCOTLAND

By June Skinner Sawyers

Alongside practical knowledge and advice are the intangible histories with which every stone of Scotland seems filled. This Maverick Guide enhances a journey through modern Scotland by revealing bits of its past, which is ripe with figures of poets and kings. It details the country's timeless features that have driven people to its shores—the ruined castles and highland cliffs—but highlights the timely attractions as well. Today, the thriving art and theater of Glasgow and Edinburgh and the recent renewal of interest in Celtic language, music, and culture are just as noteworthy.

Whether visitors are interested in golfing the famous courses of Saint Andrews, walking the battlefields of William Wallace at Stirling, or visiting Glamis castle, the haunting setting for Shakespeare's *Macbeth, **The Maverick Guide to Scotland*** is a useful tool for enhancing their travels.

608 pp. 5½ x 8½ 54 photos 19 maps Index
ISBN: 1-56554-227-4

THE MAVERICK GUIDE TO BARCELONA

By Richard Schweid

This guide describes each facet of Barcelona's personality in detail, giving tips on hotels and lodging, restaurants and cafés, sightseeing, sports, shopping, and entertainment and nightlife in the thorough manner associated with the Maverick Guide Series. Since Barcelona is the capital of Catalunya, this region is covered as well.

Introductory chapters discuss the best ways to reach Barcelona, traveling within the city, banking and changing money, procuring health and emergency services, and other valuable information for the traveler.

There is much to see and do in Barcelona, from walking the scenic streets to resting on the beach to dancing all night in lively discos. The cuisine is an important part of the Barcelona experience: It is varied and tasty, and going out to eat is an event in itself. Artistic diversions abound. Whatever the visitor's interest, this book covers it.

This new addition to the Mavericks also offers eight maps, a glossary of words in Castilian and Catalan (Catalunya's two official languages), and a sample translated menu.

160 pp. 5½ x 8½ 8 maps Glossary Index
ISBN: 1-56554-191-X

THE MAVERICK GUIDE TO MOROCCO

By Susan Searight

With much more to experience than just Tangier and Casablanca, Morocco offers delicious local cuisine in Fès and Marrakech, bargain-filled kasbahs in the Dades Valley, and prehistoric sites at Volubilis. The High Atlas Mountains, Sahara Desert, and Berber villages present diverse terrains to explore and equally distinct peoples to encounter. Regardless of location, or budget, accommodations ranging from the luxurious to the spartan are profiled to fill every possible need.

This guide utilizes the familiar Maverick format to communicate everything a first-time traveler needs to know, including the customs, history, and culture of the country, as well as how to get along with the natives in the best possible fashion. Advice is given on everything from what type of vehicle to drive in certain areas, to what kinds of clothes to wear, and even what topics of conversation are considered taboo.

288 pp. 5⅜ x 8½ 41 maps Index
ISBN: 1-56554-348-3

THE MAVERICK GUIDE
TO HAWAII: 20th Edition

By Robert W. Bone

Edited by Carol Greenhouse

WINNER OF FIRST PLACE HONORS
HAWAII VISITORS BUREAU TRAVEL JOURNALISM AWARDS

"The best guide to Hawaii, and one of the best travel guides I've ever read, is *The Maverick Guide to Hawaii.*"

Chicago Sun-Times

"It's just about as good as you can get in one package; we've yet to find a better one."

Hawaii Magazine

"They give the necessary practical information, but are also strong on local history, geography, and lore."

New York Times

The lively and informative text includes background on each island's history, the people, the language, and the best ways to travel from island to island. In addition, for the traveler who values choice, the guide provides the most current information on everything from hotels and sightseeing to entertainment and recreation.

**432 pp. 5½ x 8½ 9 Maps Appendix Index
ISBN: 1-56554-312-2**

Please tell us about your trip to Oman.

(This page can be folded to make an envelope.)

CUT ✂

CUT ✂

FOLD

RE: 2nd edition, Oman

PLACE
FIRST-CLASS
POSTAGE
HERE

THE MAVERICK GUIDES
Pelican Publishing Company
1000 Burmaster Street
P.O. Box 3110
Gretna, Louisiana 70054